HELPING

*Origins and Development of
the Major Psychotherapies*

DAVID R. COLE

*Dean, School of Applied Arts
Sheridan College of Applied Arts and Technology
Oakville, Ontario*

Butterworths
Toronto

Helping

© 1982—Butterworth & Co. (Canada) Ltd.

All rights reserved. No part of this publication may be reproduced, stored in a retrieval system, or transmitted, in any form or by any means, photocopying, electronic, mechanical, recording, or otherwise, without the prior written permission of the copyright holder.

Printed and bound in Canada
5 4 3 2 1   2 3 4 5 6 7 8 9/8

Cover design by Julian Cleva

Canadian Cataloguing in Publication Data

Cole, David R.
Helping

Includes index.
ISBN 0-409-82407-0

1. Counseling. 2. Psychotherapy. 3. Helping behavior.
4. Humanistic psychology. I. Title.

BF637.C6C34   158'.3   C82-094200-6

The Butterworth Group of Companies

Canada:
Butterworth & Co. (Canada) Ltd., Toronto and Vancouver

United Kingdom:
Butterworth & Co. (Publishers) Ltd., London

Australia:
Butterworths Pty. Ltd., Sydney

New Zealand:
Butterworths of New Zealand Ltd., Wellington

South Africa:
Butterworth & Co. (South Africa) Ltd., Durban

United States:
Butterworth (Publishers) Inc., Boston
Butterworth (Legal Publishers) Inc., Seattle
Mason Publishing Company, St. Paul

Since this page cannot legibly accommodate all the copyright notices, the following page constitutes an extension of the copyright page.

Virginia Binder, Arnold Binder, and Bernard Rimland, excerpt on pages 270-71 from the book *Modern Therapies* by Virginia Binder, Arnold Binder, and Bernard Rimland. © 1976 by Prentice-Hall, Inc. Published by Prentice-Hall, Inc., Englewood Cliffs, NJ 07632.

Robert R. Carkhuff and Bernard G. Berenson, excerpt on pages 27-30 from *Beyond Counselling and Therapy*, 2nd ed., by Robert R. Carkhuff and Bernard G. Berenson. Copyright © 1967 by Holt, Rinehart and Winston, Inc. Copyright ©1977 by Holt, Rinehart and Winston. Reprinted by permission of Holt, Rinehart and Winston, CBS College Publishing.

Joel Fischer, figure on page 137 from *Effective Casework Practice: An Eclectic Approach* by Joel Fischer. © 1978 by McGraw-Hill Book Co. Reprinted by permission of McGraw-Hill Book Co.

William Glasser, figure on page 297 from *Glasser's Approach to Discipline* by Dr. William Glasser. Reprinted by permission of the author.

J.T. Hart and T.M. Tomlinson, excerpt on pages 185-86 from *New Directions in Client-Centred Therapy* by J.T. Hart and T.M. Tomlinson. © 1970 by Houghton Mifflin Company. Used by permission of Houghton Mifflin Company.

Arthur Janov, excerpt on pages 225-27 from *The Primal Scream*. Reprinted by permission of G.P. Putnam's Sons from *The Primal Scream* by Arthur Janov. Copyright © 1970 by Arthur Janov.

Søren Kierkegaard, excerpt on pages xv-xvi abridged from pp. 27-30 in *The Point of View For My Work as an Author: A Report to History* by Søren Kierkegaard, translated by Walter Lowrie. Copyright © 1962 by Harper & Row, Publishers, Inc. Reprinted by permission of Harper & Row, Publishers, Inc.

Frederick S. Perls, excerpt on pages 219-20 from his "Introduction" to the film *Three Approaches to Psychotherapy*, Part 2. Reproduced by permission of Psychological Films, Inc.

Carl R. Rogers, excerpt on pages 182-83 from *Counselling and Psychotherapy* by Carl R. Rogers. © 1942, renewed 1969, by Houghton Mifflin Company. Used by permission of Houghton Mifflin Company. Excerpt on pages 192-93 from "15 Patterns in the Process of the Encounter Group" (pp. 15-36) and pp. 46-48 in *Carl Rogers on Encounter Groups* by Carl R. Rogers, Ph.D. Copyright © 1970 by Carl R. Rogers. Reprinted by permission of Harper & Row, Publishers, Inc.

Acknowledgments

For many years I have been glancing through the acknowledgments of texts. I'm not certain why. Perhaps because in many cases they are the only, or most, personal statement made by the author(s). And while the expressions of appreciation to often faceless names sometimes specify their significance and reason for reward, others are given even less identity. Now, of course, I understand exactly who these people are, and for whatever reason, how important each, in large or small, is to the author. I think, too, that now I understand for the first time the disclaimer that many authors feel obliged to make, absolving these others of responsibility while noting their importance to the conception, content, presentation, or editing process, or their essential moral support and encouragement.

These are the people whom I wish to acknowledge: my students, for their stimulation and inspiration; Len Rosen, for his initially flattering yet confident suggestion that I should publish, and for persistently nudging me in that direction; M. June Ross, for faithfully reading early material and providing valuable feedback and, especially, positive support; Antony M. Lipsey, for carefully reading the early manuscript and assessing its content for course and curriculum potential; James R. Sutherland, for his insightful suggestion that *self-worth* be added to the model of normal behaviour and for his astute clinical assessment of the material; Dr. Warren Shepell, for his constructive suggestions in expanding the core helping characteristics and broadening the potential audience; Dr. Wendy C. Weaver, for her critical comment regarding use of language and style, and suggestions for highlighting current issues in the delivery of helping services; Emery Nemeth, M.S.W., for his expression of confidence in the usefulness of the material; Barrie C. Wray, for his encouragement and identification as a fellow author; N. James Robertson, M.S.W., for his faith in the author and material, and assistance in obtaining early comment from colleagues regarding the text's usefulness and relevance; James B. Wickens, for his assistance throughout in the organization and presentation of the material; and finally Marilyn Eriksen, my assistant and typist, whose patience, commitment, and intelligence made this project a reality.

Author's Note

There appears to be growing awareness and responsiveness to the importance of using non-sexist language when referring in general to members of the human species. At the same time, with no non-sexist pronouns available, the "he or she", "her or him," "himself or herself" solution makes certain passages extremely awkward to read. Therefore I have used either masculine *or* feminine pronouns in alternate chapters when referring to members of our species. I have attempted to include various combinations of client and helper sex identification where the content requires such designations.

David R. Cole
July 1981

Contents

Acknowledgments	vii
The Art of Helping	xv

I: AN INTRODUCTION TO THE THERAPY MYSTIQUE ... 1

1: Human Behaviour and the Helping Process	2
Author Objectives, Biases, and Approach	2
Objectives	2
Bias	3
Terminology	4
Text Format and Content	6
Normal Human Behaviour—Who Needs Help?	8
Statistical Normality	9
Cultural-Relative Normality	9
Psychological Normality	10
The Psychologically Healthy Person: A Model	18
The Helping Process	20
The Goal in Helping Others	21
Personal Values of the Helper	25
Selecting and Training Helpers	30
Ethical Issues	33
Social Democracy: The System	33
Helpers and Clients: The Players	36
Client Needs vs. Client Rights: The New Revolution	38
Summary	41
Appendix A: Six Interview Techniques	42
Beginning Where the Client Is	43
Listening and Attending	43
Questioning and Clarifying	44
Reflecting Feeling	45
Acceptance	46
Problem Solving	47

II: THE MAJOR DISCIPLINES ... 49

2: Psychiatry and Psychoanalysis	50
A Brief History of Psychiatry	52
Psychiatric Assessment, Classification, and Treatment Modalities	63
The Psychiatric Assessment Process	63
Psychiatric Classification	66
Psychiatric Treatment Modalities	71

Sigmund Freud and Psychoanalysis ... 72
  Sigmund Freud (1856-1939) ... 72
  The Theory of Psychoanalysis ... 74
  The Therapeutic Goals, Conditions, Dynamics, and Procedures of Classical
    Psychoanalysis ... 83
Summary ... 87

3: Psychology ... 90
Psychology as Philosophy ... 90
The Birth of Scientific Psychology ... 91
The New Science of Psychology: Three Approaches ... 92
Major Contributions of Learning Theory and Freudian Psychology ... 93
  The Psychology of Learning ... 93
  Freudian Psychology and Psychoanalysis ... 93
Gestalt Psychology ... 94
Organismic Psychology ... 95
  A Holistic Approach ... 95
  Major Concepts of Organismic Psychology ... 97
  Organismic Therapy ... 101
  Communion ... 102
  Goldstein's Contributions ... 103
Existential and Humanistic Psychology ... 104
  Defining Terms and Direction ... 104
  Introduction to Existential Psychology ... 105
  Nineteenth-Century Turmoil and Twentieth-Century Indifference ... 107
  Basic Concepts and Major Assumptions Underlying the Existential/Humanistic
    Approach ... 112
  Six Implications for Psychotherapy of the Existential Characteristics
    of Humans ... 116
Summary ... 118
Appendix A: The Pioneers of Existential and Humanistic Psychology ... 119
Gordon Allport (1897-1969) ... 119
Victor Frankl (1905-   ) ... 120
Erich Fromm (1900-80) ... 121
Kurt Goldstein (1878-1965) ... 123
Abraham Maslow (1908-70) ... 124
Rollo May (1909-   ) ... 128
Gardner Murphy (1895-1979) ... 128
Frederick Perls (1893-1970) ... 129
Carl Rogers (1902-   ) ... 131
Paul Tillich (1886-1965) ... 131
Alan Watts (1915-73) ... 133

4: Social Work ... 135
Origins ... 135
Basic Social Work Values ... 135
Contemporary Casework Issues ... 136
Casework Roles and Activities ... 136
The Theory of Social Casework ... 138

The Social Casework Interview	138
Purpose	139
Worker's Observations	139
Content of Worker and Client Communications	139
Worker's Impressions of the Client	140
Worker's Self-Assessment	141
The Casework Plan	141
Casework Supervision	142
Reporting and Recording in Social Casework	142
The Purpose of Case Recording	143
The Purpose of Process Recording	143
Summary	144
Appendix A: Employing Behaviour Modification in Direct Casework With Children	144
Behaviour Categories and Modification Activities	145
Adaptiveness	145
Affection	146
Aggression	146
Anxiety	147
Attention and Recognition	148
Attention Span	149
Frustration Tolerance	149
Competition and Cooperation	150
Dependency	151
Fantasy	151
Feelings of Self-Worth	152
Giving and Receiving	152
Identity	152
Self-Control and Responsibility	153
Appendix B: Guidelines for Process Recording Casework Interviews	155
Important Factors in Process Recording	156
Comprehensiveness	156
Style	156
Accuracy	156
Avoid Spontaneous Interpretation and Assignment of Motivation	156
Purpose	157
Note-Taking	157
Reconstruction From Notes as Soon as Possible	157
Reread and Rewrite	157
Examine Observations, Purpose, and Content Before Writing Impressions and Worker's Role	157
Synthesize and Summarize	158
An Example of a Student Process Recording	158
Purpose	158
Observations	158
Content	159
Impressions	162
Worker's Role	164
Plan	164
Summary	164

III: EXPERIENTIAL, SELF-ACTUALIZING, INTRAPERSONAL THERAPIES   165

5: Rogerian Therapy   167
Carl R. Rogers (1902-)   168
Aims, Basic Assumptions, and Major Concepts   175
   Rogers's Theory of Human Growth and Development   175
   Rogerian Theory of Neurotic Behaviour   177
   The Rogerian Approach to Therapy   180
Forty Years of Rogerian Therapy   182
   Non-Directive Therapy (1940-50)   182
   Reflective Therapy (1950-57)   183
   Experiential Therapy (1957-70)   184
   Rogerian Therapy Since 1970   186
Summary   189
Appendix A: Intensive Group Experience   189
Origins   189
The Goal of Intensive Group Experience   190
Basic Assumptions and Major Concepts   191
The Role of the Group Facilitator   192
Intensive Group Process Dynamics   193
Summary   194

6: Gestalt Therapy   196
Fritz Perls (1893-1970)   196
Basic Assumptions and Major Concepts   203
   Normal Human Growth and Development   204
   The Development of Neurotic and Problem Behaviour   208
Major Dynamics of the Therapy Process   211
   The Goal of GT   212
   GT Dynamics   213
Some Methods and Techniques of GT   217
   The Pseudo-Group   217
   The Hot Seat and the Empty Chair   217
   The Five Questions   217
   The Therapist in Action   217
   GT Patient Guidelines   218
Summary   219

7: Primal Therapy   221
Arthur Janov (1924-)   224
Origin and Development   225
Aims, Basic Assumptions, and Major Concepts   227
   Absence of a Theory of Human Growth and Development   227
   The Primal Theory of Neurosis   229
Goals and Techniques   237
   Goals   237
   Therapeutic Techniques   237
Summary   241

IV: COGNITIVE THERAPIES — 243

8: Rational-Emotive Therapy ✓ — 246
Albert Ellis (1913–) — 246
Aims, Basic Assumptions, and Major Concepts — 249
  Undeveloped Theory of Normal Human Behaviour — 249
  The Rational-Emotive Theory of Neurosis — 252
Goals and Techniques — 266
  Therapeutic Goals — 266
  The Process of Therapy — 267
  Therapy Summary — 274
Summary — 274

9: Reality Therapy ✓ — 275
William Glasser (1925–) — 276
Origins and Development — 277
Basic Assumptions, Major Concepts, and Principles — 278
  Differences Between RT and Traditional Psychiatry — 278
  Evolution and Development of RT Concepts and Principles (1958-78) — 280
  The "Normal" Person — 281
  The "Neurotic" Person — 289
Goals and Techniques — 298
  Therapeutic Goals — 298
  The Process of Therapy — 299
Summary — 307

10: Transactional Analysis — 310
  The Four Stages of TA Development — 310
  The Three Schools of TA — 313
Eric Berne (1910-70) — 315
Basic Assumptions and Major Concepts — 317
  TA Concepts and Principles Related to "Normal" Human Growth and Development — 318
  TA Concepts and Principles Related to Neurotic or Problem Behaviour — 327
Aims, Dynamics, and Techniques of TA Therapy — 334
  Goals and Aims of TA — 334
  The Four Elements of TA Therapy — 336
The Process of TA Therapy — 340
  Summary of Transactional Therapy — 345

V: THE BEHAVIOUR THERAPIES — 347

11: The Behaviour Therapies — 348
Learning Theory and Behaviour Therapy — 348
  The Psychology of Learning — 348
  Stimulus-Response Theory and Behaviour Therapy — 350
  Basic Assumptions of Behaviour Therapists — 351
  Therapeutic Goals of Behaviour Therapies — 352
Behaviour Modification Using Operant Conditioning or Shaping — 352

The Free Operant	352
Specificity of Response and Stimulus	353
Response Frequency	353
Shaping	353
Reciprocal Inhibition Therapy (RIT) or Systematic Desensitization	354
The Theory of Competing Antagonistic Responses	354
The Aim of RIT	355
The RI Therapeutic Technique	356
Summary of RIT	359
Implosive Therapy (IT)	360
The Theory and Assumptions Behind IT	360
The Dynamics and Technique of IT	362
Summary of IT	363
Summary	364
Resources	365
Index	379

The Art of Helping

That if real success is to attend the effort to bring a man to a definite position, one must first of all take pains to find him where he is and begin there.
This is the secret of the art of helping others. Anyone who has not mastered this is himself deluded when he proposes to help others. In order to help another effectively, I must understand more than he—yet first of all surely I must understand what he understands. If I do not know that, my greater understanding will be of no help to him. If, however, I am disposed to plume myself on my greater understanding, it is because I am vain or proud, so that at bottom, instead of benefiting him, I want to be admired. But all true effort to help begins with self-humiliation: the helper must first humble himself under him he would help, and therewith must understand that to help does not mean to be a sovereign but to be a servant, that to help does not mean to be ambitious, but to be patient, that to help means to endure for the time being the imputation that one is in the wrong and does not understand what the other understands.

Take the case of a man who is passionately angry, and let us assume that he is really in the wrong. Unless you can begin with him by making it seem as if it were he that had to instruct you, and unless you can do it in such a way that the angry man, who was too impatient to listen to a word of yours, is glad to discover in you a complaisant and attentive listener—if you cannot do that, you cannot help him at all. Or take the case of a lover who has been unhappy in love, and suppose that the way he yields to his passion is really unreasonable, impious, unchristian. In case you cannot begin with him in such a way that he finds genuine relief in talking to you about his suffering and is able to enrich his mind with the poetical interpretations you suggest for it, notwithstanding you have no share in this passion and want to free him from it—if you cannot do that, then you cannot help him at all; he shuts himself away from you, he retires within himself . . . and then you only prate to him. Perhaps by the power of your personality you may be able to coerce him to acknowledge that he is at fault. Ah! my dear, the next moment he steals away by a hidden path for a rendezvous with his hidden passion, for which he longs all the more ardently, and is almost fearful lest it might have lost something of its seductive warmth; for now by your behaviour you have helped him to fall in love all over again, in love now with his unhappy passion itself . . . and you only prate to him! . . .

And remember, serious and stern as you are, that if you cannot humble yourself, you are not genuinely serious. Be the amazed listener who sits and hears what the other finds the more delight in telling you because you listen with amazement. But above all do not forget one thing, the purpose you have in mind. . . . If you are capable of it, present *the aesthetic with all its fascinating magic, enthral if possible the other man, present it with the sort of passion which exactly suits him, merrily for the merry, in a minor key for the melancholy, wittily for the witty, etc. . . .*

If you can do that, if you can find exactly the place where the other is and begin there, you may perhaps have the luck to lead him to the place where you are.

For to be a teacher does not mean simply to affirm that such a thing is so, or to deliver a lecture, etc. No, to be a teacher in the right sense is to be a learner. Instruction begins when you, the teacher, learn from the learner, put yourself in his place so that you may understand what he understands and in the way he understands it, in case you have not understood it before. Or if you have understood it before, you allow him to subject you to an examination so that he may be sure you know your part. This is the introduction. Then the beginning can be made in another sense.

—Søren Kierkegaard (1813-55). From *The Point of View for My Work as an Author: A Report to History,* pp. 27-30. (New York: Harper Torchbooks, 1962.)

I
An Introduction to the Therapy Mystique

"Nothing you learn here at Oxford," he told us in his opening remarks, "will be of the slightest possible use to you later, save only this: that if you work hard and intelligently, you should be able to detect when a man is talking rot. And that, in my view, is the main, if not the sole, purpose of education."

> —Harold Macmillan, former British prime minister, recalling a professor's advice.

1

Human Behaviour and the Helping Process

AUTHOR OBJECTIVES, BIASES, AND APPROACH

Objectives

This text is the outcome of five years of teaching a course on theories and methods of counselling and psychotherapy to social work and health service work students at the community college level. It began accidentally, when my students requested copies of my lecture notes. I had assigned no text, as none then available seemed suitable to my purposes. I explained that my notes might be quite difficult to follow, but recognized their desire to have something more concrete, and agreed to turn them into hand-outs. Had I fully realized the implications of this commitment, I would likely have quickly ordered a text of some sort. Instead, however, I began the process of converting my notes into material which I hoped would be useful to my students. By the end of the first year I realized that the hand-outs formed the skeleton for a text, and the following year the organization of this material began. Since then there have been countless additions and revisions to the text material, and the overall structure and format of the course has changed as well.

During the writing of this book, the content has been developed with the following objectives:

1. To expose the reader/student to a comprehensive yet concise presentation of the theory, terminology, dynamics, and methods of nine major contemporary helping approaches.
2. To present these approaches from the perspective of the originator of the particular approach using primary sources (the work of the originator). While some briefer original works might be examined or assigned to students, it was assumed that the reader/student would not have the time or inclination to explore all nine approaches in depth.
3. To create an awareness of some of the critical issues and ethical concerns facing professional helpers—that is, those who are gainfully employed to facilitate the process of human development and the achievement of individual potential.
4. To provide a brief historical perspective for viewing the contributions to

the theory and practice of helping of each of the three major helping disciplines: psychology, psychiatry, and social work.
5. To enable reader/student identification with several renowned theorists and therapists through an examination of their biographies.
6. To describe specific helping activities and techniques utilized in each approach with examples of helper and client exchanges.
7. To examine the basic elements considered essential to any helping situation.
8. To provide a list of print resources for reference and further study.
9. To provide a list of VTR and film material available in which specific approaches and techniques are demonstrated, often by their originators and with real clients.
10. To assist teachers/helpers who are responsible for facilitating the growth of their students/clients.

In that this text has been developed in concert with a specific course, some of these objectives may be course objectives too, but given the real-life situation of the classroom or work environment, the teacher and student could set others. For example, the student could look for changes in her or his self-awareness and personal growth as a result of exploring the text material two to four hours per week over a six- to eight-month period.

At the same time, I would like to emphasize that although the text has been developed in conjunction with a specific course, the material is organized and presented in such a way that it is applicable to a much wider audience. Although aimed specifically at those who are in training for traditional career roles in social and health services, as well as education, it does not exclude those in the "private sector" who seek, or whose position requires, understanding and response to a wide variety of human relations, "personnel," and morale concerns. Contemporary supervisors and managers find themselves daily in the role of counsellor and confidant as they attempt to deal with the personal problems of their colleagues, staff, and superiors which are both related and unrelated to the work environment. This major counsellor/helper role of the successful supervisor/manager in business and industry today makes the text content as relevant for them as it is for those who have been traditionally identified with the helping professions.

Bias

While one may attempt objectivity, it is perhaps appropriate to caution one's audience, at least, about known biases and prejudices. As I have stated above, the theories and procedures of each therapist will be presented from his own perspective and often without specific comment from me. However, *what* of them is presented, *how*, and *how much*, may distort their real views and techniques. While the professional and scholar may detect my bias, the new student may be at a disadvantage. Therefore, let me say at the outset that I am humanistic in approach, and am conscious of this bias in presenting the following material.

What is a humanist? Although this question is considered at some length in Chapter 3, it will suffice to state at this point that a humanistic helper holds some or all of the following beliefs and values:

1. Human life is sacred; people come first.
2. People are basically "good," in a moral sense.
3. People have an innate tendency toward growth and the fulfillment of their potential.
4. People need to be free, to participate in decisions directly affecting them, and to act autonomously.
5. People need the support, caring, respect, and love of other people.
6. The subjective, intuitive, creative aspect of human beings requires greater emphasis.
7. Self-disclosure, openness, and trust are the bases for meaningful human relationships.
8. People have a responsibility to be concerned with the condition of all lower life forms in the biosphere of which they are a part.
9. People have a responsibility to be concerned with and to work toward improvement of the human condition particularly as it relates to the young, the old, and the disabled.
10. People with problems in living, that is, social and/or emotional problems, are not sick and need not, perhaps should not, be "treated" as such within the context of the contemporary medical service system.
11. A holistic approach to the study of human behaviour is required.

This is not a complete list, but is sufficient to give an indication of the flavour of humanistic thinking. Let's now look briefly at terminology.

Terminology

During the development of this material I have used words like *therapy, counselling, helping,* and *working* interchangeably. Similarly, when speaking in general of the doer of these things, the terms *therapist, psychotherapist, counsellor,* and *helper* have been used in the same way. I believe this is appropriate since these terms describe the *process* or activity and the *role* involved, respectively. They do not describe *different* processes and activities or roles. Schwartz (1978: 344) demonstrated this rather well in his definition of a psychotherapist as:

> Someone who professionally uses physically non-invasive techniques to induce healing behavioural and/or attitudinal changes in people who seek their services.

While his adjective "healing" bothers me somewhat, and might be better replaced with *desired* or *sought for* or *requested,* to avoid the medical connotation, the definition is quite all-encompassing. In fact Schwartz suggests that it is sufficiently broad to include, at the one extreme, the shaman/witch doctor and, at the other, the traditional health practitioner. In addition he feels that the definition is suitable for the large and growing list of special counsellors (marriage, guidance, career, etc.) and therapists (art, music, learning disability, dance, etc.). Alan Towbin (1978) might even agree that Schwartz's definition could embrace his "confiding relationship" in which Towbin described his role as that of "professional confidant."

William Glasser (1965) held that therapy was not the prerogative of social workers and psychiatrists alone, and that the process of helping people deal with personal and other problems which prevented them from leading productive, meaningful, and happy lives involved teachers, clergy, friends, relatives, and volunteers. Later, recognizing the potential of the schools in resolving serious personal problems of youth, in preventing occurrence of problem behaviour, and in enhancing development of student potential, Glasser (1969) began to develop specific training programs for teachers and schools. Albert Ellis too draws a parallel between education and therapy per se, and considers that an educative model will prevail in future:

> The future of psychotherapy, in my opinion, will largely be along educational rather than along therapist-to-client lines. Therapists will tend to follow the educational rather than the psychodynamic, medical, or other models, and invent and use a wide variety of pedagogical methods to reach and affect literally millions of people (1973: 17).

A more recent paper by Paul Shane (1980: 348) reflects a similar perception of the field of education as part of the therapeutic community:

> The focus of this paper is on implications for education, but these implications have relevance as well for other modes of therapeutic intervention.

Jerome Singer (1980: 381) would appear to agree with Glasser, Ellis, and Shane. He suggests that therapists should re-examine their activities and begin to align themselves more with educators:

> There is at least some good reason to think that therapeutic orientations might be better off to recognize that we are dealing with training of *skills*, not necessarily the modification of *traits*, basic *predispositions*, or the exposing of underlying conflicts. The model of a clinician as a kind of detective which often underlies the psychodynamic orientation needs to be supplemented or even supplanted by that of the therapist as a sensitive educator.

Now, if we can include within the purview of therapy those who are involved in educating others—teachers, instructors, trainers—then we must consider parents too a part of the therapeutic milieu. Finally, those supervisors, managers, and forepersons may also be included whose jobs contain an essential element of staff training, assessment, development, and, in general, the effective utilization of human resources.

So, let us not get "hung up" on terms. The helping process may be called *therapy, counselling, helping, confiding, teaching,* or even *supervision.* At least in this text, these terms do not refer to any particular theoretical stance, discipline, or technique. Whether we speak of ourselves as *therapists, counsellors, helpers, volunteers, confidants, teachers,* or *supervisors,* we are defining a unique relationship occurring between ourselves and one or more other persons, in which facilitating the development of the unique potential of the other person is implied.

Now the person or persons in the relationship other than the therapist may be called the *helpee, student, staff, counsellee, patient,* or *client.* I prefer *not* to use the term "patient" due to the medical-illness referent implied by the term, which is considered inappropriate for one employing physically non-invasive techniques. In the text, when referring to the role or status of the individual seeking and/or accepting help in the helping relationship, the term "client" will generally be used.

Having made this distinction, it should be pointed out that in the description of specific therapeutic approaches in subsequent chapters, the terms of the theorist and practitioner will be employed. Perls, for example, uses "therapy" and "patient," while Rogers speaks of the "counsellor" and "client." In general, the greater the identification of the therapist with the medical profession, the greater the likelihood that the term "patient" will be used.

With that introduction to the text objectives, approach, bias, and use of key terminology, let's turn now to the text content and format for presentation.

TEXT FORMAT AND CONTENT

Following upon the above statement of basic objectives intended for the text, some comments regarding the selection and organization of content may help to provide an overview of the text as a whole, and how the various parts and chapters are intended to contribute to that whole.

The text has been divided into five parts.

Part I provides the rationale for the text, indicates its theoretical bias, and examines some basic concepts, assumptions, and issues considered critical to understanding the nature of the helping process. It will focus our attention on the three most important components in the helping process: the *client,* the *helper,* and *what they do together.* The third element refers to what takes place during the helping process: what is the nature of the client-therapist relationship, their communication, interaction, involvement, and activities? The objective in exploring these three components of the helping process will be to provide a general framework or perspective from which to consider *any* human interaction, not merely those which are described in the text, in terms of its helping or facilitative potential. In examining these three aspects of the helping process we will:

1. Develop a model of normal human growth and behaviour from which we may view the client.
   This is important because the assumptions or beliefs about human growth and behaviour held by each therapeutic approach or school determines the methods and activities which they employ.
2. Identify what appears to be the basic goal of helping others regardless of the specific approach involved.
3. Describe what it is that is experienced as facilitative or helpful by the client in any helping situation.
4. Identify the personal qualities and skills of the helper which are considered necessary and essential to the establishment and maintenance of any helping relationship and process.
5. Consider the significance of the helper's personal value system in the helping process.
6. Explore, briefly, contemporary ethical concerns in the helping field, such as client rights and the demonstrated effectiveness of professional helpers.

Part II examines briefly the three fields which have contributed most significantly to the development of contemporary therapy—psychiatry and psychoanalysis, psychology, and social work. There has been an attempt in this section to provide a historical perspective for our exploration of therapy and helping, to point out some of the influences of social, economic, scientific, and political events on the development of therapeutic ideas and activities, and to note the tremendous contribution made by a small number of unique personalities (psychologists, psychiatrists, physicians, theologians, philosophers, and social workers) to the helping field.

The remainder of the text—Parts III, IV, and V—examines nine therapeutic approaches in seven chapters. Each chapter is organized as follows:

1. A presentation of the theory, basic assumptions, and major concepts of the originator of the therapeutic approach.
2. A description of the therapy process and dynamics.
3. A description of the techniques and methods employed by the therapist.

In some cases, it has been possible to illustrate specific concepts or procedures with verbatim therapist-client exchanges. However, these "print" accounts of therapy do not capture very well what takes place in the actual situation. Thus, the text can only give a cognitive/intellectual account of a very complex process involving knowledge, emotion, perception, feeling, body language, tone of voice, inflection, physical contact, environmental surroundings, etc. It is for this reason that resources listed after each chapter include VTR and film material. The learning process, or helping process too, for that matter, includes three steps—explanation, demonstration, and practice—and only the first step may employ the text primarily.

We may gain an appreciation of the *what* of therapy from the text. That is, what is it? where does it come from? what does it deal with, include, contain? what are the problems, goals, issues, concerns, etc? But the *how to* of the process and the techniques involved in the various therapies presented cannot be fully appreciated without actually observing a therapist and client involved in the process. VTR and film material or live interviews demonstrate *how* it's done.

The third step—*practice*—may initially involve role-playing by students and/or clients following the demonstration of a therapy procedure and technique. Supervised practice of therapeutic or helping approaches with real clients in real situations is, of course, necessary for the achievement of minimal competence, once basic skills have been mastered.

A word now about categorization of therapies. The distinction between the personal growth therapies in Part III and the life skills therapies in Part IV is a somewhat artificial one. One might also use the terms "experiential" and "cognitive" or "intrapersonal" and "interpersonal." These therapies do not fit neatly into such categories; the categorization employed here is merely intended to highlight the dominant features of the therapies presented and enable us to organize them more easily for purposes of comparing and contrasting. On the other hand, the therapies included in Part V are clearly distinguished from those in either Part III or IV by their common theoretical basis—learning theory. Having said that, however, we will note that certain learning principles, and even learning-theory-based therapeutic techniques, do appear in the therapies in Parts III and IV, and conversely that certain psychodynamic principles and techniques involved in the therapies in Parts III and IV may also be detected in some of the therapies in Part V. While there are, then, significant commonalities to be discovered in the approaches presented, there still remains a divergence of approaches, methods, and techniques (Larson, 1980).

Finally, some attempt will be made to examine specific therapies in terms of effectiveness or appropriateness for dealing with specific concerns and problem behaviour.

With this introduction to the text objectives, bias, contents, and organization, let's turn our attention now to the three components we identified earlier which will provide a framework for examining any human interaction in terms of its helping or facilitative potential. These components are:

1. A model of normal human growth and behaviour from which to view the client.
2. Essential facilitative therapist qualities and values from which to view the therapist.
3. The goals and dynamics of the helping process.

NORMAL HUMAN BEHAVIOUR—WHO NEEDS HELP?

For historical reasons which we will consider in Part II, the helping professions, until quite recently, have utilized what might be called a "sickness" or medical model from which to view people with psychological problems. In the same way that health is defined as freedom from pathology or illness, normality has been determined more by the *absence* of strange or "crazy" behaviour than by the *presence* of certain behavioural characteristics. Thus, while we may quickly or readily agree as to what constitutes strange, unusual, or "abnormal" behaviour, we will likely find it very difficult to attain consensus on what defines normal behaviour.

For the conscientious helper this is an important consideration and not merely an exercise in academic semantics. For if we do not have a clear appreciation of what is normal human behaviour, how can we assess the need for therapeutic intervention? How can we determine the activities and goals of the helping process generally, or assist someone in dealing with specific problem behaviour? How would one determine who needs help and, equally important, whether or not we are the person to offer it?

Let's consider briefly the concept of normality and attempt to discover a perspective from which we might view human behaviour which is growth-oriented or positive in nature. Shoben's paper, "Towards a Concept of the Normal Personality" (1957), Robert White's material on competence (1959), Carl Rogers's theoretical treatise in Sigmund Koch's *Psychology: A Study of a Science* (1959), and Stanley Coopersmith's monograph on self-esteem (1967) will form the basis for our discussion and model.

Normality may be approached in three ways. Behaviour may be considered in terms of the frequency of its occurrence (statistical normality); it can be examined relative to social values or cultural norms (cultural relative normality); and it can be explored in terms of the nature of the individual organism itself (psychological normality).

Statistical Normality

A statistical definition or model is not much help to therapists who are attempting to help people with psychological problems. The statistical concept of normality simply indicates that on a scale of some sort, we may plot how often certain behaviour occurs, and label the average (mean) as normal behaviour and that which occurs less frequently as abnormal behaviour. If various types of abnormal behaviour were then ranked in terms of their acceptability by those in the average range, it would be possible to rank them from least to most acceptable.

Cultural-Relative Normality

Once we begin to rate something like "acceptability," reference is made to the opinions and attitudes of others: "Acceptable to who?" And this leads us to the notion of cultural relativism. Simply defined, cultural relativism means that an act can only be understood within the context in which it occurs. That is, what may be meaningful, acceptable, or necessary in a specific cultural situation may not be so in another. The derivation of the word "normal" includes the concept of social *norms* — informal rules or behavioural standards which have been accepted by a social group. The "normal" person then acts in accordance with group proscriptions for behaviour.

The obvious difficulty with a cultural-relative notion of normality is that it becomes meaningless. Everything and nothing becomes "normal" to someone, somewhere. This presents three dilemmas for therapists. First, is our job merely to help clients conform to the proscriptions of behaviour, that is, the value system, of the community or social group in which they find themselves? Second, what about the value system of the therapist? Should we, as therapists, communicate our values to the client? Third, how do we determine whether the client's behaviour is normal or abnormal, that is, whether our assistance is needed in the first place? What or whose grid should we use from which to evaluate the client's behaviour?

What we need is a framework for viewing normality which is value-free and which avoids the pitfalls of temporal and spatial morality. Rather than merely attempting to eliminate or decrease unacceptable behaviour by *any* standards, the goal of the therapist should be to improve, increase, develop, ensure, and promote positive *growth* in the client. Granted, this stance implies a definite value or values on the part of the therapist. But it is a value which is centred in the client rather than on something external, such as conformity to social norms.

Psychological Normality

What is positive development? Shoben (1957: 185) proposed that human "behaviour is 'positive' or 'integrative' to the extent that it reflects the unique attributes of the human animal." The two unique attributes of the human species the development of which leads to "positive or integrative" behaviour are arbitrary symbol manipulation and an extended maturation period. *Psychological normality is determined by the interplay of these two features of the human condition not shared by any other living thing.*

ARBITRARY SYMBOL MANIPULATION

While animals communicate and may have fairly high levels of sign and symbol recognition and some reasoning ability, only we humans, through the use of propositional language, can deal in the abstract. Our capacity for abstract thought and reason frees us from the concrete now-only existence of all other animals. We can think of the not-present and are aware of time. We can think in the past (remember, recall, recognize), can experience awareness in the present, and can imagine what *might* be — the future. It is our capacity for propositional speech or abstract thought that enables us: (1) to learn not only from our own experience but from the experience of others in other times and places (for primitive societies through word of mouth, for civilized societies through written symbols or print), (2) to anticipate the future consequences of our present behaviour, and (3) to imagine what *might be* even though we may have never actually experienced the fantasied event or condition.

EXTENDED MATURATION PERIOD
The other basic difference between human beings and all other animals is our initial extended dependency. We spend an inordinately long period of our development either wholly or partially dependent on others, and a further period in lengthy transition from dependency to dependability. After achieving maturity the process continues in reverse, ending in death.

Life Stage	*Characteristic Behaviour*
infancy & childhood	dependency
adolescence	independence
adulthood	dependability
senior life	independence
old age	dependency

Thus, for an extremely long time, the human person is dependent on others for basic need satisfaction in order to survive. On the other hand, the advantages of adulthood—freedom, power, status—seem to be related to acceptance of responsibility for meeting the needs of infants and children. There is established, as a result of this feature of human biology, an interdependent quality of human life, which in more complex societies translates itself further in delineation of adult roles. Adults assume the responsibility for certain aspects of living of other adults, and trade, sell, or barter in order to obtain basic need satisfaction.

POSITIVE INTEGRATIVE ADJUSTMENT
From these two potentialities—propositional language and the interdependent character of human social systems—a model of normal human behaviour may be derived which focuses on the *presence* of certain behavioural characteristics rather than on the *absence* of behaviour considered as symptoms. The characteristics of normal human behaviour which follow from our capacity for abstract thought and extended dependency are: self-esteem, self-control, intrinsic values, personal responsibility, and social responsibility.

Self-Esteem
The concept of self results from the human capacity which enables us to have awareness of our own existence. We are unique among living things in this regard. We alone know that we know. To be aware of our own existence means being able to consider ourselves as objects, to stand outside of ourselves and look back, or to look in a mirror and know that the image reflected is us. And through this process, we can observe, explore and investigate, and obtain information; make assessments and evaluations; and draw conclusions about

what and who we are, and how we operate or behave. The process by which we evaluate our sensations, experiences, actions, feelings, and thoughts determines how we think and feel about ourselves. How we think and feel about ourselves will define our sense of personal identity: what and who we believe ourselves to be now; who we should or ought to be; and who we might be or could be, in the future. The terms "self-regard," "self-acceptance," "self-worth," or "self-esteem" all describe this process.

Rogers (1959) referred to this capacity as *self-regard*, meaning the sense of well-being we experience when our behaviour reflects organismic integrity, enhancement, and the actualization of our potential. It is this capacity to experience self-awareness, appraisal, and efficacy which is included in the existential concepts of *being, transcendence,* and *ontological guilt,* which are discussed in Chapter 3. Coopersmith (1967: 4-5) refers to it as *self-esteem,* and defines it as follows:

> By self-esteem we refer to the evaluation which the individual makes and customarily maintains with regard to himself: it expresses an attitude of approval or disapproval, and indicates the extent to which the individual believes himself to be capable, significantly successful, and worthy. In short, self-esteem is a *personal* judgment of worthiness that is expressed in the attitudes the individual holds towards himself.

By making more explicit in Coopersmith's definition of self-esteem the Rogerian notion that our sense of well-being is associated with *actualization of our potential,* and the importance of this process for the establishment of *identity,* we may better appreciate the significance and importance of this self-evaluative mechanism as an essential element in normal human behaviour. Self-esteem, then, is more than simply feeling good or bad about a specific piece of behaviour or personal experience. It refers to the meaning of that behaviour or experience as a reflection of the *totality of what we are in potential, and the extent to which we are fulfilling that potential.*

We are fortunate in having available an exhaustive eight-year study on self-esteem completed by Coopersmith in 1967. His work confirmed the generally held belief in the positive relationship of self-esteem to personally effective and satisfying human behaviour. He was able to identify the child-rearing conditions which led to the development of self-esteem, and as well relate the resulting personality characteristics and behaviour to these conditions. Let's explore first the child-rearing conditions affecting the development of self-esteem.

Briefly, Coopersmith discovered that individuals with high self-esteem experienced three conditions during childhood and adolescence: (1) total or near total parental acceptance, (2) clearly defined and enforced limits, and (3) respect and room for their individual actions and behaviour within the constraints imposed by the limits. Coopersmith concluded

> that the parents of children with high self-esteem are concerned and attentive toward their children, that they structure the worlds of their children along the

lines they believe to be proper and appropriate, and that they permit relatively great freedom within the structures they have established (1967: 236).

Why would these three conditions lead to high self-esteem or positive self-regard? And how is self-regard related to positive integrative adjustment? Let's consider first the condition of parental acceptance. Carl Rogers (1959), in dealing with the development of the self, described the capacity for human self-awareness as the starting point. The very young infant cannot experience its existence as separate from its environment; the infant *person* has not yet emerged. We cannot know what the pre-symbol-using infant "thinks," if anything, but we can perceive a gradual increase in sensory awareness. The initial sense of self at this stage, or even in the early phase of symbol manipulation, which would permit the infant awareness of self as separate from the surrounding environment, is first acquired externally, and is dependent upon the responses from dependable others, such as parents. Positive regard from others is required for the initial development of positive *self*-regard.

Coopersmith has termed the caring, attentive, loving behaviour of parents *acceptance*. It would appear similar to Rogers's positive regard. But there is another important parent-child dynamic involved in the establishment of self-esteem or self-regard which is directly related to parental warmth and nurturing. This is the process of identification and modelling. The nurturing parent, while enhancing the child's self-concept directly through positive regard and acceptance, not only provides a behavioural model for the child, but establishes an *affective* relationship in which the child seeks to emulate the parent.

Coopersmith's finding that high self-esteem is related to clearly defined limits may at first be surprising, until we examine it further. He suggests that limits provide for the child a consistent source of information and cues on which to make rational judgments, assessments, and decisions. Clearly defined limits enable the child to determine the extent to which the limits have been maintained or transgressed, and the likely consequences of each. The child's locus of control becomes internalized instead of externalized. Clearly defined limits, then, promote independence, autonomy, self-reliance, self-control, and personal and social responsibility. However, in a home where the standards for behaviour are not clear, but are ambiguous, inconsistent, or conflicting, the child must continually seek assistance from others in order to determine what is acceptable and appropriate. The environment that has little structure and few definite cues on which to base behaviour does not provide us with sufficient information for rational decision making. In an unpredictable, permissive environment, children experience failure and uncertainty, become hesitant and anxious, and do not feel good about themselves.

The societal implications of producing children with high and low self-esteem or self-regard are interesting. Children with high self-esteem are likely to be a source of irritation for parents, teachers, and other authority figures. This is to be expected from children who manifest independence, tend to be outspoken, and are inquisitive. And while they may be more attuned to their own internal value systems, they appear to be at least as aware of their broader social obligations and other people as are people who are less sure of themselves. On the other hand, children with low self-esteem are likely to be "obedient, conforming, helpful, accommodating, and relatively passive" (Coopersmith, 1967: 253). They are also more likely to suffer from psychosomatic complaints and anxiety, and are less effective and more inclined to be destructive.

Let's conclude this discussion of self-regard or self-esteem with a summary of Coopersmith's findings (1967: 249-50):

> Persons with high self-esteem, reared under conditions of acceptance, clear definition of rules, and respect, appear to be personally effective, poised, and competent individuals who are capable of independent and creative actions. Their prevailing level of anxiety appears to be low, and their ability to deal with anxiety appears to be better than that of other persons. They are socially skilled and are able to deal with external situations and demands in a direct and incisive manner. Their social relationships are generally good and, being relatively unaffected or distracted by personal difficulties, they gravitate to positions of influence and authority. Persons with medium self-esteem appear to be relatively similar to those high in esteem — with a few major exceptions. They are relatively well accepted, possessed of good defenses, and reared under conditions of considerable definition and respect; they also possess the strongest value orientation and are more likely to become dependent upon others. From the context of other evidence, it appears that they are uncertain of their worth and inclined to be unsure of their performance relative to others. Persons with low self-esteem, reared under conditions of rejection, uncertainty, and disrespect, have come to believe they are powerless and without resource or recourse. They feel isolated, unlovable, incapable of expressing and defending themselves, and too weak to confront and overcome their deficiencies. Too immobilized to take action, they tend to withdraw and become overtly passive and compliant while suffering the pangs of anxiety and the symptoms that accompany its chronic occurrence.

Self-Control
Propositional language enables us to anticipate possible outcomes of intended behaviour in advance. Normal human behaviour then reflects organizing and planning to achieve desired outcomes. Language and thought enable a rational and logical examination of a variety of possible consequences of our behaviour before we take action. We are continually determining whether or not to act or what alternatives to *choose* which we may find most satisfying and rewarding. This potential for individual self-control of behaviour means a reduced need for external social control, as we have discussed above. Conformity to social norms may result not because we agree with the norm, but because conformity appears to have the greatest long-range reward for us, or, as Coopersmith suggests above, because we lack the level of self-esteem which enables our autonomous independent behaviour and adherence to our own intrinsic and subjec-

tive value system. On the other hand, if we have sufficient self-esteem, we may decide to rebel against social norms after we have considered the consequences. Rebellion too may reflect normal behaviour if it is behaviour which is organismically enhancing and self-actualizing. It would be appropriate in situations in which, after careful consideration of the alternatives, this course of action seems to be required to maintain our self-esteem and integrity. In this case, it would be normal for us to act, fully accepting that there are certain risks in doing so, and that we are prepared to take these risks. Having done so, we must also be prepared to accept any negative consequences of our behaviour without complaint, should they arise.

Intrinsic Values
We have already referred to the development of an intrinsic value system in discussing self-esteem and self-control. This internalized frame of reference or set of personal standards of what is good and to which we are drawn, and what is bad and from which we are repelled, is also made possible through our capacity for arbitrary symbol manipulation. Intrinsic values permit us to do more than assess or judge our own behaviour and actualization, however, for they provide a subjective and personal perspective from which to reflectively consider all of our experience, involving both internal and external events. Our personal value system of what in the world is desirable and advisable provides an internal standard for behaviour which decreases the need for our physical control by others, and therefore facilitates our personal freedom to explore and develop ourselves. It permits us a unique response to external events and the maintenance of beliefs or ideas which are wholly subjective or personal. Our values may be ideal, something which we do not personally achieve but to which we aspire. They may represent ideals external to us which we view as desirable or undesirable for other people and the natural environment of which we are a part. A personal value system, then, provides us with a subjective, internal focus for cognitive evaluation, as well as an intuitive/sensory/emotive awareness of all our experience such that we seek either to approach or avoid that experience.

Personal Responsibility
"Willingness to accept the consequences of our behaviour" may be rephrased as "accepting responsibility for our actions." Thus the fourth characteristic of normal behaviour is assuming responsibility for what we choose to do. Awareness and acceptance of the fact that we do have alternatives, that we do make choices, that we are responsible for what we choose to do or not to do, and that we cannot excuse our behaviour or blame other people or things if we are not the people we would like to be, means accepting personal responsibility for our own actualization.

Social Responsibility
The significance of the human organism's prolonged dependency on the nature of human relationships is persuasively discussed by Willard Gaylin (1978):

... man is not technically speaking, an individual; a social structure is a part of his biology and a necessary part of his functioning: we are a social animal not by election but by nature. Precisely because of our prolonged dependency. We could not survive as a species or develop as a type were there not a social structure to support us. While man is not quite a colonial animal like coral, he is certainly also not a true individual like an amoeba. He rests somewhere in between, and no theory of the nature of man is complete that does not recognize the obligate social structure in which he must develop (14-15).

From the standpoint of psychological development by which we identify human beings as such, beyond mere physiological and physical description this dependency period is crucial—crucial, that is, in the development of a person who loves and is lovable, who has emotions and relationships, is capable of altruism and hope . . . (7).

Caring—that is, the protective, parental, tender aspects of loving—is a part of relationship among peers, child to parent, friend to friend, lover to lover, person to animal. The parent-child aspect of caring is only the essential paradigm whose presence is necessary for the diffusion of this human quality into the other relational aspects of life. The linkages between being cared for and caring for others are crucial to remember (33).

Thus the young child who identifies with nurturing adults also learns to *want* to be helpful, loving, trustworthy, and altruistic, in demonstrating genuine concern for others. At the same time, we learn to acknowledge the need for others, and to behave so as to receive the warmth and respect which makes us feel good. As children we learn that this experience of receiving love is heightened if we reciprocate and return it, and that human relationships may be *mutually* gratifying. There is implied here, as well, in addition to explaining the development and maintenance of intimate interpersonal relationships, a more generalized social obligation for us as members of a social group to be an asset rather than a burden, and to care for and about other people as part of the normal character. The normal person then should be socially as well as personally responsible in the sense of being more than independent and autonomous, but in addition capable of accepting and responding to the needs of others.

We have considered thus far five characteristics of normal human behaviour which stem from the two unique attributes of the human species. The first four stem from our ability for propositional speech: (1) *self-esteem,* (2) *self-control,* (3) *intrinsic values,* (4) *personal responsibility.* The fifth, *social responsibility,* we saw resulting from the second attribute, our extended dependency. Now let's complete our model of psychological normality with an exploration of the sixth characteristic, *competence.*

Competence Motivation
Briefly defined, motivation is selected, directed, pertinent behaviour. In this sense, *all normal human behaviour is motivated* and *nothing occurs at random or by*

chance. While we may not have all behaviour under conscious control or awareness, *all aspects of our functioning as organisms are purposive and meaningful.*

Drive theories. We may recall from our introductory psychology course terms like "drive," "instincts," and "homeostasis." These terms belong essentially to what are called drive theories of motivation. According to drive theories behaviour is explained as a *response* of an organism to a felt *need.* The need is our experience and awareness of a tissue deficit which creates a *drive* or *urge* to satisfy the need. If the need was food, the drive state would be hunger and our response or behaviour would be food-seeking and ultimately, consummatory, once food was located. Once the tissue deficit was restored through food intake, the drive state of hunger would subside, and the response to the hunger drive—food seeking and eating—would cease. This process of quiescence→ need →satisfaction →quiescence is called *homeostasis,* and refers to the tendency of any organism to maintain an internal chemical tissue balance or equilibrium. Now, while much of our behaviour may be explained on the basis of drive and instinct theories (e.g., sexual activities, eating, sleeping, drinking, etc.), there are three types of behaviour which do not fit drive theories: exploratory behaviour, activity-arousal, and manipulation. Note that these three activities are not directly related to a tissue deficit or the organic state of the organism.

During the 1950s animal psychologists performed various experiments which demonstrated that even when all primary needs were satisfied, animals continued to explore their environment. It has now been generally agreed that there is a drive to explore (*curiosity*) and that an animal may be reinforced merely by being allowed to experience a novel environment.

Activity and *manipulation* also seem to be separate and distinct drives. Rats whose normal opportunity for movement was restricted were found to run on an activity wheel for periods which were correlated to the extent of their confinement. And monkeys, when allowed to solve a complex mechanical problem with no reward, continued to solve the problem repeatedly, seeming to enjoy the solution or "manipulation" itself as an intrinsic reward—perhaps indicating a feeling of environmental mastery.

The evidence for a new drive was reflected in the writings of psychoanalysts and in general psychology as well during this period.

Hendrick, in 1942, suggested a new instinct, the instinct to master, described as "an inborn drive to do and learn how to do." The object of this instinct, he said, was merely the pleasure in exercising a function successfully regardless of the sensual value. Kardiner, another psychoanalyst, took the opposite position to Freud's and suggested that successful and gratifying experiences, not frustrations, lead to increasingly integrated action and discrimination of the self from the external world. Mittlemann, in 1954, saw motility as a central motivating drive. He suggested the urge to make skilled motor actions in the form of posture, locomotion, and manipulation of objects by the young child reflected drives similar to oral and genital urges.

From general psychology there were a number of other theories. Kurt

Goldstein, the originator of the concept of self-actualization, believed it to be the one *master drive* with the various visceral drives being only partial expressions. Likely influenced by the Gestalt psychology of the day, he also assumed an urge to completing what was incomplete—a tendency to perfection or wholeness. The neurological work of Hebb indicated a tendency for human subjects to *seek stimulation* while attempting at the same time to *avoid excessive stimulation*. The subsequent experiments in sensory deprivation supported this conclusion. There seemed to be an optimal level of stimulation below or above which the organism would not continue to function effectively even though other biological needs were satisfied. The organism is always in a state of vigilance and activation.

The Concept of competence. After reviewing this evidence, White (1957) suggested that behaviour which dealt with effective interaction with the environment might be called *competence*. He included such behaviour as: seeking, grasping, visual exploration, crawling, walking, focal attention, perception, memory, language, thinking, anticipation, exploration, and manipulation. He defined competence as: fitness, capacity, efficiency, proficiency, or skill. He considered this behaviour as evidence of a "drive" or need state which would explain behaviour not explained by tissue deficits, need reduction, or homeostasis. This behaviour he called competence-motivated. Competence motivation was defined as the organism's need to deal effectively with its environment.

White's identification of competence as a need state, while rounding out motivation theory as a source for understanding human behaviour and complex animal behaviour generally, also provides us with the sixth and last dimension for our model of psychological normality. We have now identified six basic characteristics of normal behaviour which are intrinsically determined, and may provide us with a psychological definition of normal human behaviour.

The Psychologically Healthy Person: A Model

Characteristic   *Behaviour*
1. Self-esteem   Evaluating our behaviour as organismically enhancing, leading to the actualization of our potential, and contributing to the development of a personal identity we feel good about
2. Self-control   Anticipating
                       Planning, patterning
                       Ordering, organizing
                       Adapting, adjusting
                       Thinking before speaking, doing, etc.
                       Considering options and alternatives
                       Considering possible outcomes of options

	Choosing courses of action which are usually rewarding and successful
3. Intrinsic values	Believing in a set of personal principles and standards which act as a guide for behaviour and for evaluating experience such that we seek to approach or avoid such behaviour or experience
4. Personal responsibility	After considering alternatives and possible consequences, accepting responsibility for choice of action and our behaviour, without complaining or making excuses
5. Social responsibility	Caring for others
	Accepting others' behaviour and values
	Loving
	Receiving of love
	Respecting and recognizing the rights of others
	Involvement and participation with others
	Accepting dependency of others
	Contributing and productive
	Autonomous and dependable
6. Competence	Exploring, investigating, discovering
	Creating, sharing, building
	Trying, seeking, mastering
	Acting, doing, changing
	Stimulating, exciting
	Enjoying, satisfying
	Fulfilling, being

The psychologically healthy person, then, demonstrates the various kinds of behaviour described opposite the six characteristics listed above. This is not to say that at times we don't act without thinking; that we don't ever try to rationalize our actions or make excuses for ourselves. But generally, if we are psychologically normal, we do behave in these ways.

Suppose we do have difficulty demonstrating self-control, for example. We decide to study on Saturday night. We get our books together. We go to a quiet place. We get comfortable, and begin. Suddenly the phone rings. A party! Now what? We consider the situation. We explore the options: Stay home. Go to the party. We consider the immediate outcomes: achieving college entrance or scholarship vs. building friendships. Choice? Perhaps a compromise—study for three hours and arrive at the party late! Possible outcomes—lower grades, more social satisfaction. No loss in self-esteem.

However, if our decision was either to study *or* to attend the party and we found we were then unhappy or frustrated having made the choice, and we found this *typical* of our behaviour, we would apparently have a problem with self-control. We may not be able to complete things we begin, or don't feel "good" about the things we decide to do. If *we* are not in control of ourselves, then *who* or *what* is? Are we sick? No. But we may have a problem, and we may want to talk to someone about it. That someone may be a professional helper, a friend, a confidant, or a teacher.

Whatever the "problem," then, our model is intended to give us a framework from which to consider clients' behaviour and problems in living—problems which prevent them from growing and developing, from feeling good about themselves and others, from pursuing their goals and ideals, and from enjoying life. As helpers we will need first to address the following four questions:

1. What is the problem behaviour with which the client is seeking help?
2. What aspects of the client's existence appear to be affected by the problem behaviour in terms of the six characteristics of psychological normality?
3. Is our help indicated, and if so what might be the specific therapeutic goals?
4. What helping approach or techniques might be most appropriate?

To answer these questions requires that the client and therapist meet, that they communicate with one another in the broadest sense of that term, and that they develop a helping relationship, however brief it might be.

THE HELPING PROCESS

After some twenty to thirty years of analysis and research directed toward discovering what makes therapy helpful, there appears to be general professional agreement that regardless of the specific theory, methods or techniques involved, it is the therapist herself, as a *person*, who determines whether or not she will be helpful to others (Spielberg, 1980; Beutler, 1979; Strupp, 1978; Greben, 1977; Burton, 1972). In this section we will explore what the research literature has had to say about the therapist as a person in two areas. First, we will consider the *personality traits* or characteristics of helpers, which, when effectively communicated to the client, are helpful to the client. Second, we will examine the *values,* that is, the personal beliefs, opinions, attitudes, and standards/morals, of effective therapists, which, when they are "lived" by the therapist and communicated to the client, enable the therapist to act as a role model, which is helpful to the client. More briefly, we will look at the implications of therapist personality and values for selection and training of professional helpers. Let's begin first by outlining the general *goal* of any helping process or approach and the general *dynamics* involved in any helping process which are intended to achieve that goal.

The Goal in Helping Others

The larger, end goal of all therapy is to facilitate the growth and potential of the client to the fullest possible extent (Strupp, 1980; Burton, 1972) in the process of helping to resolve immediate problem behaviour which is experienced with pain and/or distress (Greben, 1977). While the client may approach the helping situation with a specific concern, complaint, or difficulty for which he seeks assistance, the overall therapeutic environment as well as the working on, or working through, of his initial problem has an impact on his total personality and lifestyle. Thus, even the client who seeks to overcome a fear of flying through desensitization therapy brings more of himself to the therapy situation than a set of debilitating anxieties and physical reactions. The learning-based therapist too works with a total person while concentrating attention on specific behavioural change. In the process, the therapeutic intervention does more than eliminate, develop, or improve the specific client behaviour for which the client originally sought help. Like the ripples which flow out from a pebble thrown into a quiet pool, the impact of the therapeutic intervention spreads outward and throughout the entire person. In the example given above, resolving a phobia increases the client's self-esteem: "*I did it.*" It enables him to take risks, to seek and explore with confidence. It may improve his relationships with his wife and/or family and friends. It may enable him to progress in his job or career development. It increases his sense of mastery, his ability to experience pleasure and reward, and to grow. As we have pointed out above, the helping situation, entered for whatever reason, should arm the client with new skills and abilities which, while used to deal with the problems at hand, are in a larger sense skills to employ to live effectively.

THE DYNAMICS INVOLVED IN THE HELPING PROCESS

Greben (1977), Strupp (1978), and Schwartz (1978), among others, have noted that similar basic underlying dynamics appear to be apparent in all helping methods notwithstanding claims of various schools or approaches to be doing unique things. Greben (1977: 372), for example, cites the eight basic elements to which Judd Marmor believed any and all therapies could be reduced: "a good patient-therapist relationship; release of tension; cognitive learning; operant reconditioning; suggestion and persuasion; identification with therapist; reality-testing and emotional support." Burton (1972: 4) reveals something of his own psychoanalytic bias in his list of eight basic elements considered "generic," although there is general conceptual similarity between Burton's and those of Marmor:

> (1) that reason is applied to an anti-reasoning process; (2) that verbal symbols become the method of molar transformation; (3) that pleasure and sex are the vehicle of the healing work; (4) that a form of "morality" is employed to counter superego "shoulds" which constitute the illness; (5) that love and mutual negation are the cement of the process; (6) that loneliness in one person

is used to cure loneliness in the other; (7) that an intellectual process becomes both the quest for and answer to a less than satisfactory existence; (8) that to become less "crazy" the process first calls for becoming more so.

While effective therapists from different orientations claim to do different things in the helping process, they appear to resemble one another very closely in their actual performance (Troemel-Ploetz, 1980).

How do these elements of the therapeutic process work to help the client? Carkhuff and Berenson (1967) offered the following explanation of the helping process. First, if the helper is empathic, compassionate, genuine and respecting, she creates an environment or atmosphere in which the client is enabled to explore his anxiety and hurt. Second, as the client begins to express and experience his anxiety and concern, he experiences a reduction in his inner tension level which is pleasant, rewarding, and self-reinforcing. That is, when the client speaks about his problems, he begins to feel better. He is subsequently motivated to discuss his problems in order to produce this relief from tension and pain. Third, the therapist who can create this helping climate becomes a reinforcement to the client. That is, when the client is with the therapist or helper, he feels good, or at least better. Fourth, the therapist who behaves in a caring, interested, and nurturing fashion toward the client becomes someone for whom the client develops affection, respect and admiration. The "loving," "together" therapist, then, becomes a role model whom the client seeks to emulate. Fifth, the helping relationship breaks through the client's experience of isolation, loneliness, and hopelessness and offers hope to the client for his growth and self-fulfillment.

We may begin to see from this explanation of the basic dynamics which are involved in a helping process just how crucial are the personal qualities and value system of the therapist. Whatever specific techniques she employs or interventions she makes, the therapist must do so while establishing a climate of safety and succour. In addition, the therapist is expected to support and reinforce client behaviour considered essential to the client's growth. Lastly, the therapist is expected to present a role model—an ideal for the client to emulate and identify with. How successful the therapist is in creating a therapeutic atmosphere, in establishing and maintaining a nurturing relationship with the client, in reinforcing behaviour beneficial to the client's growth and in being an appropriate role model will depend largely on *who* the therapist is and not on *what* she does, or says she does.

Personality Traits of the Helping Person
Recognition of the importance of the therapist's personality to the helping process has been late in coming. That we somehow lost sight of the significance of the humanity of the helper appears to be related to our societal preoccupation with science and technology. Psychologists and psychiatrists became so intent on being scientific and professional that they seemed to have forgotten they, and their clients, were people (Greben, 1979). The rebel therapists, some of

whom we will discuss in subsequent chapters, questioned the effectiveness of traditional psychoanalysis and sought better means with which to help their clients. The direct challenge of the new behaviour therapies twenty years ago led to the current focus on the personal qualities of the therapist as the key to therapeutic effectiveness. Unfortunately, the human service system remains populated with an army of helpers selected and trained according to principles now considered invalid.

It was not until 1967 that a team of researchers led by Carl Rogers at the University of Wisconsin, attempting to verify his "necessary and sufficient conditions of therapeutic personality change," began to uncover the significance of therapist personality in the helping process (Carkhuff and Berenson, 1976). What were at first called "dimensions" or "conditions" of therapy gradually became recognized to be characteristics or traits of the therapist. Their work initially identified three core facilitative dimensions in the helping process: empathy, respect (or unconditional positive regard), and congruence. Soon after, slight modifications were made in the descriptions of these three dimensions and four others added. These seven dimensions were empathy, respect, genuineness, concreteness, self-disclosure, immediacy, and confrontation. The identification of these core facilitative interpersonal dimensions has since provided the basis for continued exploration into helping effectiveness and skill development (Carkhuff and Berenson, 1976). Equally important to the discovery by Rogers's team of the significance of certain core facilitative personality traits of helpers was their discovery that helpers could be harmful too. Helper responses to their clients were found to *either* facilitate *or* detract from client growth. There was no *neutral* helper communication, but only "for better or worse" responses (Carkhuff and Berenson, 1967). The implication of this finding on our normal social intercourse is sobering. It means that the responses we give and receive to and from others in the course of our daily interactions do affect them and/or us, either negatively or positively. If we are not being facilitative in our interactions with others, we are detracting from them.

Spielberg's (1980) recent review of the literature now identifies ten core therapist facilitative traits which, if they are employed with sufficient skill and/or are present in the therapist to the extent that they can be readily experienced by the client, will be helpful to the client. We will notice the early Rogerian "dimensions" at the top of Spielberg's list:

1. *Empathy*—the ability to perceive accurately both verbally and nonverbally what another person is feeling and to communicate that perception.
2. *Genuineness*—being freely and deeply oneself.
3. *Respect*—for the client's individual worth, for the client's right to make his or her own choices and mistakes, and respect for the client's potential to master problem areas.
4. *Concreteness*—specificity of feelings, experiences, and behaviour.
5. *Confrontation*—a therapist may use confrontation when a client's verbal and

nonverbal behaviour seem to communicate divergent messages, like the smiling client who speaks of tremendous hurt and rejection, when a discrepancy exists between what a client is currently saying and what he or she has said previously, or when the therapist observes a difference between how the client labels his or her experience and the therapist's view of this experience.

6. *Self-disclosure*—self-disclosure does not provide a license for therapist testimonials and relentless narcissism. The focus of a self-disclosing intervention must remain on the facilitation of client self-exploration and growth.
7. *Warmth*—a concern and appreciation for the client which is behaviourally manifested both verbally and nonverbally.
8. *Immediacy*—here and now explorations of the client's feelings toward the therapist and the therapist's feelings toward the client.
9. *Potency*—charismatic, present, impactful, confident—these words all describe the potent therapist.* But potency without respect, empathy, and warmth is not necessarily helpful.
10. *Self-actualization*—the self-actualized therapist is a living model of someone who practices what he preaches (Spielberg, 1980: 58-59).

To the extent that we possess these core facilitative traits we will be helpful to others, regardless of our professional affiliation as nurses, psychologists, social workers, teachers, or laypeople, and in spite of our identification with a specific therapeutic approach such as Reality Therapy, Gestalt Therapy, or Transactional Analysis. To the extent that we do not, we will be less helpful (Spielberg, 1980).

It is instructive to note Spielberg's use of the terms "trait" and "skill" as interchangeable. Thus at one point he speaks of "core therapist facilitative traits," and in the same paragraph uses the phrase "facilitative skills." Is this appropriate? Are skills and traits identical? Is empathy, for example, a condition, a dimension, or a quality as was suggested earlier? If it is a personal quality or trait, can it also be a skill? Perhaps defining these terms will help us with the answer. A *trait*, or quality, usually refers to an enduring, consistent, or stable physical characteristic or behaviour pattern. "Empathy," then, describes a particular type of feeling or emotion, but "being empathic" may describe a consistent behaviour pattern observed in an individual's relationships with other people. To the extent that it is consistent, or relatively stable, it may be described as a personal trait. A *skill* also refers to observed behaviour. We speak of "possessing," "having" and/or "developing" skills. Skills, then, are similar to traits in that they too describe qualities of the person, but skills also imply a more dynamic aspect of human behaviour. Skill, like talent, suggests potential for development of specific behaviour which, first, is under the conscious control of the person; second, can be improved or refined with practice and commit-

---

* The ability to awaken hope in the hopeless patient, what Greben (1977), refers to as "therapeutic forcefulness," would also seem to be a part of potency.

ment; and third, is experienced by the person as organismically enhancing and self-actualizing. Considered in this way, both terms would appear to be appropriate for describing essential helper qualities, with "trait" reflecting the existence or presence of the quality, and "skill" reflecting the conscious effort for developing and improving the quality behaviourally for self-enhancement and actualization.† Using empathy again as our example, a person may or may not demonstrate empathy as a personal trait or characteristic. If it does not appear as a personal trait, the potential for skill development, even with conscious effort and practice, may not be great. Just as we do not all have the same talent or potential for the development of musical or mathematical skills, there appear to be individual differences in the presence and actualization of helping skills. When we refer to the core facilitative traits as skills, we are emphasizing the conscious development by the helper of these existing personal characteristics to a high degree, so that they can be helpful to the client.

PERSONAL VALUES OF THE HELPER

It may be somewhat artificial to discuss the therapist's values as a separate feature as though they could exist independently or apart from the total personality. Certainly they are an important and integral component of the therapist as a person, but are distinguished from personal qualities perhaps by their less tangible nature. But values, defined as the beliefs, opinions, attitudes, standards, or philosophy of an individual, are potent behavioural antecedents. The values of the therapist, then, not only govern the therapist's behaviour, they have the power of directly influencing the person seeking help. In the therapeutic or helping process, then, where the therapist is expected to be genuine, self-disclosing, and potent, is the client merely indoctrinated with the value system of the therapist? What are the possibilities for the client to develop or maintain a value system of his own?

Strupp (1980), Beutler (1979), Ansell (1977), and Carkhuff and Berenson (1967) conclude that therapy is not a value-free process, as it was once touted to be, and that indeed the values and beliefs of therapists are transmitted to, and influence, their clients. Some interesting support for this view is provided by the recent study of Shuger and Bebout (1980), who found a tendency for voluntary clients to choose therapeutic approaches which were "consistent with their own attitudes, values, and lifestyle." However, matching the client's value system with that of the therapist while avoiding the problem of propagandizing and indoctrination, or "undue influence," appears to negate the goal of therapy because it reinforces the client's existing behaviour and prevents real growth.

---

† The terms "skill" and "technique" are also often used interchangeably. In this text, "technique" is used to describe a method, procedure, or device which is not related to the personal qualities of the helper per se. See Appendix A, Chapter 1 for a discussion of six interview techniques commonly employed during the helping process.

Strupp (1980: 397-98) concludes that specific articulation of the essential values which underly therapy is required and offers the following:

1. People have the right to personal freedom and independence.
2. As adult members of a particular society, they have rights and privileges but they also have responsibilities to others.
3. To the greatest extent possible, people should be responsible for conducting their own lives, without undue dependence on others.
4. People are responsible for their actions but not their feelings, fantasies, etc.
5. People's individuality should be fully respected, and they should not be controlled, dominated, manipulated, coerced, or indoctrinated.
6. People are entitled to make their own mistakes and to learn from their life experiences.

Still, stating a value system is very different from adopting and living it. And given the fact that many or most of us have grown up without experiencing the antecedent conditions leading to high self-esteem as described above by Coopersmith, we may not have developed the highly intrinsic value system required of the helper. If we are to facilitate our clients' development of a personal value system which permits and enhances their freedom to seek and explore their own fulfillment of potential, we will need to have worked out our own personal philosophy of life and standards for behaviour. As effective helpers we seek neither to indoctrinate our clients with our own value system nor to counsel their conformity to prevailing social norms and beliefs. How might we achieve this perspective from which to objectively and realistically view ourselves, our clients and the society to which we belong? Training and supervision would be one way, and the process of our own therapy another. The work of Peebles (1980) suggests that even though those of us who aspire, or claim, to be helping persons may not *need* therapy to deal with serious concerns, our personal therapy experience as clients will help us to help others.

> This author believes that personal therapy unequivocally has a positive effect on a therapist's functioning. Above all, the personal therapy provides the therapist with the experience of being a patient with all the ambiguities and anxieties that go along with being under scrutiny and struggling to reflect on oneself. . . . The experience and process of introspection can tend to free up defenses and increase flexibility of thinking. It can enable a person to become more cognizant of and more differentiating with respect to one's emotional responses. In addition, the process of self-disclosure, along with increased self-understanding, may lead to more acceptance of self and less defensiveness with people (Peebles, 1980: 258).

Carkhuff and Berenson (1967: 201) take an even stronger stand. They suggest that not only would some type of therapeutic experience be required for helpers who themselves must overcome the destructive experience of living in a society imbued with neurotic values, but that *only* those who they describe as "fully functioning whole persons" have the right to be helpers.

Only the fully functioning whole person has the *right* to be a counsellor or therapist, for only he lives in society, yet is able to see society through the eyes of its victims, and only he can discriminate between the good and the bad. Those counsellors and therapists functioning below this level have no *right* to offer themselves as therapeutic agents and models. The fact is that most counsellors and therapists cannot successfully meet the circumstances with which their clients are coping. The interaction between such a counsellor and his client can be nothing more than a fraud.

The effective helper or counsellor then needs to *live* effectively herself. The "whole" counsellor is first a "whole" person. She is effective because she is the kind of person she is, not because she knows a lot about counselling, has years of counselling experience, or can utilize various helping techniques. Like her client, she is a growing and developing person.

Carkhuff and Berenson (1967) described the following as characteristics of whole persons or effective counsellors. We might better view them as *values* or *ideals* which we as helpers pursue, as do our clients, in the course of growing and becoming. Let's examine each of them and engage in a little introspection. Are we *whole* people in these terms? Do we agree with Carkhuff and Berenson's contention that only those with such characteristics, ideals, or values have a right to be counsellors? If not, why not? If so, what are the implications for each of us?

VALUES FOR HELPERS AND THEIR CLIENTS

1. The only consistency for the whole person is internal.

The person who is in tune with and acts on the basis of his integrity is free to modify, incorporate, and learn from venturing into the unknown, with fear, but a knowledge that his inner being will not and cannot be destroyed. Furthermore, he is not neutralized when others demand consistency. The person who has reached society's limits of tolerance for personal emergence and stops, has agreed not only to emerge no further, but also not to upset social systems, and not to expose others who have sold their integrity.

2. Creativity and honesty are a way of life for the whole person.

The whole person is fully aware that he is as creative as he is honest. Any semblance of trading or compromising responsible honesty results in an attenuated creativity. The real risk for the whole person involves honesty not being a way of life, in all his actions, with and including physical implications. A dishonest act, for the whole person, results in a dysfunction of the basic physical foundations of life: eating, sleeping, elimination and sex. Honesty in communication is not, however, without qualification, as in the case of the extremely brittle patient.

3. Although the way the whole person lives his life is seen by others to be too dangerous, too intense, and too profound, he is in tune with the fact that his real risk involves living life without risk.

Life has meaning in new discoveries, larger boundaries, deeper insights, more pain, more joy, and the realization that the whole person can only be as full with another person as he is full with himself when alone.

4. The whole person realizes that life is empty without acting.

The full person must discriminate among possible acts, make his choice, and *Act*. The most significant learning comes from acting on those aspects of life the individual fears most. For the whole person there is only security in risks. In this way, and only in this way, can the individual gain or lose. In a life without risk, no one wins, no one loses, and no one learns.

5. The whole person realizes that whatever he does is worth doing fully and well.

Full emergence depends on a full and an integrated output of energy.

6. The whole and creative person functions at a high energy level.

He employs his energy fully, resting only as much as is necessary to restore his usual vigour, so as to be able to bring to bear and tap his talents fully in dealing with crises and being productive in everyday life.

7. The whole person comes to the realization that few men are large enough or whole enough to nourish and love this creative person.

A full relationship, free of neurotic drainage, is only possible among whole people. Others, functioning at lower levels, cannot go beyond insisting that the creative person has been lucky enough to stumble on a new or novel gimmick.

8. The whole person is fully aware that any significant human relationship is in the process of deepening or deteriorating.

Stability in any relationship is only apparent. When it is not growing it undergoes changes which increase distance between those involved; this is true for parent-child, teacher-student, husband-wife, and counsellor-client relationships.

9. The whole person realizes that most men say "yes" out of fear of the implications of saying "no," and that most men say "no" out of fear of the implications of saying "yes."

The whole person can predict a great deal of behaviour from this statement, knowing that the majority of people cannot see or respond to anything but the fear of the implications of their act at a choice point.

10. The whole person is fully aware that in order to live life in such a way that it is a continuous learning and relearning process, he must periodically burn bridges behind him.

The full life requires making discriminations. To leave room for everyone in one's life is only to leave room [is to leave no room?] for one's self and, thus, retards self-definition. Clinging to past associations which drain energies only nourishes neurotic needs and diminishes creative output.

11. The whole person realizes that he is, and must be, his own pathfinder, and travel a road never travelled before.

The whole person can be alone with himself. Creative acts by definition require new and untread directions. If the person cannot live with himself, he cannot discover directions congruent with who he is; only when he does can he hope to reach for full fruition of his talents and person.

12. The whole person does not fear living intensely.

The whole person experiences greater joy and greater pain. He is aware that life is full as it is intense. He can endure and even flourish as he lives intensely, because he has fully integrated the emotional, intellectual, and physical. It is only under extreme circumstances that the whole person taps deeper personal resources and significant new learning.

13. The whole person is prepared to face the implications of functioning a step ahead or above most of those with whom he comes into contact.

Knowing when not to act or to respond in terms of his deep sensitivities requires fine discriminations: These actions depend upon whether or not the second person recognizes that the whole person can be a positive and constructive influence. The whole person's insights, because they are so far beyond the obvious, are often interpreted as being psychopathic or paranoid. Further, he is often isolated and the subject of malicious gossip picturing him as an insensitive freak, or infantile. In other instances, the least fortunate of those exhibiting unusual talent are shaped up early in life. They are usually put on reinforcement schedules so that they provide entertainment for the less potent and the impotent.

14. The whole person is aware that for most people life is a cheap game.

Psychotherapy, as another social institution, is seen by most as a means for getting people back into the game. The whole person asks the question as to whether or not he wants to help them back into the game. Furthermore, he searches ways and means to bring the "less knowing" to fulfillment in a life without games.

15. The whole person is fully aware that many of society's rewards are designed to render the creative impotent.

Striving for and then achieving societal rewards traps the creative person into living his life so that he proves to others that he was, after all, worthy of such recognition: he can no longer make new contributions; he can only rely on old ones.

16. The whole person realizes that to emerge within the acceptable levels tolerated by society means institutionalization.

Institutionalization within society renders creative acts and persons neutral and keeps them from further growth by making them a part of history. Society, after a long series of trials, moves to institutionalize the creative person operating beyond its limits.

17. The whole person realizes that he must escape traps to render him impotent.

A few of the traps involve invitations to join society at considerable compromise, living up to images, rumours and myths, and responding to all the efforts to discredit the whole person's work rather than continuing to produce.

18. The whole person is aware of the awesome responsibility which comes with freedom.

The whole person must do more than know all that there is to know about his life and work in order to stay whole and extend his boundaries. He must go beyond the known to meet his responsibilities to his own integrity knowing that without this he cannot act responsibly, with and for another (Carkhuff and Berenson, 1967: 198-201).

SELECTING AND TRAINING HELPERS

On the basis of the foregoing discussion of the import of the therapist's personality and value system in the helping process, we might assume that these factors would be given priority in the selection of those accepted for training. This does not appear to be the case. Academic achievement and cognitive skills continue to take precedence in the selection of those being trained for both the traditional helping fields such as psychiatry, psychology, and social work, and those in which helping *roles* define their professional status, such as teaching, nursing, and law. The key question of course is, "Can facilitative personality traits and personal values supportive of the helping process be learned in a training program of *any* kind?" How much personality and value change can be expected to occur in a training program, even if this *were* the focus? The suggestion is made above that the mere presence of the facilitative traits is not enough. Rather, we have determined that they must be highly developed as personality skills to be helpful to the client. Given that students are prepared to work toward such changes in personal traits and value system, can training programs significantly improve or develop such facilitative personality skills and values, and how long does it take?

Spielberg's (1980) evaluation of graduate students in social work and clinical psychology discovered the following:

- Graduate training did result in some small improvements in the student's production and discrimination of facilitative responses.
- Length of their graduate training, however, was not associated with increas-

ing improvement. That is, second-year social work graduate students did almost as well as third-year clinical psychology students and fourth-year graduate psychology students were no better than third-year psychology students.

- While all graduate students continually improved on their ability to *discriminate* what were facilitative responses throughout their training program they did not continually improve their ability to *produce* such responses themselves. In fact, on the evaluation scales used, only 2 per cent of all graduate students made responses considered to be minimally facilitative. This would imply, using Carkhuff and Berenson's all-or-none theory, that 98 per cent made minimally *detracting* responses.

Spielberg (1980: 67-68) concludes that the reason for the poor showing in production, in comparison with discrimination, of facilitative responses by graduate students seems to be related to the theoretical emphasis in the graduate education of professional helpers:

> Courses are most concerned with the transmission of cognitively oriented information. The emphasis is on theory, with the assumption that somehow the student is able to translate this knowledge into proved clinical skill. It is as if swimming were taught from a theoretical perspective; describing, analyzing and studying the various aspects of swimming. Students would be able to recognize good swimmers and discuss some of the technicalities of effective strokes. However, the students would have done little swimming themselves. The training models which have demonstrated effectiveness have all involved laboratory type experiences (actually "swimming" under skilled guidance; Carkhuff & Truax, 1965a, 1965b; Truax & Carkhuff, 1967).

Learning to "swim," or to make helpful responses at and beyond the minimally facilitative level with clients, requires *doing* and practising. This actual performance of facilitative personality traits such that they become skills, under "skilled guidance," is called *supervision*. Unfortunately, the odds that a student will be able to work with and be supervised by a skilled and effective helper are poor. Spielberg (1980: 59) reports, for example, that, "the chances that a trainee will be taught by a therapist who is himself either ineffective or harmful are two out of three." The importance of the supervision process, which is critical in the training of helpers, is made even more tenuous by the fact that the nature of that experience too is dependent upon the special personal qualities of the principal teacher. Greben (1979), recognizing the significance of the supervision process in the training of therapists, makes several suggestions which may help to resolve this circular dilemma:

- Make explicit among the staff of training programs the significance of personal traits and values to the supervisors of student helpers, so that they can be aware of the need to focus their attention on enhancing the student's potential skill development in these areas.

- Expose the students to teachers who themselves possess these qualities and values and demonstrate them in their work with both clients and students.
- Expose the student to more than one supervisor so as to provide several possible role models. The purpose of this is to prevent the negative effects of either overwhelming emulation and adoration on the part of the student, or possible feelings of omnipotence or rivalry on the part of the supervisor.
- Include as part of the supervisory function opportunities for supervisors to meet and share experience, and to identify and discuss ways of handling areas of common concern in supervision.
- Include as part of the supervisor's responsibilities certain administrative tasks pertaining to the client so that supervisors remain oriented to the practical realities of meeting client needs and do not present or promote an artificial idealized response to client problems. Students need to learn what is appropriate and realistic under the circumstances and context in which they are working.

In summary, Greben (1979: 511) says:

> From the student's point of view, the development of his own therapeutic stance, style and capacity are best encouraged through the intensive repeated interaction with a number of teachers who rank high in those qualities which, it appears, are indeed therapeutic. The student should be encouraged to read the papers of the few of those highly competent therapists who have displayed in addition to their therapeutic effectiveness, the ability to understand and conceptualize and describe those capacities. He should be exposed to teachers who know they are competent, but who are willing to challenge the neurotic (transference) idealization of their capacities, teachers who accept the view that some future therapists are born with more capacity, but all can have their innate capacity grow and develop through mutual efforts on the part of both student and teacher.

Similar criticism of the training of British social workers is made by Millington (1981). Basing his comments on reports of the Central Council for Education and Training in Social Work (CCETSW), he suggests that the absence of clearly stated and/or accepted learning objectives for social work students reflects a lack of integration in social work theory and practice which create student conflict and confusion. In particular, he discusses the question of whether the social worker, recognizing the social and economic constraints which restrict the potential for client change, acts with clients to maintain the status quo, and thus is an agent of *social control*, or whether the worker is an agent of *social change*, attempting to alter the society and/or community in the interest of the client. The greater education and knowledge base of the social worker gives the worker a much stronger position of power than the client's. This power, if unrecognized by the social worker, may result in a relationship of subtle coercion, manipulation, and control of the client by the worker, rather than what we have called a helping relationship in which the client's autonomous growth is facilitated. How can such power struggles and potential manipulation be avoided? Millington suggests emphasizing in the training of social workers certain basic social work values related to the client-worker relationship, such as the use of the process of negotiation and contracts, the communication of respect for the client, the importance of full disclosure by the worker of the basis for her behaviour with the client and others. We can identify in these "values" some of the core personality skills and therapist values we described earlier. So the British too, while recognizing the importance of personality and values in the establishment and maintenance of a helping relationship, are struggling with the problems of selection and training of helpers.

> The management of such a relationship places a great responsibility upon the social worker and it is to be hoped that the processes of selection and training will have produced individuals possessing the personality, values and knowledge required to discharge it adequately. There is, however, little evidence that this is in fact the case (Millington, 1981: 22).

We might conclude that, while greater attention should be given to determining which applicants for entry to the helping fields already possess the core facilitative traits and essential therapeutic value system, we need to examine too the learning environment, the requisite teacher/supervisor personalities and values, and the training focus. The emphasis, rather than on psychological theory, should be on students' further development of their existent core facilitative traits to the level of skill, under the supervision of a skilled and competent therapist/teacher.

ETHICAL ISSUES

The *Random House Dictionary of the English Language* (1966) indicates that the term "ethics" "implies high standards of honest and honourable dealing, and of methods used, especially in the professions. . . ." Let's consider briefly the ethics of helping with this definition in mind, from three perspectives: in terms of, first, the contemporary economic, social, and political conditions in North America; second, the relationship between helpers and clients; and last, individual client rights.

Social Democracy: The System

While there are those who may dislike the label "social democracy" applied to the Canadian and American political systems, it is nonetheless accurate. Both Canada and the U.S. have inherited from their British forebears a strong tradition for helping the poor, the sick, the old, and the disabled or disadvantaged. Both have strong federal, regional, and local governments involved in the provision of an extensive array of public services, many of which are universal in nature. A large number of these services have been created and are maintained to assist, protect, and rehabilitate individual citizens. Medical services and hospital care are wholly or partially provided by government. In Canada we have elementary and secondary education wholly, and post-secondary education largely, supported by government. We also have an array of special social services for those in need as well as programs to provide financial assistance on either a long-term or short-term basis. We have government-assisted home-ownership programs, retirement programs, even home-insulation programs.

There is increasing government intervention in the private sector too. Government appears to be required to further regulate and control business and industry in the interests of the individual citizen and the economy as a whole. At the same time, attempts are made to entice, stimulate, and encourage economic growth through an array of government assistance programs involving direct financial aid through devices such as tax incentives, loans, outright grants, cost-sharing, and a variety of trade and industrial development support mechanisms. The stimulus to research and technological development and to the maintenance of general economic stability by direct government spending for military and space programs in the United States cannot be overestimated. The current crisis in the auto industry represents one of the most colossal failures of the free enterprise system. Its economic impact is so far-reaching that both the American and Canadian governments have had to prop up the ailing Chrysler organization with billions in loan guarantees which it appears the public purse will be destined to repay, and with no return.

And so, not only is all not well in Canada and the U.S., but there are indications of serious trouble. For even with our socialist traditions we find deeply rooted and growing social problems and individual suffering characterize our communities. Our nations appear split with racial and ethnic tensions: black vs. white in the United States and English vs. French in Canada. Our Indian and Eskimo forebears are still painfully excluded from any meaningful recognition. In both countries the rich grow richer and the growing poor, poorer. Unemployment of 7-8 per cent now appears to be the norm. Double-digit inflation and soaring consumer credit rates promote a sense of economic powerlessness in the middle class, and fear in the poor, the disadvantaged, and the elderly.

We live in an era of rapid changes in values with the result that the "generation gap" is becoming shorter. It used to be that the "generation gap" referred to the difference in values between daughter, mother, and grandmother. Now the gap can occur between sisters and brothers as well: significant value and norm changes seem to be appearing even *between* decades. The idealism of the early sixties came crashing down for those who were to enter adolescence after the Kennedy assassinations. The Vietnam War, Watergate, and the Mid-East oil crisis brought a return to conservative values in the seventies. The optimistic progressive liberalism of the sixties has faded, and our eighties youth reflect a growing conservatism, resembling their grandparents more than their parents.

In short, we do not yet have "the good life." Ellis (1976), Frank (1979), and Carkhuff and Berenson (1967, 1976) perceive American society as neurotic, unhealthy, and psychologically abnormal and conclude that anyone who has been raised within it cannot help but suffer some neurotic distress. We fare no better in Canada, according to this excerpt from a report of The Vanier Institute of the Family (1977: 13):

> We recognize that the persistence of poverty, income disparity and unemployment as well as the limitations and inequities of our current systems of education and communication and the widespread feeling of alienation from the processes of work and decision-making in our country, all too often prevent persons from developing the capacity to reflect upon their lives, and to choose, in an authentic and responsible manner, a lifestyle appropriate to them.

So after almost sixty years of social reform in Canada and the United States (in both countries the real impetus for social programs occurred after the First World War), we are still left with widespread poverty, unemployment, disparities in educational opportunity and therefore economic opportunity, crime, delinquency, mental illness, and institutionalization of dependent populations. Our social reformers, experts, and helping professions have not yet succeeded in creating "the good life" for everyone.

What are the prospects for the lean '80s? What is the future of the human services system in this period of economic scarcity? In the United States, considerable concern is being expressed by human service professionals about reductions in public funding for social programs (Pilisuk, 1980; England, 1980; Alger, 1980). Foley and Schneider (1980) suggest that while budget cuts for public services may be anticipated during periods of economic recession, the programs most vulnerable to budget reduction or withdrawal will be those serving the less articulate and more disadvantaged members of the community. It is in their opinion the responsibility of those of us who serve such clients to become active politically and to speak out on our clients' behalf when this occurs:

> The economically disadvantaged, minorities, and those who are developmentally disabled are not going to be able to be strong advocates for programs that serve them. Professions concerned with the needs of these groups, even if they do not themselves work in the publicly supported institutions that serve them, have a responsibility to speak on their behalf in public forums such as state legislatures, meetings of county councils, boards of commissioners, school boards, etc. . . .
>
> If the public perceives that the value it receives from public services is commensurate with the price it is paying for these services, it will assume a commitment to pay the price for local services it needs and wants. People must understand what the price is and what it is for. If they do not believe that they are getting value for their money, we will continue to be faced with other Proposition 13s. It is up to us—government officials, professionals, and concerned citizens—to dramatize the value of good government and to insist on effective, effi-

cient, and needed government programs so that the public will make its long-range decisions with knowledge and intelligence (Foley and Schneider, 1980: 214).

There remains much for those in the fields of helping to do. We must accept, as part of our helping role, a greater commitment to public education, public accountability, and social and political action than we may have perceived thus far.

Helpers and Clients: The Players

We have considered the essential qualities and values of helpers which seem most directly related to helping others. How helpful are they? After almost thirty years of claims, counterclaims, and research into the effectiveness of psychotherapy, this question appears to remain unanswered.

> For almost three decades there has been a controversy in psychotherapy concerning whether or not therapy makes for real change and, specifically, whether patients might not achieve the same results without going into therapy. The controversy began with a study by J.H. Eysenck, who found that subjects had about a two-thirds remission rate whether they were in therapy or simply on a waiting list for therapy. Twenty-six years and at least fourteen related studies later, the controversy was still unsettled, and the best that the defenders of psychotherapy could say was that the two-thirds remission rate reported for people on a waiting list is much too high—that there is a remission rate for those not in therapy, but a much lower one than Eysenck reported. As for the improvement rate in therapy itself, a review of the studies since Eysenck suggested that there was only a modest change in psychotherapy patients. In addition a review of some 38 studies came to the conclusion that no one traditional psychotherapeutic method was more successful than another (Janov, 1980: 170-71).

Psychiatrist, psychologist, counsellor and social worker, employing various methods and techniques, seem equally effective. How effective is that? Not very, according to the research evidence thus far.

> The compelling question of what aspects of therapy work for what kinds of problems when practised by what kinds of therapists for what kinds of patients is probably empirically unanswerable because it is methodologically unsolvable (Kisch and Kroll, 1980: 406).

Kisch and Kroll suggest that, because it is impossible to design and conduct a research study that would determine effectiveness scientifically, we should concentrate our efforts on discovering the value of therapy from the client's perspective. Morrison (1979: 382) draws a similar conclusion, and suggests that therapists consider their clients in the role of consumers and evaluators of therapy.

> The client-consumer judgment of the clinical service received is just as important to eventual improvement of that service, as is the automobile-buyer's judg-

ment of a particular car to the eventual improvement of that product. Certainly few would deny that the judgments of automobile consumers have changed the safety and gas-economy of automobiles. Perhaps therapy clients need more encouragement to safeguard their own rights so as to avoid becoming the victims of "consumer fraud" i.e., being "sold" a service (therapy) without understanding what it is or what the risks involved are. And thus we therapists will thus work harder to find more effective therapeutic modalities.

Frank's comments on this subject, while perhaps reassuring for the professional helper, are also humbling:

> Without claiming scientific validity for it, then, I would hazard the judgment that cults, group activities, and psychotherapy on balance help more persons than they hurt. Some, to be sure, are injurious, the damage ranging from a brief period of distress following an encounter group or EST program to the horrors of the People's Temple. By and large however, most individuals seem to derive some increase in personal security and sense of significance, although in many ways it does not endure (1979: 404).

For the practising professional and budding novice, the conflicting research evidence, and, at best, modest support for the therapeutic effectiveness of psychotherapy is cause for reflection.* Does it mean that helpers by and large are not, as Carkhuff and Berenson suggested, "whole" persons and are therefore ineffective helpers? Does it account for the failure of the social reform movement during the past sixty years? Does it mean that the various helping disciplines need to reexamine their theoretical assumptions and techniques? Whatever the answers to these questions, the evidence suggests that we look with modesty at our skill and role as helpers, that we consider *when* our intervention is necessary and *whether* it is likely to be helpful or meaningful to the client, and, ultimately, that we determine whether or not it was experienced as such by the client.

Towbin (1978) has traded in his psychotherapist badge and membership card and seems to have resolved several ethical dilemmas by no longer *claiming* to help anyone. He describes his role with clients as that of professional confidant. He is there to listen and talk to the client. That *may* be helpful to the client, but is not considered the *responsibility* of the confidant.

Roger Ulrich (1978), a turncoat behaviourist-cum-humanist, deals with the issue in another way. He simply refuses to accept that what any individual

---

* The review of recent literature on the therapeutic effectiveness of professional helpers by the Office of Technology Assessment (1980: 4) reaches a cautiously positive conclusion: ". . . the available research, some of which meets rigorous methodological standards, seems to indicate that psychotherapy treatment is clearly better than no treatment. However, while the literature supports a generally positive conclusion with respect to the effectiveness of psychotherapy, there is a lack of specific information about the conditions under which psychotherapy is effective. . . ."

does in interaction with another has any more powerful or lasting effect than the act of any other individual.

Perhaps, then, the central issue in helping is the issue of ethics itself. Can the helper deal with the client honestly and honourably? If so, whether or not the client is "helped," the helper at least is not diminished.

Client Needs vs. Client Rights: The New Revolution

It is appropriate to end this introductory chapter with some comments about our slow awakening to the ethics of client rights. The extreme examples of violation of client rights are graphically presented in the film *Hurry Tomorrow* (1975), and from accounts such as that of Mrs. Lake (Rothman, 1978). Mrs. Lake was a Washington, D.C. resident who carried her worldly possessions in two shopping bags. One day she went to the Department of Justice to make a claim for a pension to which she felt entitled. (Her claim was denied.) As she was leaving the building, a police officer noticed her. The police officer thought Mrs. Lake seemed disoriented and asked her for her home address. Mrs. Lake was unable to respond appropriately, and although she had found her way to the Justice Department, the officer believed she could not find her way back home. Subsequently, Mrs. Lake was placed in St. Elizabeth's Mental Hospital for "wandering" in mind and body. Despite her persistent efforts to be released, she remained confined there for the rest of her life. A similar case occurring in Eastern Canada was reported recently in the Canadian Press (Heller and Tesher, 1980). A young man accused of attempted purse snatching was found unfit to stand trial because of mental illness and was detained in a mental hospital for sixteen years. It is estimated that some one thousand Canadians are currently "incarcerated" in mental hospitals even though they either were never tried, or were found not guilty by reason of insanity.

The extremes, as dramatic and horrific as they are, cloud the issue in a "forest for the trees" sense. They hide the grating paternalism perpetrated against those recipients of the "largesse" of the state. The socialist democracy responsible for the provision of so many social programs and services has not given freely. In return for its social services to meet social needs, it has taken away individual rights. Thus, the welfare "means" or "needs" test is a routine invasion of privacy, forcing individuals to prove to the parent-state that they are in need of assistance. "Proof" means providing any and all information and documentation requested by the state about one's most personal and private affairs. In fact, need alone may not satisfy the state. People may be required to prove as well that they are *deserving* of assistance. Only fifteen years ago periodic night raids were conducted by staff of the Ontario Department of Public Welfare on the residences of deserted wives and mothers to see if there were men living with them. And interrogation about absent spouses and social and sexual relationships continues today as part of most welfare assistance programs.

In meeting the physical care needs of the elderly in nursing and old-age homes we often inadvertently take away their right of free movement and association, their ownership of personal property, and their privacy. In the elementary and secondary schools we have restricted freedom of expression and set standards for dress and hair styles. In our educational institutions at all levels, we have developed a learning environment which demands dependent conformity rather than autonomous growth. The incursion of the state into the individual rights of its citizens in the course of delivering "social" services has occurred unintentionally (Glasser, 1978). For while there are strong constitutional safeguards in the United States, and it is hoped, in process in Canada, against abuses of government *power*, government "benevolence" was considered as either benign or as morally right. It did not occur to the various reformers, politicians, and administrators that social programs, designed to *help* people, could in any way be harmful. Because the aim and intent of social programs was humanitarian and uplifting, and the professionals and administrators involved indicated their strong personal commitment and enthusiasm, they were afforded a degree of trust by legislators denied other government program advocates. Thus, social programs and social legislation were not concerned with client rights. It was assumed that the professionals and administrators involved who claimed honest and honourable intentions would behave accordingly.

Social service program legislation, then, has failed not only to clearly define what administrators and workers *cannot* do but as well to delineate specifically what they *can* do. The absence of detailed and concrete legislation was originally intended to permit administrators the flexibility and leeway to act in the best interests of their clients. Guidelines, rather than rigid formulas, were developed in order to enable the administrator to respond flexibly to varying client needs and situations, and to prevent service from being denied due to legislative inadequacies. The unintended consequence of enabling administrators and workers to "interpret" the "rules," was to give them enormous *discretionary power* over their clients.

What eventually happens when free citizens have their rights denied, ignored, or abolished through capricious use of power? They rebel. The rebellion of the consumers and clients of the social service system began in the '60s and is continuing. It heralds, I believe, a new social revolution in Canada and the United States. It is much more significant in implication than the reform movement of the early 1900s which brought us to our current form of social democracy. The leaders of our last social revolution sought change to help others. The reform leaders today seek change to help themselves.

The '60s saw citizens' groups of all kinds spring up to demand a say in the provision of social and other services, and in the planning and administration of government programs directly affecting them. There were tenants' groups: public housing and private apartment tenants who pressed for action. There were native people's groups who demanded recognition, freedom from dependency, and compensation. There were poverty and welfare rights groups, "grey power" groups, black power groups, student and ratepayer groups, and the handicapped. Suddenly, high school principals, college deans, welfare administrators, social workers, public housing managers, doctors and hospital administrators, and politicians at all levels, were under attack. For the "clients" of the system had discovered that when school principals or deans had to choose between the interests of the student and the interests of the school, they chose the school. When welfare administrators or public housing managers had to choose between the interests of their agencies and the client, they sided with their agencies. The clients of the system had discovered that their interests and the interests of workers and administrators were not the same and moreover that they could not *trust* these people to act on their behalf. They had learned that these people had a great deal of power, and that they could, and would, use this power *against* them. Thus, the client and "helper" in the social service system today have become adversaries. The client cannot expect that the system will necessarily act in his or her best interest.

Glasser (1978) suggests that even should we eventually solve, through some kind of economic equalization system, the current problem of economic dependency experienced by many of our citizens, there will always remain those in our communities who will continue to be in need of our care and support—the elderly, the disabled, children. We cannot therefore expect to eliminate completely those social programs intended to assist those in need. What we can do, however, is to try to ensure, by developing some basic principles of operation, that whatever services we do provide will not have the unintended negative features and consequences we find in many of our social services today.

Three such principles (Glasser, 1978) might be:

1. The Bill of Rights applies to social institutions of caring and limits the powers of those institutions and their employees over the lives of the dependent.

This means that clients would be protected legally from abuse of discretionary power by administrators and staff.

2. Enforcement of client rights is not self-executing and therefore requires an external force.

An external body or agency free from financial or political control is required to act on behalf of clients in legal disputes with social agencies. Such agencies as the American Civil Liberties Union and Canadian Civil Rights Association are examples.

3. Every program designed to help the dependent ought to be evaluated, not on the basis of the *good* it might do, but rather on the basis of the *harm* it might do. Those programs ought to be adopted that seem to be the least likely to make things worse.

This third principle, called the "principle of least harm," should be the basis for every decision where intervention is being considered by the helper. Given the evidence on helper effectiveness, we would do well to stop and consider carefully, before taking action, the possible harm any intervention on our part might bring. This is particularly germane in child and family matters where often our interventions "in the best interest of the child" have proven disastrous for both child and family.

Perhaps our failure to improve the quality of life for so many of our clients through our social, health, and educational programs stems from our preoccupation with satisfying their basic needs. Perhaps we have been too concerned with *survival* and in the process, have neglected *life*. The contemporary rebellion of our clients challenges us to help them live effectively as whole persons. Anything less is not good enough.

SUMMARY

Part I has attempted to present a rationale for the text, indicate its theoretical bias, and to examine some basic concepts, assumptions, and issues which relate to contemporary helping approaches. In doing so, we have explored six basic components of helping, which when considered together provide a perspective or vantage point from which to consider the specific helping disciplines and approaches described in the following chapters.

The six basic components of any effective helping approach are:

1. A theory or model of normal human growth and behaviour from which to view the client, which includes the following human characteristics: (a) self-esteem, (b) self-control, (c) intrinsic values, (d) personal responsibility, (e) social responsibility, and (f) competence.
2. The presence of the following ten core therapist facilitative traits or skills: (a) empathy, (b) genuineness, (c) respect, (d) concreteness, (e) confrontation, (f) self-disclosure, (g) warmth, (h) immediacy, (i) potency, and (j) self-actualization.
3. A concern with and expression of essential therapist values, such as those provided by Strupp (1980: 397-98):

    1. People have the right to personal freedom and independence.
    2. As adult members of a particular society, they have rights and privileges but they also have responsibilities to others.
    3. To the greatest extent possible, people should be responsible for conducting their own lives, without undue dependence on others.
    4. People are responsible for their actions but not their feelings, fantasies, etc.
    5. People's individuality should be fully respected, and they should not be controlled, dominated, manipulated, coerced, or indoctrinated.
    6. People are entitled to make their own mistakes and to learn from their life experiences.

4. A stated goal or objective which embraces the concept of facilitating client growth and potential while helping to resolve immediate client concerns and distress.
5. A description and explanation of the dynamics involved in the specific helping process which are considered to help the client.
6. An indication of awareness of ethical issues involved in helping others, and in particular the issue of client rights.

APPENDIX A

Six Interview Techniques

In Chapter 1, we discussed the prime importance of the personality and personal values of any helping person in establishing and maintaining a facilitating relationship with the client. We identified ten core facilitating personal characteristics or traits which seem to be essential to the helping process, and noted that these personal traits need to be developed as *skills* in order that they may be helpful to the client. We have also noted that in addition to *being* a helping person with these requisite skills and values, the helper or therapist will employ various techniques or methods according to the discipline and/or therapeutic approach followed, for example, depending on whether we are social workers who use Transactional Analysis or are teachers using a Reality Therapy approach. The material that follows describes some basic techniques or devices commonly employed in helping interviews of all kinds. In using these techniques, the helper does so such that she has a vehicle for communicating her core facilitative personal skills to the client. Part of this communication of herself will be through body language, facial expression, tone of voice, etc. It will be non-verbal and powerful. An equally important part, however, is what she actually *says*. In this respect, *what* is said, that is, the specific response of the helper, is also important in the helping process. Watchel (1980) notes how little attention is generally given to the importance of the *wording* of therapist comments and responses. And yet it is to a great extent the choice of words which the therapist employs which convey her empathic understanding, her genuineness, and her respect or positive regard for the client. In presenting the following interview techniques, various approaches are suggested for employing each technique. These suggestions are not meant to be exhaustive and are basically explanatory. Where specific examples of possible verbal responses are given, an attempt has been made to use wording which would be considered appropriate and effective in the particular situation. In the long run, of course, learning to say the "right" thing, or to use words which facilitate the helping process, requires training, practice, and supervision by an experienced and effective helper who may facilitate the development of helper skill.

Six basic helping interview techniques are presented. Each technique is defined, the helper objective in using the technique identified, and some possible approaches for using the technique described.

Beginning Where the Client Is

Definition: the readiness to deal with the client's current views or perspectives, values, priorities, feelings, and goals.

Helper objective: to be prepared to respond to the client's current perceptions and the way she currently approaches and responds to the world around her, in terms of both people and things.

Possible Helper Approaches
- We might indicate initially a general understanding of the client's situation and our desire to hear more from the client about how she sees it.
- We then might ask questions based on the client's response which could help to clarify details. For example, such things as time, place, events, relationships, and feelings, may help the client to speak more freely to an obviously interested and attentive listener.
- We may follow through with questions or statements which rephrase or restate or condense what the client has said in order to ensure that we understand the client's meaning of the statement, e.g., "You were enjoying yourself." "You felt they disliked you." "The others felt this way too."
- We may summarize occasionally: "Let's see if I understand the . . ." then retrace quickly what the client has said.
- We would avoid questions which ask for *reasons, motives,* or *rationale,* e.g., "Why did you feel that way?" "Didn't you get angry?" At this point we would not be interested in motives, but wish only to obtain a clear picture of how the client feels, acts, interprets events and situations, etc.
- We would carefully and tactfully avoid answering questions which attempt to elicit our approval, support, or direction, e.g., "What do you think I should do?"
- We might indicate inability to give a specific answer at this point, but that in general our role is not to *give advice* but rather to help the client herself determine the best course of action.
- We would be careful not to "push or shove" the client but would move carefully and slowly at the client's pace. We would let the client share with us in a manner and pace comfortable to her. At the same time, we are prepared to deal with what the client is concerned with. If we decide to avoid certain areas, we explain why, if the client wishes to pursue it.

Listening and Attending

Definition: the active process through which the helper gives full attention to the client's communications.

Helper objective: to behave in a manner which maximizes receptivity and responsiveness to what the client is saying and doing, and how.

Possible Helper Approaches
- We give our full concentration to the client and maintain eye contact.
- We might lean toward the client and put our head in a hearing position with our ear toward the client slightly.
- We would keep other parts of our body reasonably still and motionless.
- We would give feedback and indicate our understanding or hearing by body motion (nod of head, movement of upper shoulders) and with facial expression (smile, frown, etc.).
- We could "loosen our eyes," and consciously relax our face and body attempting to feel and be soft, warm, and open.
- We could try and let ourself go *to* the client.
- We could use "m-hm," "yes," if verbal, or *vocal* reinforcement or feedback is necessary or appropriate.
- We could ask for repetition if we don't hear or understand, e.g., "Could you say that again—I don't think I got that," "Could you explain what you mean by . . ." or "Could you describe that again—I'm not sure I understand."

These are *listening,* not clarification or probing questions—they do clarify but the major purpose is to indicate we are listening and want to make certain we are not missing anything.

- We are attempting to say, "I am listening and find what you are saying important, interesting and meaningful and want to hear more."
- We are attempting to say "It's O.K.—I have time for you. I care about what you are saying. I care about you."

The Listener's voice is soft, quiet, and calm. It reflects the mood of the client. It is responsive.

The Listener's *attitude* or approach is (a) objective or non-judgmental and (b) neutral or open and does not demonstrate therapist values in facial expression or body language.

Questioning and Clarifying

Definition: the process through which the helper attempts to gain a clear understanding, by both herself and the client, of events, feelings, thoughts, and relationships. It is part of the "concreteness" aspect of the core therapist characteristics.

Helper objective: to ask questions which facilitate conversation. To indicate our interest and attention. To gain a clear understanding of the presenting problem dynamics. To help the client to organize material and place it in perspective. To indicate our desire for understanding and caring. To help the client explore and understand relationships and events.

Possible Helper Approaches
- We might indicate to the client at the outset that we have only a general understanding of the problem and would like permission to interrupt and question, if necessary, as the client describes the situation, in order to be sure that we do understand.
- We would seek to ask questions that do not intrude on the client's thought process or break her train of thought but rather enable her to *expand*. "Could you explain what you mean by . . .?" "I'm not sure I understand . . .?"
- We would attempt to "pick up" on what the client says, and use her language and expression. Even if we *think* we understand chronology or language, we might wish to test occasionally to be certain we and the client use words in the same way.
- We would not lead the client with our questions. Our questions would be phrased in a manner which enables the client to express her feelings or articulations in her own way, e.g., *not* "You must have felt pretty badly about that" *but rather* "How did you feel about that?"

On the other hand, we would be careful about asking questions which are too general or vague which place unrealistic expectations on the client, e.g., *not* "Why don't you tell me about yourself?" *but rather* "I'd like to know a little more about you—your family, schooling, work, hobbies, and so on. Let's start with family—how many brothers and sisters do you have?

If a client's explanation or statement is still unclear after the request to clarify, we may need to give an example or specifically state what our confusion consists of, e.g., "I'm still not sure I understand—do you mean that . . .?"

Reflecting Feeling

Definition: the process of openly describing to the client what we *think* and *feel* the client is experiencing on the basis of observed behaviour.

Helper objective: to facilitate client recognition, verbalization and expression of her feelings. To indicate that we are not afraid of the client's feelings and are prepared to deal with them.

Possible Helper Approaches
- We might express both verbally and through our own body language our *interpretation* of the client's behaviour. The important point here is that we indicate to the client that we are *guessing* about how she feels or felt or what she thought. Our interpretation or guess may be wrong. If it is correct, the client may be able to talk about it and explore the feeling more. If we are wrong, the client can set us straight and tell us how or what she was feeling.

We don't know the client's feeling; we can only make assumptions based on our knowledge of current events, and the client's past behaviour and current behaviour, e.g., "Mary, Mrs. Brown says you've been pretty quiet since she spoke with you about moving. I guess you've been thinking a lot about moving lately?"
- We might help the client verbalize feelings in her own way, e.g., "It's not easy to leave a place and people you know, is it?"
- We might accept the client's feelings and emotional expression and reward her ability to express and share her feelings with us, e.g., "Well, I guess we can get pretty angry at people when they don't keep promises."
- We might support the feelings of the client and reinforce and praise her by indicating her feelings seem appropriate to the situation, e.g., "It's good that you can talk about these things; it's hard enough to feel them and even harder to talk about them."
- We might help the client bring emotional expression and feelings into perspective and emphasize positives and strengths.

Acceptance

Definition: the process of demonstrating caring, concern, and respect for others regardless of their behaviour, in such a way that we do not appear to be either condoning or disapproving.

Helper objective: to help establish a relationship, to build trust and openness, to aid understanding of behaviour and motivation, to facilitate the client's growth and self-fulfillment.

Possible Helper Approaches
- Our basic stance would be non-judgmental. Our approach would neither condemn nor condone the client's behaviour but rather acknowledge and validate it for what it is.
- Accepting the client, however, doesn't mean being "wishy-washy." We may be required to indicate that we have values and beliefs and feelings which may differ from the client's, e.g., "I may not agree with all the rules and laws, or even follow them all the time, but it isn't a problem for me. It does appear to be a problem for you."
- We would encourage the client to express thoughts and feelings. We would let her know that she can safely express these things with us, and that we are dependable.
- If appropriate, we would spell out the ground rules of our relationship early. If we are part of a larger organization, our ability to respond to the client's needs may be limited or restricted by our professional role and the degree to which we feel we can extend ourselves.

Problem Solving

Definition: the process through which the client learns to satisfy her own needs for personal growth and fulfillment.

Helper objective: to help the client learn problem-solving steps, to deal with the current problem and future difficulties, which may be integrated within the client's own behaviour patterns.

Possible Approaches
- Whatever specific helping method is employed by the therapist, there is a point at which, after having established a relationship and facilitated client understanding of the dynamics of her problem, some action is required on the part of the client to begin to resolve her problem(s). This "action" is usually a noticeable behavioural change, and indicates that the therapy is affecting the client's behaviour—one hopes in the direction of growth. The client's action could be her decision to begin the process of therapy during an initial exploratory interview, her expression of her anxiety and distress, or her first steps taken outside the interview situation, after some weeks of therapy, to change an unrewarding and self-defeating behaviour pattern. While therapy techniques vary considerably in dealing with problem solving, the client in some form or other is assisted in:

1. Establishing goals and priorities.
2. Examining possible courses of action to achieve these goals.
3. Determining the effort and resources required for each course of action being considered.
4. Exploring the possible outcomes or implications for each course of action being considered.
5. Making a decision on the best one to pursue.
6. Acting on the decision taken.
7. Evaluating the outcome of the action taken.

II

The Major Disciplines

2

Psychiatry and Psychoanalysis

This chapter is intended as a brief introduction to the field of psychiatry. It will also highlight the most significant contributions made by Sigmund Freud's psychoanalysis to the theory and practice of psychotherapy. The purpose in doing so is threefold: first, to distinguish psychiatry from psychoanalysis while noting the enormous impact of the latter on the former; second, to consider psychiatry and psychoanalysis as treatment approaches per se while recognizing that psychiatry is, in addition, a specialty within the field of medicine; and third, through tracing the historical development of contemporary psychiatry, the oldest of the three helping disciplines (psychiatry, psychology, and social work), to note recurring, and as yet unresolved, social and philosophical issues impeding the delivery of these services to those members of society whose behaviour falls far short of the model of the psychologically healthy person described in Chapter 1.

We will begin by considering the origin of psychiatry in non-literate cultures, move quickly through the history of our "civilized" response to bizarre and disturbing human behaviour, and consider more carefully the major psychiatric developments in the United States in the nineteenth and twentieth centuries.

But before turning to history, a further word of clarification about the field of psychiatry. We have noted above that psychiatry is a branch of medicine—a medical specialty. As such, unlike the other two helping disciplines, psychology and social work, psychiatry employs both physically invasive and psychotherapeutic methods. Only the medically-trained physician may prescribe and administer physical as well as psychological or "talking" therapy. Thus, only the physician-psychiatrist has at his disposal physical treatment methods such as drugs, electro-convulsive therapy, insulin-coma therapy, and psychosurgery, intended to alter the somatic or organic condition of the client. It is this medical or somatic element in the psychiatric approach to the treatment of psychological problems which has led to the use of the term "mental illness." And it is the application of the so-called "medical model" to the treatment of psychological problems which has resulted in growing and outspoken criticism of the psychiatric profession, from within as well as from external critics, over the past two decades (Morrison, 1979). The implications of applying the medical model to the treatment of psychological problems are raised at this point, since it bears directly on the material which follows. If, for example, psychological disturbance or bizarre and unusual behaviour is thought to occur as a result of some organic or physical ailment, it would appear appropriate to consider the individual so afflicted as being *sick* or *ill*. But if the organic ailment cannot be directly "observed," and if the sick individual in fact appears physically healthy in other respects, yet demonstrates peculiarities in speech, thinking, perception, and/or emotion, then it would need to be assumed that an organic ailment is in fact present, even though not immediately apparent, and further that this ailment which is affecting these "mental" behaviours and capacities is therefore located in the individual's head. The resulting medical diagnosis is that the individual has a *mental* illness. Except in this chapter, the terms "mental illness" and "mental disease" are not used in this text. To be sure, there are organic brain conditions which result in psychological problems and impairments in other aspects of individual functioning. There is increasing evidence too that subtle and less subtle changes in brain chemistry accompany certain psychological conditions, such as depression. Still further, there is little argument that psychological functioning may be seriously affected by changes in body chemistry brought on by the ingestion of a variety of *substances,* and even through endogenous means, as in the overproduction of endorphins and the "high" experienced through successful achievement in high-risk activity. But none of these conditions imply mental "illness" or "disease" in the sense that these terms are commonly employed in psychiatry. Thus, "mental illness," "disease," or even "health," are vague, often inappropriate and inaccurate terms for describing human behaviour which appears to have no clear somatic or physical correlate.

The objection of humanistically oriented therapists to the use of the medical model in the definition and treatment of psychological disturbance or problem behaviour as *mental* illness, however, rests not so much with its accuracy or semantic suitability, as with the implications for patient care and treatment. The medical model essentially removes *responsibility* from the patient for both the origin and treatment of his problem and suggests an overly simplistic conception of the dynamics of human growth and behaviour.

Our brief excursion into psychiatric history, which follows, may help to explain how psychological problems came to be perceived as illnesses or disease. Our look back into the distant and more recent past will reveal, too, the significance of the prevailing social and economic conditions for the care and treatment of the psychiatric casualty. Clearly the evolution in treatment methods and the ability of psychiatrists to help the psychologically distressed appears less dependent upon their technical and scientific sophistication than we may have believed. The history of psychiatry, like other human endeavours, demonstrates that we can neither assume that advances made by some in the care and treatment of those with severe psychological problems find their way into the general body of theory and practice, nor that treatment progress, though slow, moves steadily *forward,* with each new gain a building block. Moreover, each "revolution" in the improvement in care and treatment seems to have often produced unintended and unanticipated negative consequences, which have further complicated an already complex situation. Thus, while there has been progress, there remain immediate concerns of monumental proportions.

A Brief History of Psychiatry

BELIEFS ABOUT CAUSES OF MENTAL ILLNESS

Psychiatry is both old and new. As a formal branch of medicine, it is new, having emerged during the sixteenth century as certain physicians directed their attention and work to the study and treatment of mental disorders, but not having appeared as a medical specialty until the nineteenth century. It is interesting to note that in the United States, the first national association of physicians was formed by the "fathers" of psychiatry in that country, thirteen superintendents of mental hospitals who first met in 1844. They began the Association of Medical Superintendents of American Institutions for the Insane, which from 1893 to 1921 was called the American Medico-psychological Association, and is now known as the American Psychiatric Association (Lewis, 1959).

But psychiatry is old, too. Its origins are as ancient as the practice of medicine itself. An examination of the treatment methods employed by "healers" in the course of human history reveals four basic approaches which in turn reflect certain *beliefs* about the *causes* of illness or aberrant behaviour (Sarason and Sarason, 1980). Two are associated with external events or conditions, and two with the internal state or functioning of the patient. These four belief systems regarding the etiology of the disease or symptoms are: supernatural or magical, organic or somatic, psychological, and environmental/social.

The supernatural or magical belief system suggests that an *external* event, source, or power, over which the patient has no direct control, has brought about the patient's symptoms, illness, or inappropriate behaviour. In cultures where such belief systems predominate, as is typical of non-literate societies, the medicine man/shaman/witch doctor is called upon to intervene. The shaman's treatment revolves around the use of his or her own magical powers to free the patient from the spell, curse, spirit, or demons which have produced the patient's illness. This belief system, while part of the prehistory of psychiatry, has not entirely disappeared. Even modern societies characterized by scientific and technological sophistication seem to maintain superstitious and magical thinking. Psychiatry and psychiatrists therefore continue to be perceived in a mystical light by the layperson, and in this sense there remains a link between modern psychiatry and religion.

The organic or somatic belief system holds that the patient's unusual behaviour is the result of some *internal* organic or physical ailment, which requires some form of physical treatment. Thus, some part or parts of the patient's body may be considered as the source of the problem and treatment is directed to that part or organ. One of the earliest known somatic treatments is *trephination,* a procedure in which a hole was made in the patient's skull, presumably to allow evil spirits plaguing the patient to escape or be forced out. Examples of trephination have been found dating to 3000 B.C. (Sarason and Sarason, 1980). Techniques for the physical treatment of mental illness, in comparison with the physical treatment of physical disease, seem to have progressed slowly, and generally to have exposed the patient to higher risks. For example, it was only a few centuries ago that witches were burned at the stake, in the belief that this was the only way to "cure" the unfortunate individual whose body had been possessed by the devil. The "cure" resulted in the destruction of the body as a necessary sacrifice to save the person's soul. While this seems an extreme "treatment" method, it is, in its crudeness, relative to modern medicine, not unlike the practices of lobotomy, electro-shock treatment, or psychopharmacology, in which there is no clear understanding of how or why these methods, when successful, result in symptom remission (Mora, 1959).

The psychological belief system holds that behaviour problems and mental illness reflect disturbance of *internal processes* such as sensing, perceiving, thinking, and feeling. The treatment of problems viewed as psychological in origin is to help the person learn or relearn to experience, sense, perceive, think, and feel in such a way that they begin or resume their personal development.

The environmental/social belief system holds that *external* environmental and social events and conditions cause individual behaviour disturbance or mental illness. In this situation, the individual's *response* to an adverse environmental condition, or to the failure of other people, such as family members, friends, or coworkers, to satisfy basic social needs, is considered inappropriate and/or unsuccessful. Treatment may require changes to be made in the patient's living and working situation and social relationships.

It is perhaps obvious by now that more than one of these four primary *causes* may in fact be present as *contributing factors* in the disordered behaviour of the patient. In the prehistory of psychiatry, the cause of mental illness was considered to be *external* to the patient and the "treatment" primarily focused on appeals and incantations to supernatural forces outside the patient. The early physicians, on the other hand, looked to *internal* physical causes and physical treatments for mental illness. In time, internal psychic events were perceived as the source of disturbances which resulted in mental *and* physical illness. And more recently, external environmental and social conditions have been perceived as producing internal psychic *and* physical illness. Still, there remain those today who continue to adopt either a biogenic or psychogenic perspective with respect to the cause and therefore treatment of mental illness, notwithstanding the apparent growing evidence to support a multivariate stance.

FROM THE ANCIENT GREEKS TO THE EIGHTEENTH CENTURY

Sarason and Sarason (1980: 23) give credit to the philosophers of ancient Greece as "the earliest writers about the psychological and organic approaches to deviance. . . ." At the time of Homer (c. 800 B.C.), mental illness was considered a form of punishment inflicted by the gods. Several centuries later, the writings of Hippocrates (460-366 B.C.), the father of modern medicine, and the three most famous of the Greek philosophers, Socrates (470-399 B.C.), Plato (427-347 B.C.) and Aristotle (384-322 B.C.), reflect an unusually early interest and sophistication in their understanding of human intelligence, motivation, emotion, and psychological conflict and disturbance. Hippocrates, for example, believed the brain to be the most important organ in the body and the site of consciousness. He wrote about depression, discussed irrational fears and psychosis, and even concluded that epilepsy was an organic brain disease. Thus, perhaps Hippocrates may also be considered the first psychiatrist in view of his ability to diagnose, classify, and even treat mental illness, as he did with understanding, rest, bathing (perhaps the precursor to hydrotherapy), and diet.

But the knowledge of the ancient Greeks, like their culture, did not survive, and with the fall of the Greek and Roman Empires, Europe entered into the Middle Ages. The intellectually enlightened approach to mental illness which the ancient Greeks had developed rapidly disintegrated in the atmosphere of anti-rationalism of the Middle Ages. By the fourteenth century, magical thinking and belief in the supernatural were widespread and being maintained and reinforced by the powerful and authoritarian Christian Church. The mentally ill, as in non-literate societies, were considered to be either possessed by evil spirits or being punished by God for evil thoughts and/or deeds. In either case, they were considered outcasts and were feared, condemned, persecuted, and scourged. At the same time there were "islands of enlightenment and reason" (Sarason and Sarason, 1980) during the Middle Ages and the Renaissance. Paracelsus (1493-1541) disputed the Church's notion of demonic possession as the cause of mental illness and, like the ancient Greeks, believed that mental illness was a natural phenomenon. He attributed mental aberrations to astrological causes related to the positions of the planets and stars.

Johann Weyer (1515-76), a physician, strongly asserted that irrational behaviour could be explained rationally, and was perhaps the first "psychiatrist" to record descriptions of patient symptoms and behaviour in a case-study format. In his book *The Deception of Demons,* he attacked the Church view of possession and asserted that treatment of the mentally ill must be oriented to meeting the needs of the patient. In his belief that understanding the individual patient was necessary in order to meet patient needs, he devoted considerable time to *talking* with patients. He concluded that *both internal psychological conflicts and problems in external human relations were underlying causes of mental illness.* In the same vein, the work of Juan Huarte (1530-89) also argued that mental illness was a psychological, not a theological, concern. In his book, *Probe of the Mind,* he offered one of the first psychologically based theories of child development.

With the seventeenth and eighteenth centuries came a return to the emphasis on reason and intellect. These centuries, called the Age of Reason and the Age of Enlightenment, saw the rise of scientific and technological endeavour for understanding natural phenomena and the decline of faith in superstition and magic. Thus, recalling the discussion on causes of mental illness at the beginning of this section, probable causes were now narrowed to three: physical (or organic) and psychological, both *internal* conditions; and to *external* events related to environmental and social factors. It is interesting that, as early as the seventeenth century, a *holistic* approach to the nature of mental illness (currently in vogue) was espoused by both Baruch Spinoza (1632-77), and William Harvey (1578-1657), the latter better known for his discovery of the circulation of the blood. This appreciation of the interrelationships of mind and body was not to achieve early acceptance, however, and the following centuries saw an either-or position taken by most researchers and practitioners, which continues for some, even today.

PSYCHIATRY AND THE MENTAL HOSPITAL IN THE U.S.
We began this section by noting that psychiatry is old and new—as ancient as the early Greeks, and as recent as the founding in 1844 of the forerunner of the American Psychiatric Association. In a sense, the history of psychiatry since the nineteenth century is also the history of the mental hospital (Greenblatt and Levinson, 1965). Psychiatric care and treatment has, in large part, been provided within hospital settings since that time. It is true that much psychiatric research and practice has been carried out elsewhere, particularly since the advent of the Second World War (Mora, 1959), and that considerable psychotherapy, primarily psychoanalytic in nature, has taken place in the private office practice of psychiatrists during the past fifty years. But the overwhelming bulk of psychiatric services have been, and continue to be, delivered within hospital settings, be they public or private institutions for psychiatric care, or general hospital psychiatric wards. It has been suggested (Williams et al., 1980), for example, that by the end of the 1950s one-half of the total hospital beds in the entire world were occupied by psychiatric patients. This number, for a variety of reasons we will discuss in due course, has now declined to one-quarter (Smith, 1976), which is still a very large proportion.

At the same time, patients in mental hospitals would be expected to represent the most severe and/or chronically disabled of the mentally ill; the severe and chronic patient is most closely identified with psychiatry. But more than identification is involved: these patients are the ones most likely to fall within not only the professional responsibility, but also the legal jurisdiction, of the psychiatrist. While the allied helping professionals participate in the care and treatment of the severely disturbed patient, it is the psychiatrist who is ultimately responsible, and who has the legal power and authority for admission and release of *involuntary* patients. Given the current emphasis on protection of civil liberties and frequency of medical malpractice suits, the psychiatrist's role in this respect is an unenviable one.

Let's turn now to the major developments in American psychiatry in the context of the mental hospital. Greenblatt and Levinson (1965) delineated three major periods in the development of mental hospitals in the United States: the moral-treatment era (1800-60); the decline and fall of moral treatment (1860-1920); and the "road back" era (1920-65), "in which a slow but accelerating effort has been made to reassert the therapeutic impulse in mental hospitals." To these three, we can now add a fourth period: deinstitutionalization (1965-present).

Moral Treatment (1800-60)
Treatment of the mentally ill in the United States during this period paralleled fairly closely similar developments in Europe. Benjamin Rush (1745-1813),

considered the "father" of American psychiatry, had studied under William Cullen (1710-90), one of the most famous professors of medicine in his time, at the University of Edinburgh. Dr. Rush joined the staff of the Pennsylvania Hospital in Philadelphia in 1783. This was not a mental hospital, although in 1752 it had been the first American hospital to admit mental patients. Rush proceeded to bring both a humanitarian and scientific outlook to the treatment of the mentally ill and to change the superstitious and punitive attitudes and practices stemming from ignorance and fear. Believing problems in blood circulation to the brain to be central to the development of mental disorders, he treated patients with bloodletting, purgatives, and emetics. He is credited with beginning the *treatment* focus in regard to mental illness in the United States, as did William Tuke in England and Pinel (1745-1826) in France (Lewis, 1959; Greenblatt and Levinson, 1965).

The early nineteenth century in the United States was a period of intense social, economic, and technological change. Industrialization was altering the small-village, rural atmosphere, and the growth of cities resulted in an increasingly heterogeneous population who were strangers to one another. At the same time, growing out of the social philosophy which prompted both the American and French Revolutions, there was a renewed faith in the human person's ability to act responsibly and autonomously and achieve success and "the pursuit of happiness." There was a decline in the Christian belief that one's destiny was predetermined by God, and a growing confidence in the human capacity for resolving human problems by human effort. Under these circumstances the old small-town responses of toleration of the unusual behaviour of some residents, and the incarceration in jails or alms houses of people with more severe behaviour problems, became unacceptable. The mentally ill became more visible in the new cities, and a humane response was now considered both appropriate and feasible. This new response required new facilities to be built to care for the mentally ill. There is some dispute in the literature about both the extent and nature of the mental hospital movement. Greenblatt and Levinson (1965) state that a number of hospitals were built in the eastern states beginning in 1817, some which appear to have been private, for example, the "Friends" Asylum, built by the Quakers; and some public state hospitals, for example, the Manhattan State Hospital, built in 1828. Williams et al. (1980), on the other hand, suggest that the state asylums came later, noting the strident and successful efforts of Dorothea Dix (1802-87), who in her lifetime was directly responsible for the construction of thirty-two mental hospitals. Williams et al. (1980) claim that this initial development of public and private facilities subsequently segregated rich and poor patients, producing a class structure within the treatment process.

This new and enlightened treatment approach to the mentally ill was of course neither comprehensive nor instantaneous. There were good treatment programs developed and institutions built in which the designs reflected the new *moral treatment* method. But there were many old facilities which remained untouched by the new philosophy and approach and in which the mentally ill continued to be incarcerated under deplorable conditions. The efforts of reformers and crusaders like Dorothea Dix were aimed at exposing these facilities which merely inhumanely housed the mentally ill, provided little care, and in which the treatment consisted of neglect and brutality.

But the better institutions of this period are remarkable for their treatment programs and effectiveness, and offer much for us to consider today. What then did moral treatment include? Here are some of the elements (Greenblatt and Levinson, 1965):

1. It emphasized compassion and understanding of the mentally ill person as someone who was not entirely responsible for her condition.
2. The treatment approach was individualized: understanding of the personal needs of the patient was considered essential. Thus it was necessary to obtain detailed information *from the patient* about her thinking, feeling, and behaviour through patient interviews.
3. Positive attitudes and attention shown by *all hospital staff* to patients was considered essential.
4. Physicians and staff held the optimistic belief that patients would in fact improve and/or recover through the application of moral treatment principles and methods.
5. The hospital superintendent was a charismatic figure and role model for others. He was expected to be directly involved in the hospital program, to know all patients personally, to take meals with them, and to live on the hospital grounds with his family.
6. There were well-developed work and recreation programs tailored to individual needs in which patients were expected to participate.
7. Patients were aided in forming their own interest groups and were responsible for organizing and conducting their own meetings and activities.
8. There were music programs and weekly dances, attended by the superintendent and staff, who participated along with the patients.
9. Patient self-respect was emphasized.

Both Greenblatt and Levinson (1965) and Williams et al. (1980) note that 50 per cent of the patients admitted to the hospitals with such programs in this era never returned.

Thus we see that many of the achievements of recent decades which invite our admiration were in fact embodied in moral treatment 100 years ago: trust of the patient, interaction between patients and staff without paralyzing fear, little or no use of restraint, a diversity of occupations and recreations, and the expectation that behaviour could become well modulated even in the severely deranged and that the future held out promise for these unfortunates if they were cared for properly.

. . . Moral treatment proceeded in the absence of tranquilizers, antidepressants, shock treatments, insulin treatment, and psychoanalytic approaches.

What was achieved through kindness, forebearance, attention to psychological needs, opportunities for expression of creative urges and satisfactions, liberty to work and to handle freely the tools of labor, and the maintenance of self-respect stands as a great lesson to us all: that it is not so much the modality of treatment or school of thought that influences the result, but primarily humanism in an atmosphere of reasonable therapeutic optimism (Greenblatt and Levinson, 1965: 1345).

Decline of Moral Treatment (1860-1920)
As we had suggested in the introduction to this chapter, social and economic forces which resulted in lost ground in the care and treatment of the mentally ill in the Middle Ages also were responsible for the gradual return to psychiatric *custody* rather than psychiatric *treatment* during this period. Factors such as the change from a social-democratic to a capitalistic ethic and "rugged conservatism" accompanied the development of the Industrial Revolution in the United States. Large-scale immigration during this period introduced new racial, ethnic, and religious groups whose language, customs, and lifestyle threatened the native American and stimulated prejudice and negative stereotypes.

The period also saw the rise of social Darwinism, a sociological theory which held that biological deficits of the disadvantaged members of society resulted in their condition. The theory held that because these people's inadequacies reflected organic deficits, attempts to change or improve their situation could not succeed. Further, it was believed that the human race would be endangered as a species if such individuals were allowed to procreate among themselves or with healthy members of society. Social Darwinists agreed that while the disadvantaged might be *maintained* by society, the process of natural selection should be allowed to occur ensuring the survival of the "healthy, wealthy, and wise" and strengthening of the human species. Social Darwinism, then, was a new pseudo-scientific buttress for the old religious doctrine of predestination.

But the most significant factor leading to the decline and eventual fall of the moral treatment method was economic. For primarily financial reasons, the following changes occurred in the patient population of the state hospitals: (a) overcrowding; (b) a change in the ratio of patients with *acute* illness (characterized by rapid onset and likelihood of rapid recovery) to those with *chronic* illness (characterized by slow onset and progressive deterioration; improvement may be possible over time but recovery is unlikely) in the new state hospitals; and (c) a shift in the financial status of the patient population from primarily middle-class to primarily poor. First, state laws unintentionally promoted the admission of the chronic mentally ill over acute patients, since the State accepted financial responsibility for chronic patients but charged the municipalities for the care and treatment of the acute cases. The municipalities, therefore, to save money, often retained their acutely ill residents in their own custodial settings—such as jails—until they could legitimately transfer them as chronic patients. Second, a class structure had been established within the public and private hospital system. Both systems charged patients for their care, but the State hospitals charged on the basis of ability to pay. This meant that the poor could afford to go only to the State hospital, while the more affluent could be admitted to the private hospitals. Lastly, because the municipalities believed that it was cheaper for them to provide "relief" to the poor within their institutions than to attempt to maintain them in the community, the borderline mentally-ill poor who might have remained in the community were institutionalized.

To meet the rapidly escalating admissions demands during this period, old hospitals were expanded and new hospitals were built on a larger scale. The old staff ratios, however, were not retained, and the moral treatment programs were not expanded to meet the needs of the growing patient population. The human-scale proportions so important to the moral treatment method had disappeared.

By 1860, a two-class mental care system was in place—the private and the public. State asylums were no longer viewed as treatment settings for all Americans, but as custodial facilities for the chronically insane poor, a group identified with despised ethnic groups who lacked political power. State governments were controlled by American born citizens who were openly hostile and prejudiced toward this group. Psychiatry by now had lost its claim to credibility. Moral treatment was seen as ineffective except for the privileged few, and previous claims of significant asylum cure rates were found to be bogus. (Williams et al., 1980: 57-58).

The results of these changes in the patient population, in the program, in staffing, and in the growing size of the state hospitals during the period is dramatically reflected in the discharge statistics of the Worcester (Massachusetts) State Hospital. Between 1833 and 1846 it was reported that a remarkable 70 per cent of patients were discharged as improved or recovered within a year following admission, *but by the late 1800s, the number had shrunk to a mere 5 per cent!* (Greenblatt and Levinson, 1965.)

Under these conditions, by the turn of the century psychiatry was considered ineffective by both medical practitioners and the lay public. Psychiatrists were viewed as only *managers* of large, overcrowded, understaffed, poorly maintained institutions where the "hopelessly" mentally ill were retained apart from society, with little or no expectation of their recovery.

Williams et al. (1980) note that despite the brief flurry of interest in psychiatric reform in the early 1900s and the eventual entry of the federal government into the field of mental illness with the creation of the National Committee for Mental Hygiene in 1909, conditions within the asylums were only nominally improved.

The "Road Back" (1920-65)

If the period of moral treatment decline in American psychiatry can be described as stagnant and destructive, the "road back" period was characterized by turbulence and growth. There are so many important events, discoveries, and developments connected with this period that we can only consider some of them, and even these only briefly.

In general, however, it may be said that the most significant developments in psychiatry occurred *outside* the mental hospital during this era; that there was little change in the physical facilities, the majority of mental hospitals still in use having been built in the period of moral treatment decline or earlier; and that both treatment and care of the chronically mentally ill improved very little until the 1950s (Williams et al., 1980). Again, economic factors seemed to be at work—this thirty-year period included both the Depression and World War II. The 1930s were lean times in which the mentally ill were simply too far down the list of priorities to receive the scarce funds needed to deliver massive social assistance programs. The Second World War required the economy of the country to be concentrated on supporting the military effort, while social programs and services languished.

During this period, psychiatry was significantly influenced by the new fields of psychology, sociology, and social work in their efforts to study and understand human behaviour and respond to individual and social problems. The major contributions of psychology and social work to the field of helping are considered in Chapters 3 and 4. Suffice to say here that their theories, methods, research, and findings on such aspects of human behaviour as intelligence, motivation, perception, learning, growth and development, language and communication, culture, attitudes, emotions, group dynamics, social organization, leadership, the family, religion, work, creativity, and helping individuals and groups to solve problems in living contributed significantly not only to the field of psychiatry, but to raising public awareness and concern regarding the nature and quality of human existence.

Neurology had a strong impact too. Work in the 1920s with brain-injured soldiers from World War I by pioneers like Kurt Goldstein in Germany led to a new integration of mind and body theories of causation with his organismic psychology. The new physical therapies (insulin coma, electro-shock, and psychosurgery) surfaced in the thirties, providing new methods for the treatment of certain forms of depression and other affective disorders.

Freudian psychology, of course, had a greater influence than any other single factor on the development of psychiatry during this time. Freud offered a sophisticated theory of human behaviour, emphasizing the psychological development of mental disorders and their treatment, aimed primarily at neurotic patients, which focused on applying reason, understanding, and logic, and which recognized the importance of the physician-patient relationship. Freud's discovery that the early life of the infant and child was significant in the development of neurotic problems in later life raised interest in the early treatment of children and families. This led to more psychiatrists becoming involved with the less severely mentally ill, and the beginning of a blurring of the lines between normality and mental illness.

During the Second World War, psychiatrists were employed by the military to assist in the identification of unsuitable recruits, to treat traumatically induced battle neuroses and psychotic behaviour, and, following the war, to assist in the psychiatric treatment of veterans who had suffered both psychological and physical injuries.

The period following the war was significant. American psychiatry was being strongly influenced by leading European psychoanalysts who had fled Nazi Germany and come to the United States prior to the war; by the developments and variations in theory and technique espoused by Freud's original followers, such as Jung, Adler, and Rank; and by the neo-Freudians. Harry Stack Sullivan's interpersonal theory, for example, emphasized the significance of the early mother-child relationship as a base for all human relations to follow. Karen Horney and Wilhelm Reich emphasized the present situation of the patient, concentrating less on the patient's past. Erich Fromm considered the importance of the social and cultural determinants in the patient's life and the patient's ability to respond to them humanistically. But within mental hospitals, and in the community, the evidence of this impact of new knowledge and talent seemed sparse, as the gap between public expectations, needs, and service delivery grew.

> By the 1950's mental health concerns had become the "in" thing, and juvenile courts expected miraculous results. The judges sought psychiatric advice in difficult cases and welcomed treatment programs under court sponsorship for children and families. But frustration grew in the courts, as voluntary residential treatment centres established highly selective admission criteria that excluded children who were educationally retarded, did badly on conventional IQ tests, did not have cooperative parents, and were members of minority groups. Disappointments increased as the limitations of mental health services in our society became more evident in the absence of basic social and economic changes. (Polier, 1980: 396).

Still, the 1950s did see some important developments in psychiatry, one in particular that gave to the psychiatrist a powerful tool. Three new treatment directions appeared at this time. The first was taken by psychoanalytically trained psychiatrists such as Fritz Perls, William Glasser, Eric Berne, and Albert Ellis who rejected psychoanalysis, considering it either ineffective and/or time-consuming, and developed their own theories and methods. The second was the development of two psychotherapeutic approaches based on psychological theory—Carl Rogers's Client-Centred Therapy and B.F. Skinner's Behaviour Modification. The third was the development of the major tranquilizers and pharmacotherapy. The first two directions not only expanded the range of treatment options, but also were to stimulate research, begin the demedicalization of psychotherapy, and pave the way for new humanistic approaches, seen in the human-potential and personal-growth movement which began in the 1960s. The third was to offer psychiatry a powerful and effective treatment method, albeit not without controversy, which brought renewed credibility, deserved or not, to psychiatrists from both professional colleagues and the lay public (Greenblatt and Levinson, 1965; Mora, 1959).

During the 1950s, a time of economic growth and prosperity, politicians and the public were positively influenced by the growing evidence from social scientists that there were major social problems in the United States requiring attention. The plight of the poor, the mentally and physically disabled, the mentally ill, and racial and ethnic minorities, flew in the face of the American ethic of equality of opportunity. A wave of liberal optimism swept in with the Kennedy era in the early 60s and was reflected in social policy initiatives carried out by the Johnson administration.

Deinstitutionalization (1965-present)
Talbot (1980) writes with alarm of the most recent development in the care and treatment of the chronic mentally ill—deinstitutionalization. Since 1955, the patient population in the United States has steadily declined from 550,000 to its current low of 180,000. The reasons for this, Talbot suggests, include the following:

1. The belief by professionals that returning patients to, or maintaining them in, the community would better facilitate the patients' treatment and avoid the harmful effects of institutionalization.
2. Psychiatrists' use of new psychopharmacological agents enabled patients' more bizarre and disorienting behaviour to be controlled so that many patients could now live outside the institution.
3. The new concern with patient rights and personal freedoms resulted in the tendency to release patients whose mental health was in doubt, rather than to retain them.
4. The shift in the economic responsibility for the care and treatment of the chronic mentally ill from the State government to the federal government through Medicare, Medicaid, and Supplemental Security Income. Thus, State governments could save money by discharging their chronic patients to nursing, boarding, and other community care facilities.

Unfortunately deinstitutionalization, while accomplishing the goal of freeing the chronic mentally ill from the mental hospital, has had the unintended consequence of failing to provide them with the minimal care and treatment previously afforded in institutions.

> By 1975 it had become clear in many American communities that deinstitutionalization was not an unqualified success. The media called attention to the wretched conditions many discharged patients lived in; governmental investigations into the lack of services for these patients followed; an outcry came from communities into which hundreds of patients had been "dumped"; and psychiatrists began openly to condemn the movement as a "national disgrace" (Talbot, 1980: 44).

Clearly, mental-health care has come full circle. More than two hundred years ago in the United States the mentally ill were allowed to wander about the community; those that got into difficulty were jailed or kept in poorhouses.

The new era of deinstitutionalization, in which patients from custodial settings are being returned to communities without adequate resources to provide for their proper care and treatment, has created a similar situation (Whitmer, 1980). It is to be hoped that we will see in the 1980s a revival of the principles of moral treatment, not in model institutions, but in the communities in which we live. In Talbot's enlightened description below of the role of psychiatry in the 1980s in caring for the mentally ill, he urges psychiatrists to adopt a multidisciplinary approach, reminds his colleagues of their responsibilities for the patient's physical care, and urges them to take an advocacy position in the provision of required services and to continue their involvement in research and education. His statement reflects the growing awareness that the care and treatment of the mentally ill is not a psychiatric *domain,* but a public responsibility which requires public participation and commitment to ensure that the necessary financial resources and existing expertise are properly allocated.

> Since care of the chronic mentally ill patient is a public health responsibility, it is incumbent upon psychiatrists and other physicians to join other mental health specialists in actively attending to the needs of this population. Although psycho-social problems are more obvious, the medical and psychiatric needs of the chronic patient also require vigilant monitoring. In addition, psychiatrists have an important role in the development of comprehensive services for the chronically mentally ill, and should be involved at all levels in program planning, public education, training, and research related to preventative care and rehabilitation services (Talbot, 1980: 50).

PSYCHIATRIC ASSESSMENT, CLASSIFICATION, AND TREATMENT MODALITIES

In this section we will consider briefly the psychiatric assessment process, some common forms of problem behaviour and their psychiatric labels or classification, and various treatment methods employed by psychiatrists. We will be aided in our examination by following the outline of selected material contained in the videotape series *This is Psychiatry* (Smith, 1976).

The Psychiatric Assessment Process

THE INITIAL INTERVIEW
The goals of the psychiatrist in the initial interview are essentially those of all helpers, and require the same basic personal skills, values, and techniques described in Chapter 1 (Stevenson, 1959). These goals are: to establish a therapeutic relationship with the patient and to obtain information from the patient which pertains to her problem.

The psychiatrist focuses his attention on four areas of patient functioning: (1) disturbances in thinking, (2) disturbances in feeling, (3) problem behaviour resulting from disturbances in thinking and/or feeling, and (4) bodily reactions resulting from disturbances in thinking and/or feeling.

At the outset, the psychiatrist attempts to be reassuring, since the patient has sought help only after concluding, or after someone else has concluded, that she is unable to handle a problem on her own. Under these circumstances the psychiatrist expects the patient will likely feel inadequate, embarrassed, or anxious. The psychiatrist attempts to gain an initial or better understanding of the problem through careful, sensitive questioning. This is a critical interview because it is essential for the psychiatrist to define the nature of the patient's problem before treatment may proceed. Since the patient may have difficulty explaining a problem she does not understand, or behaviour she is not aware of, the psychiatrist may engage in several exploratory interviews before he can define the problem and formulate a treatment plan.

Smith (1976) suggests that establishing a relationship with the client in which information and observations may be obtained requires four characteristics on the part of the psychiatrist. These are: (1) interest, (2) trust, (3) genuineness, and (4) competence. We might note here the similarity of these characteristics to the first four of the ten therapist qualities considered essential to a therapeutic relationship described in Chapter 1 (empathy, positive regard, genuineness, and concreteness).

The psychiatrist's initial conversation with the patient is oriented toward determining what the patient believes her problem is, its *severity,* and its *duration.* As this information is elicited from and relayed by the patient, the psychiatrist carefully observes all aspects of the patient's behaviour in addition to what she actually says, in particular noting disturbances in thinking and feeling, or physical problems resulting from these disturbances.

Once the complaint is clearly defined and there is some understanding of how long the patient has had her problem and why she is seeking help now, additional related information might be elicited as follows:

1. *Personality type.* How does the patient describe herself (quiet, outgoing, shy, aggressive, quick, slow, happy, frustrated, angry, etc.)?
2. *Other problem areas.* Are there other problems in addition to the one she has spoken of that also concerns her?
3. *Mood-related areas.* Are there changes or problems in sleeping, eating, sex, concentration, schooling, family relationship, work, etc.?
4. *Living and working conditions and social relationship.* What is the patient's general living routine? What are her family relationships? What kind of job does she have?

DIAGNOSIS OF PATIENT BEHAVIOUR

Diagnosis refers to the process of decision making in which the psychiatrist labels the patient behaviour in question.

Diagnosis requires gathering together all pertinent information possible from: (1) *Observations* of the patient's behaviour made by the psychiatrist in the initial and other interviews, (2) *Psychological Tests* conducted by a psychologist, (3) *Physical Examination* of the patient by a general practitioner and possibly special medical tests, and (4) *Reports* from referring agencies, individuals or institutions.

Observations of the Patient
Again, the primary interest of the psychiatrist is in the *thinking* and *feeling* component of the patient's behaviour, but in addition, he will be interested in the global or general *lifestyle* or *attitude* and approach of the patient.

In diagnosing thinking disturbances, the psychiatrist focuses attention on: (1) what the patient talks about, (2) the intelligence displayed, (3) the patient's memory, and (4) the patient's belief system.

He will also observe *how* the patient speaks, (quickly, slowly, with delays, with difficulty, easily). He will look for sense and meaning in the patient's verbalizations. Does the patient reason well, does she seem confused, alert, or lacking age-appropriate intelligence?

He may note the patient's recent and distant memory. Can the patient recall recent events as well as those which occurred some time ago? And last, he will attempt to explore some of the current beliefs or values of the patient to ascertain whether they appear unusual or strange.

In diagnosing feeling-related disturbances, the psychiatrist focuses attention on: (1) what emotion or emotions seem predominant, (2) what affect or feelings seem to be missing or hidden, (3) the intensity of feelings, (4) the stability or variability in emotional expression, and (5) the range of feeling and emotion experienced by the patient.

The body language of the patient may convey lethargy, worry, agitation, or fear. Her voice quality may indicate hostility or warmth or confirm the language of the musculature. Specific questions from the psychiatrist may reveal whether the patient behaves with spontaneity and flexibility or is rigid and constricted. Conversation may indicate the emotional range of the patient as within normal expectations, exhibiting extreme peaks and valleys, or consistently high, low, or flat affect.

In diagnosing treatment potential and motivation, the psychiatrist makes a clinical judgment of the patient based primarily on his (the psychiatrist's) professional experience. "Treatment potential" means the patient's ability to develop a therapeutic relationship with the psychiatrist. Is the patient able to develop rapport with the psychiatrist, or does she remain aloof and distant or defensive? On the other hand, does the psychiatrist feel this is a person whom he can and wants to help?

In assessing the patient's motivation for seeking help, the psychiatrist determines whether the patient's complaints are genuine or whether they suggest manipulation and malingering. Actually even a malingering patient is in need of help, but the latter motivation may have quite different implications for therapy.

Psychological Testing
Should the psychiatrist wish more exact and specific understanding of the patient's thinking and feeling dynamics and, particularly, possible indications of

organic impairment which may be related to behaviour dysfunction, he may refer the patient to a psychologist for assessment.

A full psychological assessment will provide further and more specific information related to the patient's intellectual potential and functioning, emotional functioning and conflicts, and perceptual-motor functioning.

Physical Examination
Although the psychiatrist is a medical doctor, he will refer his patient to a general practitioner for a general medical examination and, if indicated, for specific medical tests in order to determine what, if any, organic or physical ailments might be present which could result in the disturbances in thinking and feeling being experienced by the patient and/or observed by the psychiatrist.

Reports
Additional information about the patient's problem behaviour may be requested (with the patient's consent) or have been received from various community services, including social agencies, her family physician, hospitals, the police, the local school board, and her employment health service.

Final Diagnosis
Once all four areas have been explored, the psychiatrist is in a position to draw certain conclusions about the patient's problem. He is essentially looking for a *pattern* in the various observations. If there is a pattern, does the pattern of behaviour or symptoms resemble a category of, or a specific, illness? If so, then the patient's problem may be given the medical term which has been assigned to similar related behaviour patterns which have been observed in previous patients. Illness, then, is determined by the presence or absence of certain kinds of behaviour. If certain behaviour patterns or *symptoms* exist, then the patient is ill. The illness, or pattern of symptoms, is assigned the medical term, name, or label which identifies this symptom pattern.

Psychiatric Classification

The classification of psychiatric disorders or illnesses which occurs in the process of patient assessment and diagnosis is one of the most controversial aspects of psychiatry (Brill, 1965). Classification is essentially a method of organizing information for purposes of study, research, and ease of communication. It has existed in medicine, as it does in other fields of science, since the time of Hippocrates. There are a number of problems associated with medical and especially psychiatric classification, however, which appear unique. First, the labelling of a pattern of patient symptoms as an illness often leads to the labelling of the patient as though the patient and the illness were one and the same. Neurosis, arthritis, paraplegia, and myopia become neuro*tic*, arthri*tic*, paraple*gic*, and myo*pic*. Instead of the patient being perceived as a person experiencing certain symptoms, she may be perceived primarily in terms of her illness or deficit. Second, labelling, classifying or diagnosing patient symptoms may convey the impression to the patient that the symptoms are *understood* by the psychiatrist. Third, being able to classify the patient's symptomatic behaviour may be falsely interpreted by the psychiatrist as helpful to the patient. Fourth, the definition of what behaviour constitutes mental illness and is included in the psychiatric classification and labelling system, particularly in the functional and affective disorders, is not discrete or exact, because psychiatry is not a pure science and therefore reflects current knowledge as well as social and cultural values. Fifth, since diagnosis and classification involve considerable personal judgment, a patient's behaviour may be interpreted differently by different psychiatrists. Sixth, and last, classification and labelling tend to unrealistically homogenize patients, who, regardless of their similarities for purposes of classification, remain unique individuals whose needs can be expected to be vastly different.

In an attempt to deal with some of the problems of psychiatric classification, the most recent revision of the American Psychiatric Association's Diagnostic and Statistical Manual (DSM III, 1979) has been greatly improved and expanded and its organization and focus altered (Sarason and Sarason, 1980). The focus of the new manual is on helping the psychiatrist in describing the problem of the patient, rather than on interpreting it. Patient behaviour is considered in terms of five major factors, only one of which relates to the primary diagnosis. The new system takes into account the interrelation of psychological, physical and environmental factors in psychiatric problems and includes ranking the patient on functioning levels.

Let's look now at two psychiatric categories which will further illustrate the process of diagnosis, and in addition enable us to consider the concepts of functional versus organic illness or disease, functional illnesses being those which do not appear to have been precipitated by physical ailment.

SCHIZOPHRENIC DISORDERS
AND ORGANIC MENTAL DISORDERS

Schizophrenia
Schizophrenia is the term given to a group of symptoms and is difficult to define as a disease entity. Described as the "original crazy disease," schizophrenia is still today the most prevalent and serious form of mental disorder. There are estimated to be over nine million schizophrenics in the world with 4.5 million so diagnosed annually in the Western hemisphere (Smith, 1976).

Schizophrenia is divided into two types, *reactive* schizophrenia and *process* schizophrenia, depending on onset, though the symptoms are quite similar. The common symptoms are: (1) blunted, inappropriate feeling, (2) impaired concentration due to withdrawal into the self, (3) poor rapport with others as a result of withdrawal, (4) perceptual illusions or hallucinations (imagined auditory, olfactory, and visual sensations), and (5) peculiar beliefs or delusions.

The symptoms of *reactive* schizophrenia may be present in whole or in part and in varying degrees of severity. The onset is sudden, and is usually related to some form of situational stress.

In contrast to the reactive form, the *process* type of schizophrenia is slow and gradual in its onset.

For the reactive schizophrenic the prognosis with treatment is good and full recovery is possible. For the process schizophrenic, the opposite is true, and the best prognosis may be a protected existence in the community.

There is no known single cause of schizophrenia. Theories at present suggest a combination of genetic, biochemical, and psychological factors. Research indicates there does seem to be an inherited predisposition which may be triggered under the "right" or "wrong" environmental conditions. Recent evidence also suggests a strong biochemical involvement related to the metabolism of metabolic amines.

Both reactive and process schizophrenia are treated in the same way, with drugs (particularly the major tranquilizers, e.g., phenothiazines), electroconvulsive therapy, insight therapy and counselling, and community resources such as social agencies, family, work, and friends.

Organic Mental Disorders

When a person behaves strangely the cause may be physical damage to the brain and central nervous system. The effects of such damage can vary from mild to severe depending on the degree of damage involved. The mild response may be a brief reduction of specific function, such as motor incoordination or blurred vision; a severe trauma may result in a coma, or even total malfunction and death.

As in schizophrenia, we find both *acute* and *chronic* types of brain damage. The *acute* are those with *sudden* onset and are often reversible. The *chronic* are those with *gradual* onset and are permanent in nature.

The following characteristics of patient behaviour reflect acute organic brain damage: (1) Confusion. The patient is not reality-oriented and shows problems of maintaining spatial and time orientation. (2) Clouding of consciousness. The patient is vague or preoccupied and seems to lack purpose or direction. There is a tendency to concrete behaviour, rigidity, and defensiveness. (3) Misperception of reality. The patient experiences hallucinations, delusions, illusions, or reconstructions. (4) Emotional disturbance. The patient demonstrates unusual and/or inappropriate emotional response. An example of the above is the syndrome known as delirium tremens, in which acute fear, hallucinations, and illusions are present.

The following characteristics of patient behaviour reflect chronic organic disorders: (1) impairment of recent memory, (2) intellectual deterioration, (3) concrete thinking, (4) mood swings, and (5) episodic confusion.

Causes of organic mental disorders include: (1) vascular problems, such as arteriosclerosis and stroke, (2) alcohol abuse resulting in brain cell deterioration,

(3) physical trauma from accident, tumor, or infection, and (4) ideopathic or unexplained, as in senility.

Diagnosis of organic mental disorder would require psychological and neurological assessments using: (1) psychological tests, (2) testing of reflexes, (3) electro-encephalogram (E.E.G.), (4) X-ray, and (5) pneumoencephalogram.

Treatment. Since the cause of organic mental disorder is generally specific, so is the treatment. (1) First the specific cause would be dealt with by repair, replacement, or removal to restore the patient's physical health and well-being. (2) General medical procedures such as nutrition, hydration, sedation, and treatment of infection would be carried out as required. (3) Environmental factors, such as bright light or noise, which may cause concern or irritation to the patient would be removed. (4) Routine and environmental consistency may be prescribed in cases involving impairment of the patient's abstract reasoning. Protecting the patient from the normal daily demands for decision making and adaptation to change makes her less aware of, and therefore less disturbed by, her lost intellectual ability.

THE CONTINUUM OF MILD TO SEVERE FUNCTIONAL ILLNESS

We have been looking at two major psychiatric classifications of behaviour patterns, schizophrenia and organic mental disorder (psychosis), which, while they may both have an organic component, may be distinguished by the associated *known organic changes* which precede the latter. The other feature of these patterns which makes them "serious" in the sense of the patient's loss of potential is the *absence of* or *decrease in reality testing* which accompanies them.

Prior to the development of the DSM III in 1979, these more debilitating illnesses of a functional nature, which involved perceptual distortion, cognitive impairments, and affective difficulties, were grouped together under the general classification of *psychoses,* while less severe behaviour problems, such as phobias, compulsions, psychosexual problems, and overconcern with bodily functioning, were grouped under the classification of *neuroses*. The new classification system, while retaining the grouping and terminology of "psychoses," no longer uses the term "neuroses" to classify the less severe illnesses, because the term "neurosis" has come to include such a wide range of behaviour patterns that it no longer has descriptive value. Instead, illnesses formerly called "neurotic disorders" have been regrouped into more descriptive categories. Severity of the behaviour problem can now be indicated within the category assigned. This eliminates the previous difficulty in classifying a disturbance in feeling, for example. In DSM II, the earlier manual, a general problem of *unhappiness* being experienced by the patient might be considered a neurotic disorder, while severe *depression* accompanied by problems in cognitive and perceptual behaviour was classified as psychosis. The new system places both behaviour problems within the category of a disorder of feeling or an *affective disorder.*

Let's consider how the psychiatrist might proceed to diagnose and classify a patient problem of a feeling nature (an affective disorder) using unhappiness and depression as examples.

Unhappiness (Mild Affective Disorder)
Unhappiness may represent a valid response to life's normal setbacks and frustrations. When a person approaches a psychiatrist because she is unhappy, the psychiatrist seeks to answer the following questions:

- Is the unhappiness profound? Does it pervade all aspects of life, and is there no change?
- How long has the person been unhappy? Is it recent, or does it extend over a period of weeks and months?
- Does there appear to be risk of suicide? Is there a self-destructive element apparent in the patient's conversation or thoughts?
- Have other aspects of the person's life and functioning, such as work or social relationships, been affected by the feeling?
- Is the person's thinking disturbed? Does there appear to be confusion or problems in reasoning?

If from conversation the psychiatrist concludes that: (1) the cause of the unhappiness is apparent to the patient, (2) the unhappiness is not all-consuming, and (3) the patient's thinking processes are not disturbed, then he may diagnose the patient as experiencing a mild affective disorder. The unhappiness may be the result of the lifestyle or approach the patient has learned over time, or some specific trauma or event may have caused grief and a public expression of a sense of loss or failure. This person may need some professional help of a supportive and educative nature, or to reexamine an unsatisfying lifestyle, but the problem would not be considered serious.

Depression (Severe Affective Disorder of a Psychotic Nature)
Should the psychiatrist determine that:

- the unhappiness is profound,
- the onset of the unhappiness is rapid and is associated with an emotional event, either happy or sad,
- there has been a noticeable personality change
- there are self-depreciating statements made by the patient
- there are disturbances in thinking
- there are changes and dysfunctioning in somatic aspects of the patient's life, such as: sleeping (the patient wakes very early and is unable to return to sleep), eating (the patient has lost interest in food), and sex (the patient's interest has diminished),

then he may conclude that the patient is truly *depressed*.

Acute depression is not merely severe unhappiness. It is a response to an emotional event where there is a rapid onset and an *inward* retreat, rather than a *public* (outward) expression of sorrow.

Depressed persons have the above characteristics in common, though they may show wide variation in their expression of them.

The treatment of depression differs from that of unhappiness. There is evidence of organic involvement, in that changes have been noted in the chemical composition of the mid-brain of depressed patients, although it has not yet been determined that these changes *cause* depression. However, the initial treatment of depression is primarily *chemical* and/or *physical* although the following range of treatment methods may be employed: (1) psychotherapy, both personal and interpersonal, (2) environmental changes related to the patient's living and working conditions, and (3) chemical and physical therapies such as anti-depressant drugs, electro-convulsive therapy (ECT; one of the most effective treatments for depression), lithium salts if a manic phase is involved, or specific other drugs such as tranquilizers.

Psychiatric Treatment Modalities

There are three types of therapy currently practised by psychiatrists:

1. Psychotherapy, a special form of communication in which the patient is assisted in changing painful behaviour in favour of more personally rewarding behaviour.
2. Physical therapies, such as pharmacotherapy, electro-convulsive therapy, or psychosurgery.
3. Behaviour therapies, three techniques for altering specific patient behaviour based on the principles of learning theory.

Psychiatry has utilized the first two since its inception, although the range of possible techniques has grown and been improved. The behaviour therapies are a more recent addition to the treatment options available. Certainly the choice of modality will depend on the skill and knowledge of the psychiatrist, together with the treatment approach which appears most appropriate to the patient's problem. As can be seen above in the treatment of depression, more than one type of therapy may be employed at the same time.

Since the text is concerned only with non-physical therapeutic methods, the remainder of the text will thoroughly examine the major psychotherapeutic methods currently in use. Except for the social casework method described in Chapter 4, all other psychotherapeutic approaches, including the behaviour therapies, are employed by psychiatrists. They may employ one particular method, combine elements of several, or choose different approaches and/or elements in working with different patient problems.

SIGMUND FREUD AND PSYCHOANALYSIS

Sigmund Freud (1856-1939)*

Sigmund Freud was born to Jewish parents in Freiberg, Moravia (a former province of Austria, now in central Czechoslovakia) on May 6, 1856. At the age of four, the family moved to Vienna, where Freud was to live for almost eighty years. He was the oldest child in a family of five girls and three boys, born to his father's second wife. His early childhood was happy; his relationship with both parents affectionate and loving. Liberal attitudes predominated within an atmosphere of filial respect and parental authority (the conditions described in Chapter 1 for the development of high self-esteem). Freud's voracious appetite for learning and knowledge and his high level of intelligence were evident in boyhood. He is described as being a bookworm and an excellent student, who in adolescence often ate supper in his room so he could continue his reading and schoolwork with minimal interruption.

Not unlike adolescents today, Freud was undecided about what career to pursue, and uncommitedly entered medicine at the University of Vienna at the age of seventeen. He subsequently developed an interest in physiology, and after three years of study obtained a part-time research position in neurology with one of his professors, Ernst Brücke. It was during his time with Brücke that Freud became friends with Joseph Breuer, also at Brücke's Institute of Physiology. It was Breuer who had accidentally discovered that *talking* with a patient who displayed hysterical symptoms (the famous case of Anna O., whom he treated between 1880 and 1882) was as effective as *hypnosis*. Breuer had not been able to use hypnosis (the treatment of choice at the time) on Anna O., and instead had had the patient consciously recall and talk about her past life and events leading up to the development of the problem behaviour. Freud had learned of this case and been quite intrigued by it.

In 1881 Freud obtained his M.D. degree, and with some reluctance left Brücke's Institute to begin his medical practice, and to improve his failing financial position. He obtained employment in a private psychiatric clinic in Vienna where he undertook work in brain anatomy. He spent three years there as a resident in neurology, during which time he met his wife-to-be, Martha Bernays. In 1885, Freud obtained a grant to study the treatment of neurotic disorders with the famous French psychiatrist Jean Charcot. He was particularly interested in Charcot's treatment of hysteria using hypnosis. Five months later, in 1886, Freud returned to Vienna and set himself up in private practice. He and Martha were married in September of 1886.

Freud had established a good reputation as a neurologist and his practice grew rapidly. He attempted to use the hypnotic technique learned from Charcot in his treatment of hysteria, but found it ineffective. He decided to try

---

* This biographical data is extracted primarily from material contained in Ford and Urban, *Systems of Psychotherapy* (1963), based on the work of Ernest Jones, Freud's biographer.

instead the "talking" technique which his colleague and friend Joseph Breuer had been using, and for a time they worked together. It was at this point that psychoanalysis began to develop rapidly.

Between 1886 and 1890, Freud began to develop his theoretical position. His open discussion of the sexual basis for neuroses was quickly condemned and his ideas ridiculed as preposterous by his colleagues. For the next ten years, Freud worked in virtual isolation, continuing to develop his theory and approach amid great opposition and controversy. The period from 1890 to 1900 was therefore one of considerable stress, both socially and financially. He was considered a crackpot by his professional associates, and his medical practice suffered as a result. Finally, in the early 1900s, his ideas based on his clinical experience, which he had been expressing at professional meetings and in published papers for ten years, and which appeared in his first book, *The Interpretation of Dreams* (1900), began to receive some interest.

In the early 1900s he was joined by a few followers from various countries, among them Ernest Jones from England, Carl Jung from Switzerland, A.A. Brill from the United States, Sandor Ferenczi from Hungary, Alfred Adler and Otto Rank from Austria, and Karl Abraham from Germany. Soon after, the International Psycho-Analytical Association was formed.

An indication of Freud's growing popularity was his trip to the United States to give a series of lectures on psychoanalysis at Clark University in 1909. But all was not well in Vienna. By 1910, some of his disciples, particularly Adler, began to disagree with certain aspects of his theories. In time, Adler, Jung, and Rank would break entirely with Freud and begin their own approaches. While Freud strongly defended his ideas in the face of criticism, and resisted suggestions for altering them, he did make significant changes and refinements to them on his own, and also incorporated some of his followers', but only after his own clinical experience with his patients indicated earlier theories to be lacking or incomplete. The idea that all neurosis is caused by sexual trauma in childhood is an example of one of Freud's theories which he seemed reluctant to abandon, but did eventually give it up when clinical evidence demanded that he do so. When we remember that Freud stood virtually alone against the world for a decade asserting and defending himself against the most hostile personal attacks at great personal sacrifice, his intractability in later years, which caused such conflict and strife between himself and his earliest followers, is understandable.

Freud was the prototype workaholic. He started his typical workday at eight o'clock with his first patient. He continued to see patients for fifty-five-minute hours until nine or ten in the evening, breaking for a two-hour lunch and walk between one and three o'clock. Following dinner with his wife and six children, and another walk, he returned to work in his study answering correspondence and working on his papers and manuscripts until one or two in the morning.

Freud suffered from cancer of the mouth and jaw, for which he underwent surgery several times during the last sixteen years of his life. Nevertheless, he remained active and continued to write during the last painful stages of this illness, which eventually took his life. In the spring of 1938, fearing for the safety of his family from the advancing Nazi movement, which was hostile to his views and his religion, Freud moved his family to London, England, where he died the following year. Some of the major contributions he made to the theory and practice of helping follow. The legacy of his genius, however, is not to be found only, or even largely, in his own work—rather, it is in the dynamic stimulus he has provided for the creative thinking of so many others.

The Theory of Psychoanalysis†

Describing the major concepts of psychoanalysis is made difficult first by the fact that psychoanalysis is multidimensional, and second because of the continual changes Freud made to many of his basic concepts, not to mention those which others have made since. Wolman (1960: 199) described the breadth, impact and evolution of psychoanalysis this way:

> Freud studied primarily mental disorder and went on to the analysis of the etiological factors. The etiological research shed light on child psychology and the laws of human growth and development. Then came a general theory of personality dynamics, then a study of human nature through the ages and a theory that dealt with the impact on society, culture, and religion and personality, till finally psychoanalysis, originally meant as a psychotherapeutic technique, became a great psychological theory encompassing almost every area of normal and abnormal personality and entering into the fields of sociology, anthropology, history, education, and the arts.

Our discussion will focus on the "mature" stage of Freud's psychological theory (1920s), leaving treatment concepts and methods for the next section. We will begin with a description of the concept of libido and Freud's assumption of psychic determinism; consider briefly the structure and functioning of the mental apparatus—id, ego, and superego—including the concepts of conscious, unconscious, and preconscious awareness; outline his developmental growth stages; and discuss his theory of neurosis and defense mechanisms.

THREE ESSENTIAL PRINCIPLES OF PSYCHOANALYSIS

Psychic Determinism

Psychic determinism, the first principle of psychoanalysis, means that all behaviour has a causal antecedent. Behaviour, which includes all aspects of

---

† This section, as well as the next on the technique and dynamics involved in psychoanalysis, is not written from primary sources, as are the presentations of the helping approaches contained in later chapters. While the author is familiar with the major works of Freud, it seemed unnecessary to attempt to duplicate what is already available from a number of other sources. In order to obtain a sense of Freud's writing prowess and his brilliant powers of psychological observation and analytical thinking, and for the sheer enjoyment of experiencing both his simplicity and depth, two small books, *The Interpretation of Dreams* (1900) and *The Psychopathology of Everyday Life* (1904), are suggested.

sensing, perceiving, thinking, feeling, acting—both internal and external events—is not *random*. The human organism, as *matter*, obeys the same natural laws as all other matter in the universe, and all matter follows *causal* (i.e., deterministic) laws. There is an order and organization in the universe of which the human species is a part. It is assumed, then, that the psychic or mental component of human behaviour also is causally organized such that each behavioural act or event is an effect or result of an earlier precipitating event, and is at the same time the cause of succeeding events, actions, or behaviour (McCary, 1956). The principle of psychic determinism is the basis of the psychoanalytic preoccupation with the past and the search for the underlying causes for current behaviour problems.

Libido, or Psychic Energy
Freud's concept of *libido,* or psychic energy, is also critical to psychoanalytic theory. It is analogous to the concept of *energy* in physics. In physics, energy can be accumulated, transformed, and discharged, but it cannot be destroyed or consumed; it merely changes and becomes something else (Wolman, 1960). Freud envisioned psychic energy, or libido, as the *life force* in this sense, and libido may be thought of as Freud's master *drive,* akin to Goldstein's principle of self-actualization or Jung's concept of self-realization.

The energy of libido is expressed in terms of instincts. Instincts are the psychological experience of a physiological condition. The psychological experience is called a *wish,* and the physiological condition or source, a *need.* Human behaviour, then, is psychologically motivated to satisfy what is *desired* rather than simply to meet physiological *needs* (Nordby and Hall, 1974). Psychological energy develops internally, accumulates, gives rise to tension, and is discharged in behaviour aimed at obtaining the wish or desire.

Constancy, Control, or Regulation
Freud hypothesized three processes through which human behaviour is controlled or regulated. The first he called the *pleasure principle.* This concept is akin to the concept of homeostasis, in which there is a built-in tendency of the organism to maintain an internal equilibrium or balance. Freud believed that when the organism discharged accumulated psychic energy, experienced as tension, through some type of behaviour, the decrease in tension was then experienced as relief, or *pleasure.* Thus, *maintaining* a *constant* level of tension through periodic discharge of accumulations of psychic energy would be pleasant, or in the language of learning, reinforcing. The second principle of regulation and control he called the *reality principle.* The reality principle gives *direction* to our external behaviour. This has the effect of reducing internal accumulations of tension. The *reality principle* ensures that the external behaviour directed to the surrounding environment (reality) is appropriate, will achieve the desired aim, and is timely. It ensures that we don't get ourselves into difficulty in the desire for tension reduction and the experiencing of the attendant pleasure. The reality principle prevents behaviour which is chaotic, impulsive, or disorganized, through our awareness of the possible *negative* consequences of spontaneous or

impulsive behavioural expression. The third principle of regulation and control Freud termed the *repetition compulsion*. While the reality principle is capable of overriding the pleasure principle, the repetition principle is able to predominate over both of the others. The repetition compulsion occurs in response to a *past* event or experience which has been traumatic and overwhelming. It is essentially neither tension-reducing (in fact it often results in an increase in psychic energy and tension), nor is it reality-oriented. Thus it may be painful or distressing and irrational or alogical. Repetition compulsion is evident in recurrent nightmares or in recounts given by people of a very upsetting experience during which they demonstrate high levels of discomfort and a seeming unresponsiveness to support given from listeners present. It is seen too in marriage failure where people repeatedly choose mates with the same personality traits as the former partner (McCary, 1956). Freud believed this behaviour reflected a need to bring the original chaotic experience and tension under control by experiencing it over and over, so that chaotic impulses could be mastered.

In summary, then,

> behavior is guided by a tendency to reduce psychological tensions, a tendency to accommodate behavior to situational events [reality], and a tendency to repeat earlier behaviors in order to get stimulation under control (Ford and Urban, 1964: 131).

THE STRUCTURE AND FUNCTIONING OF THE MENTAL APPARATUS

The concepts of id, ego, and superego; and unconscious, preconscious, and conscious appeared quite late in Freud's theorizing (1920s) and represent the basis of his personality theory. Munroe (1955) refers to the id, ego, and superego as *structural* components of mental behaviour and unconscious, conscious, and preconscious as *topographical* components or layers of awareness involving all three. The important point to keep in mind when considering these elements, or *systems,* as they are described by Hall and Lindzey (1957), is that they are *integrated* systems which act in concert with one another such that they are normally all present in varying degrees in our behaviour with one system only rarely operating in isolation from the others (Wolman, 1960).

Id

The id is the source and centre of all psychic energy. It is the link between the purely physiological or organic aspect of human functioning and the psychological. It is the earliest developing psychological mechanism, present at birth, perhaps before, and is represented by our instinctual and reflex actions and behaviour. It is considered pure psychic energy, and is the centre of our wholly subjective unconscious awareness which follows the pleasure principle without regard to the safety or security of the total person. When somatic or psychic tension accumulates, the response of the id is to immediately discharge energy in behaviour in order to achieve tension reduction and the sensation of relief—pleasure. The *desire* or *wish* for relief of tension, referred to in our discussion of libido, is formed through the operation of the id as a symbol, hallucination, or image, which *represents* the need being experienced. The wish, or psychological representation of the experienced need, cannot reduce the tension, but is merely a conversion of the tension or energy being experienced. The operations of the id are wholly *unconscious,* and id-based images or hallucinations are not subject to awareness. Dreaming, for example, is an activity of the id. Dreams are representations of needs of which we are unaware. Even when the content of dreams can be recalled into consciousness, the contents in their representational form, which do not conform to the principles or laws of reality, appear to have no meaning without our conscious effort to interpret the real meaning of the id symbols or images.

Ego

The ego is the element in the mental apparatus and personality which is *subjective* and *objective*. If the id is the link between the somatic and psychic, the ego may be thought of as the link between our internal subjective experience and the *objective* facts of our internal and external environments. The ego is the centre of *conscious* awareness—of both internal sensing of physiological states, and external perception of situational events in the external environment. The function of the ego is to ensure the safety and survival of the person. In order to do so, it follows the *reality* principle, moderating, guiding, and directing id impulses such that expressed behaviour may achieve subjective need satisfaction and tension reduction while at the same time meeting the demands of objective reality in the most appropriate fashion. The ego is responsible for behaviour control through perception, reason, intelligence, self-awareness, and orientation in time and space; and through assessment, evaluation, and anticipation of consequences of both external events and subjective behaviour.

Finally, it is important to emphasize that the ego, while exercising a control function over id impulses, is organized to *facilitate* rather than *frustrate* their expression.

> It should be kept in mind, however, that the ego is the organized portion of the id, that it comes into existence in order to forward the aims of the id and not to frustrate them, and that all of its power is derived from the id. It has no existence apart from the id, and it never becomes completely independent of the id. Its principal role is to mediate between the instinctual requirements of the organism and the conditions of the surrounding environment; its superordinate objectives are to maintain the life of the individual and to see that the species is reproduced (Hall and Lindzey, 1957: 34-35).

Superego

We have described the id as the link between the organic and psychic aspects of our behaviour and the ego as the mediator between subjective experience and objective reality. The superego develops last, and provides additional control of id impulses through the internalization of learned social *values* and subjectively held *ideals*. It is the *unconscious* source of the experience of guilt and shame: guilt experienced as a failure to behave in terms of socially approved standards, and shame experienced when personally held values and goals are not achieved. The superego presses for perfection, and operates as our *conscience*. It contains proscriptions for behaviour in black-and-white, right-and-wrong terms. The superego enables the development of self-control in the child prior to the mature development of the ego, by the internalization of parental demands. Thus, *external* control by parents and other adult figures may be decreased as the child's superego enables the child to exercise her own *internal self*-control. Unlike ego control, however, the superego attempts to *prevent* id impulses altogether, rather than to channel or moderate them. In addition, the superego attempts to control the operation of the ego by substituting behaviour which is directed to satisfying the demands of *morality* as opposed to *reality* (Hall and Lindzey, 1957).

The Unconscious, Conscious, and Preconscious Mind
Freud did not discover or invent the idea of unconscious mental activity. His and others' experience with hypnosis confirmed that such mental activity did exist and that it offered an explanation for certain kinds of human behaviour, which until that time were not understood. It *was* Freud, however, who perceived the significance of unconscious mental activity, not only in the etiology of neurotic disorders, but for understanding all of human behaviour. Freud envisioned consciousness as a continuum: unconscious mental activity is that which we are unaware of and cannot be aware of without special effort, and even then not completely; preconscious mental activity is that which we are unaware of, but *can* become aware of by refocusing our attention; conscious mental activity is that which we are aware of at any given moment.

The unconscious was conceived of as the layer of the mental apparatus which contained certain memories of past events and experiences, impulses, and sensations occurring in the id, and the material from the superego. However, the most important psychic materials in the unconscious are *repressed* feelings, impulses, and thoughts. We will examine the process of repression more fully in discussing Freud's theory of neurosis and the defense mechanisms.

The preconscious is the layer of mental activity which is immediately *available* to conscious awareness, but which is not being given attention. It includes the stimulation occurring within our bodies, such as our heartbeat, the feeling of our tongue in our mouth, or the sensations experienced in swallowing. It includes, too, stimulation being received from the external environment, such as the tick of a clock or the smell of food cooking, which is present, but which we preconsciously selectively ignore when engrossed in a good book. It also contains impulses from the id pressing for action, possibly visceral sensations of hunger; and superego "shoulds," "oughts," and "musts," of which we are not consciously aware.

THE PSYCHOSEXUAL STAGES OF DEVELOPMENT

One of Freud's major contributions was his discovery of the significance to the total personality of early infant and child experiences. The psychosexual stages were conceived of as defining the aspect of the child's behaviour which reflected the greatest tension, need, or conflict, and therefore pleasure, at a particular period in the child's development. Thus, for the newborn, the most critical needs are somatic, and as the infant has no consciousness, the pleasure principle operates without regard to reality to bring about tension reduction and somatic need satisfaction, which is experienced as pleasant. As the new infant grows, there is a progression from behaviour based in id, which seeks generalized comfort, to a focusing of id on a specific organ or part of the body, called an *erogenous* zone, and finally with the gradual development of superego and ego functions, the eventual preoccupation with ego concerns in adult life. There are four stages of psychosexual development: (1) oral, (2) anal, (3) phallic, and (4) genital.

Oral Stage

Freud gave the first year of life this designation, believing the most important subjective experience to be hunger-satisfaction, leading to active interaction of the infant with the environment in feeding. While the infant was viewed as pure id, giving immediate response to all and any instinctual urges and reflex action, the organ or primary site of pleasure was assumed to be the mouth. Thus, although the awake infant was perceived as a seething cauldron of uncontrolled drives and impulses indiscriminately being discharged in chaotic behaviour in the random pursuit of immediate tension relief, the mouth was the source of food and therefore a primary, perhaps *the* primary, source of pleasure. The mouth too is the infant's contact point of union with the mother through suckling, and the sucking reflex itself seems to be satisfying and tension-reducing even when no food is required. The use of the "soother" provides ample evidence of the latter. In the first year, then, the infant is seen as a receiver, as a consumer, as one who takes in but gives little back, and as one who is dependent on others for the satisfaction of basic needs, for feeling comfort, for relief from tension and distress, and for experiencing pleasure. Freud believed that these characteristics were retained within the personality and modified by later experience, and, in some individuals, characterized later adult behaviour. He used the term *fixation* to refer to a failure of the person to achieve full genital adult development. Since in normal development our early experience is not eliminated in growth, but is merely modified and integrated within the personality, oral-stage behaviour may be evident in our actions, desires, or sensations. In times of stress, we may demonstrate characteristic behaviour from this or other earlier psychosexual stages. Such demonstrations are called *regression*. Regression, if episodic or situational, may be positive or negative for the overall functioning of the individual, but if it persists over an extended period as the characteristic response to stressful situations, it would be considered a behaviour problem.

Anal Stage
The anal stage begins at about two or three years of age. During this period the anus becomes the site of tension and, with reduction of tension by elimination, pleasure. Freud again postulated the development of a number of other character traits which arise out of the child's focus of attention on the elimination process. For example, toilet training involves a struggle between the parent and the child. It is the first act under the child's control from which the child derives a sense of power, since elimination or retention of feces is looked on with concern by the parent. The way in which the struggle is resolved may determine the nature of our future relationships with authority figures. The evacuation of feces gives rise to feelings of *ownership* by the child. Feces are the child's creation, and the child may be distressed to see them disappear in the toilet, and/or refuse to give them up. Thus part of the anal character development relates to the giving or holding in or back, qualities seen in later life. Fixated anal-retentive persons may be seen as cheap or stingy, or stubborn and withholding of themselves, or as uptight, rigid, and obsessive. Fixated anal-evacuative persons may be considered messy, disorganized, and destructive and/or as receiving pleasure from giving to others, but having little to give, and being unable to retain much of anything. Feces, then are the child's first possession, and therefore may be given as the first gifts. The child who completes toilet training and becomes retentive—evacuates on cue, and gives the parent the gift of the feces—does so in exchange for parental love and approval. Freud believed *tenderness* is predicated on the child learning to be anal-retentive. Tenderness results from the child's desire to preserve and possess the object of gratification, and to care for it (Wolman, 1960). Satisfactory resolution of the toilet-training conflict sees the child's feelings of tenderness transferred to special objects like bottles, blankets, and stuffed toys, and later to parents, siblings, and pets. In the mature adult the desire to *possess* is sublimated in the desire to *preserve* and *protect* the love object.

Phallic Stage
This stage begins between three and five years of age and is completed about the age of six. At this point, sexual pleasure becomes focused on the genital organs, which both male and female children discover and manipulate or masturbate. Ego control over sexual and aggressive urges occurs at this time, as does the establishment of sexual identity. Freud believed that at this point the development of males and females differed. For the male, Freud described the events of this stage as the Oedipus complex, and for females, the Electra complex.

Freud believed that in the Oedipal conflict, the boy, experiencing his developing genital sexuality, desires to possess his mother, who is his primary love object, and to replace his father as the mother's sexual partner. The boy develops during this period a strong love relationship with his mother, and growing anger and hostility toward his father. As this conflict intensifies, the child fantasizes, perhaps aided by real parental censure, but more likely through identification with the father (the child imagines what his own response would be were someone about to possess, or steal, something that belonged to him), that his sexual desires for his mother are dangerous, and punishable by the father. The fantasized threat of punishment for his wish, perhaps castration or harm of now his most important organ, his penis, results in gradual *repression* of this desire, and replacement of a desire for sexual union with his mother by demonstration of extreme tenderness and affection. This resolution of the conflict enables the child to reestablish his relationship of love with his father, complete his identification and modelling with him, and to subsequently seek an appropriate other female love object for sexual union and gratification. Since Freud believed we are initially bisexual, several other scenarios may occur in the phallic stage which result in either a failure to make a definite sexual identification and the retention of the bisexual status, or the development of a homosexual orientation.

The Electra complex is essentially the reverse of the Oedipal conflict. However, it is more complicated for the girl in three respects. As with the boy, her primary love object is her mother. Unlike the boy, she must give up her primary love object, her mother, to possess her father. When she learns that she does not have a protruding penis, she assumes she has lost it, and blames her mother for letting this occur. She seeks a sexual relationship with her father, but at the same time resents him for being a male and possessing the penis she lacks. Freud considered that penis envy disappeared through compensation at the time of the birth of a woman's first child, especially if it was a boy (Hall and Lindzey, 1957).

Genital Stage
The genital stage occurs in adolescence. The attention of the adolescent is directed away from home and family, and the parents are no longer viewed as the primary love objects. As well, the adolescent, who as a child was narcissistic and self-centred, begins to direct love outward, and to appreciate others altruistically for themselves rather than for what they can do for him or her. It is a time of further exploring and practising independence and autonomy, and as well, for assuming new responsibilities in which dependability is expected. Thus, adolescence is a transition period, in which new adult roles are being assumed. It is the final transition in the development from the uncontrolled mass of infantile id urges to the socialized ego adult. In adult life, all psychosexual stages will be in evidence and contribute to the total adult personality and behaviour.

FREUD'S THEORY OF NEUROSIS
Very simply, Freud viewed neurosis as arising from approach-avoidance conflicts leading to the development of *anxiety*. The role of anxiety is key, since all approach-avoidance conflicts may not lead to anxiety. Only those approach-avoidance conflicts that involve events which threaten the physical and/or psychological integrity of the individual and over which the individual has no con-

trol cause anxiety. The precipitating events which invoke anxiety responses may be either events external to the person in the environment, or internal psychological events. Thus, the conflict may be between id impulses for tension reduction (approach), and ego control for purposes of self-preservation (avoidance). The conflict may occur between ego behaviours (approach) and superego restrictions (avoidance), or may represent external threatening stimulation or events (approach) from which the individual is unable to escape (avoidance).

But intense anxiety is a dysfunctional response of the individual. Powerful anxiety is immobilizing. As a result, the individual learns from experience as an infant and young child to recognize situational cues and signals both internal and external, which indicate the onset of intense anxiety. This results in what Freud terms *signal anxiety,* a mild sensation of threat which stimulates an avoidance response prior to the onset of debilitating anxiety (Ford and Urban, 1964).

Signal anxiety is recognized by the ego, and the ego responds with what Freud called *mechanisms of defense*. We have already discussed fixation and regression above; five additional ego defense mechanisms are: (1) repression, (2) denial, (3) reaction formation, (4) projection, and (5) displacement.

Repression

Freud originally termed repression *resistance*. He noted that his early patients had difficulty recalling and/or speaking about the anxiety-evoking events, desires, or impulses associated with the occurrence of their problem behaviour. Because these experiences were not forgotten and could be fully discussed under hypnosis, Freud believed the patient had actively pushed such memories and sensations out of consciousness to avoid the pain and emotional discomfort they involved. However, since the psychic energy associated with these events could not be dissipated by merely pushing them into the unconscious and out of awareness, these impulses, thoughts, and desires continued to press to be discharged in behaviour. Since the real need, desire, feeling, or thought was unacceptable to the ego, and the psychic energy could not be discharged in its original form, the original impulses were disguised or changed so that they would not be recognized by the ego and could therefore be manifested in behaviour. Such disguised manifestations, then, appeared as the patient's symptoms. Repressions are resistant to change because they are not available for reality testing by the ego. Thus, something repressed by the child may no longer represent a threat to the adult ego, but since the repressed material does not enter consciousness, the repression continues, and the resulting inappropriate behavioural symptom is retained (Hall and Lindzey, 1957).

Denial

In denial, the individual *substitutes* what she *wishes* for the real situation. The person may deny the existence of thoughts, feelings, behaviour, or impulses which may be apparent to others, but are refused awareness by the denying person. Denial is not the same as unconsciously forgetting or unconsciously lying, because in denial we are convinced that our beliefs represent reality.

Reaction Formations
Reaction formations also represent substitutions for real feelings, impulses, or beliefs. Reaction formations, however, result in the polar opposite of the unacceptable behaviour. For example, a man uncertain of his masculinity may adopt a Don Juan role in an attempt to convince himself and others of his sexual prowess.

Projection
Projection is the process by which individuals attribute to others characteristics, behaviour, feelings, or desires which they find unacceptable in themselves. The projection of their own unacceptable behaviour onto others is also an attempt to justify it. "Everyone is a little dishonest," means, "I am dishonest, feel guilty, and fear I will be punished."

Displacement
Displacement occurs when a response is directed to a substitute object instead of to the originally chosen object. For example, if we are unable to demonstrate love and affection to significant people, we may do so instead with pets.

The Therapeutic Goals, Conditions, Dynamics, and Procedures of Classical Psychoanalysis

TREATMENT GOALS
The goal of psychoanalysis is to enable the patient to become conscious of previously repressed material in order that she may recognize and become aware of: psychologically determined wishes and desires, self-evaluative thoughts and feelings, and environmental demands of reality, and be able to choose rationally the most self-satisfying and rewarding behaviour response (Ford and Urban, 1964).

CONDITIONS FOR THERAPY

Limitations of Classical Psychoanalysis
Classical psychoanalytic therapy was developed for the treatment of hysteria, a neurotic disorder. With modifications to the classical technique, Freud considered it also effective in the treatment of phobias or obsessional neurosis. It was thought to work best with educated patients between 15 and 50 years of age. It was considered inappropriate for psychotic patients, or for other patients who for whatever reason were unable or unwilling to "cooperate" (Bernstein, 1965). This would include mentally disabled patients, patients suffering depression, or patients who had been "forced" into therapy, but were unmotivated. Since it is a technique requiring an extensive and protracted time commitment, five days

a week for a period of two to five years, it is inappropriate for crisis cases, or where a long-term commitment to basic change is unlikely, as in older persons.

Patient Prerequisites
In addition to the age, motivational, and intellectual factors noted above, Freud believed patients should also have the following characteristics (Ford and Urban, 1964): (1) be in a state of pain and distress, (2) be agreeable to participate in the method of free association, (3) be able to form a relationship with the therapist, (4) be unrelated to the therapist, (5) be able to pay for the therapy, and (6) be independent of parents or other relatives who might interfere in the therapy.

On the other hand, there are certain conditions which pertain to the therapist: (1) The therapist is expected to give the patient his undivided attention. (2) The therapist does not return either affectionate or hostile responses received from the patient but should maintain complete affective neutrality. (3) The therapist does not *introduce* conventional morality into his responses. (4) The therapist remains alert to *all* aspects of the patient's behaviour; he does not selectively attend.

Abstinence
In classical psychoanalysis, the patient is required to abstain from behaviour which may bring substitute relief from her pain and suffering. In Chapter 6, for example, we will note that Fritz Perls was forbidden by his analyst to get married until his analysis was completed. The rationale for such prohibitions is to ensure that the tension level and distress experienced by the patient remains sufficiently high to maintain the patient's motivation to *work* on her analysis. Analysis is difficult. It is begun because the person hurts. As the therapy proceeds, and the patient begins to feel better, there is a tendency to stop. Abstinence from external substitutes for analytic relief from tension is intended to maintain a sufficiently high tension level so as to maintain the patient in therapy until the analysis is complete. On the other hand, there is also the danger that the patient will find the analysis *too* gratifying and develop a dependency on the analyst and analysis (Bernstein, 1965).

DYNAMICS OF THERAPY
There are five basic dynamics which together form the basis of psychoanalytic treatment. They are: (1) exploration or interpretation, (2) working through, (3) acting out, (4) transference, and (5) countertransference.

Exploration or Interpretation
This is the work of the analyst. As the patient, through free association, verbalizes what comes to consciousness, the therapist listens to and observes the patient carefully and attempts to deduce, from his knowledge of the patient, understanding of problem behaviour, clinical experience with other patients,

and self-awareness gained through his own analysis, what the patient is revealing. The analyst acts as an interpreter of the real messages in the patient's verbalizations, which are hidden or disguised from the patient's consciousness as a result of the process of repression. This is a complex process which requires continual assessment on the part of the therapist as to what of the material discussed by the patient requires interpretation, when, and in what manner. When the patient is silent or refuses to accept an interpretation, this behaviour is also interpreted and is considered to be *resistance* to experiencing the repressed stimuli.

Working Through
While the patient initially resists or denies the interpretations of the therapist, anxiety is increased when the therapist continually points out the patient's avoidances. The increase in anxiety occurs as the patient comes closer to acknowledging or accepting the interpretation and the avoided material reaches consciousness. Finally, when the patient can no longer deny the repressed material and is able to accept the interpretation, the patient and therapist discuss the significance of the avoidance for the patient. This discussion is called *working through*. In working through, the goal is to have the patient learn to identify not only what was being avoided, but what the real *desire* or wish was that the patient had repressed (Ford and Urban, 1964). This is the gaining of *insight* into the nature of the conflict and is experienced with emotional release and spontaneous verbalization by the patient.

Acting Out
The object of psychoanalytic therapy is to engage in *verbal* recall of repressed material in order to bring into conscious awareness, and therefore under conscious control, impulses and behaviour which produce pain and discomfort for the patient. The patient is therefore forbidden, as in the case of abstinence above, to make any important decisions or take any significant actions without first discussing them in therapy. This injunction against independent action is made to prevent the patient from *acting out* in a repetitive and compulsive manner the symptoms which have brought her to the therapist originally. The only way the patient can be helped to cease her inappropriate behaviour is by talking about it, since she is unable to recognize her own self-destructive actions.

Transference
Transference is a form of acting out in which the patients "transfer" to the therapist "the characteristic attitudes and expectations which they have developed in the course of their lives and which operate in the present to interfere with their capacity to live a normal and satisfactory life (S. Freud, 1912a)" (Bernstein, 1965: 1187). This acting out is considered appropriate because it enables the full range of patient behaviour to be demonstrated in the safety of the treatment situation, as it is being experienced. Thus the transference dynamics provide a here-and-now balance to the past orientation in psychoanalysis.

Countertransference

Countertransference may be defined as "the repetition of previously acquired attitudes toward the patient, such attitudes being irrational in the given situation" (Cohen, 1955: 539). In psychoanalytic therapy, in which the therapist is expected to remain involved but objective and neutral, countertransference is considered a therapist problem and a serious impediment to therapy. Countertransference is characterized by the therapist's anxiety in the presence of the patient. It may occur when the therapist has his own unresolved personal problems, or when the patient communicates anxiety to the therapist. Whatever the reason, it is necessary for the therapist to deal with the countertransference so as not to destroy the therapeutic relationship.

PSYCHOANALYTIC PROCEDURE

Two procedures identify the classical psychoanalytic approach: (1) the use of the couch and (2) free association.

Use of the Couch

Bernstein (1965) suggests that the use of the couch in analysis may be a carry-over from Freud's early period, when hypnosis was used in the treatment of hysteria, but maintains that it is still appropriate in establishing certain conditions required for the treatment procedure. Reclining in a horizontal position, with the therapist out of her direct gaze, the patient may attend to her own thoughts and feelings, undistracted by the therapist's facial expressions, eye contact, and body language. Because the therapist is out of sight he need not be concerned that the patient will make incorrect inferences from his body language, and may therefore be more relaxed himself and able to focus his attention wholly on the patient. This sharper focusing facilitates the therapist's cognitive processing of the content of the patient's verbalizations and his responses to them. Thus a patient's dislike of the couch is interpreted as resistance, because objectively the couch provides the most comfortable position for analytic work for both the analyst and patient.

Free Association

The technique of free association requires the patient to become as relaxed as possible and to begin to speak about whatever comes to mind. She is not to censor anything, but to speak as much as possible her thoughts, feelings, or sensations as she is aware of them. She is not to rule out something because it seems trivial or silly, and is not to feel embarrassed or ashamed of expressing anything. What the patient expresses are not hidden secrets or guarded thoughts, but rather a stream of seemingly unconnected bits and pieces of memories, experiences, events, and situations which jump back and forth in time from the present to yesterday to childhood to last week. The job of the therapist is to listen to the so-called random, chaotic flow of disconnected material, and discover the recurring themes, the connections in time, the areas of conflict, the events that carry emotion and evoke a change in mood, and so on.

Thus, the therapist observes the patient's apparently disjointed verbalizations as we do when we sit before the pieces of a giant puzzle, and searches for the bits that go together in terms of colours, shades, contours, and distinguishing patterns. What the therapist finds, as we find when we stare at the pieces of the puzzle for a time, is that there is in fact a *pattern* in the patient's "free" associations, a pattern which is gradually consciously re-revealed to the patient, as the patient unconsciously reveals it to the therapist.

The following is an example of the nature of free association from a small segment of the reconstructed associations of a well-educated patient:

> The patient begins with a brief report of the previous day—a sort of routine in his analytic sessions. Nothing special: he had a conference with his boss about a going project. He didn't quite like the boss's policy, but it was not too bad and who was he, in the hierarchy of his institution, to contradict the boss? By now this was an old issue in the analysis: did he habitually give in too easily, or did he evaluate correctly the major contours of his job? In any event, the conference was just a conference like any other. He'd had a dream—something about an ironing board, but that was as far as he could go. Association to ironing board? Well, we have one. "Matter of fact, my wife said our maid irons badly. She could iron my shirts better herself, but I don't think she could and I'm sure she wouldn't. Anyhow, my shirts look all right to me. I wish she wouldn't worry so much. I hope she doesn't fire that maid." The patient suddenly hums a bit from *Lohengrin* and has to hunt for the words on the request of the analyst. It is the passage where Lohengrin reveals his glorious origin. ("My father, Parsifal, wears his crown and I am his knight, Lohengrin.") Patient: "Now I think of that last report X [his boss] turned in. That was my work—only I can't say so. That ironing board—my mother was ironing. I jumped off the cupboard, wonderful jump, but I sort of used her behind as support—she was leaning over. She told father I had been disrespectful and he gave me a licking. I was awfully hurt. I hadn't even thought about her old behind—it was just a wonderful jump. Father would never let me explain. My sister says he was proud of me. He never acted that way. He was awfully strict. I wish he hadn't died when I was so young—we might have worked things out (Munroe, 1955: 39).

SUMMARY

We began this chapter by considering the historical roots of contemporary psychiatry. In doing so, we briefly examined the concept of mental illness and explored four belief systems regarding the *causes* of mental illness, noting the gradual shift from either/or biogenic and psychogenic positions to the widely held contemporary view that physical, psychological, and environmental factors together are involved. Our quick look at the development of psychiatry and the uneven progress and advances made in the care and treatment of the severely mentally ill made evident the importance of the prevailing social conditions and highlighted recurring issues which continue to surface. Tracing the history of the mental hospital in the United States, we identified four periods:

1. moral treatment (1800-60)
2. the gradual decline of moral treatment (1860-20)
3. the "road back" (1920-65)
4. deinstitutionalization (1965-present)

Although major improvements and advances in treatment procedures have occurred since 1950, enabling effective community-based care programs even for the seriously ill patient, availability of community resources for this purpose appear inadequate. Thus the apparent economically-motivated thrust of deinstitutionalization of the mentally ill has, in effect, decreased the availability of effective psychiatric care and treatment programs to this high-risk population. The old domination of psychiatry in the treatment process appears to be giving way to a collegial approach with allied helping professionals. There is a new realization that mental illness is not the private domain or sole responsibility of psychiatry, but rather is a public concern. As such, psychiatrists along with other helpers are being drawn into patient advocacy and political action. In the second part of the chapter we outlined the psychiatric assessment and classification process and identified various treatment modalities in use. The diagnostic process was discovered to concentrate on obtaining information regarding the *thinking* and *feeling* aspects of the patient's behaviour and included four sources of data:

1. psychiatric interview
2. psychological testing
3. physical examination
4. other specialized medical tests

Four *types* of mental illness were discussed to illustrate the nature and usefulness of psychiatric classification. Schizophrenia was used as an example of a *functional* illness, that is, one *without* an apparent physical cause, and organic mental disorder, to reflect mental illness *with* a known physical basis. These were considered severe illnesses, known as psychoses. The continuum of severity in illness was illustrated using unhappiness and depression, two affective disorders, the latter being psychotic in nature.

Treatment modalities were only briefly discussed. The psychiatrist has at his disposal the most powerful armamentarium of treatment options of all helpers. In addition to the physical therapies described, all the "talking" therapies and behaviour therapies are employed by psychiatry.

Lastly, we considered the major concepts of psychoanalysis and psychoanalytic treatment principles, beginning with a brief biographical sketch of Freud himself. The theory of psychoanalysis was discussed in terms of:

1. basic assumptions about human behaviour and development (psychic determinism, libido, and the principle of constancy)
2. the structure and functioning of the mental apparatus (id, ego, superego; and the unconscious, conscious, and preconscious mind)
3. the psychosexual stages of human development (oral, anal, phallic, and genital)
4. the theory of neurosis and ego mechanisms of defense (repression, denial, reaction formation, projection, displacement, fixation, and regression)

And finally, psychoanalysis as a therapy was described in terms of goals, conditions, dynamics, and procedures for treatment. Although psychoanalysis today is alive and well, the real contribution made by Freud appears to be in the stimulus provided by his ideas to others, since many of his concepts have not stood up to scientific scrutiny, and classical psychoanalysis as a method of psychotherapy appears to be of limited value in comparison with newer approaches (Singer, 1980).

3
Psychology

The contributions of psychology to the field of helping are of two kinds. First, other helping disciplines have borrowed, incorporated, and employed in their own approaches selected principles or theories from various areas of psychology. Second, a number of psychologists have themselves employed the knowledge of their field to develop new and unique helping strategies.

Psychology differs from the helping disciplines described in Chapters 2 and 4. For while psychiatry, psychoanalysis, and social work developed as *methods and techniques* for the purpose of *changing* behaviour, psychology per se concerns itself with the *study* of behaviour. Thus, while the new clinical psychology is involved in behaviour assessment and change, it retains a strong scientific and research bias and identification. Since the field of psychology did not begin as a therapeutic approach or method, and since the study of human behaviour offered such a vast and complex area of exploration, it expanded in a number of directions and produced an enormous amount of information and theory. At the same time, the work of those in the helping disciplines attracted the attention of psychologists, stimulating some to search for their own helping approaches. In this chapter we shall examine three such approaches which figure prominently in the helping methods discussed in Parts III and IV. In Part V a fourth approach, which forms the basis for three powerful methods of behaviour change, will be explored. These four approaches are: (1) Gestalt psychology, (2) organismic psychology, (3) existential or humanistic psychology, and (4) learning psychology and behaviourism.

Let's begin our exploration with a brief history of psychology up to the development of the Gestalt school.

Psychology as Philosophy

Modern psychology dates from the end of the nineteenth century. Prior to that time, psychology was considered a part of philosophy. And the issue which had for centuries occupied the attention of philosophers was the "body-soul" or "mind-soul" dilemma: if there is a "soul," what is its relation to the "body," and what happens to the "soul" when separated from the body in death? These questions were in the realm of metaphysics, which concerned itself with attempting to understand the universe and the meaning of life. But there was no *proof* for the theories and ideas of the metaphysicians. Their explanations of such phenomena as the nature of emotion, reason, memory, perception, and sensation were subjective and theoretical. As a result, toward the end of the nineteenth century there were as many psychological or metaphysical theories as there were philosophers, and no way of proving which theories were correct and which were not. Psychology as philosophy was at a dead end, but psychology as science was just beginning.

During the latter half of the nineteenth century, while psychologist-philosophers were continuing to speculate about the nature of humans and human behaviour, great strides were being made in the natural sciences. The new laboratory methods being successfully employed in physics and biology first intrigued and finally were adopted by psychologists. With the new empiricism came several advantages not previously available for the study of psychological events. These were:

1. Control over the conditions under which events occur
2. Control over the scheduling and frequency of the event's occurrence
3. Repetition of the occurrence under the same conditions to verify earlier results
4. Description of conditions under which events occur so that others can duplicate results
5. Variance of the conditions under which events occur to discover the effect and variance on resulting events (Woodworth & Schlosberg, 1958).

This was the way to discover the truth about human behaviour and experience. The *scientific method* adopted by psychology would turn the discipline from preoccupation with speculation and theory to concentration on facts and truth.

The Birth of Scientific Psychology

In this climate, in 1879 in Leipzig, Germany, the first psychology laboratory was established, and Wilhelm Wundt was named as its head. He was an ideal choice, being well versed in psychology, philosophy, and physiology. Both he and his pupil Edward Titchener, who later taught Abraham Maslow at Cornell University, defined the subject of psychological investigation as human *consciousness*.

Although their approach was empirical, employing observation, experimentation, and measurement, their *method* for studying consciousness was introspective, involving self-observations. This introspective approach raised several difficult questions. For example, is introspection the *best* method for studying consciousness or experiencing? Does consciousness cover all of the behaviour of interest to psychologists? Doesn't introspection continue to split man into mind and body—i.e., muscles, bones, and nerves belong to the physical field, while emotions, feelings, perceptions, and memory belong to the mental field.

Wolman (1960) suggests that three major challenges to introspectionism, which occurred simultaneously at the turn of the century, helped to broaden the scope, and form the bases, of contemporary psychology. These were the development of intelligence tests in France by Binet and Simon, and in the U.S.A. by Thorndike, Therman, and Yerkes; the study of animal psychology; and psychiatry.

The development of intelligence tests did not employ introspection and yet produced measures of mental capacities and functioning which could be used to predict future behaviour and achievement. The work of animal psychologists suggested that certain behavioural investigations conducted on animal subjects could lead to interesting hypotheses and might have application for higher biological species, including humans, even though animal behavioural studies obviously did not involve introspection. Early psychiatrists such as Charcot and Janet demonstrated that their patients were capable of displaying love, hate, and fear without *conscious* awareness of the existence of their own inner experience. A psychology which consisted only of the elements of conscious awareness, then, would leave out some important aspects of human behaviour. In addition to these criticisms, there were those who railed against the artificial, austere nature of the introspective experimental laboratory method which seemed so removed from the complexity of "real" human behaviour.

The New Science of Psychology: Three Approaches

Psychology as introspectionism did not survive the challenges outlined above. As a result this fledgling field, with its borrowed scientific methodology, entered the twentieth century without a central focus. And while it would continue to concern itself with certain philosophic questions and values, it was now successfully established as a separate discipline. The absence of a singular focus, however, meant that psychology developed along several different lines concurrently.

Thus, groups of psychologists concentrated their attention and study on three major features of human behaviour: learning, "mental illness," and perception. The three approaches to the study of human behaviour arising from these concentrations were: (1) the psychology of learning (behaviourism and conditioning), (2) Freudian psychology (psychoanalysis), and (3) Gestalt psychology and phenomenology.

To these, we have added organismic psychology and existential-humanistic psychology. Organismic psychology has been included because of its importance to psychological theory generally and to current helping strategies in particular. It reflects the work of one person and in this sense differs from the other four approaches which each identify the work and study of large numbers of psychologists. Existential-humanistic psychology, the fourth major approach, which, like organismic psychology, developed during the 1920s and 1930s, represents the most recent approach to the study of human behaviour.

MAJOR CONTRIBUTIONS OF LEARNING THEORY AND FREUDIAN PSYCHOLOGY

The Psychology of Learning

The names of Pavlov, Watson, McDougall, Guthrie, Hull, Skinner, and Wolman are associated with this approach. These psychologists and their followers embarked upon a rigorous empiricism in which there was no room for the consciousness of the introspectionists. They focused instead on "outer" as opposed to "inner" experience. Overt behaviour—stimuli and responses, actions and reactions—was their object of concern and study. The learning theorists occupied themselves with exploring the totality of human behaviour, and their work attempted to explain or interpret all aspects of human behaviour in terms of conditioning, biology, and physiology. All of our behaviour, they said, was *determined* by the facts of our physical existence and past experience. If so, then given knowledge of the physical condition and potential of an organism, as well as its past experience in a given situation, one should be able to predict the organism's behaviour in a similar situation.

In short, the behaviourists and early learning theorists made three highly significant contributions to the field of psychology and to helpers generally:

1. They demonstrated the importance of careful observation and analysis of *external* behaviour in the study (or understanding) of *internal* events.
2. They demonstrated the importance of the past learning experience of the organism on present behaviour.
3. They were the first psychologists to develop a general theory and method of behaviour change.

Freudian Psychology and Psychoanalysis

Freud, too, developed a theory and method for behaviour change. His efforts were aimed at a specific problem behaviour called neurosis. While the discoveries of the behaviourists were not applied to behaviour problems per se until much later, Freud's concepts and principles gained instant attention and were quickly employed in both psychiatry and social work. In contrast to the behaviourists' quantitative, empirical, laboratory approach to the study of human behaviour, Freud used a qualitative and clinical case study method. In fact, Freud's entire psychological theory was developed on the basis of his work with a very small number of patients. Nevertheless, his theories and concepts had an enormous impact on the development of psychotherapy. He began with a theory regarding the origin and treatment of specific behaviour problems and ended with a theory of human nature which encompassed all aspects of human behaviour. Freudian psychology is reflected in many of our contemporary helping theories and methods.

Consider the following contributions made by Freud:

1. He focused attention on infant and child development and the importance of early infantile experience on later personality development.

2. He identified the critical importance of human sexuality and aggression in understanding human behaviour.
3. He originated the concept of *unconscious* motivation.
4. He initiated the concept of repression and defense mechanisms.
5. He created a treatment method—psychoanalysis—for dealing with neurosis.
6. He stimulated the creative work of numerous followers who in turn made their contributions to the field.

GESTALT PSYCHOLOGY

Gestalt psychology developed as a rejection of nineteenth-century experimental psychology. It was initiated by three German psychologists—Max Wertheimer, Wolfgang Kohler, and Kurt Koffka—following the First World War. The basic principle behind Gestalt psychology was that the way in which an object was perceived was determined by the total context or configuration in which the object was embedded. Perception was the result of *relationships* among various components in the perceptual field rather than the result of the individual *characteristics* of the separate components involved (Hall and Lindzey, 1957). Hence the famous quote "the whole is greater than the sum of the parts."

The Gestaltists were in direct opposition to experimentalists like Wundt. Behaviour or events, they said, *could not be isolated* for study, since isolating them from their context or relationships would change their meaning and function. Humans, in particular, were not simply complicated machines which could be studied by taking the pieces apart, because the pieces became different when they were isolated from the whole. There is a certain parallel here to the sociological concept of cultural relativity, which states that an act can only be understood within the context in which it occurs.

The second major principle of Gestalt psychology is called "closure." Gestaltists believed that the brain would attempt to *complete* whatever was *incomplete* in order to make sense out of what is perceived. However, they did not see perception as incremental, built on by bits and pieces of information. Perception, they said, occurred instantaneously as something from the environment took precedence and *emerged* or became dominant.

Actually, the Gestaltists were only half right. There does seem to be, as they suggested, an either/or element present in perception. Instant recognition does seem to occur *after* a period of confusion, when we *suddenly* see, not by steps in a gradual and incremental fashion, but all at once—in a flash. What was not perceived a moment before is perceived suddenly. Imagine yourself in a dimly lit room. You peer through the darkness trying to make out shapes and forms. The various objects in the room, in this case, do not *slowly* become clear and vivid and recognizable, but rather they *suddenly* appear to you.

The third major principle of Gestalt psychology was that perception was automatically *meaningful*. However, while the principles of "closure" and "relationship" were correct, the principle of "automatic meaningfulness" was not. The meaning of a perception is an active process which requires the focusing, attention, awareness, and motivation of the perceiver.

We find early Gestalt principles evident in most contemporary psychotherapies for sound reasons. The Gestaltists were the first psychologists to warn against the use of a purely mechanistic approach to understanding human behaviour. They emphasized the importance of understanding the *context* in which behaviour occurs and the *relationship* of the various elements involved in any psychological event. Behaviour may appear strange when viewed out of context. We therefore need to understand the circumstances in which problem behaviour has occurred. Second, the Gestalt principle of "closure" is apparent in a number of contemporary helping theories. The idea of a drive or tendency of the organism to complete what is incomplete is compatible with personal growth therapies. It is used to explain or understand complex behaviour such as problem solving, task completion, goal attainment, perseverance, and attention. Third, Gestaltists emphasized *understanding* as opposed to analysis, description, and explanation of human behaviour. Their focus was on the *meaning* of the behaviour to the person demonstrating it.

The Gestalt school was short-lived, overtaken by the empiricism of the day. Its principles of "relationship," "closure," and even "meaningfulness," however, have remained as fundamental psychological principles.

ORGANISMIC PSYCHOLOGY

A Holistic Approach

Organismic psychology was the creation of Kurt Goldstein (see Appendix A at the end of this chapter for a brief biography). His work is not usually afforded the same status as that of the learning theorists or the Gestalt or Freudian psychologists, but has been included in this presentation because of the importance of Goldstein's contributions to the field of psychotherapy. Like the Gestaltists, Goldstein developed a holistic approach to the study of behaviour, and began his work in Germany following the First World War (1914-19). In fact, he did some early work with Gelb, a Gestalt psychologist, and both he and the Gestaltists taught at the University of Berlin in 1930 (Hall and Lindzey, 1957). Goldstein was not a Gestaltist, nor was he a psychologist. He was by training a neurologist. His entry into the field of psychology resulted from his work with brain-injured soldiers who were war casualties. The organismic approach considered that any behaviour, whether normal or pathological, was an expression of "the organism to realize all its capacities in harmony—in other words, its nature. The degree to which this realization is fulfilled is dependent upon the relationship between the organism's capacity and the demands of the outer and inner worlds, that is, on how much the organism can come to terms with them" (Goldstein, 1959: 1333).

The Gestalt principle of "relationship," which was based on the study of perception alone, was confirmed by Goldstein as a principle which governed the behaviour of the *entire* organism. His work demonstrated that the human organism functions as an *integrated and unified system,* and that the separation or dysfunction of any part would not only alter the characteristics of that part, but would alter the functioning of the other parts of the organism as well.

If one was to employ an experimental laboratory approach of breaking complex organisms into discrete parts for study, Goldstein argued, it would be necessary to know what effect the isolation of the part from the whole has on the functioning of the part once isolated.

Being a neurologist, Goldstein approached his study of the behaviour of the organism through the study of the nervous system. This system, he maintained, functions as an integrated unit in a state of constant excitation. Any activity or behaviour of an organism reflects changes taking place in the organism as a result of responses made to external and internal stimuli. More important, Goldstein found that stimuli which are experienced by a particular part of the organism, while affecting that part in a special way, also change or affect the *entire* nervous system. For example, the eyes are specially adapted to receive light stimulation. However, while the retina changes with various levels of light stimulation more dramatically than any other part of the nervous and perceptual system, stimulation of the retina affects the *total* nervous system as well. We could compare this process to figure-ground; the figure being the specific sense organ response and the ground being the rest of the sensory-nervous system. Any change in the figure also alters the ground, and in the same way, changes in the ground affect the figure. For example, when our hands are very cold, we lose some of our sense of touch and have difficulty moving our fingers deftly.

Goldstein found, too, that there was *constancy* in these figure-ground relationships in that the same figure always produces the same ground. The organism, then, typically responds to stimuli in a consistent way. In addition to constancy, he discovered that organisms respond to new stimuli with increased excitability for a brief period only, and then they return to previous response levels. There is, then, a tendency for organisms to maintain an *equilibrium.* It has since been demonstrated that there is an optimum level of activation and arousal, or excitation, of the nervous system, required for normal functioning. If sensory input is too high or too low for the organism to maintain equilibrium, unusual behaviour and experiences occur. Similarly, Goldstein discovered that *isolation* of certain parts of the sensory nervous system altered organism equilibrium. His observations of patients with specific injuries which resulted in incomplete sensory-nervous systems revealed behaviour similar to that of organisms in laboratories where certain sensory-nervous functions had been removed.

In summary, where certain sensory-nervous processes are isolated from the total organism due to trauma or operative procedures, the following effects are found:

1. The reactions to stimuli in an isolated part are abnormally strong. There appears to be a dampening effect on each *part* of the system by its *connection to the total system*. Thus, while the eye may not "see" if certain neural pathways fail to integrate it with the perceptual apparatus, it may, if it continues to receive blood, continue to live and function. The retinal responses to stimulation, however, under these circumstances, are not of the same intensity as with an intact eye.
2. Reactions are of abnormal duration. There appears to be an equalizing role of the total system which enables the organism to return quickly to a state of equilibrium and maximum potential for response to new stimuli. The response to new stimuli of an organ already highly excited or responsive is reduced. For example, our ability to listen to someone's comment at a rock concert, or when listening to someone else, is impaired by the sounds we are already hearing.
3. Reactions are related to the stimulus in an abnormal way. In brain-injured patients this was observed in their tendency toward certain forms of obsessional behaviour.
4. As a result of a disturbance of the normal figure-ground process the reaction of an isolated part of the organism either exhibited abnormal rigidity or evinced alternate reactions to the same stimulus.
5. The detachment of a part of the organism produces a simpler, more primitive type of reaction.

Major Concepts of Organismic Psychology

No discussion of Goldstein's organismic approach would be complete without mention of the concept of *self-actualization,* which he originated. Less often discussed, but of similar importance, are his analyses of what he called the *abstract and concrete attitude, anxiety,* and *catastrophic reaction.* While these concepts were formulated as a result of his experience with patients with organic brain damage, in later years he demonstrated their implications for understanding patient behaviour where the problem was "functional" in origin or non-organic, as with neurosis and schizophrenia.

SELF-ACTUALIZATION (SA)

While Goldstein used this term over a thirty-year writing span, its meaning remained essentially the same. SA was a *drive;* the only drive of an organism to fulfill its potential. In this sense, any behaviour or activity of the organism is considered or viewed as an attempt, at least, of the organism to develop or experience its intrinsic nature, or to be what it is in potential.

This single-drive theory for understanding behaviour enables us to consider normal and abnormal behaviour from the same perspective. That is, we need not assume certain motivation for abnormal behaviour and some other kind of motive for normal behaviour. Both the "sick" organism and the "normal" or healthy organism are attempting to realize their potential. The difference between the two is that because of its abnormality the "sick" or abnormal organism is unable to realize its full potential. With growth blocked the only course left would appear to be mere existence or survival. The abnormal organism then, Goldstein concluded, becomes concerned with *self-preservation* or maintenance of the status quo, while the healthy organism demonstrates concern with *self-actualization*. The organism which is preoccupied with preserving its existing state recognizes its lost capacities and becomes defensive, fearing further losses. The individual's behaviour in such a case would be characterized by withdrawal and constriction, and clinging to routine, safety, and security. The self-actualizing, intact, healthy person, on the other hand, does not strive for *maintenance*, but seeks *new experience*, manifests *spontaneity*, and demonstrates *creativity*.

THE ABSTRACT ATTITUDE

Goldstein (1959) found that patients with brain lesions in the cortex demonstrated particular difficulty with a capacity he called the *"abstract attitude."* Normal human organisms relate to the world on a concrete *and* an abstract level. The *concrete* level is shared with all other animals. It involves the use of expressive and anticipatory symbols. The *abstract* level is unique to humans and involves the use of arbitrary symbols. (This capacity was discussed in Chapter 1 as a basic attribute of the normal human being.) Arbitrary symbol manipulation enables people to transcend the immediate situation; to conceptualize; to respond to the not-present. The normal person can shift easily from the concrete to the abstract attitude depending on the situation; the brain-injured patient cannot. Many brain-injured patients lose this capacity to adopt the abstract attitude, and while their initial behaviour may not appear to be different from the normal, further observation will reveal the person to be less spontaneous, less active, more defensive, and less flexible and adaptive. For example, the brain-injured person may be unable:

1. To assume a definite mental attitude on request, such as disappointment
2. To account for his actions and ideas
3. To shift reflectively from one aspect of a situation to another, for example, to consider how another person feels
4. To keep in mind various aspects of a task or of any presentation simultaneously, which requires either recall or prediction of events
5. To grasp the essential of a given whole, that is, break it up into pieces, isolate them, and synthesize them
6. To abstract common properties reflectively, such as weight
7. To perform concepts, or symbols, and to understand them
8. To evoke voluntarily previous experiences or images

9. To adopt a "what if" approach in order to respond to the "merely possible"
10. To detach the ego from the outer world or from inner experiences (Goldstein, 1959: 773-74).

As would be consistent with organismic theory, such loss in abstract functioning does not occur in isolation from the rest of the person, but affects emotional and concrete performance as well.

ANXIETY AND CATASTROPHE

What happens to the brain-injured patient who fails to solve or deal with a simple problem which requires the use of the abstract attitude? Goldstein found that the patient suddenly became agitated, began breathing heavily, became restless and very concerned, *or* became sullen, evasive, or angry. He called this response "the catastrophic reaction" (Goldstein, 1940). Goldstein discovered that the patient could not account for this anxiety reaction, and did not connect it to the failure to complete the task. These observations led to Goldstein's brilliant analysis of the concepts of anxiety and fear—central concerns in the fields of psychiatry, abnormal psychology, and theology. It is significant that although this analysis was gained through his early work with brain-injured patients, it is directly applicable to the understanding and treatment of various forms of non-organically related problem behaviour in both children and adults.

Goldstein (1940) stated that, while anxiety is characteristic of all animals, fear is characteristic of humans alone because the abstract attitude is necessary for the sensation of fear. Fear, he said, impels an organism to either attack or run. It is a motivating emotion. The way in which we respond depends on what choice we make. Choosing a course of action requires consideration of the alternatives, and of the implications of our decision. In order to choose, we must be aware of ourselves and of our relation to the object of fear.

With anxiety, however, we have only one reaction—flight—because although we *sense* danger, we are unaware of its *source* or *object*. Anxiety is fear of the unknown. What is it, then, about an object that causes fear? It is not the object itself, for the same object may be approached with fear in one case and not in another. It appears to be the situation itself, or the particular nature of the relationship between the organism and the object. Fear, says Goldstein (1940: 93), is "the experience of the possibility of the onset of anxiety." Fear occurs when we realize that if we don't do something, the situation may change to one causing anxiety, and an anxiety-producing situation is one in which we are unable to do anything to protect ourselves except run.

How is this explanation demonstrated in the behaviour of brain-injured patients? Very simply. The impairment of the abstract attitude prevents the patient from looking into the future, of giving to himself an account of his actions. If he were merely afraid, he would be able to do this. His reaction, because he is unable to assume a future orientation, is one of anxiety, that is, a vague sense of danger to his existence brought on by an awareness of his impaired ability to realize some of his essential capacities (Goldstein, 1940).

How does the patient cope with this anxiety? Since the catastrophic reaction is so debilitating to him, the patient attempts to avoid having it disrupt his behaviour. This means that he must find some way to organize his environment so that he can meet its demands with the use of his limited capacities. In other words, he *structures* a world in which he can live more comfortably. This, of course, must be a world in which he is free from stimuli which might set off a catastrophic reaction.

One way in which the patient can do this is to withdraw from the disturbing "total world." He does so by narrowing his environment to one which does not make demands upon him that he cannot fulfill. Goldstein noticed that his patients avoided situations which *might* lead to catastrophic behaviour. This they could not do through conscious effort, since this would have required planning which in turn would have required the use of the abstract attitude, which the patient did not have. Instead, avoidance was accomplished through the use of what in animal learning are called *anticipatory symbols* (this term is not used by Goldstein, but it is the process to which he refers (Goldstein, 1940: 97). The patient recognizes certain physical cues in his environment which were present when his previous catastrophic reaction descended upon him. These cues become *associated* with his anxiety reaction. Thus the real danger is not understood. The cues, however, warn him of impending danger and he withdraws or escapes while he can. This behaviour, Goldstein discovered, was developed as the patient learned to cope with his injury. For this reason, the newly injured patient seemed to have a much more difficult time, having to experience anxiety until he could establish his own cues for avoidance.

The avoidance of catastrophic situations by withdrawal does not mean that the patient becomes vegetative and inactive. On the contrary, such patients appear very active. Their activity, however, is seldom of much value in itself. Rather, its value seems to lie in the protection it offers from *unexpected* contacts with the environment they cannot handle. Thus, so long as patients keep themselves engrossed in tasks they can accomplish, they seem to be protected from the novel or the unknown. Functionally, this type of performance is identical with certain types of neurotic behaviour; only the etiology is different.

Another way of avoiding a catastrophic situation was the patient's pathological orderliness. His life was kept intact by a total adherence to the motto "a place for everything and everything in its place." This rigid control of his environment permitted optimal use of the concrete attitude—of automaton behaviour—and kept judgment, decision, and adaptability to an absolute minimum.

In summary, a vague sensation of danger or tension experienced by Goldstein's patients resulted in an avoidance response to the situation, learned through the use of anticipatory symbols. The patients narrowed their world in order not to experience tension. This resulted in stagnation or the maintenance of the status quo. Preservation of what capacities they had left and a concern for survival characterized their lives. The primary drive for the normal person is not self-preservation, but rather self-actualization of those potentialities through which individuals can realize their essential natures to the highest degree. This requires a *constant state of arousal and tension*. For the normal, then, tension and mild anxiety mean growth; for the abnormal they mean stagnation.

Organismic Therapy

Although Goldstein is not usually considered a psychotherapist, and although his major contributions to the helping field were made early in his career in the 1930s, the insights into neurotic behaviour and normal psychology gained from his work with brain-injured patients justify a brief examination of some of his later views on therapy. He gives an excellent treatment of the organismic approach to therapy in the *American Handbook of Psychiatry* (1959: 1333-47). Here, only a brief outline of some of the major points will be presented, such as the concept of health and sickness, the choice of the patient, the search for causes, and the patient-therapist relationship.

THE CONCEPTS OF HEALTH AND SICKNESS
Briefly, the organism can be said to be sick when it is in a state of disorder—when it is no longer capable of fulfilling the capacities which are inherent in it. (Those characteristics or attributes essential to the human person are discussed above and in Chapter 1.) Symptoms are the expressions of the organism which indicate its inability to adequately respond to the demands made upon it. The various symptoms of the sick organism are accompanied by anxiety which results not from the experience of failure to react adequately to external stimuli, but from the perception of danger, real or imagined, which the organism experiences when it is not able to realize its essential nature. *From this standpoint, sickness can result from either somatic or psychological malfunctions.*

The symptoms of the patient may be interpreted as adjustments which he makes in responding to his environment with modified capacities. In this sense, a basic trend is seen in the organism toward realizing its essential nature. That is, the organism uses what potentialities it has and adapts its behaviour such that these existent capacities will be preserved. It is possible to say, then, that the brain-injured patient is healthier once a state of ordered behaviour is attained by which he can function within a limited environment. The brain damage continues to exist but the patient has learned how to shape his environment in such a way that he can meet its demands satisfactorily. The brain-injured person avoids realization of how greatly his world has narrowed *except when thrown unexpectedly into a situation which triggers such realization* and a catastrophic reaction.

The neurotic or non-organically involved psychologically distressed person, however, *does* realize the extent to which he has narrowed his world to avoid anxiety.

THE CHOICE

When the neurotic reaches an awareness of the extent to which his defense mechanisms and his restrictions are preventing him from realizing his essential nature, he must make a choice—a choice between learning to live with some of the anxiety and experiencing the realization of his capacities to some extent, or through restriction keeping his anxiety at a minimum and suffering the corresponding lack of self-fulfillment and "good" feelings. Neurotic defenses may prevent the patient from feeling really bad, but they also prevent him from feeling really good!

According to Goldstein, whether the individual can make the choice for self-realization will depend on three factors. First, it depends on his premorbid personality structure. Therapy will make him aware of his total personality. He must be able to accept his limitations and recognize life's values in spite of them. He must see a possibility for self-actualization. Therapy will help him to meet his conflicts with *fear* rather than with crippling *anxiety*. Secondly, the capacity for choice depends upon how fully the personality is involved in the illness. If the illness embraces the total personality, such as in the case of the impairment of the abstract attitude, the capacity will be greatly reduced. Lastly, the choice will depend on how greatly past experience is connected with the present condition and with the solution of present conflicts.

SEARCH FOR CAUSES

Goldstein speaks of therapy as present-oriented rather than past-oriented. He is aware that the present conflict will be influenced by the effects of previous experience and so should not be ignored, but cautions that past experiences related to the present do not correspond to the actual past experienced situations. It is important to consider carefully whether the past behaviour and experience of the patient is significant to therapy in terms of the self-actualization of the patient in the present.

Communion

Communion is Goldstein's term for the patient-therapist relationship. He sees this relationship as the same whether the patient's illness is organic or functional. In the case of a patient with a neurotic problem, the relationship is arranged so that the patient experiences it as a common enterprise of himself and the therapist, in which the therapist leads *only* because he has learned how to deal with difficult problems. Therapeutic success, however, depends upon the active participation and cooperation of the patient. In this situation the patient is made aware that his problems are not alien to the therapist but are common to many people and that although they may be demonstrated in many ways, through a variety of symptoms, they arise primarily as a result of disturbances in interpersonal relationships. He learns in the therapist-patient relationship the value of mutual human relationships and of the necessity for sacrifice. (Goldstein does not explain what he means by "sacrifice" specifically, but refers to it as "the price man has to pay for being an individual." He is perhaps making reference to a form of altruistic love. In this sense the person who loves altruistically is a giving person. A person can only give what he has or is. Thus, to give of ourselves freely, the more complete or whole we must be, as persons and individuals (cf. characteristics of whole persons, Chapter 1). It is this important experience and relationship which the patient takes away from the therapeutic situation: if the therapy is successful, the patient will be able to develop communion with other people in his life.

It should be especially noted that the therapist does not simply act as a mirror reflecting passively to the patient his difficulties and conflicts and enabling the patient to develop insights. Nor is Goldstein's approach one in which the therapist directs, but remains professionally aloof from the patient. Organismic therapy involves the active participation of the therapist, who, as a result of the relationship, should be a little different than he was before. Goldstein states that a friendship should develop out of therapy which may continue long after treatment has ended. In describing the experience of communion, he says:

> one could call it the experience of a unity of individuals—a unity which does not eliminate them as such but on the contrary promotes their full development. It disentangles the individual from many irrelevant experiences and from many conflicts of the past and present, it makes him free to realize the essentials of life in general and of his individual existence in particular, the basis of self-realization.
>
> We consider communion as the presupport for every successful treatment, precisely because, in such a situation, we are dealing with an expression of one of the fundamentals of human existence, the possibility of understanding and accepting each other. The union is based on the normal drive in man to help and be helped out of which originates the mutual concern and thus the guaranty of self-realization in the highest possible degree for the particular human being and the other (Goldstein, 1959: 1346).

Goldstein's Contributions

In summary, here are the major contributions made by Goldstein's organismic approach to psychology and psychotherapy:

1. Goldstein founded his psychology upon human nature. He looked at human beings as organisms with certain biological characteristics and unique potentialities which characterize their existence.
2. He was the forerunner of "normal" psychology and demonstrated the fallacy of considering the "normal" person as simply pathology-free. His work suggested instead the existence of two essentially different primary drives in the normal and abnormal person. *The drive for self-preservation, when primary, is abnormal. The drive for self-actualization, when primary, is normal.* One is not simply an absence of the other. They are two totally different states.

3. He rebelled against an atomistic and reductionistic approach to the study of human behaviour and demonstrated how both the parts isolated for study or treatment, as well as the total remaining physiological systems, function differently when isolated from the whole organism than when a part of it. He felt that reductionists failed to take this into consideration and tried to apply their knowledge of parts to construct knowledge about people as a whole.
4. He was the first to demonstrate the significance of the human capacity for abstract behaviour and the far-reaching implications which this capacity has for both normal and neurotic behaviour.
5. He developed clear and concise concepts of anxiety and fear, how they could be distinguished, how they functioned, and how they affected patient behaviour and treatment.
6. With the creation of the concept of self-actualization he paved the way for a psychology of the normal organism, and a psychology of growth and being.
7. He made a major contribution to the diagnosis, treatment, and rehabilitation of brain-injured patients.
8. In his therapy he emphasized the second unique attribute of humans: their need for communion.

Goldstein's careful analysis and prolific work in the field of organic disorders and related behaviour problems paved the way for a sound theory of neurotic behaviour and functional psychoses. More than that, he provided a foundation on which to build a psychology of *health*, a psychology of the *normal*, to replace the sickness/mental illness model that had characterized the helping professions during their first fifty years.

EXISTENTIAL AND HUMANISTIC PSYCHOLOGY

Defining Terms and Direction

Let's begin this section by first considering the terms "existential" and "humanistic." Although it may sound confusing, *existential is humanistic, but humanistic may not be existential*. The term "humanistic" might describe any psychological approach, theory, or belief which has as its focus the human person. Thus, any helping strategy, philosophy, or even religion, might be considered humanistic. Since the term "existential" implies a concern with human *existence*, existential concerns may be encompassed by the general term "humanistic."

In considering the impact of existential concepts and principles on contemporary helping approaches, the work of Rollo May, the leading exponent of existential psychology, will be explored. It is important to keep in mind, however, that existential psychology refers to an *approach* to *understanding* human behaviour rather than to a specific therapy or technique. While May, for example, does define certain *conditions* for existential therapy, he does not suggest a specific therapeutic method. Similarly, there is no single humanistic theory or method of therapy or helping, but rather a number of discrete approaches which share similar values and basic assumptions regarding the human person and the human condition. In Parts III and IV we will explore six such approaches. For this purpose, and to capture more fully the implications of the existential movement on the development of the humanistic approach, Appendix A at the end of this chapter might be consulted. This material explores briefly the biographies of eleven famous pioneer humanists from several fields whose work continues to influence the development of modern helping methods. They are: Gordon Allport (1897-1969), Victor Frankl (1905-   ), Erich Fromm (1900-1980), Kurt Goldstein (1878-1965), Abraham Maslow (1908-1970), Rollo May (1909-   ), Gardner Murphy (1895-1979), Fritz Perls (1893-1970), Carl Rogers (1902-   ), Paul Tillich (1886-1965), and Alan Watts (1915-1973).

Introduction to Existential Psychology

The significance of existential philosophy on modern western culture during the past fifty, but particularly in the past thirty, years is enormous. It has helped to integrate our social sciences, stimulate our theologies, challenge our political and economic institutions, and spark an explosion of artistic creativity in music, art, literature, theatre, and architecture. It gave us a new perspective from which to view ourselves, a new understanding or self-awareness which opened up new options for action, increased our choices and thus our freedom.

Rollo May, the American psychoanalyst who is identified as the leader of the existential approach to psychotherapy in the U.S., points out that this therapeutic approach differs from other types of therapies in two ways: first, it is not the invention of one man and, second, it is not a technique as such, but rather a theoretical basis for approaching human problems. The two major theoretical areas of concern are (1) the nature of human existence and (2) the nature of reality (May, 1958).

WHAT IS EXISTENTIALISM?
Existential psychology and art is concerned with the human condition. Specifically, it is concerned with understanding the human species as a whole as *both* subject, that is, as a thinker and actor or something which knows it knows; and object, as something which is also acted upon. It is a rejection of conceptions of the human person as *either* subject *or* object. The Cartesian notion of human existence, for example, was expressed by the phrase *"Cogito ergo sum"*—"I think therefore I am," a rationalism in which our existence was defined wholly as subject. Science, on the other hand, tended to be concerned with people only as objects or things. Existential thought was a reaction to, or rebellion against, both of these extremes.

The term "existence" comes from the Latin *existere* meaning "to stand out or emerge." The existentialists were, and are, concerned not only with the *essence* or qualities of people in terms of certain static mechanisms or substances and elements, but with people as *being*, in the sense of *becoming*. This is a dynamic view of the human person. The human "being," for the existentialist, is the human person in the *process* of living and dying. The word "being" is used always as a verb rather than as a noun (as in eating, sleeping, walking).

The uniquely human dilemma, articulated for the first time by the existentialists, is that we are *aware* of the fact that we *exist* at this moment in time and space and must *choose* or *decide* what we are going to do about it. Note that our awareness (subject) requires and/or enables our experience and acknowledgment of our finiteness, that is our essence (object) as part of our being/becoming.

This is a very different conception of the human person than those which had been held by either the rationalists or the logical positivists. (The rationalists defined the human person in terms of reason and intellect; the positivists, through the application of the scientific method.) This conception resulted from the dissatisfaction of various philosophers with the answers provided by existing theorists, and was expressed during the latter part of the nineteenth century simultaneously by several theorists and practitioners in Europe who came to their conclusions independently. But before we review something of the situation at the time which may have helped to stimulate these ideas, let's first complete the discussion of the two major concerns of existential thought. We have been examining the concept of human existence. Now let's briefly consider the existential view of the nature of reality.

EXISTENTIALISM AND REALITY

May (1958) pointed out that existentialism is not a comprehensive philosophy or way of life but is rather an attempt at understanding reality. It is really not so much a creation or invention as a *response* to certain issues or dilemmas or conflicts which are found only in Western culture. When Karen Horney writes of *The Neurosis of Our Time* or Carkhuff and Berenson suggest we live in a "sick" or neurotic society, they are making the point that our modern Western culture is based on certain assumptions or premises about the nature of reality which, if not wholly incorrect, are at least incomplete. According to the existentialists, it is our inability to understand reality that is at the centre of our cultural confusion.

May describes the problem of Western thought as an overconcern with essences, that is, with the characteristics of things—their weight, length, shape, substance, etc. Modern science has concentrated its efforts on such concerns. Thus we believe we *know* what something *is* if we can describe its *qualities*. This approach may be logical; may even result in laws; but the *existence* of the thing has to be omitted in the process of objectification. For example, the proposition that 3 + 3 apples = 6 is true. But it is equally true if we substitute pigs. That is to say that a proposition can be true and logical in the abstract, without having any reality.

Since the essence approach to understanding reality has worked so well in certain areas of science we have adopted it as the method for understanding *all* reality. Yet, to apply the empirical method when dealing with human beings means adopting a detached viewpoint in which the actual living individual must be omitted so that only the essence remains. If we study ourselves only as objects, what results may be true, but not real. The dilemma for the behavioural sciences is to be able to bridge the gap between what can be proven to be abstractly true and what remains to be unknown, that is, existentially real, for the given living person. Much of the work of psychologists has been and continues to be concerned with truth in this sense. But well-done experimentation, often on animals, does little to help us understand the reality of human existence.

Both Kierkegaard and Nietzsche perceived this split between truth and reality in Western culture and attempted to show that reality cannot be investigated in a detached and abstract manner (May, 1958). They suggested instead that human existence be studied from both a subjective and an objective base. "We must not only study a person's experience as such, they held, but even more we must study the man to whom the experience is happening, the one who is doing the experiencing" (May, 1958: 14). Here we have the basis of Gestalt, organismic, and even psychoanalytic depth psychology. However, the concept is the same. We cannot understand a particular act or event in isolation, or as it may appear to the objective observer. The behaviour can only be understood by understanding the person, the person's motivation and/or what the behaviour means to the person. Thus a behavioural description may be objectively true, but may not reflect reality.

For the phenomenologist, reality is what exists, but in facts, events, experience. There is no judgment imposed as to whether the "fact" is true or false. If it is reported it is considered as existing, at least for that individual. Reality is *subjective*. This is the position articulated by Carl Rogers.

For the scientist, reality is what exists *objectively* outside the person and can be proven true.

Existentialism, on the other hand, is concerned not only with facts or truth, but also with reality-existence. *Reality is neither a wholly subjective experience nor a wholly objective truth, but rather a relationship between one's internal awareness and an external truth.* With this introduction to the key concerns of existential psychology—human existence and reality—let's consider briefly the cultural climate at the end of the nineteenth century which influenced the development of existential thought and its relevance for contemporary western society.

Nineteenth-Century Turmoil and Twentieth-Century Indifference

THE EXISTENTIAL CRISIS

While May (1958) refers to it as "compartmentalization" and the Josephsons (1962) as "alienation," the central problem within modern western society is considered by existentialists to be *our loss of integration within ourselves, with other people and with our environment.*

Thus, as was indicated earlier, existentialists attempt to create awareness of our estrangement from ourselves and our loss of personal identity, in a world preoccupied with "externals." They observe our aloofness from meaningful relationships with other people and the increase in loneliness, social isolation, and loss of beliefs and values. And they call attention to our separation from nature and our physical environment, from which separation arise our feelings of powerlessness and meaninglessness.

We may think of it as a contemporary condition, but our alienation from ourselves actually began prior to the nineteenth century. With the collapse of the feudal system in Europe and the beginning of the Renaissance in the late sixteenth and early seventeenth centuries, the possibility of "individuality" was born. For the first time in human history, individuals could exist alone and apart from their social group. The rise of mercantilism meant we could alter our social status, something which previously had been fixed in the feudal caste system. The opportunity for mobility allowed us to pursue an *individual* identity as opposed to guild or craft *group* membership only, as had been the case until this time. During the same period, we became further individualized by scientific developments, separating ourselves from nature and learning to control it as an object for our own purposes (Josephson, 1962).

Thus, the same conditions which led to our opportunity for development as unique individuals also led to the beginning of our *separation* from others and our environment.

During the Renaissance, reason and intellect were considered our supreme achievements, and we gloried in our own brilliance in science. But our art suffered. The literature, art, and music of the period reflects a romantic quality which is pedantic, mathematical, pretty, and contrived. It was not concerned with "here and now" but rather with reminiscences of the past and fantasies of the future. As this preoccupation with science and rationality continued, technology advanced, and machines, rather than tools, became the implements by which we forged our new relationship with nature and the surrounding environment. This new relationship, in which we perceived ourselves as *over* or *against* nature, culminated in the Industrial Revolution of the mid-eighteenth century. But as we moved further away from a oneness with nature in favour of attempting to use, control, and master it for our own purposes, so too did we use and control ourselves and others. Thus, the *potential* for individual human growth brought about by the end of the feudal system collapsed only four hundred years later at the beginning of the twentieth century. The significant point here is that, had Western civilization evolved differently following the end of feudalism, our modern existential dilemma of alienation might not have occurred. Hence the humanistic or existential psychologists' contention that people in psychic crises are merely reflections of a neurotic society, or "crazy" culture. And here we have the existential basis of all contemporary helping methods: to help people discover and be what they are, learn how they may form meaningful relationships with others, and experience themselves as part of their natural environment.

The Industrial Revolution seriously altered our sense of personal identity and our concept of work. The machine, unlike the tool which joined us to the natural environment in a creative act, *separated* us from nature. The machine operated independently, impersonally and, to some extent, autonomously. But in addition, the machine required a *disciplined* worker—a worker who could "adapt" to the rhythm of the machine. The tool had been at the mercy of the craftsman, but the worker was at the mercy of the machine. Thus, a person as worker became an object, like a machine. And the better he could perform as a machine, the better worker he was thought to be.

The worker was "rewarded" not for what he produced, but for his *labour*. Thus, when the work itself became a mechanistic, externally regulated process, like that of a machine, the worker changed too. This change was the subjective aspect of the worker's involvement in work and in his direct relationship with the natural environment or raw material. This was the major contention of Karl Marx: the alienated worker who had lost control not only of the conditions of his work, but also of the fruits of his labour, had become *alienated from himself*. Under capitalism the worker did not own the work environment, the tools, the raw materials, or the product. These "things," or objects, were therefore not a part of him, since they did not belong to him, but were the property of the plant owner. Further, the worker's labour, since the product does not belong to him, does not belong to him either. It is the decision of the owner whether the worker is allowed to labour, under what conditions, for how long, and in what way. Therefore the worker is separated from his own efforts and in this sense is alienated from himself. Finally, he becomes alienated from others because his only relationship with them comprises objective transactions involving things, commodities, or money.

But our alienation and dehumanization has not come about merely as a result of our new identity as cogs in the wheels of the new machine age. In order to manage and administer the new complex technology and economic interests, a new rationalized social and organizational structure was developed. It was the most effective method of administration yet conceived—*bureaucracy*. Bureaucracy too helped to divide the human person into subject and object. While the bureaucratic method is highly rational, to fit the Cartesian belief that only in reason and intellect do we demonstrate our true identity, it *depersonalizes*. Bureaucracy is not concerned with individual feelings, beliefs, hopes, and fears. It is concerned only with what specific skills we have which may be utilized to efficiently accomplish the objectives of the organization. The effects of bureaucracies on the individual, then, are quite similar to those experienced by the worker in industry. But in addition to the depersonalization they too create, bureaucracies, due to their vertical hierarchical nature, concentrate incredible *power* in the hands of a few, with the result that coercion and manipulation of the less powerful majority permeates all social relations. The "system" destroys trust, promotes deceit and game-playing, and rewards the aggressive sycophant who has defined his subjective existence according to what the organization defines as success.

Success, under these conditions, can only be measured externally in terms of visible indicators. Thus, the worker further identifies with things or the material objects which bureaucratic identification and dehumanization bring. As members of modern society, we have become collectors of things, conspicuous consumers of objects which have no meaning, but which powerfully symbolize our estrangement from self, others, and the world.

We could trace too the spiritual upheaval of the mid-nineteenth century and the rise of Protestantism. The Catholic Church, for good or bad, for centuries did offer many people a sense of spiritual direction and belonging or community. The Church's power and influence, and its bureaucracy, were also questioned, and today there are those who would say the Church is gone, and in its place is a social institution which has all but replaced the spiritual function. Science has won. We have no faith, no belief, only knowledge and facts.

We referred earlier to the nineteenth century as an age of turmoil and indifference. In any period, the prevailing social conditions and values are articulated by its philosophers, writers, artists, musicians, and playwrights, and this period was no different. While the Industrial Revolution was in high gear there were some who cried out against its inhumanity. The atrocities of child labour—the separation of children from their families, from their childhood and, for many, from their lives—was one of the "causes" taken up by novelist Charles Dickens. Dickens was a social reformer. He used his pen to reveal the plight of the poor, the weak, and the powerless. He exposed the machine age and its inhumanity and the crass value system of the English entrepreneurs. Other writers described the tragedy of the industrial towns with their smoke and water pollution and the separation of people from nature and their environment. There were those, like Shaw, who exposed the capitalist ethic, the ineffectual church, and the corrupt political system of the time (e.g., Dostoyevsky, Chekhov, Dumas, Hugo).

But the rationalists did not heed the warnings of the few who spoke out against the depersonalization of the new capitalism, and bureaucratic systems. They had faith in technology, in science, and in man's reason and intellect. Whatever problems existed were temporary. Man would deal with them in time. Science and technology were the answer. And those with power and influence were convinced this was so, until the beginning of the twentieth century.

But the turmoil of the times was perhaps best depicted and forecast by a small group of painters—the French impressionists, and later expressionists, who have become almost synonymous with the term "modern art." They moved away from the academic, highly rationalized, and contrived art of the baroque and rococo periods.

The breakaway from romantic themes began with the neo-classical art of Jacques Louis David (1784-1825). His style was classical, but the expression more personal and the themes unique. It was the French lithographer and painter Honoré Daumier (1808-79), however, who was the first to express poignantly the social unrest of the time. Of his painting *Third Class Carriage*

(1860), which displays an unusual insight into the plight of the "common" man, Gardner (1959: 659) says:

> Never before had the peculiar pressures of modern life, especially as they affect the classes so largely cut off from the benefits of a materialistic culture, been so penetratingly and persuasively depicted.

While his technique and style was not accepted by the prevailing "art" community and French school of the time, as would be the case of those to follow, he powerfully influenced the development of what is now called modern art. The following names will be familiar to you: Edouard Manet (1832-83), Edgar Degas (1834-1917), Paul Cézanne (1839-1906), Pierre-Auguste Renoir (1841-1919), Paul Gauguin (1848-1903), Henri Rousseau (1844-1910), Vincent Van Gogh (1853-90), Georges Seurat (1859-91), Henri de Toulouse-Lautrec (1864-1901), Henri Matisse (1869-1954), Pablo Picasso (1881-1975). Does it not seem unusual that so many French artists should refuse to accept the prevailing art styles? They painted what they saw and felt. It was not truth, but it was *reality* —the reality of their subjective perception, and experience of objective events. It was the same approach which gave impetus to the work of the Group of Seven in Canada following World War I. (The Group of Seven was really nine. It began with Lawren Harris, Arthur Lismer, A.Y. Jackson, Fred Varley, J.E.H. MacDonald, Franklin Carmichael and Franz Johnston. Tom Thomson is considered one of the Group even though he died in 1917, prior to its formation. A.J. Casson later replaced Franz Johnston, who left the Group and Toronto for Winnipeg in 1926.)

Music, too, was affected. The classical and romantic themes of Beethoven, Mozart, Bach, and Handel were replaced by the new sounds of composers like Stravinsky, Prokofiev, Britten, Mahler, Glier, and Weill.

But with the outbreak of World War I in 1914, the belief in man's salvation through the exercise of reason and intellect vanished. There were those who would begin to question the academic rationalism of the day, and Freud's pessimistic view of man as a volcano with a thin veneer of control seemed to strike a responsive chord. While Gestalt psychology and the work of Kurt Goldstein in the 1920s were to offer a different conception of man, almost forty years and another world war would pass before this conception was articulated in American psychology. This time, it was not in defiant rebellion, but rather as a spiritual offering in humility and devotion, that a number of American psychologists, psychiatrists, psychoanalysts, and theologians began over a period of ten years to share their existential observations and beliefs and offer prescriptions for the troubled souls of their fellow humans, in the hope that we might yet save ourselves and the earth from our growing destructive power. Having experienced since that time two more major wars (Korea, Vietnam) and numerous other minor ones (Suez, Israel, India-Pakistan, Greek-Cypriot); with the recent perfection by the U.S.A. of the ultimate "clean" nuclear device which is the epitome of our dehumanized world culture—it kills people but leaves "things" intact; and the new political war tactic—terrorism—our apparent twentieth-century indifference to our self-destruction either at our own or others' hands, is disturbing. The appearance of calm and order in the Victorian period was achieved through suppression of individual freedom by a rigid class system in which the power elite chose to be unaware of reality. Today, a rigid class system no longer exists for us; personal and social freedoms abound; and the general level of understanding of our precarious existential condition is growing, with the aid of mass education and the media. It is to be hoped that this increasing existential awareness will, before we annihilate ourselves in one way or another, overtake the controlling majority who have as yet not fully realized what it means to live as human beings.

Basic Concepts and Major Assumptions
Underlying the Existential/Humanistic Approach

This section will examine six concepts described by May (1958) which characterize man's existence and are therefore central to the existential approach: (1) being/becoming, (2) death or non-being, (3) ontological guilt and anxiety (the freedom to choose), (4) being-in-the-world—understanding the meaning of experience, (5) time, and (6) transcendence.

BEING/BECOMING

The definition of "being" is complex. We have indicated earlier that in English a better word might be "becoming" in order to indicate the dynamic, in-process aspect; something in potential and with a future orientation. Being might be called "the life force," but is not synonymous with drives, instincts, or motives. May suggests that being is what remains when all the qualities or characteristics of a life form are taken away.

Being is more than human awareness, since it is required for the process of awareness to take place. It might be better described as our self-consciousness. But awareness of our being brings with it the realization of our responsibility for our own becoming. The experience of our being, the goal of therapy, is required in the process of satisfying our own needs and resolving our problems. It is the experience of our being that enables us to see ourselves as subject and object for the first time, to recognize that we must choose what to do, and that we are free to decide what we will become. At the same time, the experience of our being does not involve value judgments. Being is neither good nor bad. It is what is. Our being is therefore authentic and real. It is not a reflection of what we have been told we should or ought to be. It is an internal point from which we can assess ourselves. It is the centre of intrinsic satisfaction, or the sense of feeling good about our being/becoming, not by comparison with external objects, but through experiencing more fully our own existence. This concept of being we will see contained within Rogerian Therapy, Gestalt Therapy, Primal Therapy, Reality Therapy, and Transactional Analysis.

DEATH

For the existentialist, being and non-being, or death, cannot be separated. For us to experience our existence or being, we must at the same moment recognize the fact that we may also *not exist*. This is perhaps the most significant contribution of the existentialists. For Western society seems to have refused to deal honestly and openly with the concept of death, just as the Victorians refused to deal openly with emotion and sex. In failing to come to grips with our transient and tenuous momentary existence and our ultimate death, we experience our being and living as unreal and shallow. But once we recognize the reality of our non-being, our lives take on an immediacy and vitality. Ignoring and denying the finiteness of our existence we let life slip by without taking charge. Thus we must first acknowledge the reality of death before we can actualize our being and relate ourselves meaningfully to others and our environment. May points out that it is precisely this capacity to confront non-being which enables us to deal constructively with potentially destructive anxiety, hostility, and aggression. To deny that such experience or behaviour exists or to attempt to avoid them either by running away or by obedience or conformism is to deny the authenticity of our own being. But to deny our own being means to live a neurotic or shadow existence, unreal and unfulfilling, and potentially dangerous to others and the environment.

ONTOLOGICAL GUILT AND ANXIETY

May defines anxiety as the "experience of the threat of imminent non-being." Again, there are problems in translating the original concept into English and the German word *angst* may be better translated as "anguish" or "dread," to convey the stronger meaning implied in *angst*. The German concept better defines this experience than our word *anxiety*, which usually refers to the emotion of fear without an object, or fear of the unknown.

Existential anxiety, then, is not the *result* of external threat, but rather a threat to the *being* of a person. In this sense, it may be experienced as a wholly intrinsic process. Thus May says (1958: 52):

> . . . anxiety occurs at the point where some emerging potentiality or possibility faces the individual, some possibility of fulfilling his existence, but the very possibility involves the destroying of present security, which thereupon gives rise to the tendency to deny the new potentiality. . . . If there were not some possibility of opening up, some potentiality crying to be "born," we would not experience anxiety.

Thus, as we shall see below, the concept of anxiety is tied to the concept of freedom. Anxiety can arise only if the individual is *free* to choose to fulfill an emerging potentiality. Of course existential anxiety can be quickly stemmed by choosing not to fulfill our emerging unique potential, and instead to seek the safety of conformity with others. This choice results in our loss of personal freedom. (It is interesting to note here the similarity of Goldstein's description of the origin of anxiety (see page 99) to that of May.)

But to choose not to be the person we are and can be, to choose to deny our potential, results in the experience of guilt. Failure to become what we are results in ontological (being) guilt, in contrast to the common moral guilt, and is a condition of human existence. Thus it appears that we are faced with the experience of either anxiety or guilt. If we choose to fulfill our potential it means risk and anxiety. If we choose to deny our potential it means safety and guilt.

But choosing to fulfill our potential also brings increased self-esteem, happiness and even joy. Choosing safety means self-denial, defensiveness, and loss of existing potential. Like the dynamics in the helper-helpee relationship, there is no neutral. Choosing to actualize is positive in its effects. Choosing to deny potential is negative and detracting. We do not remain static; rather we *lose ground*.

The concept of ontological guilt applies as well to one's relationships with others and the environment, in addition to one's relationship with oneself. In terms of our social relationships we experience ontological guilt when we fail to meet the needs of others, fail to understand, fail to demonstrate caring, trust, and love. For, as we discussed in Chapter 1, it is part of the human condition to be related to others in this way. Similarly, we experience ontological guilt as we separate ourselves from nature as a whole, and attempt to manipulate it for selfish gain, thereby causing pollution, extinction of other life forms, and the destruction of the delicate balance of the ecosystem of which we are a part.

BEING-IN-THE-WORLD—
UNDERSTANDING THE MEANING OF EXPERIENCE

The existential therapist attempts to understand the patient in the context of his *World*. The person and his World are seen as *one* with each defining the other, as with the Zen concept of Yin and Yang. The person cannot exist without his World and vice versa. But by World, more is meant than the environment. May defines World as "the structure of meaningful relationships in which a person exists and in the design of which he participates." World then includes past events and all other deterministic forces which affect us as we relate to them. "World is never something static," writes May (1958: 60), "something merely given which the person then 'accepts' or 'adjusts to' or 'fights.' It is rather a dynamic pattern which, so long as I possess self-consciousness, I am in the process of forming and designing."

Existential therapists distinguish three modes or aspects of World which exist simultaneously: (1) *Umwelt*, (2) *Mitwelt*, and (3) *Eigenwelt*. The *Umwelt* is the world of object around us. It is the world of *nature* and the world in which we would continue to exist if we had no self-consciousness. It includes the biological or physiological aspect of the person: drives, needs, and cycles. It is the person as object. But while the existential therapists, unlike the phenomenologists, accept the validity of the *Umwelt* and its implications for the human race, rejecting the phenomenologists' tendency to ignore objective reality, neither do they attempt to force all human experience into the *Umwelt* as have the scientific rationalists.

The *Mitwelt* is the aspect of World which involves human interrelationships. The important point here for existential therapy, which is elaborated by

May in the film *Rollo May and Human Encounter*, is the process of "relationship" which characterizes the *Mitwelt*. While we may "adapt" or "adjust" to the *Umwelt* as one object may be required to give way or "respond" to another as it impinges upon it, the nature of the interaction between persons, beings, is not as objects. In the *Mitwelt*, the process of relationship involves what May calls "encounter." And in encounter *both* persons are *changed as a result* of the nature of the relationship. If this does not occur, then one or other of the persons involved are responding as though the other person were an object. Responding in this fashion means the person is not involved in relationships but rather in *manipulation*.

The *Eigenwelt* is that aspect of World that is unique to human beings and requires self-awareness or self-consciousness. It is the personal, subjective experience of World which gives it meaning. This particular aspect of World has received the least attention by western society and in fact is considered as less valid or significant than that which may be abstractly proven true and given consensus.

These three aspects of World are present simultaneously. In fact, should one or more of them be emphasized to the exclusion of the other(s), the reality of World is lost. Psychoanalysis dealt primarily with the *Umwelt*, the world of instincts and urges. The later interpersonal therapies and existing relationship therapies deal primarily with the *Mitwelt*. The *Eigenwelt* is dealt with by Gestalt therapy, existentially oriented therapies, and eastern religions and philosophies only.

In *Rollo May and Human Encounter*, May gives specific examples of self-self encounter and outlines four characteristics of self-other encounters. These are what are known as "I-thou" relationships. These relationships are of particular interest to helpers.

The term "encounter" is used by May to describe a relationship in which we understand and feel the experience of another person. In this sense, it resembles empathy or love. But in addition to this quality, it includes at the same time a feeling of affirmation of oneself as a result of this experiencing of another person. When we do encounter someone, we experience our own being more intensely and positively. The four characteristics or aspects of relationship which must be present in order for encounter to occur are:

1. Empathy—an instantaneous knowing of the other person as your eyes meet.
2. Friendship—a love relationship growing out of empathy, of give and take.
3. Eros—more than sex, eros involves an appreciation of the physical reality of another person and an awareness of the possibility of physical intimacy and union with them. It may be both heterosexual and homosexual in quality.
4. *Agape*—is the Greek word for charity. It means to affirm the welfare of others before our own. It includes the idea of caring or altruism and stems from doing for others without specific personal gain or reciprocity except in feeling good about it.

If all four elements are present the relationship is an encounter. If one or more aspects are missing then there is a relationship of manipulation rather than encounter. If none of these aspects are present then there is no relationship. May laments that for western society the norm of human relationship is manipulation and not encounter.

TIME

Although the concept of time is important in all therapies, it is approached uniquely by the existential therapists. The concept of space has been given the primary attention of those concerned with human behaviour, with time viewed as a similar dimension and dealt with in the same way. The existential therapists, however, have made time the most critical dimension of human existence. Since, as we have earlier described, the existential concept of being is emergence of potential, for the human person in the process of developing potential, the future becomes more important than either the past or the present. The past and present are not ignored by the existential therapist, but they are viewed in the context of what the future may mean for the individual. Thus, what the client selects to recall or remember from the past, or what he is doing now, only makes sense if he can also appreciate what he views as his future. Thus, the human person is considered to be determined by past events, only to the extent that he decides to alter his potential or emergence in the future, on the basis of these events. He might just as easily choose to ignore the same past or present events and select the same or a different pattern for his becoming.

TRANSCENDENCE

Transcendence refers to the human ability to step outside or beyond the immediate situation in fantasy or imagination using our capacity for propositional speech or arbitrary symbol manipulation. It is this capacity that enables us, among other things, to see ourselves as both subject and object at the same time. It enables self-awareness and self-consciousness. That is, it enables us to evaluate ourselves against our own standards, to compare ourselves with ourselves over time, and to develop, as Shoben suggested, ideals. The capacity for transcendence is therefore a part of the normal human being. But our capacity for transcendence may also become distorted. That is, we can become too subject-oriented as well as too object-oriented. When this occurs, the range of neurotic behaviour that results signals the loss of integration of subject and object aspects of being: the person experiences distortion in time orientation; refuses to tolerate even mild anxiety, expressing guilt in excuses and denials; and fails to achieve fulfillment of potential in all three World aspects.

Six Implications for Psychotherapy of the Existential Characteristics of Humans

May (1958) outlines six features of existential therapy which follow from the existential conception of human existence.

First, he points out that there is no specific set of techniques or principles used by all existential therapists or even used by any one therapist with all patients. What techniques they do employ, they use to meet the specific needs of the particular patient in treatment. This does not mean that existential therapy is vague, undirected, abstract, or philosophical. In fact, May claims that it is characterized by its concrete reality orientation.

Second, psychological processes such as repression derive their meaning from the patient's particular life situation. In other words, the patient's behaviour is not placed on an existing grid for the purposes of analysis and understanding. Rather, the therapist attempts to understand the repression in the context of the patient's grid/life situation. For example, a client's behaviour might be said to reflect the norms of his social group. The existential therapist would seek rather to understand the behaviour in terms of the patient's intrinsic value system. It may reflect group norms, but what else does it reflect and what does it say about the client's freedom to choose to perform the behaviour or to refuse it?

Third, the relationship of therapist and patient is considered *real* rather than a performance of roles. This relationship is called "presence." The key to presence is the therapist's attempt to understand a person as opposed to his seeing a patient as an object to be analyzed. This does not mean that presence is achieved without prior study and knowledge of human behaviour. Rather, presence is the aim of a helper with extensive knowledge about human beings to better understand the real person before him.

Fourth, the goal of therapy, as indicated earlier, is to help the patient develop his own potential. Thus the therapist's job is to help discover what is preventing emergence. But the process by which this may occur requires the therapist to have awareness of what is preventing his own becoming.

Fifth, since the goal of therapy is to enable the patient to become aware of the reality of his existence, the job of the therapist must be to make all his interventions in the context of facilitating the patient's awareness. If what the therapist says or does is not in the context of the patient's existence, the intervention has no meaning for the patient. The therapist's task is to ensure that what he does is directed to "confronting" the patient with his existence, so that this remains as the central focus and the patient is not allowed or enabled to avoid or evade subjective awareness. This particular implication, and its corresponding technique, is evident in both Gestalt and Reality Therapy.

The sixth and last implication for therapy is the need for commitment on the part of the patient. At the beginning of therapy, the patient must decide that he wants to grow and become, and discover who and what he is. He must decide that he will try to become the person he is and achieve awareness of the reality of his being. It is crucial that the patient understand that the therapist is not omnipotent and cannot save or protect him from all harm, especially from himself, and that if he, the patient, decides to take his own life, for example, the therapist may in all likelihood be unable to prevent him from doing so. The point here is that the patient must understand at the outset, and agree, that he will take his own existence seriously.

SUMMARY

Beginning with a brief historical outline of the origins of modern psychology, this chapter has focused on two of the five major approaches to the study and understanding of human behaviour from which contemporary helping strategies were developed. These five approaches are:

1. Learning theory and behaviourism
2. Freudian psychology
3. Gestalt psychology
4. Organismic psychology
5. Existential and humanistic psychology.

It is significant that Freudian psychology, organismic psychology, and even existential and humanistic psychology to a large extent, were developed by non-psychologists. Both Freud and Goldstein, for example, were physicians trained as neurologists, and only four of the eleven "pioneers" (Allport, Maslow, Murphy, and Rogers; see Appendix A) were trained primarily as psychologists. Still, whatever their training or identification, they have all advanced the field of psychology dramatically and substantively.

Since Part V will deal with learning-theory-based helping methods and Chapter 2 has considered Freudian psychology and psychoanalysis, only a brief summary of the major contributions of these approaches was repeated in this chapter. Similarly, Gestalt psychology was dealt with simply, in view of its more limited impact on current therapeutic methods, notwithstanding Lewin's Gestalt-based contributions to group work methods. The Gestalt principles of "relationship," "closure," and "meaningfulness" remain evident in various helping strategies.

The remainder of the chapter was devoted to exploring organismic and existential-humanistic psychology. Goldstein's major contributions to psychology and helping were discussed and identified as:

1. the origin of the concept of self-actualization
2. the development of a psychology of the healthy person
3. the neurological basis for a holistic approach to understanding human behaviour
4. the development of a psychology and treatment approach which was founded on the two unique human attributes of (a) arbitrary symbol manipulation and (b) dependency; or as Goldstein called them, the abstract attitude and communion
5. refinement of the concept and dynamics of human fear and anxiety.

Rollo May's work in existential psychology formed the basis for a presentation of basic existential concepts and their implications for contemporary helping theories and methods. The basic concern of the existential approach, people's estrangement from themselves, others, and their world, was examined from a historical perspective. As in organismic psychology, the existential approach focuses on the unique human attributes which define human existence, and parallels between these approaches can be seen in such existential concepts as being/becoming, ontological guilt, and anxiety and transcendence. The most significant contribution of the existentialists was their recognition of the importance of death, and their corresponding focus on the future.

APPENDIX A

The Pioneers of Existential and Humanistic Psychology

This material has been assembled to accompany Chapter 3 for several reasons. First, examination of the lives of the pioneers of existential and humanistic psychology demonstrates the breadth of this approach and expands further some of the basic concepts and principles explored thus far. Second, it seems particularly appropriate that we consider these theoreticians and practitioners *as people* in this section. It is interesting to note how similar many of their experiences were, even though they did not, in most cases, work together. Certainly we cannot help but be impressed by the strong representation in the group of those of Jewish and German origin and by the impact of Nazism on their lives and work. Lastly, since we have noted in Chapter 1 the significance of the personality of the therapist on effective helping, we should be interested in learning not only *what*, but also *who*, the founders of contemporary psychotherapy were and are. In Chapters 5, 6, 7, 8, 9, and 10, where appropriate and where information has been available, a brief biographical sketch on the founder of each helping approach has been included.

GORDON ALLPORT (1897-1969)

Gordon Allport was born to a Protestant family in Indiana and spent his childhood and youth in Cleveland, Ohio. His father was a physician. He had three brothers, the oldest of whom also became a psychologist and with whom he did some early collaborative work.

Allport received his undergraduate degree in economics and philosophy in 1919. He spent the next year in Istanbul teaching sociology and English and returned to Harvard to complete his Ph.D. in 1922. He spent the following two years studying in Berlin and Hamburg in Germany, and at Cambridge in England. This was likely not by accident—interesting work was being done in Germany at the time in Gestalt psychology, and of course in psychoanalysis by Freud in Vienna. Allport's breadth of travel and cultural sophistication were unusual in those days, especially for such a young man.

Allport returned from Europe again and became an instructor in social ethics at Harvard. Two years later he went to Dartmouth College as an assistant professor of psychology and four years later returned to Harvard, where he remained. With his teaching background in sociology, social ethics, English, and psychology, and his early interest and residence in Europe, it is not surprising that he was in the forefront of the establishment of Harvard's Department of Social Relations, which attempted to integrate psychology, sociology, and anthropology. As might be expected of an academic with his eclectic background, he did not follow the mainstream interests or approaches pursued by his contemporaries. While psychologists in the 1940s were either emphasizing increased scientific rigour and quantification or were enamoured with the ferreting out of unconscious motivations, Allport was advocating the importance of the qualitative study of the individual case and emphasizing the significance of conscious motivation. He continually railed against his colleagues who borrowed models from the natural and physical sciences to study human behaviour. Although the scientific method was important for Allport, he maintained serious reservations about whether human behaviour would ever be completely understood through scientific means alone. Due to the value he placed on the unique complexity of every individual, Allport believed that each human or social problem had to be approached according to the specific particulars or conditions involved. He did not search for a system suitable for understanding and therefore handling all behaviour or social problems. He believed each must be seen as unique, and a unique and individual solution obtained.

Allport was a fighter. He refused to partake of the narrow empiricism with which his contemporaries were occupying themselves and, moreover, he demonstrated in his own prolific work the dangers in their approach. He continually cautioned against borrowing models for study from other disciplines, particularly those emphasizing quantification. He constantly emphasized the importance of conscious as opposed to unconscious motives, particularly in understanding the "normal" person. He emphasized qualitative case study and extolled the importance and value of the unique individual. He focused attention on the present as most important in understanding human behaviour and cautioned against preoccupation with the past of the individual.

During his lifetime, Allport received many professional and academic honours, was president of the American Psychological Association, and wrote or co-authored ten books and numerous articles.

VICTOR FRANKL (1905-   )

Victor Frankl, a Jew born in Germany in 1905, was not well known in America until his book *Man's Search for Meaning* appeared in 1965. His basic tenet is that people's essential motivation is to discover or create meaning for their existence—hence Frankl's inclusion with humanists and existentialists whose basic concern is human behaviour and existence. While he claims to have evolved his basic views of human behaviour prior to the Second World War, it is significant that he spent three years in Nazi concentration camps, including Auschwitz. Frankl observed in the camps that the only survivors were those who could make some sense out of the intolerable situation they were in. Since the situation itself was so devastatingly crushing and futile, survival seemed dependent on one's ability to focus attention on a reason for continuing the struggle for life. Physical strength and prowess was not the key; survival seemed to depend rather on the strength of a personal belief system which enabled the individual to transcend the horror of the present situation. Frankl discerned that although all the prisoners experienced the same overwhelming deprivation, individual differences did not decrease. Instead, as people of all walks of life and backgrounds were reduced to a common preoccupation with the satisfaction of the most basic needs, differences increased: some prisoners became saints and others, beasts.

In summary, Frankl's contribution, as simplistic as it may seem, is significant because it had not been expressed in quite this way before. Human existence must have some kind of meaning. If people cannot find value or meaning or purpose in life, they stop growing and becoming, begin to decline, and eventually atrophy and succumb. Frankl's ideas have been accepted and included in most therapeutic approaches today in which client activity, planning, goal setting, action, participation, and stimulation are involved in reestablishing acceptance of personal responsibility and productivity, and in establishing a value and belief system which facilitates an answer to the why of existence.

ERICH FROMM (1900-80)

Born in Frankfurt, Germany in 1900, Erich Fromm studied psychology and sociology, receiving his Ph.D. from the University of Heidelberg in 1922. He subsequently trained in psychoanalysis in Munich and later at the famous Berlin Psychoanalytic Institute. (An M.D. degree was not yet required to qualify as a psychoanalyst.) Fromm, a Jew, left Germany for the U.S. in 1933, became a lecturer at the Chicago Psychoanalytic Institute, and later moved to New York, where he began private practice. During his lifetime Fromm has written several books (*Escape From Freedom* (1941), *Man For Himself* (1947), *Psychoanalysis and Religion* (1950), *The Sane Society* (1955), and *The Art of Loving* (1956)), and taught at various universities (Hall and Lindzey, 1951).

Fromm is one of the neo-Freudians who, while trained in strict psychoanalytic theory and practice, developed his own approach and principles. The neo-Freudians' contribution was in demonstrating the limitations of psychoanalytic theory, which insisted that all human behaviour could be traced to instinctual, biologically regulated drives. They also felt that too much attention had been devoted to unconscious motivation and too little to the conscious reasoning processes which characterize human behaviour.

Fromm focused his attention on the human condition and the uniqueness of our existence which separates us from all other living things, even other people. He cited five human needs which result directly from our unique situation among living things: (1) the need for relatedness, (2) the need for identity, (3) the need for transcendence, (4) the need for rootedness, and (5) the need for a frame of orientation.

The need for relatedness stems from the fact that we are separated from nature. Our growth process is not automatic, is not based solely on instinctual, biologically regulated drives. We must therefore create our own relationships with our environment and work out how we will fit into nature, of which we are a part and which we cannot deny or ignore.

The need for transcendence means that humans have a need to create. It is our ability to create new things that makes us more than other creatures. For Fromm, destruction reflects the same need for transcendence. Destruction occurs only when creative needs are frustrated. In the same way that animals cannot transcend and create, neither do they destroy. Only humans create and destroy as we attempt to transcend.

The need for roots is a need for a sense of belonging, acceptance, and recognition by others. It is perhaps stronger than the need for identity, the sense of being a unique individual person, in that we often sacrifice the need for uniqueness or deny it. Thus we may choose to give up our personal identity in order to sense belonging by becoming a "company man," a nationalist, a party politician, etc.

Finally, the need for a frame of orientation refers to our method of perceiving the world. Our value system provides consistency in our approach and response to our World.

Having developed this conception of human nature, Fromm then considered the relationship of people to the social and cultural situation in which they live. This is Fromm's most significant contribution, for he has repeatedly demonstrated that *how* people go about satisfying these basic human needs will be *determined* by the values and conditions prevalent in the society in which they live. There is in Fromm's work a strong degree of social or cultural determinism.

If societal values are such that we are unable to satisfy our basic needs, then society alienates us from ourselves. "Both capitalism and communism, for example, try to make man into a robot, a wage slave, a nonentity, and they often succeed driving him into insanity, antisocial conduct, or self-destructive acts" (Hall and Lindzey, 1962: 129-30). Under such circumstances, Fromm would define the society itself as "sick" when it fails to satisfy the basic needs of people.

Fromm has written and spoken convincingly for almost forty years on the relationship of human beings to themselves, to other people, to nature and to the society in which they live. His message is simply this: human beings with their uniquely human attributes of propositional speech and prolonged dependency have certain basic psychological needs which must be satisfied if people are to fulfill their potential-essence. Society has been created by people to meet or fulfill these needs and thereby fulfill their essence. No society has yet been devised which meets the basic needs of human existence, but it is possible to create such a society.

KURT GOLDSTEIN (1878-1965)

Kurt Goldstein was born in Germany in 1878. He studied medicine at the University of Breslau and obtained his M.D. degree in 1903. On graduation, Goldstein concentrated on research rather than private or clinical practice and worked with several noted medical researchers in Germany. In 1906 he accepted a teaching and research position at the Psychiatric Hospital in Koenigsberg, where he remained until 1914. During this time he did a great deal of research and writing, culminating in his appointment as professor of neurology and psychiatry and Director of the Neurological Institute at the University of Frankfurt.

During the First World War (1914-18) he became Director of the Military Hospital for Brain-Injured Soldiers. It was during this work that Goldstein's organismic theories were developed and the concept of self-actualization formulated. It was not until 1933, however, that he set out these ideas in book form in what has become not only his most important work, but also a significant contribution to contemporary psychology. The translated English version, *The Organism*, was published in 1939.

As with Perls, Fromm, Lewin, and other Jewish scientists and professionals who saw the danger, Goldstein fled Germany as the Nazis were seizing power, and emigrated to the United States in 1935.

Between 1935 and 1940 Goldstein continued his work in research and teaching in neurology, psychiatry, and psychopathology at New York City's Montifiore Hospital, at Columbia University, and at Harvard.

During the Second World War he spent the years 1940-44 in Boston at Tufts Medical School and returned to New York in 1945.

His later years, 1948-54, were spent in researching and writing in the field of language disturbances. He became more closely identified with psychology than with neurology or psychiatry during this time. Although closely identified with Gestalt psychology as a result of his organismic theory and some of his perceptual work, he did not consider himself a Gestalt psychologist.

The preceding section has outlined the major ideas and concepts of organismic psychology. These can be summarized as follows:

1. There is a built-in tendency of the organism—the human person included

—to realize or actualize its nature, that is, to become what it is in potential. This he called the principle of self-actualization.
2. The above principle Goldstein saw as the single and only motivating force. All behaviour could be seen as an attempt by the organism to fulfill its nature.
3. The organism operates as a unity. While specific parts of the organism have specific functions, they operate together such that there is an interactive effect of one part of the organism on all other parts.
4. Any specific behaviour of the organism does not reflect isolated response or activity of that aspect of the organism alone, but reflects the response of the total sum of the parts of the organism in interaction with that part.
5. Since the organism responds or acts holistically, investigation of symptoms as a reflection of a problem of a specific part of the organism is misleading and incomplete.
6. The healthy organism is characterized by arousal, activation, and a tendency to growth—*self-actualization*.
7. The unhealthy organism is characterized by attempts to decrease arousal and activation and a tendency to maintain equilibrium—*self-preservation*.
8. Awareness of one's inability to self-actualize—to fulfill one's nature—results in uncomfortable anxiety and tension.
9. Avoidance of uncomfortable anxiety and tension can be accomplished by denial of awareness and a rigid ordering of one's existence.

ABRAHAM MASLOW (1908-70)*

Abraham Maslow was born April 1, 1908, into a poor Jewish family in Brooklyn, New York. He was the first of seven children and seemed to be close to neither his mother nor his father. Maslow described his mother as "schizophrenic" and was frightened of his father, and spoke of himself as being neurotic for his first twenty years. As a child he was lonely, isolated, depressed, and physically unattractive. Maslow was amazed later in his life that he had managed to turn out so well despite his unhappy childhood. And of course he was the victim of anti-Semitism, which in those days was blunt, cruel, and open, even from his elementary school teachers.

Maslow may have survived these experiences because he was bright and could escape some of the harsh reality of life by reading books: the library was his sanctuary. But his childhood isolation and feelings of inadequacy disappeared as he entered high school. There he found new and interesting subject matter, more qualified teaching and a range of extra-curricular activity. It was an atmosphere in which he was recognized and rewarded for his intelligence and in which there was an outlet for his curiosity and enthusiasm for science. He remained shy and introverted, but he was not unhappy.

---

* This material has been developed largely from Colin Wilson's *New Pathways in Psychology* (1972).

In 1926 at age eighteen Maslow enrolled at New York City College in law, at his father's insistence. Maslow, however, was not interested in law, and after spending three semesters and doing poorly because of his disinterest, he dropped out. He tried Cornell the next semester, and though he enjoyed being at university away from home, he did not like the required courses, and so returned to City College.

At nineteen Maslow discovered three things: that he could be loved and accepted by a female (he had strong inferiority feelings regarding his physical appeal and had not kissed a girl until he was nineteen); that he was very interested in classical music (he began attending two concerts a week); and that New York City was an intellectual and artistic centre. Maslow steeped himself in theatre, music, and books and attended lectures being given by visiting intellectuals, who were his heroes.

But this lifestyle was short-lived. His constant companion after his return from Cornell had been Bertha, his one and only love. Maslow wanted to marry her, but his parents, feeling she was not good enough socially for him, disapproved. For some unexplained reason, Maslow responded to their disapproval by running away and enrolling at the University of Wisconsin. His love for Bertha was so strong, however, that he returned to New York in 1928, married her, and returned to school.

It was at Wisconsin that Maslow's interest in psychology was established. He had attended lectures in psychology at Cornell, but the introspective method of Titchener and Wundt being taught at the time did not appeal to Maslow. Shortly thereafter he read an article by John Watson on behaviourism which interested him. For Maslow, behaviourism suggested the possibility that human beings could be improved scientifically. Ethical questions aside, the possibility of improving people, and subsequently the world, were appealing to a person whose interpersonal experiences so far suggested that people could use some improving.

Maslow's undergraduate experience was unique. He even wrote several papers on his work involving clinical laboratory animal research typical of the time. But the most interesting paper he wrote was one which had been accepted for publication a year before he received his Ph.D. in 1933. It was called "Psychoanalysis as a Status Quo Social Philosophy." Imagine such a topic from an undergraduate in a psychology department which was dominated by the traditional experimental-learning approach! The opportunity was incredible. Because of the Depression, there were only ten students and four professors in the department. Under these conditions a close peer-like relationship developed between students and professors. Maslow felt acceptance and belonging for the first time.

Upon graduation, Maslow was fortunate to obtain a job with E.L. Thorndike, the student of Watson who was at Columbia.† Maslow's experience with

---

† It is interesting to note that Columbia University played an unusually large role in the education and experience of the humanistic pioneers we are discussing. All of the American pioneers obtained degrees from, or, as in the case of Maslow, lived and worked in the shadow of, this institution. Allport, Rogers, Murphy, and May obtained their Ph.D.s from Columbia.

Thorndike was also positive. Maslow apparently achieved the second-highest score ever achieved on one of Thorndike's intelligence tests, but it was likely as much Maslow's soft and humble manner which endeared him to these "father-figure" greats in psychology as it was his intellect. Maslow remained with Thorndike for only eighteen months, and in 1937 accepted a position at Brooklyn College. He was to remain there for fourteen years.

Maslow's years at Brooklyn College were good. He had decided to opt for intrinsic satisfaction in contrast to material success. He liked being back in New York. He liked the culture and most of all the intellectual stimulation it offered. As we have seen, the German psychologists and psychiatrists fleeing the Nazis all arrived in New York. Maslow took the opportunity to learn from them all. He met, talked, and developed friendships with Max Wertheimer (founder of the Gestalt school), Erich Fromm, Karen Horney, Kurt Goldstein, Ruth Benedict, and Alfred Adler.

It was at Brooklyn College that Maslow did his most satisfying work, and where he articulated the two contributions to psychological theory for which he has gained lasting attention. These were his "hierarchy of needs" theory of motivation, and his later work on "peak experiences" and characteristics of self-actualizing people described in *Toward a Psychology of Being* (1968).

In 1961 Maslow moved to Brandeis University in Massachusetts and remained there until 1969, a year before his death. These years at Brandeis were not satisfying. Maslow found his students uninvolved in the learning process and, typical of the mid- and late sixties, "rebellious and elder-rejecting." In a life that had had its peak experiences, Maslow's seemed toward the end to resemble its beginning. He found himself again unwanted, isolated from his peers, and lonely. He left Brandeis in 1969 to accept a fellowship with the Laughlin Foundation in California. He died of a heart attack in June 1970 at age sixty-two.

Maslow was an unusual individual. Essentially an introvert, an intellectual, and an academic, he remained optimistic about the future of the human race and the possibility of a humanistically oriented society or world even through his own personal experiences in his later years were unrewarding and disappointing. He is remembered for his contribution in the field of motivation and personality theory, although he did significant work with Harry Harlow at Wisconsin in the 1930s. Although he was educated in the experimental tradition, and was at one time a behaviourist, Maslow's intellectual thirst led him to a continually widening perspective and appreciation of the human condition. His keen interest in music, theatre, literature, politics, and philosophy carried him beyond the narrow microcosm of the behaviourists. His association with the German "refugees" added the Freudian, gestalt, organismic, and existential perspectives to round out his perception of the human condition. The criticism by professional colleagues that he had turned from psychology to philosophy is a valid one. But equally valid would be Maslow's rejoinder that their psychology could not describe nor understand, and certainly not facilitate, improvement in the human condition.

The following five basic needs identified by Maslow resemble closely those outlined by Fromm which were discussed earlier. They are:

1. Physiological needs (food, water)
2. Safety needs (security, stability)
3. Belongingness and love needs (affection, identification)
4. Esteem needs (prestige, self-respect)
5. Self-actualization.

These needs were of "lower" and "higher" order in the sense that basic needs must be satisfied before higher-order needs would be experienced and satisfaction sought. It was also felt that the hierarchy would be reflected in human development, with lower-order needs predominant in the infant and child and the higher-order needs characterizing adult behaviour.

As with the other humanists, Maslow developed an early interest in normal psychology and the healthy person. This work in the 1950s studying "successful" people was a first—all other case study up to that time dealt with pathology and the abnormal. While this research has been criticized methodologically, Maslow did discover the following characteristics found in self-actualizing people (note the similarities to Carkhuff and Berenson's characteristics of "whole persons" described in Chapter 1):

They have more efficient perceptions of reality and are more comfortable with it.

They accept themselves and their own natures almost without thinking about it.

Their behaviour is marked by simplicity and naturalness and by lack of artificiality or straining for effect.

They focus on problems outside themselves; they are concerned with basic issues and eternal questions.

They like privacy and tend to be detached.

They have relative independence of their physical and social environments; they rely on their own development and continued growth.

They do not take blessings for granted, but appreciate again and again the basic pleasures of life.

They experience limitless horizons and the intensification of any unselfconscious experience often of a mystical type.

They have a deep feeling of kinship with others.

They develop deep ties with a few other self-actualizing individuals.

They are democratic in a deep sense; although not indiscriminate, they are not really aware of differences.

They are strongly ethical, with definite moral standards, though their attitudes are conventional; they relate to ends rather than means.

Their humour is real and related to philosophy, not hostility; they are spontaneous less often than others, and tend to be more serious and thoughtful.

They are original and inventive, less constricted and fresher than others.

While they tend toward the conventional and exist well within the culture, they live by the laws of their own characters rather than those of society.

They experience imperfections and have ordinary feelings, like others (McConnell, 1974: 631).

ROLLO MAY (1909-   )

Rollo May was born in a small town in Ohio and took his undergraduate degree at Oberlin College, graduating in 1930.

He spent some time in Greece following graduation and, after returning to the United States, became a student advisor at Michigan State University in 1933. From 1934 to 1936 he was a student counsellor at the City College of New York. In 1936 May decided to enter the ministry, and he began to study at Union Theological Seminary in New York City. He obtained his Bachelor of Divinity degree in 1938 and was ordained as a Congregationalist minister. It is interesting that May and Rogers not only both had theological training, but they also attended the same seminary. It suggests an early concern and interest in the spiritual and phenomenological aspects of human behaviour and existence. May obtained his Ph.D. from Columbia in 1949.

Between 1948 and 1955 he was a teacher, then a supervisor, at the William Alanson White Institute for Psychoanalysis, Psychiatry and Psychology, with which he is still affiliated. May has since taught at numerous universities, been active in professional associations, received various awards, and published considerable material.

His first book, *The Meaning of Anxiety*, appeared in 1950, and four others followed, the most recent, *Power and Innocence*, in 1972. He is identified professionally as a psychoanalyst and existential therapist and still resides in New York City.

May is perhaps the leading North American exponent of existential psychology. In this role he has indicated the significance of existential philosophy in understanding contemporary social issues and individual problems.

GARDNER MURPHY (1895-1979)

Like Rollo May, Gardner Murphy was born in a small town in Ohio. His father was an Episcopal minister. Murphy obtained his B.A. degree from Yale in 1916, his M.A. from Harvard in 1917, and his Ph.D. from Columbia in 1923. Murphy became an instructor in the psychology department at Columbia in 1921 and proceeded through the ranks, becoming an assistant professor in 1929. He remained at Columbia until 1940 earning a reputation as an outstanding lecturer and brilliant teacher. A number of prominent psychologists, including

Carl Rogers, were his students. He became professor of psychology at City College of New York in 1940 and remained there until 1952. From 1952 to 1968 he was Director of Research at the Menninger Foundation. At the time of his death in 1979, he held a faculty post at George Washington University in the District of Columbia.

Murphy's work has been both prolific and expansive. Hall and Lindzey (1962) described him as truly eclectic, using all the basic principles and postulates of modern psychology in developing his "biosocial" theory of personality. "It would be difficult," they say,

> to find anyone who has matched this extraordinary achievement of writing four major books in as many diverse branches of psychology (history of psychology—1929, survey of experimental social psychology—1931, personality theories—1932, introductory psychology—1933) within a five year period. It shows Murphy's encyclopedic knowledge of scientific psychology, his capacity for digesting, organizing, and systematizing a wealth of empirical and theoretical material, and his firm conviction that there is a basic unity among the diversities of psychological fields and viewpoints (Hall and Lindzey, 1962: 505).

Again, we see that characteristic breadth of the pioneer humanists whose interests typically spanned several fields of study. Murphy was recognized as a leader in the field by his colleagues, served as president of professional associations and editor of scholarly journals, and was a recipient of academic honours and awards. His humanitarian concerns and values are evidenced in his activity as one-time president of the Society for the Psychological Study of Social Issues, his writings on the role of psychologists in world affairs, and his role as consultant to UNESCO. The field of parapsychology has been legitimized somewhat by Murphy's recognition of, and interest in, psychical research. He has conducted research into a number of paranormal phenomena such as telepathy and clairvoyance and served as president of the London Society for Psychical Research.

Murphy's significance and contribution to humanistic psychology stems from his pervasive eclecticism and capacity to pull together virtually the whole science of psychology in formulating a personality theory he called "biosocial." His stature as a scientist and academic gave strength and support to the humanistic movement, and his later writing and efforts directed to social problems and the responsibility of psychologists in directing their attention to solving such problems could not easily be dismissed by those who considered the humanists and existential psychologists as fuzzy-minded idealists and dreamers.

FREDERICK PERLS (1893-1970)

A later chapter has been devoted to "Fritz" Perls's creation, Gestalt Therapy, and includes a detailed look at Perls himself. This account, then, will be brief.

Perls was born in Germany to middle-class Jewish parents. His early life was happy although his parents' marriage was not a good one. He entered medical school only to have his studies interrupted by World War I. He did not resume them until 1919. Perls was appalled by the human carnage of war, and experienced severe anti-Semitism and alienation for the first time.

He received his M.D. in 1920 and entered a bohemian social life, associating with artists and political dissidents. Perls was unsettled and unhappy in postwar Germany and made a trip to the U.S.A. to visit relatives. The trip was a disaster and he returned to Germany in 1924. During this entire period, Perls continued to live with his parents, reflecting his social and professional insecurity.

At thirty-two, partly as a result of an unhappy love affair, he entered psychoanalytic treatment, the new vogue. Between 1925 and 1932 Perls continued his analysis and maintained a meagre medical practice. By this time, he himself had become a full-fledged analyst, but remained beset with self-doubt and feelings of inadequacy.

By 1933, with the Nazi rise to power, Perls was forced to flee Germany with his family, without possessions, and emigrated to South Africa. Here he was successful socially, economically, and professionally, but not spiritually. By late 1946 he left his family and emigrated to the U.S.A. He established a practice in New York and achieved in a relatively short time the lifestyle he had enjoyed in South Africa. Perls had by now developed his own therapeutic theories and approaches. While he was a successful practitioner and had a small following of adherents, his more traditionally oriented colleagues refused to accept him and his approaches.

By 1956, at 63 years of age, Perls felt defeated and discouraged at the lack of interest his Gestalt Therapy received from the professional community. He left New York and his family again to live in Miami.

During the next eight years, Perls experienced the lowest point in his life and work. He seemed to become a wanderer. He gave lectures, did demonstrations, and travelled around the U.S.A. trying to spread the good word of Gestalt Therapy. Only a few listened and were impressed.

Not until 1964, with the creation in California of the Esalen Institute, a loose therapeutic community, did Perls at last achieve the attention and recognition he sought.

It was short-lived. He did experience six good years, but in 1970, after a brief illness, he died of cancer at the age of 77.

Perls's theories and practice reflect some unique experiences not shared by other "pioneers" discussed here. For example: (1) He was a patient and later a friend of Karen Horney and Wilhelm Reich, both neo-Freudians who were pupils of Freud. (2) He was a part of the Bauhaus group in Germany during the 1920s, which included leading German intellectuals like Freidlander (the existential philosopher), and the existential theologians Martin Buber and Paul Tillich. (3) His wife was a graduate student in Gestalt psychology. (4) He worked for a time in Frankfurt with Kurt Goldstein.

In Chapter 6 the implications of these events and others in his life and work will be further explored.

CARL ROGERS (1902-   )

Since Chapter 5 will examine Rogerian Therapy in some detail and includes a biographical sketch on Carl Rogers, the information presented here will only attempt to put Rogers in perspective with the other pioneers.

Rogers was born in the United States to a middle-class fundamentalist Protestant family with strong religious beliefs and conservative values. Although interested in the ministry, Rogers did not complete his theological training, and transferred instead to child psychology at graduate school. Rogers developed an early interest in Freudian psychology and became deeply involved in psychoanalytic theory and practice following receipt of his Ph.D. in psychology from Columbia University.

For almost ten years, he worked as a psychologist in a child guidance clinic in Rochester, New York, where the analytic and humanistic approach of social work impressed him more than the experimental mechanistic approach of his psychologist colleagues.

In 1940, he published the first case-oriented book on therapy. In it he described his experiences in working with disturbed children. However, it was not until he reentered the academic world and began teaching at Ohio State University the same year that he realized he had developed a theory and method of helping that was unique.

Rogers's theories and techniques have evolved continually over the past thirty years, and he has subjected them to rigorous scrutiny and research. He has been a prolific writer and a dauntless fighter for a humanistic approach to the study of human behaviour and has made significant contributions to psychological theories of motivation and the therapeutic process.

PAUL TILLICH (1886-1965)

If we have been impressed by the academic stature and import of the pioneers discussed thus far, Paul Tillich's impact in the fields of theology, philosophy, and political and social science is even more astounding. He wrote some twenty books from 1932 until his death in 1965, two of which were published posthumously; and published over three hundred journal and magazine articles during his lifetime. There have been as well several books, countless papers and articles, and over thirty doctoral dissertations written *about* him and his work. Lo (1970: 13) writes:

> As a man whose starting point was always existential, Tillich endeavoured tirelessly from this perspective to pull together through his method of correlation

the centuries-long problems of the harmony and the unity between theology and philosophy, religion and culture, church and the world, sacred and secular, symbols and art, and God and man.

The relevance of Tillich's work to humanistic psychology may perhaps be demonstrated by this brief sample of his ideas. In *The Courage To Be* (1952) he suggested that human beings experience three anxieties: (1) the anxiety of death, (2) the anxiety of guilt, and (3) the anxiety of meaninglessness.

The anxiety of death arises from our finite existence and our knowledge that death is inevitable. The anxiety of guilt arises from our awareness of the gap between what we are and what we could be. The anxiety of meaninglessness arises when we sense the purposelessness of much of what we do from day to day.

Tillich was not speaking about pathology or mental illness. However, he was suggesting that these anxieties are a part of the human condition and represent "normal" human functioning. In all three forms, he says (1952: 41) "anxiety is existential in the sense that it belongs to existence as such and not to an abnormal state of mind as in neurotic (and psychotic) anxiety."

Tillich was born in a small German village where his father was an Evangelical Lutheran minister. His childhood (until age 14) was spent in such rural communities, though the family moved from his birthplace when he was four. As with Rogers, May, and Murphy, this early rural background seemed significant in establishing a sense of relatedness to nature and a respect for its mysteries. His relationship to his strong and authoritarian parents was good, although there was a long struggle, which took the form of "philosophical" discussions, with his father before he was able to achieve true autonomy from him. Having won it, Tillich seemed bent on maintaining his independence of thought and action for the rest of his life.

In 1900 the family moved to Berlin where his father had been called to a new important post, and Tillich continued his education in the classical tradition. He attended the Universities of Berlin, Tübringen, and Halle from 1904 to 1909, and in 1911 he received his Ph.D. in theology from the University of Breslau.

Following his graduation, he served as an assistant pastor for a few years, but volunteered as a chaplain when the war broke out in 1914. As with Perls, the war had a drastic effect on Tillich. He discovered that Germany was not a unity as he had assumed, and that there was considerable social unrest—the average man saw the church as allied with the ruling aristocracy, ambivalent about the sick, and uncaring about the poor and middle classes. Tillich also became critical of Germany's war effort and motives. Following the war he became preoccupied with movements for social change and concerned and identified himself with the suffering populace.

From 1919 to 1924 he lectured in theology at the University of Berlin. His topics were unusual, however, in that he related religion to art, philosophy, Freudian psychology, and sociology. Between 1925 and 1933 he taught at the Universities of Dresden, Leipzig, and Frankfurt. During this time he had met

Heidegger and was introduced to his existential philosophy, wrote several papers and books, and became recognized as a leading German scholar. He also became politically active, joining the National Socialist Movement in 1929 in opposition to the Nazis. When he began to write and speak openly against the Nazi movement he was identified as dangerous to their cause. When they took power in 1933, Tillich was suspended from his professorship at the University of Frankfurt. He emigrated from Germany to the U.S.A. in the same year with his family, and shortly thereafter was made professor of philosophical theology at Union Theological Seminary (the same seminary attended by Rogers and May). He held this position for the next twenty-two years until his retirement.

From 1955 to 1962 he became University Professor at Harvard. Tillich had no teaching duties, but delivered lectures on selected topics and continued his writing. His lectures were enthusiastically received: when he gave his last one there in 1962, several hundred students crowded into the hall (MacLeod, 1973).

His last appointment was at the University of Chicago in 1963. He held this post and remained active until his death from a heart attack in his eightieth year.

His three most important books are *The Courage To Be* (1952), *Love, Power and Justice* (1954), and *Biblical Religion and the Search for Ultimate Reality* (1955).

ALAN WATTS (1915-73)

Born at Chislehurst, England in 1915, Alan Watts obtained his early theological education in Britain and had written two books on eastern religion and philosophy (*The Spirit of Zen*, 1936; *The Legacy of Asia and Western Man*, 1937) prior to emigrating to the U.S.A. in 1938. He was married for the first time the same year (then later divorced and remarried twice, becoming father to six children by these three unions). He obtained his master's degree from Western Theological Seminary in 1948, and a Doctor of Divinity at the University of Vermont in 1958. Between 1944 and 1957, Watts held various university posts, including Counsellor and Episcopal Chaplain of Northwestern University, and Professor of Comparative Philosophy and Dean at the University of the Pacific, San Francisco. He travelled widely during the 1960s, lecturing in Canada, Europe, Japan, and the United States. Watts is important in that he brought to western thinkers some of the essential beliefs, values and philosophies of eastern religions, particularly Zen Buddhism, and was considered to be the best western interpreter of Zen.

Watts became a leading figure in the consciousness-raising movement which was popular during the 1960s and might be credited with the current continuing interest in both Indian and Oriental religious groups and their following in both Canada and the U.S.A. His work was of interest to the humanistic psychologists and psychiatrists who had begun to focus on the human existential dilemma which had been created for western societies as a result of our own fallacious belief systems or inadequate philosophical structures. He felt that psychotherapy, as a process directed at helping people to find meaning in their existence, was for the western person what religious experience was for the Indian or Asian. When our western religious institutions could not meet this need, people turned to psychotherapy. Hence Thomas Szasz's labelling of psychotherapy as "the new religion." But more than showing how eastern philosophies and religions deal more effectively than traditional western belief systems with existential concerns, Watts demonstrated the positive, growth-inducing, and enlightening effects on people which eastern philosophies and religions could facilitate. There was in eastern philosophy an appreciation of mystical and spiritual experience which is essential for human self-fulfillment, but which westerners had come to view as something to be avoided or denied.

Although he wrote some seventeen books, Watts's most popular works were *The Way of Zen; Nature, Man and Woman*; and *Psychotherapy, East and West*.

4

Social Work

ORIGINS

The field of social work evolved in industrialized countries in the late 1800s from certain individuals' concern and compassion for the poor and disabled. The Church had for centuries been a source of refuge and care for the "less fortunate," but the late 1800s also saw a secular corps of volunteers established who attempted to help those in their communities with material aid and kind words. This was originally an urban phenomenon. In rural areas, people were assisted in crises by friends and neighbours. In the cities, however, those in need were often alone with no one to succour them.

Gradually, under pressure from social reformers, and partly as a result of World War I, additional public funds were made available to meet the needs of widows, dependent children, veterans, the elderly, the poor, and the "insane." Volunteers began to be supported by paid staff who were responsible for administering these social programs. These staff were the first social workers. The Canadian Association of Social Workers was founded in 1928. Then came the Depression, and the resulting wide-spread unemployment required the development of major social assistance programs during the 1930s. Thus, out of economic catastrophe arose a new social ethic and a tremendous impetus to the field of social work (Armitage, 1975).

But the 1920s and '30s were interesting times too from another perspective. It was a time of rethinking nineteenth-century concepts of human nature and the dramatic development of one particular approach to understanding human behaviour: Freudian psychology and psychoanalysis. The fledgling field of social work latched on to Freudian psychology, and for the next forty years Freudian concepts and dynamics dominated social-work theory and practice.

BASIC SOCIAL WORK VALUES

While the definitions and methods of social casework have been in continual dispute by practitioners within the field since its inception, social workers have been consistent in agreeing on the basic values which underly their approach (Fischer, 1978).

First, there is a fundamental concern with the uniqueness, value, and dignity of the individual in terms of his interactions with his environment.

Second, there is a continuing search for a scientific base for practice, and an openness to the knowledge which can be incorporated from other fields.

Third, there is a focus on the people and problems which many other professions have ignored or given up on.

CONTEMPORARY CASEWORK ISSUES

Fischer writes (1978: 48):

> The term interpersonal helping provides a broad umbrella encompassing a number of the activities which traditionally have been included under such designations as casework, psychotherapy, and counseling and guidance. These activities have been performed by social workers, psychiatrists, counselors, and psychologists. However, in areas where research has been conducted, primarily involving views and attitudes toward clients and preferences for and use of therapeutic techniques, little or no differences arising from professional affiliation can be detected (Strupp, 1955, 1958, 1960; McNair & Lorr, 1964; McNair et al., 1963, Eels, 1964; Henry et al., 1970; Fischer et al., 1975). Even more importantly, there is no evidence that the profession of the helper leads to any difference in effectiveness in helping clients (Poser, 1966; Meltzoff & Kornreich, 1970). There may be professional differences in status and prestige, and ability to influence colleagues, but no differences that can be attributed to professional affiliation in terms of the ability of professionals to help their clients.

Thus, as we saw in Chapter 1, while traditional casework has not been proven to be an effective intervention method in helping clients, it appears to be as good as any other method employed by professional "helpers." Fischer (1978) suggests that in light of this knowledge, caseworkers must begin to examine what other helpers are doing, and whether or not other methods fit the traditional casework ideal. This does not necessarily mean that they will cease to be caseworkers.

> Whatever the source of knowledge, caseworkers will still be caseworkers, by virtue of their professional affiliation, values and philosophy, and because their social functioning perspective will likely lead them to engage in a far broader range of interventions than members of other professions (Fischer, 1978: 49).

(See Appendix A to this chapter for an example of how behaviour modification may be adapted to the social casework method.)

CASEWORK ROLES AND ACTIVITIES

The three major roles/activities of the caseworker are: clinician/behaviour-changer, consultant/educator, and broker/advocate (see Fig. 4·1). These roles have not changed during the evolution of social work. They are as relevant today as they were for the early volunteer.

FIGURE 4·1
A Framework for the Derivation of Casework Activities

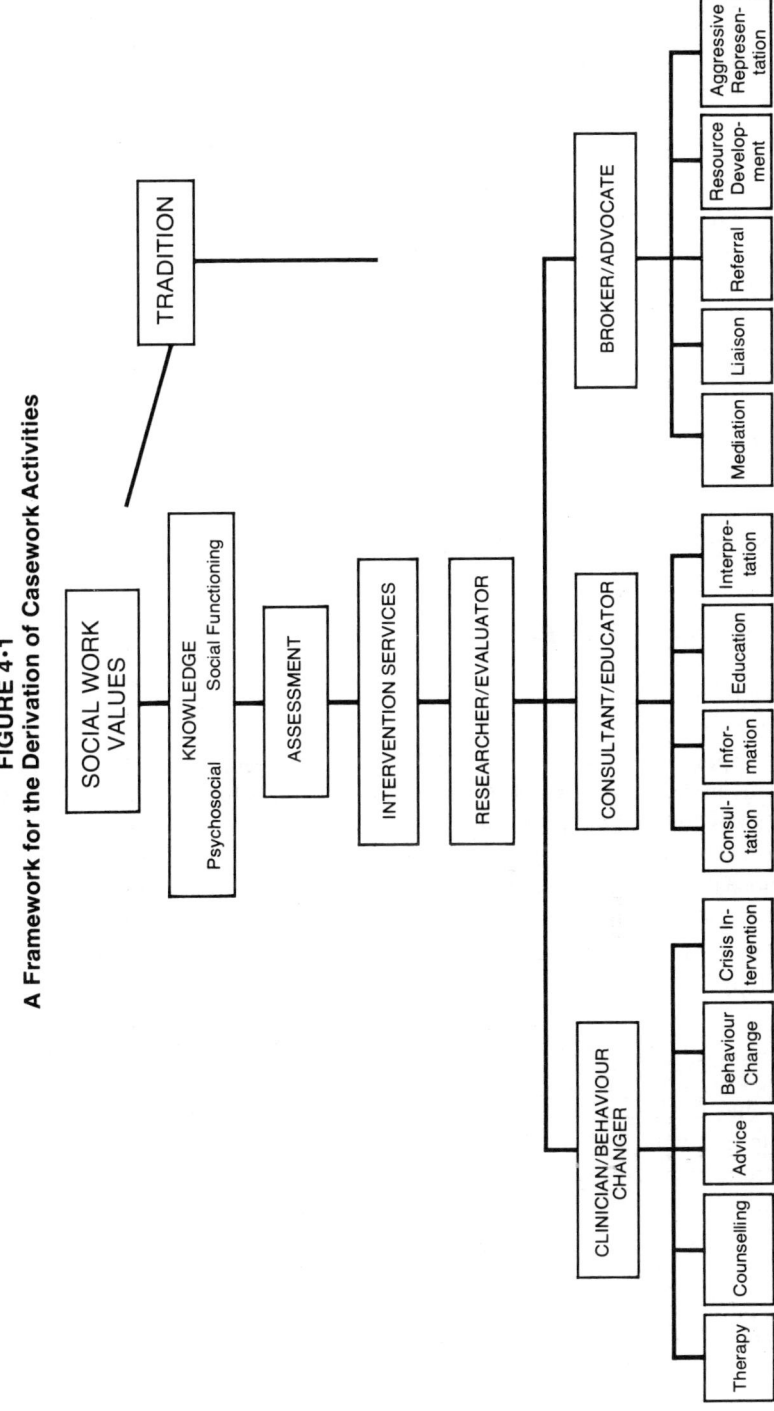

From *Effective Casework Practice: An Eclectic Approach* by Joel Fischer (1978). Reprinted by permission of the publisher, McGraw-Hill Book Co., New York.

They do show a difference between the basic roles of caseworkers and those of other helpers. The caseworker is more involved in the consultant-educator role and assumes almost singularly the role of broker/advocate within the helping profession. Hence the disparaging "do-gooder" label.

All roles require expert interpersonal, human-relations, and communication skills. These activities imply the presence in the caseworker of the personality skills necessary for establishing and maintaining a helping relationship and effective deployment of the basic interview techniques described in Chapter 1.

In addition to the basic roles, the caseworker performs the supportive activities of: assessment, intervention services, and research/evaluation. These activities, too, are found in traditional casework and will be discussed within the context of the traditional social casework interview below. This chapter, however, will concentrate on the traditional social casework method, primarily in terms of the clinician and consultant roles. Fischer's comments should be kept in mind, however: as we explore subsequent approaches and techniques, notice how many of them lend themselves to a casework approach. *The strength of the casework method lies in its ultimate ability to incorporate "technique" from other helping methods and in its breadth of helping roles, from therapist through teacher to advocate.*

THE THEORY OF SOCIAL CASEWORK

Unlike many of the therapeutic approaches we will examine, social casework does not have a specific set of basic assumptions and a defined theory. The basis for this approach is found in the social sciences and medicine: psychology provides the principles of individual human growth and behaviour; sociology provides an understanding of human interaction, culture, and basic societal institutions; and psychiatry (using principles of abnormal psychology combined with psychoanalysis and the arts of medicine) provides a perspective for identifying and classifying various forms of maladaptive behaviour and, to a lesser extent, for determining etiologies and suggesting treatment or prevention strategies.

THE SOCIAL CASEWORK INTERVIEW

Assuming the helping person has a good understanding of the psychological principles involved in human growth and development, can appreciate the basic concepts of sociology, has explored problem behaviour from the perspective of psychiatry and abnormal psychology, has developed some basic helping interview skills, and has some understanding of community resources, he might then employ these abilities as a social caseworker. The method he would use is called the social casework interview.

As we noted earlier, while various helping techniques may be incorporated into the social casework method, the traditional social casework interview contains the following features (Dwyer and Urbanowski, 1965):

1. A clear perception of the purpose of the interview by both client and worker
2. The worker's observation of the client and himself prior to the interview
3. The content of the client and interviewer communications during the interview itself, including a description of behaviour, feelings, body language; facts and events related by the client or worker; options explored; decisions made; and termination
4. Worker's post-interview impressions of the client and his problem
5. A subjective assessment by the worker of his effectiveness in the interview
6. An outline of the plan the worker will attempt to carry out in helping the client.

Purpose

An interview may be defined as "a conversation with a purpose." For every interview, then, the worker has begun by determining in advance what the purpose or objective of the interview is. This purpose should be clear in the mind of the worker and be communicable in either written or verbal form. The purpose might include the relatedness between that interview and any others prior to it. It should include a statement of the function of the agency or the setting in which it occurs (context). It might include a brief description of the client in terms of his problem, known capacities (strengths, liabilities), and motivation. It should include the nature of the worker's relationship with the client.

Worker's Observations

Since attention to observed behaviour is fundamental to all helping methods, the worker's observations are a key aspect of the interview process. The social casework method requires the worker to give careful attention to the *appearance* of his clients and their reactions to the immediate environment. This means both the physical environment of people and things and the emotional environment or atmosphere which exists just prior to the interview. These observations might include the way the client looked (e.g., distraught or happy), the way he was dressed, the way he moved, the way he spoke, and the way he greeted the interviewer. In addition the worker would observe his own pre-interview behaviour, such as his apprehension, apathy, frustration, hunger, impatience, or anger.

Content of Worker and Client Communications

The worker pays attention to all the communications occurring during the interview, including factual information offered by the client and responses made by both the client and himself. He tries to appreciate his own and the client's feelings which emerge during the course of the interview and the non-verbal communications used by both. The content of the interview, then, while including the actual dialogue spoken by the client and the specific verbal responses by the worker to what the client has been saying and doing, refers to all that the worker perceives as occurring in the client, himself, and their environment during the course of their conversation. During their dialogue, the worker attends to more than simply what the client discusses, the nature of the client's problem, and possible problem solutions. Structurally, the content includes the worker's method of beginning the interview, directing the course of the conversation, and the manner in which the interview is terminated by the worker.

Worker's Impressions of the Client

The worker's impressions of the client are constructed following the actual client interview. They are both diagnostic, in attempting to clearly understand the development and current status of the client's problem and/or behaviour, and prognostic, in assessing the strengths and resources available to the client and worker in formulating the most effective approach to helping the client. The worker's client assessment and treatment plan is based on the information received directly from his client during their conversations and (with the consent of his client) from other helping agencies, professionals, and community services with whom the client has been involved or to whom he may be referred. Only with an understanding of the client as a whole person can the worker begin to determine a helping strategy appropriate to the client.

In examining his client as a whole person the worker would consider the following eight factors: (1) physical health, appearance, and capacities, (2) intellectual functioning and potential, (3) intrapersonal behaviour—behaviour and feelings about self, (4) interpersonal behaviour—behaviour and feelings about others, (5) social relationships—family and friends, (6) talents and skills, (7) education and work history, and (8) living environment.

1. In assessing *physical health, appearance, and capacities,* the worker would indicate impressions and/or facts regarding the client's current and past health history; his physical appearance (attractive, tired, gaunt, overweight) and any physical disabilities and their effect on client behaviour (e.g., hearing loss, visual or motor difficulty).

2. Assessing *intellectual functioning and potential* may involve actual knowledge of an intellectual assessment and/or may indicate the worker's impression. Also important is his impression of current and potential functioning under optimal circumstances.

3. *Intrapersonal behaviour* refers to the client's sense of self-awareness, self-esteem or confidence. It includes his values: what things are important to him and what his priorities are. It includes as well noting the presence or absence of the following feelings or characteristics: anxiety, hostility, trust or suspicion, fantasy life, frustrations, wishes and dreams, and independence and autonomy.

The worker's job here is to indicate what, how, and under what conditions these client feelings or behaviours are demonstrated and what the implications are for overall client functioning and self-actualization in respect to the casework process.

4. The worker's description of *interpersonal behaviour* would indicate client behaviour in various types of interpersonal situations involving: competition, cooperation, aggression, embarrassment or shame, love and affection, responsibility, and praise and recognition.

5. In assessing *social relationships* the worker would outline briefly his client's social support system. He would comment on the relationship of the client to his family: are they supportive or rejecting? Similarly he would wish to know something about his friends. What friends does the client have? Are they close, peripheral? Are they facilitating or destructive to the client's growth?

6. *Talents and skills* might include activities such as music, theatre, storytelling, crafts, mechanics, sewing, athletics, cooking, writing, listening, etc. It should also include work skills such as typing, machine operation, teaching.

7. In assessing *education and work history* the worker should include the client's level of education and training and success or interest. Also included might be the nature of the work the client has done and the interest and motivation for these and other work roles.

8. The client's *living environment* should be considered in light of its relevance to the overall problem. Should the client's environment be improved, maintained, altered, etc.?

If the worker considers these eight factors conscientiously for each client, he will discover that he has usually a great deal of information with which to begin to help his client. Not only will this complete picture help in relating to the client and planning casework, it also will make the worker more aware of attitudes and feelings about the client which may affect his role positively or negatively.

Worker's Self-Assessment

Following each interview, the worker reflects on his use of interview techniques and casework skills and judges his effectiveness in this interview as a helping person. This process assists his self-evaluation and supervision.

The Casework Plan

The casework plan is a brief statement of the plan being considered to assist the client. It may include various referral agencies for follow-up. It may outline areas to be covered with the client in the next interview. It may indicate problem resolution and case closing, or some indication of long-range treatment plans or goals being suggested for the client.

CASEWORK SUPERVISION

While the social casework method manifests itself in the casework interview, casework supervision remains a vital ingredient of the casework process. In traditional, and many contemporary, social service agencies, clients are initially screened by an intake worker. If service is to be extended, the intake worker obtains essential basic client information, prepares a file and forwards the client data to the department concerned. The department supervisor receives the "case" and allocates it to one of his caseworkers for response. The process or relationship which develops between the caseworker and his supervisor is called *supervision*.

The casework supervisor, usually a Master of Social Work with at least five years of experience, is considered to be exactly that—a master. Since the helping process is very much an *art* to be *mastered,* the novice, student, or working professional looks to the Master of Social Work for guidance and skill development. In the same way as the painter, musician, or sculptor seeks to improve his technique and skill by study with criticism from accomplished artists, the caseworker sharpens his skills through the casework supervision process.

The caseworker meets regularly with his supervisor at specific times to discuss client interviews and case progress. The supervisor listens to the worker's assessment and plan and offers support, guidance, and direction to the worker. The supervisor may ask the caseworker to explain his analysis of the client problem, and perhaps to defend it against suggested alternative analyses or interpretations offered by the supervisor. The worker may request the supervisor's assistance in responding to a difficult situation and in general seeks confirmation and feedback from the supervisor regarding his role, activities, and effectiveness. The casework supervision process, because it examines so closely the conscious and unconscious feelings, thoughts, attitudes, motivations and values of the caseworker, has obvious therapeutic implications. Casework supervision requires continual self-examination, exploration and understanding by the worker. The dynamics involved in therapy outlined in Chapter 1 also apply to casework supervision. In the supervision process or "encounter," both the supervisor and caseworker learn more about their strengths and liabilities as persons and as effective helpers.

REPORTING AND RECORDING IN SOCIAL CASEWORK

Urbanowski (1974) distinguished and described two basic types of records utilized by the social caseworker: case recording and process recording.

Both of these reporting procedures are important to casework supervision. *Case recording* refers to the client's file record which is maintained by the social agency. *Process recording* is a special student learning tool. Case recording is usually a brief written account of an interview, intervention or event of significance in the helping process of a particular client which is added to the file record. If an interview is recorded, it might include the general subject headings included in the above section on the social casework interview, but generally it is a condensed and distilled account of only the aspects of the interview considered essential and significant to retain. The format for case recording is not universal, and each agency develops its own.

Process recording, on the other hand, is essentially a learning tool in which the total interview is described in narrative form in as complete and accurate detail as possible. It is an exercise to help the beginning worker increase his awareness and attention. The novice helper is naturally self-conscious. His denial of his anxiety and apprehension, or his preoccupation with ignoring it, distracts him from the real focus of the interview—the client. The process recording tool enables him to analyze the interview after the fact and discover his own inadequacies and strengths. It also enables his supervisor to support and guide him. It helps the novice worker to talk about his concerns openly and gain confidence through supervision. Thus, as the worker learns to direct his attention to the client's behaviour rather than to his own, he becomes more effective in the helping process.

Case recording and process recording differ, then, in format, content, and purpose. Case recording is required to ensure the professional accountability and professional development of the practising caseworker (Gordon, 1946). Process recording is a learning procedure used by the student helper.

The Purpose of Case Recording

Professional accountability. Case recording provides a mechanism for indicating client progress and casework results by the worker through which he acknowledges his accountability to his profession, to the agency employing him, to other professions involved in his client's therapy, and to the client himself.

Professional development. Case recording provides a vehicle for the worker's professional development since it enables analysis and evaluation of his methods and effectiveness, by himself and his supervisor.

The Purpose of Process Recording

The novice helper's objectives in recording the client interview are: (1) To increase his awareness of his client's behaviour and surroundings, and to increase his effectiveness in responding to that behaviour; and (2) to establish a framework for the development of an organized and disciplined approach to the problem-solving process.

Appendix B, which includes an excellent example of a student process recording, will be of interest to students wishing to explore further this learning process.

SUMMARY

In this chapter we have briefly discussed the origin of social work, noting its development from a volunteer movement to professional status. We have considered the basic values underlying social work, values which have remained constant even though much change has occurred in the methods it has employed, and in the programs it has served. Appendix A, which follows, shows how the caseworker may adapt other helping strategies to meet specific client needs. We identified the major casework roles as clinician, consultant, and broker, and the major casework activities as behaviour changer, educator, and advocate. It was pointed out that social work theory developed through selectively employing principles and concepts borrowed from psychiatry, psychology, sociology, and psychoanalysis. The bulk of the chapter concentrated on the technique of the traditional social casework interview and the process of casework supervision. The importance and significance of case reporting and recording were outlined. Guidelines to effective process recording are provided in Appendix B.

APPENDIX A

Employing Behaviour Modification in Direct Casework With Children

This revised guide was originally developed by the author with the assistance of Rosemary Carew, M.S.W., for the Special Treatment Foster Home Program of the Catholic Children's Aid Society of Metropolitan Toronto in 1971. It had been recognized that along with the foster care provided by specially selected parents and families, and the more intensive attention given to these children and families by staff within the home and in special monthly meetings, direct casework might also be beneficial for many of the children.

In order to help ensure that this direct casework activity might be maximally effective, this guide was developed. It was intended to assist the child caseworker:

1. to define the problem areas being experienced by the child
2. to determine what techniques and materials might be used in attempting to help the child modify this behaviour
3. to develop specific objectives for direct casework
4. to maintain a record of the child's progress.

The following types of behaviour were identified and selected as representative of those with which many emotionally disturbed children seemed to have problems:

Adaptiveness	Dependency
Affection	Fantasy
Aggression	Feelings of Self-Worth
Anxiety	Frustration Tolerance
Attention and Recognition	Giving and Receiving
Attention Span	Identity
Competition	Self-Control and Responsibility

The guide is exactly that and obviously cannot be considered a recipe for the definition, description, or modification of these activities. It is intended only as an aid for the experienced child caseworker.

An evaluation summary sheet such as that appearing at the end of the appendix is designed to assist in recording the behaviour observed following each session in order to determine progress and the setting of casework goals.

BEHAVIOUR CATEGORIES AND MODIFICATION ACTIVITIES

Adaptiveness

Adaptiveness is defined as the ability of the child to meet the demands of new situations and experiences. In assessing the child's adaptive behaviour, the worker would note the child's reaction to specific events in the therapy environment and monitor his response to demands for change at the introduction of new routines, events, or procedures over time. The worker's objective is to assist the child in achieving age-appropriate responses to new situations.

Some possible modification activities and levels of activity would be:

1. Preparation of the child verbally, through demonstration, through encouragement and praise, through understanding, and through empathy and support
2. Gradual introduction to new things such as toys, activities, people and places
3. Gradual decrease in the preparation and introduction to new situations and activities, until
4. The child achieves an easy and comfortable transition to new experiences, and
5. He seeks on his own initiative new experiences and explores situations independently.

Affection

Affection is defined as the child's ability to express feelings of warmth, caring, and concern, and to accept and respond to these feelings from others. The worker would assess the child's affectional behaviour as appropriate, indiscriminate, or withholding. If either of the latter two conditions exist, the worker's objective would be to assist the child to feel and express age-appropriate affect from and for others.

Some possible modification activities and levels of activity would be:

1. Establishment of relationship between child and caseworker
2. Verbal indications of caring, liking
3. Non-verbal demonstrations of affection through touching, holding, sitting with, sharing, giving of treats
4. Opportunity for child to give and share thoughts, feelings, and things. The therapist must *create* situations in which the child is given the opportunity to share in these ways. For example, if given crayons, does or will the child share them with the therapist?
5. In play with dolls, puppets, and animals, the child is given an opportunity to express spontaneously both positive and negative feelings.
6. Provision of opportunities for the child to demonstrate affectional behaviour with peers, initially through careful structuring of the situation and encouragement by the therapist and later spontaneously.

Aggression

Aggression is defined as overt acts of hostility with conscious intent to harm or destroy. It would be observed as destructiveness, self-abuse, fighting, or any behaviour which interferes with the activities or possessions of others. The objective of therapy would be to assist the child in developing internalized controls, so that negative feelings may be expressed in socially appropriate ways.

Some possible modification activities and levels of activity would be:

1. Non-verbal activity which encourages non-verbal expression of aggression (e.g., drawing, finger-painting, plasticine, puppets, dolls).
2. As the relationship with the child develops, the therapist may assist the child in verbalizing feelings, perhaps through having the child interpret or talk about expressive material which the child has created (e.g., pictures, models, child-selected play-materials).
3. The therapist accepts the child's angry and aggressive feelings, indicates this to the child verbally, and praises his ability to express them in a safe situation. In this situation limits are very important and the child needs to be given an explanation of his need for limits. For example, "You can shout, yell, or throw things [if possible], but you can't hurt others, yourself, or me. You may get angry at me or others, but I won't let you hurt me, or others,

or yourself. If I did, you would feel badly later and if I let you do things which would make you feel bad or hurt yourself, I would not be helping you. I care about you and because I care, there are certain things I won't let you do."
4. The therapist helps the child to find ways to verbalize his aggression and anger in various play situations. For example, the child can "safely" express anger with toys and fantasy. Use of puppets, dolls, drawings, and toys may enable the child to "act out" and role-play.
5. When the child can deal with anger in play, he may be ready to learn to begin to express his negative feelings in real situations. Gradually, he may be introduced to situations which are ego-involving and threatening, for example, game-playing with win-or-lose components, or authority situations where disappointment and frustration may be encountered.
6. Gradually the child may be encouraged to express anger toward specific people: first toward the worker or therapist, and eventually toward other significant adults such as parents or foster parents.
7. The therapist assists the child in handling anger and aggression with his peers in simple play, and gradually in increasingly complex competitive play situations.
8. The therapist continues to help the child express hostility verbally so that repression is avoided and a buildup is unlikely. The child is helped to achieve a balance and accept as "OK" the fact that he may have both negative and positive feelings in interpersonal situations, and that it is important to verbally express *both* in socially appropriate fashion.

Materials such as paper, pencils, crayons, paints, brushes, plasticine, puppets, dolls, doll house, doll furniture, picture books, magazines, blocks, tinker toys, magic markers, sandbox, cars, trucks, dinky toys, simple games, Old Maid, Fish, ring toss, balls, and bean bags may be used in therapy.

Anxiety

Anxiety is defined as fear of the unknown. The anxious child typically appears tense, quiet, withdrawn, and rigid or hyperactive and uncontrolled. The objectives of therapy are to reduce anxiety and enable free and easy response to the environment.

Some possible modification activities and level of activity would be:

1. Setting limits—verbal indications to the child of the therapist's awareness and acceptance of the child's behaviour and fears; stating rules and limits or boundaries of behaviour and the reasons for them; establishing an environment which maximizes the child's sense of safety and his ability to succeed and experience competence.
2. Maintaining limits and controls—firmly dealing with the child's physical

and verbal testing behaviour, while continuing to accept empathically and with reassurance the child's anxiety.
3. Maintaining limits—primarily through verbal controls, recognizing carefully the child's ability to respond successfully and establishing realistic expectations which the child can attain.
4. Maximizing success—introduction of new experiences designed to increase the child's feelings of self-esteem, confidence and mastery which are age-appropriate and socially rewarding.
5. Non-verbal expression of fears—providing opportunities for expression of fear and anxiety through play and fantasy.
6. Verbal expression of fears—providing means which encourage verbal expression of previously unexpressed fears and anxieties.
7. Discussion and "working-through" of the child's fears and concerns.

Materials such as art supplies, simple games, puppets, dolls, blocks, sandbox, rocking chair, table and chairs, clay, music, and mechanical toys may be used in therapy.

Attention and Recognition

The child who has an excessive need for praise, acceptance, and recognition from others either demonstrates unusual demands for attention and recognition from adults and peers or appears to deny his need for attention and recognition. The objectives of therapy are to establish a sense of self-esteem which is positively based and realistic and does not depend solely on external evaluation from others.

Some possible modification activities and levels of activity would be:

1. Giving positive reinforcement to small pieces of behaviour, for example, sitting still long enough to hear instructions. The therapist may give encouragement and praise spontaneously through verbal comments, smiles, and body language. He may respond as required to continued demands for attention until the child's need is satisfied. In the case of a withdrawn child, the therapist may need to find behaviour to reward which is simple and easily repeated. The therapist may attempt to reinforce desired behaviour while ignoring undesired behaviour.
2. Gradually offering reinforcement less frequently while attempting to maintain the desired behaviour and to build reinforcement on more significant behaviour. For example, in game play, verbal encouragement becomes less general and praise is made increasingly contingent upon more sophisticated behaviour which is, however, still within the child's ability.
3. Reserving external recognition and attention for only age-appropriate significant behaviour, whether sought after or not.
4. Establishing goals and plans with the child that are increasingly longer-range, with attention and praise occurring at time of completion or intermittently as appropriate.

Attention Span

Attention span is defined as the ability to maintain attention in an activity which the child finds interesting while excluding other sources of distraction. Attention span may be considered a problem for the child when he is unable to maintain sufficient interest or length of sustained involvement in age-appropriate activities to experience completion or enjoyment. The objective of therapy is to enable the child to develop the ability to experience the degree of involvement required for successful task completion.

Some possible modification activities and levels of activity are as follows:

1. The therapist might find a task in which the child desires to become involved, such as a game, TV show, or play activity, and measure the time the child's interest was sustained in the activity.
2. Once a base is established, the length of time of involvement may be extended through encouragement and praise, and/or a reinforcer such as food.
3. The therapist gradually introduces the child to stimulating, enjoyable, and non-threatening tasks where success and/or completion is experienced, for example, watching a cartoon together, talking about it while watching, and enjoying the conclusion; or simple play with plasticine.
4. As the child's attention span improves for non-structured and/or play activities, the therapist introduces tasks which require skill and mastery, such as beadwork, colouring, building, and music.

Materials such as music, TV, drawing tools, games, blocks, books, cut-outs, colouring books, paint, toys, mechanical toys, dolls, puppets, old clothes, balls, marbles, and food may be used in therapy.

Frustration Tolerance

Often confused with attention span, *frustration tolerance* is the ability to postpone immediate gratification or reward; to persist and persevere until a task or goal is completed, even in the face of failure, without giving up too quickly. The child with low frustration tolerance typically behaves in a hyperactive, defeatist, self-denigrating, angry, uncooperative, erratic, inconsistent, and stubborn manner. The objectives of therapy are to increase the child's ability to postpone gratification, improve perseverance, develop problem-solving skills, and improve self-esteem.

Some possible modification activities and levels of activity are as follows:

1. The therapist might find situations in which the child can experience task completion quickly and easily, and be rewarded by praise and recognition and a sense of mastery.
2. Gradually the tasks involved may become more complex and require more

time to give the child satisfaction. For example, the child might first be asked to draw a clown or simple figures, and later to colour or copy figures. Next, simple puzzles might be introduced, then, gradually, more complex ones.
3. Once the child has begun to persevere and succeed in tasks alone, game play—first with the therapist, then with other children—may be introduced.
4. As he masters game skills and competitive situations, the child may be introduced to academic areas.

Materials such as books, games, blocks, pencils, crayons, and paint may be used in therapy.

Competition and Cooperation

Competition and cooperation is defined as the ability to interact in achievement-oriented situations where the child's behaviour is being compared with that of others. Problems may be inferred when the child's inter-personal behaviour with both adults and peers in such situations is characterized by conflict and frustration. The objective of therapy is to enable the child to enjoy and succeed at social interaction requiring cooperation and competition.

Some possible modification activities and levels of activity are:

1. Involvement with the child in non-competitive activities in which he is competent, such as painting, drawing, doll play, and clay modelling.
2. Introduction of activities where cooperation, but not competition, is required for completion and success, such as building with blocks, puppet play, cars, or play with a doll house.
3. Involvement of the therapist and child in separate activities which have minimal competitive aspects and are devoid of win or lose qualities. The therapist and child can compare their art, printing, drawing, building.
4. Introduction of simple games where the chance factor is high, such as Old Maid, Fish or dice games. Care should be taken to avoid the use of specific skills which may disadvantage the child.
5. Introduction of simple games where skills which the child has are involved, such as ring toss, ball play, puzzles, bowling, ball gun.
6. Introduction of cooperative-competitive games with more than one player, such as Chinese checkers, snakes and ladders, dice games, avalanche.
7. Gradual expansion of the complexity of skills required and the number of players in various play and "work" situations.

Materials such as pencils, crayons, paints, blackboard, chalk, brush, modelling clay, dolls and furniture, puppets, farm, blocks, games, and cards may be used in therapy.

Dependency

Dependency is defined as a need for external direction and support. The dependent child is unable to demonstrate age-appropriate independent behaviour and to define and follow through with individual goals. The objective of therapy is to assist the child to develop age-appropriate personal autonomy in thought and action.

Some possible modification activities and levels of activity are:

1. Total acceptance of dependency (doing for and responding to the child with warmth and care as required).
2. Involvement of the child as a partner and helper in satisfying personal needs. The therapist is directive and initiates activities.
3. Involvement of the child in task and activity selection and choice, with the child given simple instructions to carry out independently.
4. The child is encouraged to choose activities and the therapist becomes non-directive.
5. The child is encouraged in and given the opportunity for increasingly complex and competitive task involvement and completion, such as play with others or involvement in cooperative projects where individual tasks are defined.
6. The child is encouraged to make plans and initiate requests for autonomous age-appropriate behaviour.

Materials such as chalk and blackboard, pencil and paper, crayons, cars and trucks, blocks, balls, dolls, games, sandbox, table and chairs, rocking chair, blanket, and food may be used in therapy.

Fantasy

Fantasy is defined as conscious or unconscious fabrication or distortion of reality. The fantasizing child's behaviour is characterized by daydreaming or a tendency to withdraw or to alter the real facts. The objective of therapy is to assist the child to respond to reality appropriately.

Some possible modification activities and levels of activity are:

1. Involvement of the therapist with the child's fantasies. The therapist questions, understands, and shares interest in the fantasy without indicating disapproval of it, so that the child's fantasy becomes a shared experience rather than a means of escape.
2. The therapist carefully begins to require the child on occasion to rationalize his fantasy and to point out or question the reality of his fabrications. This may be done in the third person or as an abstract exercise rather than as a direct questioning by the therapist himself.
3. The therapist begins to become more direct in leading the child into involve-

ment with reality as opposed to fantasy. Play materials may change from puppets, crayons, and dolls to game play and situations involving more gross motor activities, and those requiring recall and memory of real events experienced.

Materials such as pencils, paper, crayons, paints, puppets, dolls, cars, trucks, blocks, doll house, clay, balls, sandbox, and old clothes may be used in therapy.

Feelings of Self-Worth

Self-worth is defined as self-esteem, feelings about oneself, and competence behaviour. The child who has a poor sense of self-worth will make verbal statements and actions in everyday activities at school and play, with peers and adults, which denote poor self-image, lack of self-confidence, and low self-esteem. The objective of therapy is to maximize experiences in which the child feels success and minimize those in which he might experience failure.

Modification activities and levels of activity used in therapy would be similar to those used to help the child with adaptiveness, anxiety, competition, dependency, and identity.

Giving and Receiving

The child who has trouble giving and receiving cannot accept from, give to, and share with others self, experiences, and belongings.

Some possible modification activities and levels of activity to be used in therapy would be:

1. Exercises in simple giving, receiving, and sharing of objects of play or food, such as clay, paper, gum, candy, crayons.
2. Exercises in simple giving to, receiving from, and sharing with the therapist ideas, actions, and responses, using puppets, dolls, story telling, word games, songs, or drama.
3. Exercises in simple giving, receiving, and sharing of self through physical contact such as touching, holding and cuddling.
4. Rewarding the child for specific acts with others which demonstrate efforts and success in giving, sharing, and receiving.

Identity

The child's identity is defined as his feelings of who and what he is, including his sense of family, race or ethnic origin, sex role, and religious affiliation. The child's behaviour may indicate that his self-concept in terms of sex, family, or racial community may be weak, absent, or negative. The objective of therapy is to help the child work through and accept who and what he is.

Some possible modification activities and levels of activity are:

1. Use of simple, unstructured play material to introduce to the child, or obtain from him, feelings and ideas of various aspects of his identity.
2. While using more structured materials, the therapist might indicate and/or seek responses from the child regarding his self-concept as it relates to specific identity factors for him, such as his family constellation, background, race, and sex role.
3. The therapist might then begin to provide additional factual information of a positive nature to fill in gaps and clarify misinformation or negative stereotypes. Some direct discussion of racial, sexual, or ethnic stereotypes may be required.
4. With factual information at hand, feelings and concerns may be dealt with more openly and concretely and a responsive plan determined, to deal with the real identity concerns that require resolution.

Materials such as games, costumes, drama, and stories may be used in therapy.

Self-Control and Responsibility

Self-control and responsibility are defined as the ability to respond to routines, limits, and environmental and social restrictions and expectations. Children who demonstrate difficulties following rules and accepting limits, whose behaviour appears disorganized, who fail to anticipate the consequences of their behaviour, and who refuse to accept responsibility for their actions have a problem with self-control. The objective of therapy is to develop age-appropriate self-control and personal responsibility.

Some possible modification activities and levels of activity are:

1. Exploration by the therapist of the degree to which the child has internalized controls.
2. If controls are weak, and additional external routines and limits (structure) are required, the limits will need to be carefully explained and the child assisted in their maintenance. Thus the therapist will need to be prepared to accept from the child a higher degree of dependency at this time, the object being to gradually move the child toward independent and responsible behaviour which is realistic and achievable.
3. Initially, control may be required occasionally through physical restraint by the therapist. It is important to avoid setting demands or expectations for control which are unrealistic. If the child cannot control either aggressive or withdrawal behaviour due to perceived threat or anxiety, external control may be required in the form of holding or cuddling while talking to the child until he feels safe enough in the situation to regain self-control and begin to act independently.
4. As the child gains in confidence and his internal controls become strengthened through relationship, the child may be able to respond to *verbal* control more easily, and gradually physical coercion or touch from the therapist

BEHAVIOUR MODIFICATION RECORD SUMMARY

Name: **Date:**

                                              Length of Session:

Modification Activity:

Materials Used:

General Comments:

Specific Behaviour	**Modification Level**	**Comments & Observations**
Adaptiveness		
Affection		
Aggression		
Anxiety		
Attention & Recognition		
Attention Span		
Competition		
Dependency		
Fantasy		
Feelings of Self-Worth		
Frustration Tolerance		
Giving and Receiving		
Identity		
Self-Control and Responsibility		

may be eliminated. That is, the child may then follow verbal instructions, respond to verbal direction, begin to understand conceptual symbolic nuances, and act accordingly with some degree of independent responsibility. This does not mean that the child may be expected to be unexpressive. Shouting, screaming, and swearing in anger and frustration may indicate a tremendous move toward being able to internalize control from a previous stage when hitting, biting, and destructive acts were the only means by which the child was able to express these feelings.
5. At this point, the child may be encouraged to express his feelings verbally and to control physical acts of violence or withdrawal behaviour, both self- and other-directed, and to accept greater responsibility for his behaviour. Initially such things as puppets, drawing, ball play, painting, and non-competitive games may be useful here. Considerable verbal assurance is required from the therapist that it is safe for the child to express himself in these situations. Praise and recognition from the therapist will be important in helping the child to recognize his gains and his ability to exercise self-control, verbal expression, and independence of thought and action.
6. The verbal controls of the therapist may be gradually decreased as the child gains skill in demonstrating responsible behaviour, although he may still require the therapist's non-verbal signs and symbols for assistance. The desire here is to help the child to make the transition from verbal to non-verbal symbolic cues as reinforcements for internalized social controls. The therapist at this point may wish to practice non-verbal cues and signs and body language with the child. Role playing or make-believe may be appropriate. Thus the child may learn cognitively the meaning of various facial expressions used by adults and peers and practice them himself. He can also practice talking about social expectations in various situations. For example, how do we behave at meal times, when guests are present, with small children, when receiving gifts, when we lose games, or in school?
7. The child is given opportunities to experience his newly acquired controls and to practice in new situations, first with the therapist present and later alone with peers and adults.

APPENDIX B

Guidelines for Process Recording Casework Interviews

Process recording typically produces great apprehension and concern in students. The most widely expressed concern is in remembering or recalling accurately and comprehensively the events and dialogue of the interview. In fact, we all do exactly this every time we convey or repeat a conversation to others who have not heard it before. We are involved in the same process when we relate a joke, tell a story or describe to others some encounter or experience we had. We all have the capacity or ability to remember and restate accurately a complex series of events in which we are a participant. Of course, the anxiety level of the budding helper lowers confidence and, in addition, there is normal concern over being "evaluated" by one's mentor. Still, my experience with students, even under these circumstances, has been that they can do much better than they believe possible until they try. In fact, they continually amaze themselves at the high quality of their recordings.

IMPORTANT FACTORS IN PROCESS RECORDING

The following ten points cover some of the important factors to keep in mind when preparing a process recording of a client interview:

Comprehensiveness

A process recording is a full and complete account. Remember that you are describing what has occurred to persons who were not there. Describe the event or situation in as much significant detail as possible so that you are confident others are perceiving it through your eyes. It is better in the beginning for the account to be too long than too short.

Style

Use a narrative style, in the third person and the past tense, with full sentences and correct grammatical form and structure. Check spelling and punctuation. Remember that this is a professional document which demonstrates your awareness of your accountability to your profession, placement, and client.

Accuracy

Give special attention to recording factual information which will provide a graphic description of events, behaviour, and feelings. In particular, the content section should include as much verbatim content (placed in quotation marks) as possible of the actual dialogue between the client and yourself.

Avoid Spontaneous Interpretation and Assignment of Motivation

Record exactly what is perceived, where, when, how, with whom, and with what result. Refrain from making leaps from observations of behaviour to interpretations of behaviour, and/or assessing or assigning motivation to the client. For example, rather than stating that the client was nervous, describe the client's behaviour, such as trembling hands, facial tic, small voice, which you might label as nervous. It is important to determine whether your interpretation or labelling of behaviour is shared by others who read your account. Let others make their own judgment based on your observations and descriptive report. The same is true of assignment of motivation, for example, "He was obviously upset by the long wait."It is possible that the behaviour labelled as "upset" could be anger or fear or frustration, and this behaviour may or may not be related to a long wait. It may be related to some traumatic event totally unrelated to the immediate situation. Once the behaviour is described, a label might be assigned with caution using terms such as "appeared," "seemed," "suggested." The same is true with suggestions of motivation, for example, "Mrs. Black's outburst *may have* occurred at this point because. . . ."

Purpose

The purpose of the interview should be known by the worker before the interview begins. Specific points might be written down as a guide and reminder for reference during the interview.

Note-Taking

While it may not be possible in all situations, clients are accustomed to, or expect, note-taking during an interview. This can be mentioned by the interviewer and a brief explanation given if appropriate and necessary.

Reconstruction From Notes as Soon as Possible

Recording will be easiest and most accurate if notes are obtained in interview. Where this is not possible, the need to reconstruct the interview in written form soon after will be even more urgent. The longer the time lag between interview and reconstruction, the more vague will be the perceptions and the greater the loss in accuracy and comprehensiveness.

Reread and Rewrite

Once you have put down in rough the verbatim reconstruction of the Observations and Content of the interview, some polishing, attendance to grammar, spelling, etc. will be required before final form.

Examine Observations, Purpose, and Content Before Writing Impressions and Worker's Role

From the Observations and Content will come the material for the Impressions section. You are permitted in this section some educated guesses about, and judgments of, the client's behaviour. Look for gaps, inconsistencies, conflict, cause-effect relationships, strengths, weaknesses, growth potential. In assessing your role, review the purpose of the interview and comment on your achievement of objectives. Were they accomplished? How? If not, why not? What about the interview did you do well? What would you like to have done better?

Synthesize and Summarize

In the statement of plan, restate or summarize the whole interview process and result in a sentence or two and indicate briefly the plan for the next interim or long-term objective.

AN EXAMPLE OF A STUDENT PROCESS RECORDING

The following account, prepared by a second-year student, contains the essential elements of good process recording and may be useful as a model. Descriptive detail in the recording has been altered to protect the identity of the client.

Purpose

The worker had been asked by her agency to visit Jane and assess her eligibility for financial assistance. The client had phoned the agency two days prior to the worker's visit. She had explained to the worker in the office that she was eight months pregnant, had left her husband, and was unable to support herself financially. Jane explained that she was now living with her parents but that they were in some financial distress and could not provide for her at this time.

Observations

Jane was 21 years old but appeared even younger. She was approximately 5'2" tall. The worker estimated her normal weight at about 110-12 lbs (her bone structure seemed small). However, the "little bundle of joy" she was carrying put her present weight probably nearer 125-28 lbs. The worker felt (from a professional standpoint) that Jane was probably closer to "term" than she had signified to the office worker. From the appearance of her pear-shaped abdomen, the baby seemed to have dropped in her uterus and was on his descent down the birth canal. The fact was probably verified during the interview when the client had to make frequent trips to the bathroom. Jane's round "cherub"-like face was framed by soft shoulder-length blonde hair, her large deep-set brown eyes dominated her expressive but pale face. She wore what appeared to be new blue jeans and a freshly laundered white blouse. She walked with the definite gait of a proud mother to be (her back swayed and her head held high).

Jane greeted the worker warmly at the door with a friendly engaging smile. (The worker wondered who was putting who at ease!)

The client asked the worker to go through the kitchen. (This could have turned out as a dangerous walk for both worker and client.) The hall and the entire downstairs of the house did not appear untidy—it *was* untidy. Milk bottles, newspapers, toys were strewn from the front door to the kitchen table and they were joined there by piles of dirty dishes. Sitting surrounded by this array of confusion was a woman in her late forties; a gaunt, pale woman with a scarf unsuccessfully concealing large pink hair curlers. Her tattered faded trousers were complemented by an egg-stained overblouse. Jane quietly, without looking at the woman, introduced her to the worker as her mother.

The contrast between mother and daughter's appearance was very apparent. However, the worker realized later that the mother had her hands full babysitting three youngsters and a husband that did not appear too active. It did cross the worker's mind that Jane could (although pregnant) have perhaps cleared the table for her mother. Jane's mother quickly left the room although Jane did say that it was fine by her if she wanted to stay. Jane and the worker pushed the pile of dishes aside in order to complete the necessary paper work.

Content

Worker: How are you feeling, Jane?
Jane: Oh, fine, thank-you. Except that I feel so fat (Jane laughs and holds her stomach). You know, he is always kicking me just here. Can you feel that? (Client takes worker's hand and places it directly under her rib cage. The worker is immediately punched by a little active wandering foot!)
Worker: He certainly is ready to start walking out of there (the worker and Jane both laugh). I gather you have decided it's going to be a boy.
Jane: Jim and I would both like a boy. (A big smile lights up her face.)
Worker: Jim? Is that your husband's name?
Jane: Oh, sorry! Yes, Jim is my husband.
Worker: (At this point worker feels Jane is wanting to discuss her husband in more detail.) Would you like to tell me a little about Jim and your relationship?
(Jane shifted her position on the chair and leaned intently towards the worker, keeping direct eye contact while talking.)
Jane: Well, as I told the worker in your office, I left him last week. My nerves were getting really bad. He was always picking on me.
Worker: How did he pick on you, Jane?
Jane: Oh, I don't know. He grumbled because he said I am not so much fun as I was. I guess he is upset because I don't want to go out and party like I used to before I was pregnant. (Jane slumps back in her chair and pushes her abdomen out towards the table and drops her head.)
Worker: Yes, I guess pregnancy does slow women down. How do *you* feel about not going out to parties?

Jane:	Oh, it bothers me, I guess, but Jim is the one that really bothers me when he gets so angry with me. I was getting so upset my family doctor suggested I go to see a counsellor at the psychiatric outpatient clinic at the hospital. So I went.
Worker:	Did you feel that you got any help by going to the clinic?
Jane:	Yes, a little I guess, but he wants to see Jim too. (Client lowers her head and looks at her hands which are moving slowly over her abdomen.)
Worker:	Does Jim know that you are going to the hospital?
Jane:	Oh yes, I told him.
Worker:	Did you tell him the counsellor had asked him to go with you?
Jane:	Yes, but he just got mad all over again. That's why I decided to leave and come home last Friday.
Worker:	He was cross that you asked him to go to the clinic with you?
Jane:	That and other things. I guess the real thing last Friday was because I wouldn't go to the show with him on Thursday. But I was just too tired—so I came home.
Worker:	How do you feel about your decision now?
Jane:	Oh, I don't know. My mum is glad to have me home and she really spoils me, you know (client lowers her voice and looks in direction of the living room), but my stepfather is worse than Jim. He says I am lazy and just want a handout. He is always picking on me too.
Worker:	That must not make you feel too good, eh Jane?
Jane:	Yes, it really does upset me. But my mum is good to me although she has never liked Jim, even before we were married—she has been on at me ever since to leave him.
Worker:	Do you think you will leave him?
Jane:	Oh, I don't know. (Smile disappears completely and her voice sounds terse.)
Worker:	Jane, you know if you do leave Jim permanently and you do need our assistance for a long period of time we will ask that you go to court after your baby is born for legal custody and support from your husband.

(Jane's whole body stiffened, her large eyes appeared suddenly much larger as the pupils dilated. The tears welled up in her eyes and could no longer be controlled and they cascaded down over her flushed cheeks. (The worker felt like a real "heel," but it was part of the stipulation for documentation of deserted mothers.))

Jane:	(Brushing the tears away from her cheeks.) I don't want to do that. It is Jim's baby too. He wants to see the baby too, you know.
Worker:	(Takes client's hand in her own.) Nobody is going to stop Jim from seeing his baby even if you do get custody. However, if this idea of the court action bothers you, I am sure that we can still assist you on a temporary basis, at least until your baby is born. You will have

	had time to think things through in your mind. Maybe we could talk a little longer and see if we can come up with some good ideas. Would you like that?
Jane:	(The tears have subsided and the smile is reappearing.) Yes, please.
Worker:	When is the baby due, Jane?
Jane:	In about six weeks, I guess.
Worker:	How do you feel about your delivery?
Jane:	Scared a bit, I guess.
Worker:	I think that is only natural, especially with first babies. I know I was a little anxious with my first baby.
Jane:	Was your mother around you when you went into labour?
Worker:	Yes, Jane, she was there. I went home to my mother because I was a little anxious.
Jane:	Yes, I am glad my mother is here to help me. But I miss Jim too. He says he will be at the delivery.
Worker:	How do you feel about him being there?
Jane:	Oh, great. I really miss him, you know. I guess I really am mixed up. I am scared and I want my mother around and yet I want Jim too.
Worker:	Why did you leave Jim?
Jane:	I told you. He picked on me.

(Silence. The worker thought she would give Jane time to think about why she left him.)

Jane:	(The puzzled expression leaves Jane's face and she starts to smile.) I think I know what you're thinking.
Worker:	What am I thinking?
Jane:	(Both client and worker start laughing.) I guess I really was plain scared and used Jim's picking as an excuse to get home to my mother to look after me. Because I really do love him, do you believe that?
Worker:	Yes, Jane, I do believe you both have good feelings for each other.
Jane:	But he does pick on me sometimes. How would he like to be pregnant?
Worker:	That would be a miracle, Jane!

(Client smiles and appears more relaxed.)

Worker:	Have you heard from Jim since you left him?
Jane:	Oh yes, he calls all the time asking me to go back, but I told him unless he goes to the counsellor with me I will not go back. He says if I don't go back he will not send me any money until the baby arrives.
Worker:	Sounds as if you are both doing some bribing!
Jane:	Yes, I guess. But I don't think my bribe is a bad one, do you?
Worker:	Well, maybe you could just suggest it again, but not use it as a threat.

Jane:	Yes, that's a good idea. Do you think you can help me until the baby is born?
Worker:	Well, Jane, let's get these papers completed and I will get back to the office and talk to my supervisor. However, Jane, I would like you and Jim to talk and maybe get some help with your problems. It is very important that you get things settled before junior arrives. He deserves a good life, you know, with people who are going to be responsible for him.
Jane:	Yes, I know, Mrs. Barnes. Thank you for spending time with me.
Worker:	Call me at the office if you have any questions. I delivered several babies when I was a nurse so maybe I can come up with some answers for you.
Jane:	Oh, good. I will definitely call.
Worker:	Goodbye, Jane.
Jane:	Goodbye, Mrs. Barnes. Thank you again.

Impressions

PHYSICAL HEALTH, APPEARANCE, AND CAPACITIES
Jane's attractive "madonna-like face" had the warm healthy glow that only a mother-to-be portrays. Her posture was good; in spite of her increased weight she held her body and head erect. Jane had had an uneventful physical history with regard to her pregnancy—a little morning nausea in the early months. Prior to leaving her husband she had not been sleeping well and her doctor had prescribed a mild sedative, which she no longer finds necessary. Her only physical complaint appeared to be her frequency of micturition, which had increased significantly in the last two weeks. Jane had had no premature contractions (the worker explained the signs and symptoms of these false labour pains). However the client (as noted in the interview) had been aware of and excited by the fetal movements.

INTELLECTUAL FUNCTIONING AND POTENTIAL
Jane had completed her grade 12 education and from her quick bright answers to the worker's questions appeared to be an intelligent girl. Her intelligence was made more evident by her own diagnosis of her situation (her desire for her husband complicated by her apprehension of the pending delivery and consequent dependence on her mother).

Jane was very obviously aware and conveyed to the worker that her mother did not approve of her husband and was encouraging her to stay at home and discontinue the relationship.

INTRAPERSONAL BEHAVIOUR
Jane appears to be generally a very confident and enthusiastic girl with high self-esteem. Although at the present time she seemed a little uncertain of her

hasty decision to leave her husband, her dependency on her mother, the worker felt, was only temporary, due to her condition. Her baby seemed to be number-one priority to her, with her husband following as a close second. Jane appeared to be an outgoing and genuine young lady who responded to most situations in a mature manner. She showed no negative feelings towards her husband and only passing moments of distrust concerning their future relationship.

The client was a little apprehensive regarding her forthcoming delivery, which in the case of a first labour appeared to the worker to be quite natural. Jane showed some anxiety which manifested itself only in the enlargement of her eyes (bewilderment) and the tone of her voice. This occurred when the worker spoke of her legal adoption of the baby. Jane told the worker that she had become very upset and unhappy in her relationship with her husband in the last month, and her family doctor had suggested that she attend a psychiatric clinic for counselling. These sessions had, she felt, helped her, but she wishes Jim would attend with her.

INTERPERSONAL BEHAVIOUR
Jane showed considerable love in her warm description of her husband and expected baby. She was kind and considerate of her mother and told the worker she appreciated all the help her mother gave her. Jane spoke about good times she and her husband had when their friends dropped by. Her best friend was also expecting a baby and Jane spoke of their warm relationship and shared anticipation. Jane appeared to get along well with her mother. She was able to be tolerant of her stepfather regardless of his derogatory remarks. Jane has two sisters in high school who are living at home. She spoke fondly of her siblings.

TALENTS AND SKILLS
Jane described herself as a "real outdoors girl." She played tennis with her husband, and loved to swim. Under normal conditions she liked to ride her bicycle downtown (she explained this was a little awkward now!) Jane is also able to type well and prior to her pregnancy held a secretarial job.

EDUCATION AND WORK HISTORY
Due to her age and grade 12 level of education, Jane has only worked for a year and a half prior to her pregnancy.

LIVING ENVIRONMENT
As described previously, Jane's mother does not appear to pay particular attention to housework. The house is a semi-detached two-storey home. Jane's mother babysits for three young children to supplement her income (which may explain the toy display that nearly levelled the worker on entering the house). Jane's stepfather worked periodically. At the time of documentation he was asleep on the couch.

Worker's Role

From the outset of the interview the worker felt there was a bond between herself and the client. It was easy for the worker to show empathy, having been a first time mum and one who had run home to Mother! Also a nurse, the worker remembered the fears of many young mothers at the birth of their first children. The worker questioned her part in helping Jane make any decisions—she felt that Jane had those decisions made before the worker appeared on the scene! However she had been an empathetic and genuine sounding board.

Plan

To assess the situation, process the documentation. The worker will ask her supervisor to assist this client at least until after delivery. Jane is young and this is a big undertaking for any girl, which should not be complicated by financial stress. Worker intends to visit the client in the hospital. Worker is sort of drawn to little baby boys.

Summary

On December 15 Jane had a 7-lb. baby girl! She returned to Jim and they are both seeing a counsellor. All three appear very happy.

There are some fairy tales even in social work!

III

Experiental, Self-Actualizing, Intrapersonal Therapies

In Part I we discussed some of the basic concepts and issues involved in the helping process and identified elements considered essential to any helping approach. In Part II, we explored the contribution to contemporary therapeutic methods made by the fields of psychiatry, psychology, and social work. Parts III, IV, and V will examine the theories and methods of specific therapies.

In Parts III and IV, each chapter is devoted to one therapy, and in Part V, three behaviour therapies are presented. These chapters are organized as follows:

>Founder—a biographical sketch
>Basic Concepts and Assumptions
>Theory of Normal Personality
>Theory of Neurosis
>Process and Technique of Therapy
>Summary

The three approaches which have been grouped together in Part III have been described as "experiential, self-actualizing, and intrapersonal therapies." This is an arbitrary grouping in that while these therapies are similar in theory and aims, their methods and techniques are unique. They are, however, all characterized by a focus on the intrinsic emotional/feeling/sensation aspect of the client's behaviour in contrast to the cognitive/intellectual, social/environmental, or other component of the client's behaviour. Here first, are some of the similarities in assumptions, aims, and concepts of Rogerian, Gestalt, and Primal Therapy.

SIMILARITIES
• All three place the origin of neurotic behaviour in infancy and early child-

hood and recognize the significance of parental approval in shaping personality development.
- All three have an organismic base to the theory, with Gestalt Therapy reflecting a strong organismic quality, Primal somewhat less, and Rogerian least of all.
- Both Rogerian and Gestalt Therapy assume a single primary drive for self-actualization. While Janov, the founder of Primal Therapy, does not explicitly suggest a drive to self-actualization, his belief in the release of the natural "instincts" of the individual suggests a similar idea.
- All three approaches reflect the aim of therapy as enabling the person to be what he or she is.
- All three see the role of repression and suppression as key to the development of neurosis.
- All three include the concept of defenses or defense mechanisms and discuss the importance of anxiety.
- All three focus in some way on the defenses of the client.
- All three are present-oriented, in the sense of dealing with what the client is experiencing now, even though this may include past memories.
- All three view the client as split or dis-integrated, with therapy focusing on enabling the client to become re-integrated and whole.
- All three view society as neurotic and have expressed a social action orientation.

DIFFERENCES
- Theoretically, Rogerian Therapy is the strongest in terms of the organization, articulation, and scientific validation attempted.
- Rogerian Therapy is the only approach of the three to have a fully developed personality theory. Gestalt Therapy does not deal extensively with normal development, and the normal character is almost totally absent in Primal theory and approach.
- All three are ex post facto theories, but Rogerian and Gestalt are strengthened by their deductive method; Janov arrived at Primal Therapy inductively.
- Language and terminology used to describe various similar concepts, dynamics and methods differ considerably, and unique language is prominent in both Gestalt and Primal.
- The actual therapeutic process and techniques are the strongest distinguishing feature of the three approaches. Rogerian Therapy focuses on the communication of certain personal qualities of the therapist to the client to enable the client to self-actualize. Gestalt Therapy focuses on the external behaviour of the client and enables the client to become aware of her or his own potential to be. Primal Therapy focuses on the dismantling of client defenses and the experiencing of past hurt and rejection now.

5
Rogerian Therapy

> *I have avoided noisy confrontations whenever possible. When I was told early in my career, that it was absolutely impossible for a psychologist to carry on psychotherapy, because this was the province of the psychiatrist, I made no attempt to meet the issue head-on. Instead, I first used the term treatment interviews to describe what we were doing. Later the label counselling seemed more acceptable. Only after years of experience, and the amassing of a considerable body of research by me and my colleagues, did I openly speak of the fact—by then obvious—that we were doing psychotherapy. I had walked softly through life, making relatively little noise until I had arrived at my destination—and it was too late to stop me. I do have a stubborn streak.*
>
> —Carl Rogers, 1977: xi–xii

Carl Rogers's significance and contribution to the field of psychotherapy parallels that of Sigmund Freud. Freud dared to expose the mysteries of neurotic behaviour common to Western cultures for all of us to see and ponder. Rogers dared to expose the *mystique* of the process of therapy itself to scientific scrutiny and public awareness. The importance of this feature of Rogers's work cannot be overestimated. It was through Rogers's efforts that the focus on the dynamics of the therapeutic situation turned from the patient to the therapist. And it was subsequently learned that what the therapist or helper *does* is not the key to client improvement, but rather what the therapist or helper *is* as a person. The eventual discovery that the personal qualities of the helper were paramount to effective helping began with Rogers's bold and brave accounts of his own client interviews and therapeutic process. Not until this time (1942) had the helping disciplines begun to seriously scrutinize their own behaviour and its impact on client responses.

Now, having credited Rogers with the identification of what appears to be the most significant feature of the helping process, it should not be assumed that therefore Rogerian Therapy is the best. We have gained, however, from Rogers's initial ideas, his influence on others, and his own direct research and clinical effort, a fundamental principle governing the therapeutic or helping process. While Rogerian Therapy is distinguished from others primarily by its reliance on this principle *alone,* all effective helping methods recognize its significance and incorporate it within specific techniques. Rogerian Therapy, then, is distinguished from other contemporary helping approaches not by what is present, but by what appears to be missing.

In almost all helping approaches there are two major roles or techniques involved on the part of the helper. First, the helper is involved in questioning or interrogating the client (what, where, when, how, how much, why). Second, the helper is involved in telling, advising, directing, suggesting, or guiding the client. Rogerian Therapy involves neither of these roles or techniques, but only the therapist's intense communication of wanting to understand and *be with* the client in his distress. As we shall discover below, this communication for the most part takes place without resorting to either the traditional question-and-answer interaction or advisor-advisee relationship.

Finally, before we look briefly at Carl Rogers as a person, a word about the term "Rogerian." You may be more familiar with Rogers's approach as *client-centred* therapy. The word "Rogerian" has been employed in the text as a more generic term to describe Rogers's work over a span of more than forty years. As we shall see below, there appear to be three distinct periods or phases to his work during this time, with the term "client-centred" defining accurately only the second period (Hart and Tomlinson, 1970). The term "Rogerian," then, while non-specific, seems at the same time more appropriate for an approach which has been in the process of development and refinement for almost half a century.

CARL R. ROGERS (1902-   )

Carl Ransom Rogers was born in a Chicago suburb, the fourth of six children. His parents were both university-educated, which was unusual at that time, but they were not a sophisticated family, and Rogers (1972) refers to them as "anti-intellectual." Religion and the Protestant work ethic seemed to provide the basis for the family structure. By the time Carl was born, the Rogerses were a comfortable upper-middle-class family, financially secure through his father's thriving construction business.

Carl remembers the family as a close-knit unit, where warmth and love existed among an unusual array of prohibitions:

> They were both devoted and loving parents, giving a great deal of time and energy to creating a family which would "hold" the children in the way in which they should go. They were masters of the art of subtle and loving control. I do not remember ever being given a direct command on an important subject, yet such was the unity of our family that it was understood by all that we did not dance, play cards, attend movies, smoke, drink, or show any sexual interest (Rogers, 1972: 30).

A most interesting revelation from the son who was to go on to create *non-directive* and *client-centred* therapy!

Rogers was always an A student, read at the fourth-grade level before starting school, and was an imaginative, introspective, and solitary child, with almost no social relationships outside his immediate family. To keep things that way, and to protect their children from the evils of the big city, Mr. and Mrs. Rogers moved the family to a farm west of Chicago when Carl was entering adolescence.

Living on a farm developed in Rogers an abiding interest in nature and science. His father's farm was somewhat of a hobby. He wanted it to be a model of modern agricultural science, and brought agriculturalists from the universities to train his help in the most up-to-date methods. Rogers read his father's agricultural journals and gained by the age of sixteen a thorough understanding of the scientific method.

He entered the University of Wisconsin in 1919 to study agriculture. Although he roomed with his brother Ross, his university studies saw the beginning of his separation from his family. He became a member of a YMCA church study group and found in it his first meaningful relationships outside his family. It was in the same year that he began writing to Helen Elliot, a girl he had known since elementary school and had dated a few times as a freshman at Wisconsin, where she was studying art. This relationship was to grow quickly: they would be married in 1924.

In his sophomore year, Rogers decided to follow his religious interests and consider preparation for the ministry. He switched his course from agriculture to history. Midway through his sophomore year he was selected to attend a YMCA conference in China. With great enthusiasm, he embarked on a six-month tour of the Orient that was to complete his emancipation from his family.

> After this six months trip I was able freely, and with no great sense of defiance or guilt, to think my own thoughts, come to my own conclusions, and to take the stands I believed in. . . . From the date of this trip, my goals, values, aims, and philosophy have been my own and very divergent from the views which my parents held and which I had held up to this point (Rogers, 1972: 38-39).

After a six-month bout with an ulcer on his return, which Rogers attributes to his "gently suppressive" family environment, he returned to university in the fall of 1922, and became engaged to Helen on a weekend visit home in October that year. He graduated with a bachelor's degree in history in 1924, and two months later Carl and Helen were married.

Rogers now thwarted his family on two counts. First, he had decided to pursue his graduate work at Union Theological Seminary (UTS) in New York because of its liberal reputation and intellectual leadership. Second, he had decided to get married before completing his education because he felt Helen should experience it with him. His father wanted him to attend Princeton Seminary, a centre of fundamentalist thinking, and had opposed the marriage since in those days it was considered inappropriate for a man to marry while still attending school. However, his parents were generous, assisting the young couple with expenses and giving them gifts.

The first year at UTS was refreshing and stimulating but Rogers began questioning his suitability for the ministry.

> I realized that my own views had changed tremendously already and would very likely continue to change. It seemed to me that it would be a horrible thing to have to profess a set of beliefs in order to remain in one's profession. I wanted to find a field in which I could be sure my freedom of thought would not be limited (Rogers, 1972: 42).

So, for the second time in his university career, Rogers transferred: this time out of UTS and into Teachers College, Columbia University, where he had already been taking some courses, to study clinical and educational psychology. This same year, 1926, their first child, David, was born.

Upon graduating from Columbia in 1928 with his M.A. and while continuing to work on his doctorate in psychology, Rogers began his professional career as a psychologist with a child guidance clinic in Rochester, New York. He spent twelve very important years there. The birth of their second child Natalie completed his family, and during this time his unique therapeutic approach was born as well. Rogers described this period as one of isolation from academic psychology, and as such, one of freedom from the strictures and discipline of any particular field. But it was at the same time a highly stimulating and pragmatically creative environment in which he played his part as a team member in a typical community social service agency:

> Our colleagues in the social agencies, schools, and the courts knew little and cared less about psychological ideologies. The only element which carried weight with them was the ability to get results in working with maladjusted individuals. The staff was eclectic, of diverse background, and our frequent and continuing discussion of treatment methods was based on our practical everyday working experience with the children and adolescents, and adults who were our clients (Rogers, 1959: 188–89).

It was during the latter part of this period that Rogers was influenced by the then controversial ideas of Otto Rank, whom he subsequently met briefly. Rank's views assisted him to further organize his thoughts about, and experience with, the process of therapy.

It would appear that his intellectual freedom and his lack of strong professional identity during this time enabled him to perceive a seemingly inherent *orderliness* to the therapeutic process. Thus his approach was conceptualized only after he became impressed by his own repeated observations and experience of certain events in the therapeutic situation regardless of the client or the problem presented. It did not follow from a "eureka" experience in which he suddenly grasped insight into the nature of the process, nor from a cognitive activity or single case or patient phenomenon which he then set out to "prove" through inductive reasoning. Rather, Rogers's approach originated deductively from his and others', invariably social workers', repeated observations and experiences with their clients in the treatment process. It was born from the real-life urgency they felt to better understand what was occurring in the therapeutic situation so that they and other helpers could better respond to the distress of their clients.

It was in this context that Rogers published his second book, *The Clinical Treatment of the Problem Child* (1939).* This was essentially a case-oriented manual based on his own work with disturbed children and was significant because little other material of a case nature was available at the time.

In 1938, after a reorganization of social agencies in Rochester, Rogers won his first battle with psychiatry and was named director of the new Rochester Guidance Centre. And although he was satisfied with his work there, he had visions of a university appointment. When in 1940, largely on the basis of *Clinical Treatment of the Problem Child,* he was offered a full professorship in psychology at Ohio State University, he accepted. His return to academia and his interaction with students impressed upon him two things. First, he became aware for the first time that he had developed a point of view in psychology and psychotherapy that was distinctive and uniquely his own. Second, neither his inexperienced students nor his traditionally oriented colleagues were about to accept readily what his twelve years of clinical experience had taught *him*. It was this impetus which led to his next book, *Counselling and Psychotherapy* (1942), in which he set out the major elements of client-centred therapy and which signalled what has remained his life's work: the empirical study and understanding of the therapeutic process, of human interaction, and personality development.

In 1945 Rogers left Ohio State, accepting an invitation to head a new counselling centre at the University of Chicago. He was to spend another twelve very important years there until 1957. It is this period which resulted in his wide recognition as a leading therapist, theorist, teacher, and researcher, and during which his stature in and contribution to psychology and psychotherapy were firmly established.

But Rogers has had his moments of self-doubt and emotional trauma too. In the midst of this most productive and satisfying period of his life he reports that he encountered two years of "intense personal distress" associated with his failure to help a seriously disturbed client.

> Gradually I realized I was on the edge of a complete breakdown myself, and then suddenly this feeling became very urgent. I *must* escape. . . . I went home and told Helen that I must get away, at *once*. We were on the road within an hour and stayed away two or three months, on what we can now calmly refer to as our "runaway trip." Helen's quiet assurance that I would come out of this distress in time, and her willingness to listen when I was able to talk of it, were a great help. However, when we returned I was still rather deeply certain of my complete inadequacy as a therapist, my worthlessness as a person, and my lack of any future in the field of psychology or psychotherapy (Rogers, 1972: 57-58).

---

* Rogers's first book, *Measuring Personality Adjustment in Children* (1931), was based on the research for his Ph.D. thesis and was published by Teachers College the year he received his doctoral degree (Current Biography, 1962).

With help offered from one of the members of the Counselling Centre, Rogers was able to work through his self-doubts "to a point where I could value myself, even like myself, and was much less fearful of receiving or giving love." His assessment of that experience is that it significantly helped him as a therapist to be "consistently and increasingly free and spontaneous" with his clients.

It is interesting that Rogers has found it so difficult to ask for help for himself, as though he was not supposed to need it. He reflects on this characteristic thirty years later:

> I have been more able to ask for help. I ask others to carry things for me, do things for me, instead of "proving" that I can do it myself. I can ask for personal help. When Helen, my wife, was very ill, and I was close to the breaking point from being on call as a 24-hour nurse, a housekeeper, a professional person in much demand, and a writer, I asked for help — and got it from a therapist-friend. I explored and tried to meet my own needs. I explored the strain this period was putting on our marriage. I realized that it was necessary for my survival to live *my* life, and that this must come first, even though Helen was so ill. I am not quick to turn to others, but I am much more aware of the fact that I can't handle everything within myself (Rogers, 1980b: 12).

It was during the Chicago period that Rogers's reputation brought many invitations for him to travel to various universities. He was a visiting professor at UCLA, Harvard, Brandeis, and Berkeley. In 1957 he returned to the University of Wisconsin for a five-month appointment as the honorary Knapp Professor. This provided him with time to do some synthesizing of his own work and to continue to search for the basic elements in the helping process. He also gave seminars to graduate students and faculty in counselling, psychology, and education. His impact was immediate. Virgil Herrich, the education professor who had arranged his appointment, now tried to lure Rogers to Wisconsin on a permanent basis. While appreciative and flattered, Rogers did not wish to leave the Counselling Centre at the University of Chicago. In response to Herrich's persistence, Rogers finally wrote a job description that would tempt him, believing that no such position could be created. The job involved ". . . appointments in both psychiatry and psychology, opportunity to train psychologists and psychiatrists, time for therapy and research with psychotic and normal individuals (the two extreme groups where I felt my experience was deficient), and other improbable requirements" (Rogers, 1972: 60). The cross-appointments in psychology and psychiatry were particularly significant in view of the stranglehold psychiatrists had on the field of psychotherapy and the battles which Rogers himself had fought and won against psychiatrists' attempts to deny him his position first as head of the Rochester Guidance Centre and again at the Counselling Centre. The fight with psychiatry was one of two significant "struggles" reported by Rogers (1974) in his paper to the APA in 1973 on receiving the Distinguished Professional Contribution Award. The other was his struggle with behaviourists, particularly B.F. Skinner. Both struggles represent basic differences in the philosophy of human behaviour rather than scientific disputes. Rogers's position is humanistic and existential, the behaviourists' and psychiatrists', deterministic. Herrich managed to work out the appointment that Rogers had outlined, and Rogers, after careful consideration, decided to accept it. In 1957 Rogers and his wife moved to Madison, Wisconsin.

For the next seven years Rogers remained at the University of Wisconsin. His research with schizophrenics was completed, although not without some serious problems encountered through unethical behaviour on the part of one of the members of the research team he had selected. His participation in the Department of Psychiatry was very satisfying and enabled the kind of cooperative resolution of disciplinary jealousies and differences he had hoped would occur. His experience with the Department of Psychology, however, was disappointing and frustrating. The Department was essentially learning-laboratory-oriented and unsympathetic to clinical psychology. Rogers had hoped to achieve with his clinical graduate students a resolution of differences existing between experimental and clinical psychology similar to that which he had achieved between psychiatry and psychology. His comments are instructive in that they still define the situation in graduate education in most universities today, twenty years later.

> What I did not foresee or recognize was that the department had come to place such stress on "rigorous" examinations, on failing large proportions of students, that no-one in any field could turn out a significant number of Ph.D.s. In the department as a whole—though it took me a number of years to recognize this—about one out of seven of our carefully selected graduates ever received the Ph.D. Some were failed, some of the most creative minds and the best clinicians left in disgust, and I was in the peculiar position of training graduate students who had only a minute chance (a chance which did not have too much to do with merit) of obtaining a degree. I made every effort in my power to change what appeared to me as both an incredibly wasteful and foolishly punitive system, but without avail. A majority of the department would put through some liberalizing change, only to have it negated by some new policy (all, of course, in the interest of "high standards"). In April 1963, I finally resigned from the department, retaining only my appointment in psychiatry. I felt I would be lacking in integrity to do otherwise. As persons, the members of the department constituted an interesting and often likeable lot. Collectively, they were destroying everything I valued in the development of scientists and practitioners (Rogers, 1972: 61).

In 1964 Richard Farson, a former student at the Counselling Centre who appears in the award-winning *Journey Into Self* (1968) as a co-facilitator with Rogers, pressed Rogers to join the Western Behavioral Science Institute (WBSI) in California. This was a new non-profit organization devoted to humanistically oriented research in interpersonal relations, on whose board Rogers had served as a director. With his work on schizophrenics completed, having had some success in cross-disciplinary education but having failed to facilitate the graduate learning process in clinical psychology at Wisconsin, Rogers decided to accept this invitation. He saw it as an opportunity to work with like-minded colleagues, and to turn his attention now to working with "normal" people. The vehicle for such work and study would be the encounter group, which Rogers had discovered while at Chicago, and which involved adapting his therapeutic approach ". . . to the facilitation of learning and the self-enhancement of the well-functioning person" (Rogers, 1972: 65). His book *Carl Rogers on Encounter Groups* (1970) outlines his theories of the process and dynamics of this method based on his experiences.

In 1968, with the resignation of Farson as Director of WBSI, the informal collegial climate of the organization changed and Rogers, along with several other staff members, founded the Centre for Studies of the Person (CSP) at La Jolla, California. We might note that when Rogers founded CSP, he was already 66. However, in a 1977 article he wrote that he considers only his Chicago period at the Counselling Centre as involving as much personal growth, although not as much personal satisfaction, as this one. With five books and forty papers published during the ten years *after* he turned 65, not to mention the lectures he gave, the group sessions he led and organized, and his continual study of and participation in professional issues, Rogers does not seem suited to retirement.

> I recognize that I have been unusually fortunate in my health, in my marriage, in my family, in my stimulating younger friends, in the unexpectedly adequate income from my books. So I am in no way typical. . . .
>
> As a boy I was rather sickly, and my parents have told me that it was predicted I would die young. This prediction has been proven completely wrong in one sense, but it has come profoundly true in another sense. I think it is correct that I will never live to be old. So now I agree with the prediction. I believe that I will die *young* (Rogers, 1980b: 16).

Rogers is an amazing man. He is a skilled and prolific writer, having produced more than a hundred articles and ten books in a fifty-year span. He is a philosopher, a scientist, an explorer, and a humanist. He has been powerfully influenced by Freud, Rank, Goldstein, Kierkegaard, Maslow, Perls, and others. Science and religion have deeply affected his own developing philosophy and life focus.

He appears to have been very much a fighter, "stubborn," as he says, suffering at times the loneliness and pain of one who forges his own way. At the same time Rogers is powerfully charismatic. He communicates integrity; he exudes warmth; he demonstrates genuineness, openness, and personal honesty. He appears somehow to characterize in his behaviour the essence of his approach, as one who is experiencing the joy of self-fulfillment and human encounter. He has continually reworked his ideas, theories, and methods for forty years, reflecting his openness to new experience. He has subjected his approach to rigorous scientific scrutiny and has faithfully communicated and shared his research and personal thoughts with others.

AIMS, BASIC ASSUMPTIONS, AND MAJOR CONCEPTS

With Rogers's work now spanning a fifty-year period, an examination of basic tenets and beliefs must necessarily reflect change in emphasis and direction while tracing the core aspects which have persisted. Let's first examine his approach at the midpoint in his work (1959). This was a relatively mature stage in his theoretical development, and although some changes in application have occurred, his basic assumptions have not altered significantly in the past twenty years.

As discussed in the introduction, then, we will examine the:

1. Rogerian theory of human growth and development (personality integration)
2. Rogerian theory of neurotic or maladaptive behaviour (personality disintegration)
3. Rogerian approach to therapy (personality re-integration); the goal of therapy; the conditions for the therapeutic process; and the characteristics of the fully functioning person.

Rogers's Theory of Human Growth and Development

We should remember that Rogers's personality theory emerged ex post facto from his clinical experience. He has had to work backwards, observing and experiencing the behaviour of his clients during the course of therapy from beginning to termination, and pull together the common features of their development. Here are the basic assumptions Rogers has held.

BASIC ASSUMPTIONS
1. Our *subjective* experience constitutes reality and it is this experience to which we respond regardless of its objective nature.
2. We are motivated or impelled by an inherent, solitary, primary drive to develop or actualize our potential to be what we are, fully and completely.
3. We interpret our experiences as either good or bad, good experiences being those which lead to our maintenance or enhancement, that is, our actualization; and bad experiences being those that do not.
4. We learn to approach "good" experiences and to avoid "bad" ones.
5. We are *aware* of our experiencing and therefore of ourselves.
6. Our self-awareness develops as we interact or relate to our environment and, in particular, with other people.

7. As our self-awareness increases during infancy and early childhood, we develop a *need* for positive regard from others. Positive regard is defined as warmth, liking, respect, sympathy, and acceptance. This need is reciprocal. That is, in satisfying the need for positive regard in others we may also elicit this response from them for ourselves.
8. The need for positive regard from others is of such significance to us and so powerful that we may choose to satisfy this need even when it means denying other basic needs essential for our maintenance and enhancement. Consider here our response to the loss of a person whose love was particularly important to us. We may be so profoundly distressed by our inability to have them satisfy this need that we become depressed and cease actualizing. On the other hand, recognition and acceptance from significant others may be so important to us that we attempt to be the kind of person they want us to be rather than the person we really are.
9. Positive regard from others results in the experiencing of self-regard. Our personal identity or sense of self develops from our experience of positive regard.
10. Self-regard may be experienced independently of any interaction with others. Once we have developed a personal identity, we can experience ourself as a person when we are alone.
11. When our self-experiences are interpreted by significant others as *more* or *less* worthy of positive regard, then our self-regard also becomes selective. That is, when other people evaluate our behaviour in terms of how deserving it is of their approval or respect, we begin to evaluate ourselves in terms of "goodness" and "badness."
12. When a self-experience is sought or avoided solely because it is valued either positively or negatively in terms of self-regard, we have learned what Rogers called "a condition of worth." In other words, whenever we do something or don't do something simply on the basis of how we believe it will affect our self-esteem or self-regard, we have learned that we are loved or prized for some things and not for others. These are *conditions* for receiving positive regard from others. When we behave in terms of these conditions, even to the point of evaluating ourselves on these terms, the locus of evaluation is *outside* of us and reflects the needs of others. *When we behave as others wish us to, we must deny the natural tendency we have to base our behaviour and experience on the maintenance and enhancement of ourselves, or the actualization of our potential.*
13. If we experienced, on the other hand, only *unconditional* positive regard, no conditions of worth would arise and self-regard would also be unconditional. Our basic need for positive regard, then, and our subsequent self-regard, would always be in *congruence* with our organismic tendency for self-actualization. The demands of our external and internal environments would be the same, and we would be psychologically normal, fully functioning, and self-actualizing.

We can see that Rogers's personality theory comprises a number of basic assumptions concerning the nature of reality (phenomenological) and the nature of the human organism (organismic), which build logically upon one another. Rogers's personality theory is strongly influenced by Goldstein's Organismic Psychology (see Chapter 4), earlier Gestalt Psychology, and a phenomenological and existential bias. In addition we may detect to a lesser extent some Freudian concepts, although they are not labelled as such, and even some behaviouristic material. The four most significant features of his personality theory from the perspective of therapy are:

1. The assumption that reality is subjective or at least that we behave in accordance with our *perception* of what exists. It doesn't matter, then, what is objectively true. If we wish to understand the client's problem, we have to understand how *he* sees it.
2. The assumption that we are motivated by a single, innate, primary drive to self-actualization. Implied here is the notion that we will automatically develop our potential under the "right" conditions. By establishing these conditions in therapy, the client will become self-actualizing. Thus the "non-directive" aspects of the Rogerian approach. The therapist does not have to tell the patient what to do, and need not advise or recommend or guide.
3. The assumption that we have a basic need to be unconditionally loved, accepted, wanted, and respected by other people. By giving this love in therapy, we can satisfy a basic human need. Thus there is a strong emphasis on relationship and the communication of therapist qualities of love, respect, genuineness, and empathy to the client.
4. The assumption that our self-concept and sense of personal worth is dependent upon the nature of the love, acceptance, and respect we experience from others. The client's self-concept can be changed by a therapeutic experience in which he experiences unconditional positive regard.

Rogerian Theory of Neurotic Behaviour

Rogers's analysis of the process underlying personality dis-integration involves three stages:

ISOLATION OF THE SELF-CONCEPT FROM EXPERIENCE
Because we need to experience self-worth, we begin very early in infancy to perceive our experiences in terms of the conditions of worth we have learned in our interaction with others. Experiences which reflect our conditions of worth we perceived *accurately,* and they may be eventually symbolized in awareness. That is, we may speak or think about them. But experiences which do not reflect conditions of worth are perceived *selectively* and may be distorted to con-

form to our conditions of worth. They may even be denied in part or whole to awareness. The result of this process of beginning to selectively experience our world, including ourselves, is that we cease to be the integrated organism which we are initially at birth. The most powerful expression of this split in experiencing and self-concept can be seen in the two-year-old child who periodically demonstrates depersonalization when he speaks about himself in the third person. This rarely occurs when the behaviour or experience of the child reflects conditions of worth, but may occur when it does not. For example, a child who has wet his pants may come to his mother saying, "John wet his pants." By using his own name, "John," he seems to disown the behaviour and experience, thus retaining his self-regard.

The implications of this process are substantial, as Rogers states (1959: 226):

> From this point on his concept of self includes distorted perceptions which do not accurately represent his experience, and his experience includes elements which are not included in the picture he has of himself. Thus, he can no longer live as a unified whole person.... Behaviour is regulated at times by the self and at times by these aspects of the organism's experience which are not included in the self....
>
> This, as we see it, is the basic estrangement in man. He has not been true to himself, to his own natural organismic valuing of experience, but for the sake of preserving the positive regard of others has now come to falsify some of the values he experiences and to perceive them only in terms based upon their value to others. Yet this has not been a conscious choice, but a natural—and tragic—development in infancy.

The estrangement from ourselves which impedes our ability for true self-direction occurs in infancy, not by choice, but as a natural consequence of a child-rearing tradition in which unconditional positive regard is unlikely, if not impossible! Are we all a little "disturbed," then? Rogers claims we are, and he is not alone in this perception. We shall find close theoretical parallels in the work of Perls, Janov, Ellis, and Berne.

DISCREPANCY BETWEEN SELF-CONCEPT AND BEHAVIOUR
In a similar fashion to the process described above in which the self and experience become dis-integrated, we also disconnect our *behaviour* from our selves. So long as behaviour is consistent with the self-concept, it is accurately symbolized in awareness. That is, we are fully aware of it and can speak and think about it. But some of our behaviours maintain, enhance, and actualize aspects of our experience or self which are not part of our self-concept. This is behaviour which, while unacceptable to significant others, does reflect our essential nature or organic self. These behaviours, as a result, may not be perceived as self-experiences, or are perceived in a distorted or selective manner such that they may be considered acceptable and therefore a part of the self-concept.

THREAT AND DEFENSE MECHANISMS

Obviously, we cannot on the one hand behave or experience in such a way so as to satisfy our need for self-regard while at the same time actualizing, maintaining, and enhancing aspects of our experience or self which are either absent from, or in contrast to, our self-concept, without some difficulty. We cannot be in two "places" at the same time. In such situations, we feel uncomfortable. Rogers calls such experiences "threatening." The nature of the threat is that if the experience were symbolized in awareness we would discover we were not the person we would like to be, or think we are. We would recognize that we would not be deserving of others' approval or respect and would therefore be unable to satisfy our need for positive regard and self-regard. We would then experience *anxiety* and fear rather than a vague sense of discomfort. The sense or feeling of concern, however, prevents this anxiety reaction. (You may wish to review Goldstein's comments on anxiety in Chapter 4 in this regard.) Remember that anxiety is a crippling and disorganizing emotion—it prevents either attack or defense.

The defense which the sense of threat does stimulate is designed to prevent the debilitating effects of anxiety and disorganization. Upon sensing threat, we begin to *selectively* perceive or distort our experience in such a way that our awareness of it conforms to our self-concept and our conditions of worth. As a consequence of employing such defense, our experiences, behaviour, and perceptions become more rigid and our perception of reality distorted.

SUMMARY

Personality dis-integration begins in infancy and is characteristic of our society. It occurs because our basic need for love and approval from others is satisfied only conditionally rather than unconditionally. To obtain love and approval, we try to become the person others would like rather than the person we are. But we can never completely eliminate the real person we are and our innate tendency to maintain, enhance, and actualize our basic nature or being. Thus, we experience a continual tension and function inadequately, in a state of disunity and disharmony. The *discrepancies* between what we are and what we must be in order to receive love and approval would create disorganizing anxiety *if we were aware of them*. We are prevented from experiencing anxiety by sensing these discrepancies as *threatening* and preventing awareness through denial or distortion of both the experience and of reality. Various defense mechanisms are employed for this purpose.

Well, if we are characterized by dis-integration and internal disunity, how might we become whole again? How do we regain our focus and unfetter our innate tendency to self-actualization? Here is Rogers's answer (1959: 226):

> The path of development toward psychological maturity, the path of therapy, is the undoing of this estrangement in man's functioning, the dissolving of conditions of worth, the achievement of a self which is congruent with experience, and the restoration of a unified organismic valuing process as the regulator of behaviour.

The Rogerian Approach to Therapy

THE GOAL OF THERAPY
The goal of the Rogerian approach to therapy is to release an already existing capacity for self-actualization in a potentially competent individual.

THE UNDERLYING ASSUMPTIONS
The basic assumptions underlying the Rogerian approach to therapy are:

1. The individual has the capacity to guide, regulate, direct, and control himself providing that certain conditions exist. Only in the absence of these conditions is it necessary to provide external control and regulation of the individual.
2. The individual has the potential to understand what it is in his life that is related to his distress and anxiety.
3. The individual has the potential to re-organize himself in such a way as to not only eliminate his distress and anxiety, but to experience self-fulfillment and happiness.
4. The individual's potential for self-actualization will be experienced in any interpersonal relationship in which the other person is congruent during the relationship, experiences unconditional positive regard toward, and empathic understanding of, the individual; and is successful in communicating some of these qualities to the individual.

THE CONDITIONS OF THERAPY
Because the client himself already possesses the capacity for self-actualization, the role of the therapist is merely that of facilitating the client's natural tendency for growth by creating an environment or conditions in which this tendency may emerge. These conditions are both *necessary* and *sufficient* for constructive personality change to occur. The therapist does not do anything *to* the client. She merely creates a situation in which the client's own growth tendency may re-emerge and become self-directing.

Rogers (1959: 213) listed the following elements as both necessary and sufficient for therapy regardless of the characteristics of the client:

1. That two persons are in *contact*.
2. That the first person, whom we shall term the client, is in a state of *incongruence*, being *vulnerable*, or *anxious*.
3. That the second person, whom we shall term the therapist, is congruent in the *relationship*.
4. That the therapist is *experiencing unconditional positive regard* toward the client.
5. That the therapist is *experiencing* an *empathic* understanding of the client's *internal frame of reference*.
6. That the client *perceives,* at least to a minimal degree, conditions 4 and 5,

the *unconditional positive regard* of the therapist for him, and the *empathic* understanding of the therapist.

The term "experiencing" which appears in conditions 4 and 5 means the reception by the therapist of whatever sensory or physiological events are impinging upon her from within and without at that moment. It suggests not merely an intellectual or cognitive assessment or appreciation of the situation, but rather a total involvement of herself in the situation. Rogers's subsequent comments seem to suggest that the most important quality of the therapist is that of congruence or wholeness herself as a person. However, for therapy to be effective, part of this congruence must be the therapist's ability to experience unconditional positive regard and empathic understanding in the relationship. This latter point is also emphasized. It is expected that the therapist may not be completely congruent or whole at all times. This is likely impossible. But if she can at least be congruent, be completely and fully herself in her relationship with the *client*, she can be of therapeutic assistance.

THE PROCESS OF THERAPY

Rogers described the following typical client responses to the preceding set of conditions for therapy:

1. The client gradually becomes more free to express his *feelings* both verbally and with body language.
2. His expressed feelings increasingly refer to himself.
3. He becomes more adept at describing and defining the sources of his feelings and perceptions.
4. His expressed feelings increasingly refer to the disparity between his concept of himself and his actual experiences.
5. He begins to experience and be aware of the threat involved in this awareness.
6. He begins to experience fully, in awareness, feelings which have in the past been denied awareness or have been distorted.
7. He begins to reorganize and reconsider his self-concept such that previously denied or distorted experiences are integrated and assimilated.
8. As his self-concept continues to be reorganized and expanded, he is able to include new experiences which previously would have been too threatening to reach awareness. He becomes less defensive.
9. He becomes increasingly able to experience the therapist's unconditional positive regard without feeling threatened.
10. He begins to feel an unconditional positive *self-regard*.
11. He begins to experience himself as the centre of evaluation.
12. He reacts to experience more in terms of what it means to his own self-actualization and less in terms of conditions of worth set by others.

Thus, during and following therapy the client should become *less:* defensive, vulnerable to threat, tense, and anxious; and *more:* realistic and objective, effective in problem solving, able to risk new experience, congruent, self-confident, accepting of others, open, in control of his behaviour, mature, creative, adaptive, expressive, and positively self-regarding.

FORTY YEARS OF ROGERIAN THERAPY

Hart and Tomlinson (1970) suggested that Rogerian Therapy evolved during thirty years of practice and research and really comprised three different approaches with distinct characteristics. The early stage (1940-50) they termed *non-directive* therapy; the middle period (1950-57), *reflective* therapy; and the final stage (1957-70), *experiential* therapy. Although these periods or stages may be somewhat arbitrary and ideal, they do assist us to better understand Rogerian theory and therapy.

Non-Directive Therapy (1940-50)

In the early stages, the goal of Rogerian Therapy was the client's gradual achievement of insight into his behaviour and situation (as in psychoanalysis). The role of the therapist was to facilitate the emergence of insight through the creation of a permissive, non-authoritarian situation in which the client could gradually explore his problem at his own pace. The acceptance of the client by the therapist and the avoidance of therapist interpretations of client behaviour was intended to enable the client to decrease his defensive behaviour so that he could become aware of his problems and conflicts. The therapist's active interventions were directed toward helping the client to experience his thoughts and perceptions more clearly and accurately. Here is an example of the early non-directive style (Hart and Tomlinson, 1970: 6-7):

Client:	I don't know how, though—I think they'll work out pretty well. Darned if I can make it out (looking at his notes). (Pause) Oh, that had to do with a girl I got to talking to! She said she hoped that there would not be a strip-tease to the floor show, and I was trying to analyze why she objected to it. I guess maybe she didn't want any competition. Either she would feel that the girl would be superior to her, or she had secret desires in that direction which she could condemn in someone else but not in herself.
Therapist:	Doing a little evaluating of others' motives as well as your own, hmm?
Client:	Oh, yes. I've always done that. Well, I've always analyzed others perhaps a little bit more than myself. (Pause.) Well, to sum all this up; I think I should seek out every and all healthy situations and enter into them. I noticed a curious thing. When I made a resolve that I would take the hard way, and even though it might be the long way too, although I made the resolve in a vacuum, I got a release (laugh) so that way back in the last

	analysis, one experiences only one's own nervous system, so that it seems to be the resolve that counts, but at the same time that resolve does have to be nourished by the outward situations. And I suppose once in a while a person can resolve in a vacuum when they really sincerely mean it, but it's too hard to keep meaning it in a vacuum.
Therapist:	And also, as you pointed out before, perhaps your earlier notion of doing something in a vacuum was really not too much a desire to make a resolve, but more a desire to get away from making a resolve.
Client:	M-hm. Well, there's all sorts of masks. (Pause.) What do you think of my prescription? Do you care to add anything to that?
Therapist:	No, I think that—well, we might be able to add details to it, but I think that that is the prescription that really will count toward more long-time satisfactions. I think you're right—it may be a hard road, may be a long road. But—at least it's the only road. It's a road that you feel pretty well convinced now offers more satisfactions in the long run than in the other direction (Rogers, 1942: 411-12).

Reflective Therapy† (1950-57)

Although the therapist continued to create a non-threatening atmosphere in which the client could explore his conflicts and problems, the major difference in the second stage was in the therapist's focusing attention on the *feelings* being expressed by the client rather than on the *content* of his verbalizations. Instead of concentrating on *what* the client was saying, the emphasis was on sensitively *reflecting* the *feeling* aspects of the client's communications. Hart and Tomlinson (1970: 8), quote from Rogers in describing the therapist's role in this stage and provide the following example:

> . . . Counsellor participation becomes an active experiencing with the client of the feelings to which he gives expression. The counsellor makes a maximum effort to get under the skin of the person with whom he is communicating, he tries to get within and to live the attitudes expressed instead of observing them, to catch every nuance of their changing nature; in a word, to absorb himself completely in the attitudes of the client. And in struggling to do this, there is simply no room for any other counsellor activity or attitude; if he is attempting to live the attitudes of the other, he cannot be diagnosing them, he cannot be thinking of making the process go faster. Because he is another, and not the

---

† If the term "Rogerian" is used to encompass all three stages, then a more appropriate term for the second stage would be "client-centred" rather than "reflective." The use of the term "client-centred" to describe Rogers's overall approach is misleading; note the active involvement of the therapist in the third stage.

client, the understanding is not spontaneous but must be acquired, and this through the most intense, continuous, and active attention to the feelings of the other, to the exclusion of other types of attention (as quoted in Rogers, 1951: 29).

Therapist: That catches a little more of the flavour of the feeling, that is, it's almost as if you're really weeping for yourself. . . .

Client: And then of course, I've come . . . to see and to feel that over this, see, I've covered it up. (Weepy). But . . . and . . . I've covered it up with so much *bitterness,* which in turn I had to cover up. (Weeps.) That's what I want to get rid of! I almost don't *care* if I hurt.

Therapist: (Gently.) You feel that here at the basis of it, as you experienced it, is a feeling of real tears for yourself. But that you *can't* show, mustn't show, so that's been covered by bitterness that you don't like, that you'd like to be rid of. You almost feel you'd rather absorb the hurt than to . . . than to feel the bitterness. (Pause.) And what you seem to be saying quite strongly is "I do *hurt* and I've tried to cover it up."

Client: I didn't *know* it.

Therapist: M-hm. Like a new discovery really.

Client: (Speaking at the same time.) I never really did know. But it's . . . you know, it's almost a physical thing. It's . . . it's sort of as though I−I−I were looking within myself at all kinds of nerve endings and−and bits of, of . . . things that have been sort of mashed. (Weepy).

Therapist: As though some of the most delicate aspects of you−physically almost−have been crushed or hurt.

Client: Yes, and you know, I do get the feeling, oh, you poor thing. (Pause.)

Therapist: Just can't but feel very deeply sorry for the person that is you (Rogers and Dymond, 1954: 326-27).

Experiential Therapy (1957-70)

Hart and Tomlinson (1970) suggested that at the time of their writing the experiential stage was still in process. This stage grew partly from a general shift by Rogerian therapists away from using specific techniques for reflecting feeling and partly from the failure of the reflective or client-centred approach to work effectively with either schizophrenic clients or with well adjusted "normal" clients. It had been reasonably well demonstrated by this time that so long as the six major conditions for constructive personality change existed, *how* the therapist communicated her essential therapeutic personality traits (see Chapter 1) was not important. There was a move therefore toward greater openness on the part of the therapist directed toward the "experiencing" of both the client and herself and their relationship.

The term "experiencing" is defined by Hart and Tomlinson (1970: 11) as:

> . . . the apperceptive mass of the individual's subjective life, the implicitly felt and directly known inner sense that is the source of personal meanings. It is a process of internal sensing rather than a something.

This concept is similar to what Gestalt Therapy calls "awareness" and what existential therapists would call "being." Here is an example of an experiential therapy client-therapist exchange (Hart and Tomlinson, 1970: 14-16):

> I found GET in the dayroom and she joined me with such dejected heaviness that I found myself having to pull within myself to dig for some reserve strength. Neither of us talked as we went down the stairs and through the tunnel. GET walked with what seemed like sagging hopelessness. I walked with dread of the hour ahead because my own loneliness now seemed small compared to hers and I felt inadequate to help or comfort her.
>
> . . . I sat with all these feelings and found the silence soothing. My fear lessened as I let in the quietness, but my pain grew with a new wanting to reach out somehow to GET who sat so close and yet seemed so far off and shut away inside her loneliness. I felt so unalone in my loneliness and I wanted to share that unaloneness with her somehow. I looked at her downcast face and hoped that she would look up. I don't know how long I sat there looking at her before I broke the silence . . .
>
> (After 15 minutes of silence)
> Therapist: You look as though you felt very much alone . . .
> Client: (No response).
>   (After several minutes of silence)
> Therapist: When I say *alone* rather than *lonely* I mean more than lonely . . . as though you were so lonely that you can't bear to tell anybody how lonely you are . . .
> Client: Hm-mm.
> Therapist: So it makes you all alone in it.
> Client: Course it don't help it any either.
> Therapist: It's awfully hard to reach out of loneliness sometimes . . . I don't quite know what you meant but . . . if you feel as though people don't want to hear or don't care . . .
> Client: No . . . Nn-nn . . . It seems like everybody has got an ear but I don't have no words to say . . . nothing to say . . .
> Therapist: You mean you feel you don't have anything to *offer* anyone?
> Client: Hm-mm . . .
>   (Silence for 2-3 minutes.)
> Therapist: I guess what I'm trying to say is you don't have to offer or be able to give anything . . . just sit with it and it may feel less alone . . . I think sometimes it's awfully hard to find words to say how . . . I guess I'll put it: I sometimes find it hard to find words to say how low I feel when I'm low . . . so that I can't

	reach out to somebody who might be able to understand . . . but . . . sometimes it helps just to sit with somebody I know would understand if I could talk about it . . . especially somebody who doesn't ask "What's the matter? How do you feel? What do you . . . ." when I just plain feel like crying for no reason . . . just sit . . . So I'll shut up . . . All I'm trying to say is I *care* . . . I care and I'm sorry everything is so hard for you now.
Client:	It isn't so bad . . . it's better than it used to be.
Therapist:	The sun isn't exactly shining through is it? (This is a reference to an earlier interview when GET told me that her mother once complained that she, GET, always expected the sun to shine on her.)
Client:	Last week it just seemed that I had something to say every minute we were down here . . . and today . . . nothing . . . I'm trying to find . . . can't remember what we talked about . . .
Therapist:	I do . . . You were thinking about the future . . . What you'd like to do . . . You were doing some very realistic, very honest thinking about what you might be able to do . . . and ended up getting yourself pretty discouraged.
Client:	I still think that I'd kinda like to be a lady boxer . . . because I've got the temper for it I think . . . It seems like I'm always angry . . .
(Silence for 3-4 minutes)	
Therapist:	"It seems to me like I'm always angry". . . . It seems to me like I'm angry when everything seems too hard . . . when I can't find sunlight . . . when I wish somebody would take care of me . . . when everything seems to go wrong . . . and when I get feeling very *alone* with that whole dark picture . . . I think you've felt alone for some 20 years. . . .

Note the difference here in the role of the therapist from that of the first two periods: the therapist does not clarify or reflect, but rather tries to *experience* the feelings of the client and express to the client what these feelings seem to be as well as showing feelings the therapist herself is experiencing.

Throughout the three stages of Rogerian Therapy, therapist goals and roles have changed to reflect the increasing significance of therapist genuineness or congruence to the therapeutic relationship and process. Figure 5·1, following the schema presented by Hart and Tomlinson (1970: 4), highlights the major features of the three stages.

Rogerian Therapy Since 1970

Rogerian theory seems to have changed very little in the past twenty years. Rogers (1977) has maintained the essential elements of both his 1959 therapeutic

FIGURE 5·1
The Three Stages of Rogerian Therapy

Therapy	Therapist Goals	Therapist Roles
Non-Directive —cognitive orientation (insight) 1940-50	1. Creation of a permissive atmosphere 2. Acceptance of client 3. Non-interpretive 4. Help clarify for client his thoughts & feelings 5. Help patient develop insight (knowledge) *about* self	1. Listen to what is said—passive 2. Non-judgmental 3. Empathic 4. Warm 5. "Soft" 6. Non-confronting 7. Non-sharing of self 8. Feedback objective—rephrasing, repeating, clarifying, questioning *what* is said

Client-Centred or Reflective
—emotional orientation
(self-concept)
1950-57
	1. Development of conditions necessary and sufficient for constructive personality change
	  a. Empathic understanding of client's inner feelings—attitudes
	  b. Demonstration of unconditional positive regard
	  c. Demonstration of genuineness
	  d. Communication of a, b, and c to client
		1. Empathic understanding of client's thoughts & feelings
		2. Soft, warm
		3. Listens actively
		4. Non-confronting
		5. Sharing self
		6. Non-interpretive
		7. Feedback is subjective indicating how therapist believes client *feels*

Experiential —existential/encounter orientation (humanistic) 1957-70	1. Establishing a therapeutic relationship 2. Reflecting patient experiencing 3. Expressing therapist experiencing 4. Patient growth as a unique individual and as a group member	1. Empathic, understanding 2. Listening actively 3. Confronting 4. Sharing as authentic friendship 5. Interpreting if appropriate 6. Feedback is subjective 7. Non-technique-oriented 8. Prizing, loving, caring

and personality theories. The six necessary and sufficient conditions for constructive personality change or growth remain, with greater attention now paid to a larger number of therapist personal qualities: genuineness, respect, empathy, concreteness, self-disclosure, immediacy, confrontation, warmth, and self-actualization. Research evidence, as we saw in Chapter 1, has confirmed the therapeutic importance of all of them.

There are three additional areas in which Rogerian Therapy *has* developed further during the past ten years. Two of these relate to applications of the

Rogerian approach and the other to the theory itself. We referred earlier to Rogers's recent interest in and commitment to social action and social reform. We see this activity in his more recent writing (1977, 1980a, 1980b, 1980c) and in his involvement in encounter group* experiences, as opposed to individual client therapy, since 1970. Here is part of an interview with John Wood (1972: 20):

> Wood: If you were 17 today and in high school, how do you think you would be behaving?
>
> Rogers: I would very likely be a social activist of one kind or another: quite a rebel, I guess. . . . I would be far more rebellious toward education than I was. I would realize how stupid most "education" is. I think I would be a drop-out from conventional education—headed toward an experimental school of some sort.
>
> . . .
>
> Wood: What is the burning social issue for you now?
>
> Rogers: The war. I feel so strongly about that. I think we'll look back on this period in our history as one of the most shameful we've been through—unless we pass all the way through to a military dictatorship, which is not impossible. Then history will be completely re-written. It all goes against everything in me.†

His recent book *Carl Rogers On Personal Power* (1977) further indicates his political stance and a developed rationale for viewing participatory democratic principles as fundamental to the development and fulfillment of human potential. At this time he appears more optimistic:

> I don't know of any political party or government which operates fully on this basis, but I do believe there is a movement toward more participation in government and a growing distrust of authoritarian institutions of every kind. So I do not despair (Rogers, 1980a: 9).

The third interesting theoretical development is his recent discussion (1977) of the actualizing tendency from a biological and organismic perspective. It is interesting because while it is valid and appropriate that he should buttress his psychological theory of human growth and development with a biological base, he is late in so doing. With this addition, an important one, Rogers's theory of human growth and behaviour resembles very closely those of Fritz Perls and Eric Berne, and is compatible with the more recent physiological theories of Arthur Janov and William Glasser.

---

* Appendix A to this chapter describes the theory and process of the encounter group relying largely on his work *Carl Rogers On Encounter Groups* (1970).

† It is interesting that Perls expressed the same concern in 1966, believing the U.S.A. on the brink of fascism. And as we enter the eighties, we note a definite swing to the political right in the bastions of liberal democracy: the U.S.A., Britain, and even Canada.

SUMMARY

The following statement nicely summarizes Rogers's theory of the therapeutic process and the role of the therapist:

> If I can create a relationship characterized on my part: by a genuineness and transparency, in which I am my real feelings; by a warm acceptance of and prizing of the other person as a separate individual; by a sensitive ability to see his world and himself as he sees them; then the other individual in the relationship: will experience and understand aspects of himself which previously he has repressed; will find himself becoming better integrated, more able to function effectively; will become more similar to the person he would like to be; will be more self-directing and self-confident; will become more of a person, more unique and more self-expressive; will be more understanding, more acceptant of others; will be able to cope with the problems of life more adequately and more comfortably.
>
> I believe that this statement holds whether I am speaking of my relationship with a client, with a group of students or staff members, with my family or children. It seems to me that we have here a general hypothesis which offers exciting possibilities for the development of creative, adaptive, autonomous persons (Rogers, 1961: 37-38).

APPENDIX A

Intensive Group Experience

Encounter is a way of learning about oneself through feedback from others.
—Carl R. Rogers, 1969

ORIGINS

It is interesting that the intense group experience we often refer to as *encounter*, and may have come to think of as an extreme, almost cult-like, procedure, originated not as a therapeutic device, but as a means for improving industrial productivity and management effectiveness. The techniques and process have been refined and improved since their introduction thirty years ago, and we now find encounter group methods employed for a variety of purposes, including traditional group therapy, organizational development, sensitivity training, human relations training, marriage counselling, pastoral counselling and religious experience, and group conflict resolution. It is potentially a powerful means of *initiating* personality and value change in a very short time, usually three to five days.

The encounter or T-group experience began with Carl Rogers in 1946 and Kurt Lewin in 1947, independently, but for much the same reasons. Both were attempting to meet the need for human relations skills in business, industry and government. There had developed during World War II considerable interest in troop and worker morale which led to high productivity and effectiveness. The end of the war created new problems of returning a wartime economy to peace, and of reintegrating soldiers into that economy. There was the need to restructure large complex organizations, and to retrain hundreds of thousands of soldiers and workers.

In 1947 Kurt Lewin, then at Massachusetts Institute of Technology, set up a summer human relations training program for managers at Bethel, Maine. The term "T-group" comes from these early *training* groups. This program grew in size and scope and is now the well-known National Training Laboratories (N.T.L.) located in Washington, D.C.

THE GOAL OF INTENSIVE GROUP EXPERIENCE

Lewin discovered that the individuals who came away from their work and homes and spent a few weeks at Bethel, Maine to learn about human relations —or be *trained* in human relations—were deeply affected by these sessions. In a short time, those attending the sessions developed strong feelings for one another, with trust and caring characterizing their relationship. It is important to remember that this was not the original objective of these early sessions. This "group thing" occurred spontaneously, and only after it had occurred several times did Lewin and his associates begin to appreciate and explore this phenomenon as an important factor in itself.

Charlotte Bühler described these experiences thus:

> In the so called T-group one met relatively normal persons who, in their interaction, discovered their own and other people's weaknesses, strengths, and humanness.*

At the same time, a similar experience with intensive group process was occurring at the University of Chicago. It was between 1946 and 1947 that Rogers's Counselling Centre at Chicago had become involved in retraining D.V.A. counsellors to help them cope with the flood of returning soldiers. Unlike Lewin, Rogers consciously decided to use intensive group experience and to use it for the kind of result Lewin had stumbled on. Rogers hoped that the intensive group experience would get at attitudes from an emotional and

---

*Charlotte Bühler, "Humanistic Psychology as a Personal Experience," *Journal of Humanistic Psychology* 19 (1979): 5-22.

experiential rather than cognitive perspective. He wanted people to feel certain things which would help them change attitudes that might be self-defeating in a counselling relationship, and he wanted them to feel and change quickly. The system worked so well with the D.V.A. counsellors that he began a series of summer workshops for those interested in such an experience.

Thus, even though Lewin and Rogers had different purposes, the intensive group experience resulted in much the same kind of interpersonal experience for the groups involved. Thus was the encounter group discovered. We find in intensive group theory, then, a mixture of Lewinian thinking, Gestalt psychology, and Rogerian Therapy.

BASIC ASSUMPTIONS AND MAJOR CONCEPTS

Rogers (1970) lists eight hypotheses he claims are shared by methods which employ intensive group process:

1. Climate of Safety
   A facilitator can develop in a group which meets intensively a psychological climate of safety in which freedom of expression and reduction of defensiveness gradually occur.
2. Expression of immediate feeling reactions
   In such a climate many of the immediate feeling reactions of each member toward others and toward oneself tend to be expressed.
3. Mutual trust
   This safety to express real feelings, positive and negative, results in a climate of mutual trust with each member moving toward greater acceptance of his total being, emotional, intellectual, and physical, as it is, including its potential.
4. Change in attitudes and behaviour
   With less need to maintain rigid defenses, new approaches and risks can be taken which result in the possibility of changed professional methods, administrative styles, interpersonal relationships, etc.
5. Understanding and openness
   With reduction in defenses, people begin to listen more to what others say, hear more, and understand others better.
6. Feedback
   A climate of openness and listening enables one to attend to feedback and learn how one appears to others and what one's impact is in interpersonal relationships.
7. Innovation, change, and risk are possible
   With improved freedom to be, communication with others is better, and risking new ideas, concepts, and directions is facilitated, encouraged, and possible, and not seen as a threat.

8. Transfer
   Experiences in the group tend to be carried over into other situations such as work, family, and social.

THE ROLE OF THE GROUP FACILITATOR

Rogers (1970: 46-48) describes the role of the group facilitator as follows:

> I tend to open a group in an extremely unstructured way, perhaps with no more than a simple comment: "I suspect we will know each other a great deal better at the end of these group sessions than we do now," or "Here we are. We can make of this group experience exactly what we wish," or "I'm a little uneasy, but I feel somewhat reassured when I look around at you and realize we're all in the same boat. Where do we start?" In a recorded discussion with a group of other facilitators I stated this view as follows:

> Partly because I do trust the group, I can usually be quite loose and relaxed in a group even from the first. That's overstating it somewhat, for I always feel a little anxiety when a group starts but by and large I feel, "I don't have any idea what's going to happen, but I think what's going to happen will be all right," and I think I tend to communicate non-verbally, "Well, none of us seem to know what's going to happen, but it doesn't seem to be something to worry about." I believe that my relaxation and lack of any desire to guide may have a freeing influence on others.

> I listen as carefully, accurately, and sensitively as I am able, to each individual who expresses himself. Whether the utterance is superficial or significant, I listen. To me the individual who speaks is worthwhile, worth understanding; consequently he is worthwhile for having expressed something. Colleagues say that in this sense I "validate" the person.

> There is no doubt that I am selective in my listening, hence "directive" if people wish to accuse me of this. I am centred in the group member who is speaking, and am unquestionably much less interested in the details of his quarrel with his wife, or of his difficulties on the job, or his disagreement with what has just been said, than in the meaning these experiences have for him now and the feelings they arouse in him. It is to these meanings and feelings that I try to respond.

> I wish very much to make the climate psychologically safe for the individual. I want him to feel from the first that if he risks saying something highly personal, or absurd, or hostile, or cynical, there will be at least one person in the circle who respects him enough to hear him clearly and listen to that statement as an authentic expression of himself.

> There is a slightly different way in which I also want to make the climate safe

for the member. I am well aware that one cannot make the experience safe from the pain of new insight or growth, or the pain of honest feedback from others. However, I would like the individual to feel that whatever happens to him or within him, I will be psychologically very much with him in moments of pain or joy, or the combination of the two which is such a frequent mark of growth. I think I can usually sense when a participant is frightened or hurting, and it is at those moments that I give him some sign, verbal or nonverbal, that I perceive this and am a companion to him as he lives in that hurt or fear.

INTENSIVE GROUP PROCESS DYNAMICS

Rogers (1970) describes fifteen stages which the intensive group experiences and through which they appear to progress chronologically.

1. Milling around
   This describes the initial stage of disorganization, confusion, and perhaps mutual embarrassment or discomfort of group members at their first meetings.
2. Resistance to personal expression or exploration
   Even when personal attitudes are expressed the group does not pick up or facilitate.
3. Description of past feelings
   Even with the ambivalence of the group in risking feelings, some expression of feelings does begin to occur, but of past events.
4. Expression of negative feelings
   The first expression of here and now feelings are negative.
5. Expression and exploration of personally meaningful material
   After negative feelings are expressed someone in the group breaks the ice and reveals himself in a significant way.
6. Expression of immediate interpersonal feelings in group
   Members finally begin to express immediate feelings toward another member of the group. These may be positive or negative.
7. Development of a healing capacity of the group
   Members begin to show a helpful, facilitating role in dealing with the suffering of others.
8. Self-acceptance and beginning of change
   Members begin to recognize and/or freely state who they are and what they are doing. "I am hurt." "I do like to mold people."
9. Cracking of facades
   Polite words disappear, and the group moves beyond mere intellectual understanding. The expression of self by some indicates that basic encounter is possible. The group members begin to demand realness from one another.

10. Feedback
    Members get rapid and instant feedback from others as to how they are perceived and what responses they produce—positive and negative.
11. Confrontation
    Group members "level" with one another and give direct and genuine feedback.
12. Helping others outside the group
    Dyads outside the group develop intensity and sharing.
13. Basic encounter
    With their own tears, laughter, embarrassment, and anger, group members begin to demonstrate an experiencing and sharing of the feelings of other group members.
14. Expression of positive feelings and closeness
    Members express feelings of warmth and love openly.
15. Behaviour changes in the group
    Group members demonstrate changes in their gestures, tone of voice, attitudes, and values at the end of the process, becoming more spontaneous, open, and caring than they were at the beginning.

SUMMARY

The intensive group experience has been demonstrated to be a powerful method for *initiating* individual, group, organizational, and even religious and social-political change. It is essentially a technique which, as Bühler described, enables people to discover their own and other people's strengths, weaknesses, and humanness. It suggests that when we are able to be the people we really are with others, we not only discover our similarity, but also find we like ourselves and others more as they really are, and can communicate with them more effectively. Conflict and misunderstanding are replaced in such situations by cooperation, tolerance, and mutual respect. The individual seems to become more authentic, self-directing, creative, and happy.

At the same time, there are cautions. The intensive group experience may be perverted and distorted such that the members are manipulated and controlled by *leaders* rather than facilitators, who seek to strengthen and convert members to a value system which is external to the group member. Whenever intensive group experience is used or sponsored by a socio-political or religious organization it is suspect.

Note that the term "initiated" has been used to describe the personality or value changes which may occur with intensive group process. This is perhaps the most serious criticism of the technique. While lasting changes *may* occur as a result of a brief encounter group experience, they do so because the group member is able to integrate these changes into his lifestyle when he leaves the group and returns to his family, friends, and work situation. This reintegration process may be very difficult for the member on his own because his everyday relationships and experiences are not those of the encounter group. Thus, some group members may seek individual or group therapy subsequently in order to bolster their initial efforts at personal growth. Others may periodically seek an intensive group experience in order to "recharge" and therefore at least maintain their growth pattern. Some may not be as successful, and without the support of the group they will slip back to their pregroup status.

Thus, while certain cautions and criticisms must be expressed, the potential benefits of this process, particularly in the area of conflict resolution among racial, ethnic, or national and political groups, suggest that it should be used more widely.

6
Gestalt Therapy

> ... the principles of Gestalt therapy are coherent conclusions based on the observations of one's own behaviour and the behaviour of others. In our case, the central conclusions have to do with Gestalt (or figure) formation, contact and the contact boundary. The therapy consists of bringing to awareness the ways in which the client keeps Gestalts from forming freely, and its aim is creative, aware behaviour, forming figures of grace, beauty, coherence, richness and liveliness out of the world that exists in—and outside us.
>
> —Dr. Joel Latner, *Subject To Change*, Vol. 4, no. 1 (1982): Gestalt Institute of Toronto.

The significance and importance of the work of Frederick Solomon (Fritz) Perls to the theory and practice of contemporary psychotherapy seems somehow to have eluded both the academic and professional communities directly affected. This is not to suggest that Perls has been ignored, but rather that attention to, if not acceptance and recognition of, his ideas and contributions seems to have been slow in coming. Certainly Perls's early paper (1948) in the second issue of the new *American Journal of Psychotherapy* could have been improved in presentation or format, even perhaps in organization; but the concepts and discussion reflect brilliance and competence. It is possible, of course, that Perls's insightful material, then a decade or two in advance of his field, either went unnoticed or was not clearly understood by his contemporaries. Perls's significance, however, does not reside merely in the fact that he was ahead of his time. For Gestalt Therapy reflects as well an appreciation and conscious integration of the essential concerns of the five major schools of psychology not apparent in any other contemporary therapeutic approach. Not only does Perls's therapeutic process and technique follow directly and logically from his theories of personality and neurosis, they elicit too an immediate and intense encounter between patient and therapist in their pursuit of growth and well-being. Let's turn now to a look at Fritz Perls, the originator of Gestalt Therapy.

FRITZ PERLS (1893-1970)

Gestalt Therapy's goals of personality integration, wholeness, and self-realization are reflected in Perls's own lifelong struggle to pull *himself* together and experience full integration and development of his potential. His personal life was characterized by a continuing series of unusually significant events and encounters which, while potentially enriching, were often disorienting and unsatisfying. They provided the substance for his subsequent theory and practice. In order to highlight these events, they will be noted as such in the discussion that follows. We are fortunate in having two substantive sources of biographical data on Perls: the autobiographical statement *In and Out of the Garbage Pail* (1968), and Martin Shepard's intriguing biography, *Fritz* (1976). Walt Anderson's "Fritz Perls Revisited" (1973) provides some additional material.

Perls was born on July 8, 1893 in Berlin. Germany at the time of the Kaiser was composed of a rigid social system and class structure dominated by Victorian manners and classical concepts of education and culture. It was a time of fierce competition among the powerful middle-class industrial, merchant, and banking interests and heralded the decline of colonialism and with it, heightened international political tension. German society was about to enter a period of immense social and technological change for which it was unprepared.

Perls began life in a middle-class Jewish ghetto. He had two sisters, one three years his senior who had a sight defect from birth and whom he never liked, and another a year and a half older than himself who was a childhood playmate and with whom he was close. He had a good relationship with his mother but a bad one with his father. His father, a travelling wine salesman, was an arrogant Don Juan figure who had little time for his wife and family and appeared to resent their dependency and restrictions. As Perls's parents grew older, their marriage grew worse, but because they regarded divorce or separation as unthinkable, they remained together in strife and conflict. Perls's early childhood, however, seemed happy. His grandparents and other relatives were good influences, and his parents were sufficiently well off to provide outside cultural stimulation through theatre, schooling, and books.

As Perls entered adolescence, his relationship with his father deteriorated and he rebelled against both his family and school. He was aggressive, unruly, and abusive and was finally expelled from school at the age of thirteen. After spending a brief period as an apprentice to a tailor, Perls was sent to another school where there was greater academic and personal freedom. He was successful in this atmosphere, which offered a refreshing contrast to the then typical rote memory approach of the classical *gymnasium*. Upon graduation he entered the University of Berlin and began the study of medicine. His studies were to be interrupted, however, by the first of the significant events which were to shape Perls's life and influence his later theory and practice: in 1915, at the age of twenty-one, Perls was inducted into the German army and introduced to the horror of warfare and the humiliation of anti-Semitism. In the beginning, because of a medical problem, he was fortunate in escaping front-line action, but as the tide of the war turned in 1916 he was posted to the front as a medic. He had been distressed by the human suffering and tragedy he witnessed as a Red Cross worker in the rear, and found the front lines to be a shocking, and eventually a dehumanizing, experience.

Here, for the first time in his life, he was considered a Jew—his second significant experience—although his family had never been religious and Perls did not identify himself as Jewish. He was slighted and shunned by anti-Semitic superior officers. When the war ended Perls was severely disillusioned. He was lonely, having lost close friends in the war. He felt alienated politically, and, having seen the war effort benefit the German arms producers and sellers at the expense of the German people, he began to seriously question for the first time the motives and judgment of his country's political and military leaders.

Perls returned to university after the war and in 1920 at the age of 26 he received his M.D. degree. The post-war German economy was in ruins and life was hard. Perls became associated with the bohemian class of Berlin: he practiced medicine during the day and hung out in cafés and clubs in the evening. This was to be his third significant experience. Along with other German intellectuals, teachers, writers, and artists, he became part of the famous Bauhaus Group of dissidents and political radicals who challenged the values of the day —outdated and destructive German nationalism, selfish profiteering by industrialists, and their dehumanizing capitalism. But although the Bauhaus Group achieved a powerful influence culturally and philosophically, leaving behind significant and lasting work in literature, art, architecture, music, and theatre, it had little impact on the German political and economic systems.

During this time, as part of the Bauhaus Group, Perls had his fourth significant experience: he met Sigmund Friedlander, a German existential philosopher. Perls had not been satisfied with the answers to significant questions offered through his classical schooling. He did not find "truth" in his classical studies. But Friedlander provided an alternative: he introduced Perls to the idea of simplicity. Friedlander espoused what might be termed "German Taoism," defining reality or truth as a centre point or balance which is a fusion of opposites. Opposites were understood as defining one another in the sense that one cannot exist without the other (Yin and Yang). This concept of reality as competing polarities with a centre point remained with Perls and later became a significant part of his therapeutic theory and practice. It also stimulated his interest in Gestalt and organismic psychology and his adaptation of the concept of closure to mean the centre or zero point at which an organism is in a state of optimal functioning. Either a surplus *or* a deficit—either polarity—in the organism is *necessarily an impediment to optimal functioning* (homeostasis). But just as significantly, as he would later indicate, the concept of polarities would help to explain (or better, discover and *describe*) the pathological. The "neurotic" would come to be identified by the *polarities of behaviour displayed*—either too much or too little. The presense of opposites would signal the existence of the other extreme of the behaviour as only *unexpressed* rather than *non-existent*. Therapy then would concentrate on making the denial or repression *explicit* to enable experiencing of unexpressed behaviour and eventually achievement of an *integration of the polarities* or the *centring* of the person.

In 1923 life in Germany was still a struggle, and Perls was personally unsettled. With a view to emigration, he accepted an invitation to visit relatives in New York. However, he was no happier there. Because he spoke English poorly, he felt isolated and lonely. In 1924 he returned to Germany.

In 1925 Perls, at age thirty-two, was still living with his parents. He was a frustrated, unhappy person; insecure socially, sexually, and professionally. Then he met a woman who triggered in him an emotional rebirth. He was totally disoriented by his relationship with her: at the mercy of his emotions, experiencing extremes of lust, anger, jealousy, and shame. In 1926, after some months of emotional trauma, he decided to enter the then new psychoanalytic treatment. This was Perls's fifth significant experience. It introduced Perls not only to psychoanalysis and Freudian psychology but also to Karen Horney, who was his first therapist, and who would later break with Freud and develop her own approach. Horney suggested that Perls leave Berlin, advising him that his analysis would proceed more easily if he were separated from his traumatic love affair. He accepted Horney's advice and moved to Frankfurt.

Perls spent only one year in Frankfurt, but it was the sixth significant experience in his life and one of the most important. For Perls decided on Frankfurt in order to work with Kurt Goldstein, the originator of organismic psychology and the concept of self-actualization.

Perls benefitted from his contact with Goldstein in several ways. First, he developed further his interest in a holistic approach to understanding human behaviour, which had been initiated by the concept of simplicity espoused by Sigmund Friedlander. Second, he was introduced to various applications of the principles of Gestalt psychology. Third, and equally important, he became involved with two theologian-philosophers who have played a key role in the development of existential or humanistic psychology: Martin Buber and Paul Tillich. Lastly, it was at one of Goldstein's seminars that Perls met his wife-to-be, Laura, a graduate student in Gestalt psychology. Her family did not like Perls, his ideas, or his lifestyle, and never accepted him.

Perls left Frankfurt in 1927 for Vienna to be trained himself as an analyst. After returning to Berlin, Perls and Laura married in 1929. Still plagued by a sense of personal insecurity, and lacking confidence, Perls again turned to Karen Horney in 1932 and on her suggestion began to see Wilhelm Reich, a leading psychoanalyst. This was Perls's seventh significant experience, for Perls's own later approach displays characteristics of Reichian therapy, such as drawing the patient's attention to immediate behaviour (posture, gesture, muscular tension) observed by the therapist rather than merely dealing with memories and associations from the past, as was typical of psychoanalysis at the time.

By 1933 the Nazi movement was seriously threatening Jews. Perls and his family fled to Norway leaving behind all their possessions, money, and friends. For six months they experienced extreme hardship, living in one room, until Perls was offered help from two American psychoanalysts, A.A. Brill, Freud's theoretical interpreter in English, and Ernest Jones, Freud's biographer. Brill offered to help Perls to come to the U.S.A., and Jones, to get him a position in

South Africa. Perls, recalling the dissatisfactions with his earlier American experience, decided on South Africa.

The Perlses established themselves rapidly in Johannesburg. A second child was born and all was well. Both Fritz and Laura had flourishing practices. They built a Bauhaus-inspired home complete with swimming pool and led the "good" life. In 1936, Perls travelled to Czechoslovakia to deliver a paper on oral resistance at the World Psychoanalytic Congress. For the first time in his life, he was feeling confident and assured and looked forward to gaining professional acclaim for his paper. But he was disappointed, for not only did his colleagues reject his theory and paper, he was coolly received by Freud as well. When he met Wilhelm Reich, whom he both admired and revered, he was further disillusioned, as Reich, also a German refugee, was himself depressed and did not seem pleased to see Perls. He returned to South Africa feeling angry, rejected, and disillusioned. This was the eighth significant experience: he had failed to win approval, recognition, and support from his colleagues and "heroes." The following ten years were difficult ones. Although economically and socially successful, Perls sensed that something was missing. He felt personally empty and unsatisfied. His marriage began to deteriorate, and he grew apart from both Laura and his children. Finally, he began to feel restrained and confined by his role as a parent and husband. During this period Perls wrote his first book, *Ego, Hunger and Aggression* (1940), expressing views contradictory to psychoanalysis. This was the ninth significant experience and was the foundation for his later approach. As Shepard states (1976: 49):

> The final section of *Ego, Hunger and Aggression* he entitled "Concentration Therapy." Within these pages Fritz elaborated upon those concepts that, when attended to, brought him some peace of mind. These had to do with focusing awareness in the present moment, stopping unproductive historical ruminations and blame, and realizing the nature of projections. This part can be read either as a unique self-help book or as a primer which underlies and explains the "magic" that Fritz performed in his subsequent work with patients. Chapter by chapter he suggests procedures to help the reader realize the importance of the moment, of internal silence, of simple task observations, of body concentration, and of how one externalizes inner conflicts.

These procedures still form the basis of his approach.

In 1946 Perls contacted Karen Horney, his first analyst, who was then in New York. She agreed to sponsor him for emigration from South Africa. Shortly thereafter, Perls left for the United States with plans to have Laura and the children join him as soon as he was settled. During the twelve years in Johannesburg he developed his own theory and therapeutic technique, later to be called Gestalt Therapy, and concluded that he was not content only to play the father-husband role. At the age of fifty-three he had decided to build a new life.

During the next ten years Perls resided in New York City. He succeeded almost instantly on his arrival in establishing a practice. But it was not long before the routine pattern of life there resembled that in Johannesburg from which he had sought his escape. Fritz and Laura became involved in an American bohemian intellectual set which focused on personal honesty and experimentation in human relationships. This group of wealthy dilettantes, artists, writers, actors, professors, and students were, in a number of value areas, a decade or so ahead of their time. One of these value areas was sex. The group experimented sexually and Perls, always a very sexual person, apparently gave this aspect of himself free rein. These experiences led him to begin to question the traditional anonymity of the therapist as a person in the therapist-patient relationship. How could the therapist-patient relationship be real, if only one of the participants, the patient, was real? Thus, Perls became more aware of his own "roles" and "games," and of his lack of integration, consistency, or continuity. Increasingly he attempted to pull together his social and professional roles, acting more like a psychoanalyst in social encounters and more like a person in the office, in order to lead one life instead of two. But although he may have achieved greater personal integration, his professional status was damaged: the William Alanson White Institute of Psychoanalysis refused him full membership and recognition.

Perls had reworked, rewritten, and renamed his early material on concentration therapy with the considerable assistance of Paul Goodman and Ralph Hefferline from Columbia, and the new theoretical work was published as a collaborative effort in 1951 with the title *Gestalt Therapy*. By the time the book appeared in print, the new approach was already being used and the Gestalt Institute had been formally established. Perls spent a great deal of time travelling around the country lecturing to groups who would listen, but he did not obtain the attention and recognition he felt his theories and approach warranted. Finally, in 1956, at age sixty-three, Perls seemed to give up. This was the end of his tenth significant experience. At last, he had managed to articulate a new theory of personality and psychotherapeutic process, and to begin to achieve a degree of personal integration. For the former he was generally ignored and for the latter he was rejected.

In poor health, Perls left New York in 1956 for Miami. Depressed, withdrawn, and bitter toward his professional colleagues, feeling that Gestalt Therapy would never have the impact he had hoped for, Perls saw few patients, travelled little, and lived an impoverished, lonely, and futile existence. Then, at sixty-five, Perls met Marty, a thirty-two-year-old woman patient, and experienced his second emotional rebirth and eleventh significant experience. Their relationship was the most important Perls had ever known, and for two years he and Marty explored together a range of experiences, at times assisted and/or enhanced by drugs.

Perls had been revitalized by his relationship with Marty and in 1960, assisted by a former student, Jim Simkin, Perls established himself in Los Angeles. Simkin also helped Perls cut down on his use of LSD, which he had been taking regularly since 1957. This was, of course, long before hallucinogenic drugs became popular. Although Perls had initially experimented with

LSD as a means of increasing his awareness, heavy use of the drug over several years produced frequent bouts of paranoid and hostile behaviour, which even his close associates found intolerable. Simkin also helped Perls to relaunch his professional career. But while he was mildly successful, Perls's group work and consulting really only resembled what he had left behind in New York and Miami. Dissatisfied again with the routine, he planned a world trip in 1962. He travelled to Israel and Japan, spending two months in Zen training in Kyoto. This was likely stimulated by the then widespread interest on the West Coast in Eastern religion through the influence of people like Alan Watts and Rollo May, but may also have reflected his early exposure to Friedlander's German Taoism.

On his return to Los Angeles Perls was asked to be one of the first participants in the Human Potential Movement, later to be called the Esalen Institute after a local Indian band. The first conference was an interdisciplinary event designed to introduce to one another people who were considered to be in the forefront of their fields of music, dance, sociology, psychology, and body awareness. It was not open to the public.

Perls returned to the Institute in 1964 to teach Gestalt Therapy. Esalen was to become his Mecca and his twelfth significant experience, for it was there that Gestalt Therapy finally made an impact on the therapeutic community. Gestalt Therapy was not the only thing at Esalen. There were Yoga, meditation, religion, nude therapy, and sensory awareness. But it was the Esalen exposure that enabled Perls to gain his long-awaited recognition. For the next four years Perls held court at Esalen. But his involvement with the "community" was bittersweet and eventually he decided to move out and establish his own Gestalt commune at Cowichan, British Columbia. The Gestalt Institute of Canada Commune was his crowning achievement, but he was to spend little time there. On returning from a trip to Europe in February 1970 Perls became seriously ill. He entered hospital in Chicago March 6 and died of cancer eight days later at 77 years of age.

Fritz Perls experientially grasped the basic concepts and dynamics of his approach and lived them as best he could. And living them caused much of his pain and distress. Had he given up and knuckled under to the pressures of his professional colleagues, had he resigned himself to the comfortable life of an analyst and family man, Gestalt Therapy and its significant contributions to the understanding and treatment of human misery would have remained either undeveloped or unnoticed. Still further, while Perls's life seems to have been filled with an inordinate amount of confusion, suffering, insecurity, unhappiness, and disappointment, it was also a life rich with significant experiences and opportunities. And in his final years, he appears to have achieved the joy and self-fulfillment he had been doggedly seeking: full awareness and the realization of his potential to be.

From this careful review of Perls's unusual life experience we find him influenced by, and having incorporated, the five major schools of psychological thought in Gestalt Therapy.

First, from his training and practice in Freudian psychology and psychoanalysis he incorporated basic concepts such as repression, resistance, denial, ego, projection, introjection, and general principles underlying neurotic behaviour and the importance of dreams. However, he discarded the psychoanalytic treatment method as unproductive and ineffective.

Second, he incorporated the major principles and concepts of organismic psychology learned during his association with Kurt Goldstein. His medical background and work with Goldstein paved the way for a strong biological base for his theory and approach to human behaviour.

Third, he utilized the principles of closure and unity and the applications of Gestalt psychology learned during his stay in Frankfurt, and from his wife Laura, who was a Gestalt psychologist.

Fourth, he employed the behaviourists' phenomenological focus on the study and description of *only presently existing externally observable behaviour and events*. Perls concluded that the only way we had of attempting to study and understand internal events (thoughts, repressions, denial, projection, emotions, etc.) was through careful observation of external behaviour. Because the organism operates as a unity, internal events will be reflected in the external behaviour of the organism.

Fifth, he assimilated the existential concerns and concepts espoused by the existential philosophers and theologians he had known, such as Friedlander, Buber, and Tillich, whose ideas were to form the base for the new humanistic psychology of the 1950s. Thus we find in Gestalt Therapy a concern with splits and holes; with attention and awareness; with integration, centredness, polarities, or opposites; with "being"; and with the here and now.

It is the strength of Gestalt Therapy's theoretical base, which incorporates all schools of psychology and biology, and the relative simplicity of the resulting therapeutic technique, which identifies Perls's genius and the significance of his approach.

BASIC ASSUMPTIONS AND MAJOR CONCEPTS

While Perls's approach and technique is well rooted theoretically, and includes all of the major schools of psychological thought, it is difficult to find in his own work a logical, ordered, and systematic presentation of the basic assumptions on which Gestalt Therapy (GT) is founded. What follows then is an attempt to provide a systematic examination of the major concepts and assumptions of GT in a developmental context.

Unlike Rogers, Perls did not develop both a theory of normal human growth and development per se and a separate theory of neurosis or problem behaviour. Perhaps this is appropriate from an organismic-gestalt perspective. That is, the opposite is defined by a discussion of either polarity—normal or abnormal. However, it might assist our own exploration of GT concepts if some distinction is made. Let's examine some of the characteristics which Perls ascribed to the healthy person, with the understanding that this is not an integrated personality theory as such. We will then discuss the development and characteristics of neurotic or problem behaviour from the perspective of GT.

Normal Human Growth and Development

Quite simply, the human person is viewed primarily as an *organism*, that is, as a living being that has organs, has an organization, and is *self-regulating* from within. The organism requires a *physical* environment (air, water, etc.) and a *social* environment (friends, associates, identity, belonging, membership), and it *interacts* with these environments. But as well, the organism is *in itself* composed of a number of complex *systems* involving different types of cells which interact with one another (circulatory, respiratory, musculatory, sensory, nervous, etc.). Their interaction is organized in such a way as to serve the functioning of the *total* organism. The organism therefore *always acts as a whole*. It is not a summation of liver, heart, cells, brain, etc., but rather an integrated coordination of complex systems.

These physiological systems do not co-exist independently and autonomously, but rather exist only in *synthesis*, in integration with one another, forming something more and different than what they are either together or in summation: the total organism. The implication of this basic assumption, of course, is that the functioning of the total organism, because of the *limitations* of this structural characteristic, can and will be adversely affected by the faulty operation—too much or too little, surplus or deficit—of any part or system of the organism. Further, the organism will reflect this functioning impairment in its external behaviour which can be observed sensorily by others. At the same time, the organism cannot be separated from its *environment*, physical or social, without serious effects, perhaps even death. If deprived of oxygen or water the organism ceases to exist. If the young infant is not cared for by adults, she dies. If the adult experiences rejection, she suffers. We must, then, always consider the physical and social environment in which we live as a part of ourselves. We always carry it around with us.

SELF-REGULATION, COMPLETING GESTALTS,
SENSATION, ATTENTION, AND AWARENESS
As was indicated above, the organism is considered to be potentially self-regulating, that is, to have a built-in internal control mechanism or principle which enables it to achieve maturation or realization of its potential. This is essentially the primary and singular self-actualizing drive postulated by Goldstein and espoused as well by Rogers. But Perls adds to this concept the idea of the gestalt as the mechanism or process through which the self-actualizing drive or tendency is achieved. The term *gestalt* might be better understood as a need-satisfaction cycle, with the emerging incomplete gestalt being the need-recog-

nition, and the need-satisfaction being closure or the gestalt completion and subsequent disappearance. Thus the gestalt is a sensory-biological activity or process. Perls (1969a: 15) describes the process and its implications for therapy as follows:

> The world, and especially every organism maintains itself, and the only law which is constant is the forming of gestalts—wholes, completeness. A gestalt is an organic function. A gestalt is an ultimate experiential unit. As soon as you break up a gestalt it is not a gestalt any more. . . . If you analyze, if you cut it further up, it becomes something else.

For example, an engine disassembled is a pile of engine parts, not an engine. The parts assembled are more than the sum of the parts, they are something else.

> . . . organismic self-regulation is very important in therapy because the emergent, unfinished situations [Gestalts] will come to the surface. We don't have to dig: it's all there. And you might look upon this like thus: that from within, some figure emerges, comes to the surface and then goes into the outside world, reaches out for what we want, and comes back, assimilates and recedes. Something else comes out, and again the same process repeats itself (Perls, 1969a: 21-22).

Thus, there is in Perls's theory a homeostatic, drive-reduction component.

> So we . . . consider the organism as a system that is in balance and that has to function properly. Any imbalance is experienced as a need to correct the imbalance (Perls, 1969a: 16).

But this is not a static, passive organism which rests in between emerging gestalts. For Perls sees the sensory process as the primary means of orientation to the internal and external environment. The sensory mechanism, then, rather than waiting to be stimulated, is viewed as reaching out or searching continually for the emerging gestalt. It is the means by which we experience the reality of our existence or *awareness*.

AWARENESS

The concept of awareness is very important in GT and merits further exploration. Perls (1969a) described it simply as the subjective experience of one's self inside, and the otherness outside, the ego boundary. But a more detailed description and discussion is provided by Yontef (1976: 67-68), which includes several corollaries of this concept involving the whole human person:

> Awareness is a form of experiencing. It is the process of being in vigilant contact with the most important event in the individual/environment field with full sensorimotor, emotional, cognitive, and energetic support.
>
> Corollary one: "Awareness is effective only when grounded in and ener-

gized by the dominant present need of the organism" (Yontef, 1976: 67). In other words, without this level or degree of awareness we may be unaware of how or if the need is being met and fail to experience the real impact of the event. Examples: eating while reading, worrying about an exam while at the movies, thinking about work while having sex.

Corollary two: "Awareness is not complete without directly knowing the reality of the situation and how one is in the situation" (Yontef, 1976: 67). This refers essentially to responsibility in the sense of being "response-able." It means that we cannot be responsible without being *aware* of our situation. Being aware includes knowing cognitively, feeling and sensing, appreciating our alternatives, and *choosing* to be as we are. Awareness then means self-acceptance; to choose to reject ourselves means a lack of awareness. If we are dissatisfied with ourselves, and *aware*, we are also aware of what we are doing to create and perpetuate the situation. If we are aware of what we are doing to create and perpetuate our problems, we have obviously made a choice to retain the problem in order to be what we are.

Corollary three:

Awareness is always here and now and always changing, evolving, and transcending itself. Awareness is sensory, not magical: it exists. Everything that exists does so here and now. The past exists now as memory, regret, body tension, etc. The future does not exist except now, as fantasy, hopes, etc. In GT we stress Awareness in the sense of knowing what I am doing, now, in the situation that is, and not confusing this is with what was, could be, should be.

. . .

The act of *Awareness* is always here and now, although the content of *Awareness* may be distant. To *know* that "now I am remembering" is very different from slipping into remembering without *Awareness*. *Awareness* is experiencing and knowing what I am doing now (and how) (Yontef, 1976: 68).

Awareness, then, is the process through which we achieve our being and our becoming. It is the primary requirement for our personal growth, development, and actualization of our potential.

LEARNING

Perls (1969a) envisaged the human learning process as primarily a sensory as opposed to a cognitive process. He felt that learning occurred through our sensory *experience* of a situation or event and was therefore similar to the concept of *discovery*. And while he agreed that learning may *appear* to occur, as evidenced by behavioural change, through drill or repetition, the habit formation which resulted from these methods he saw as essentially non-human; as mere training, not real education. He pointed out, however, that if we discover the *meaning* of the drill, the drill results in closure, which in turn results in discovery ("Aha!") which then becomes a human experience. Thus, in therapy Perls attempted to have patients learn to *discover* themselves, or to experience *awareness*, and thereby to sense the meaning and closure of their emerging gestalts. At times he used drill or repetition to facilitate the closure process.

This discovery process was contrasted with the information-gathering process used or sought by our human "computer." Perls considered facts or knowledge secondary information useful only to those who had "lost their senses." Such people, he felt, could not experience *directly* their sensations. Without this capacity they are unable to achieve awareness and therefore cannot experience reality. But Perls believed that for most of us, *sense data*, not cognitive input or factual information, is what enables understanding. Concepts do not enable understanding, they merely explain. The difference between the two is similar to the difference between feeling and thinking. The chapter you are reading attempts to explain GT, but to *understand* it you would have to *experience* GT so that you might discover its meaning.

COMMUNICATION, ENCOUNTER, AND CHARACTER

Organisms sharing a common segment of the environment (attitudes, geography, language) or whose two worlds overlap in some way can communicate with one another. Where this occurs the *I* and *You* changes to the *We*. The *We* does not exist in itself but neither is it *I* and *You*. The overlapping of the two worlds or encounter produces a common (ego) boundary and each person becomes a part of the other in the process.

This encounter does not occur if the two persons have what Perls (1969) described as "character." Character is a rigid organismic system or pattern. Behaviour of people who have character is predictable. Their predictability prevents them from approaching the world spontaneously and creatively with all available potential. They have a predetermination to respond in a specific patterned fashion. Unfortunately our society rewards and demands predictability, which is contrary to healthy organismic functioning. Creative, spontaneous, and productive behaviour identifies the mature organism.

SUMMARY

The human person is a self-regulating organism designed to actualize its potential. It orients itself to its internal and external environment by the employment of an active sensory system. The needs of the organism are signalled by an emerging gestalt which is experienced by the organism as discomfort, disequilibrium, confusion. Attention to the emerging gestalt in the form of awareness enables the organism to satisfy the need, complete the gestalt cycle or achieve closure, and enables the organism to regain its balance and internal harmony, so that the next emerging gestalt may be attended to and completed. The human organism learns through experience or discovery. The learning process is primarily sensory as opposed to cognitive. Human communication and encounter requires the presence of spontaneity and creativity on the part of those in communication.

But as Perls (1948) pointed out, even the best parents are seldom able to merely facilitate the development of the child's inherent potential. Instead, the individual is gradually shaped into the kind of person who meets with the approval of both her parents and society. Learning focuses on cognitive processes rather than sensing and discovery and human encounter is made impossible by the development of "good" character. Let's turn now to an examination of Perls's theory of neurotic behaviour. It will be interesting to note the similarity of Perls's and Rogers's ideas in this regard.

The Development of Neurotic and Problem Behaviour

PERSONALITY DIS-INTEGRATION

For Perls (1948) the root problem of human beings, at least in the Western hemisphere, is the *dual* character of their personalities:

> The deep split in our personality, the conflict between deliberate and spontaneous behaviour, is the outstanding characteristic of our time. Our civilization is characterized by technical integration and personality deterioration. . . .
>
> If the assumption is correct that the split personality is the normal, perhaps even unavoidable product of our time, doubt arises as to whether or not an integration is possible, or if so, whether or not it has market value or at least survival value (Perls, 1948: 567).

It sounds very like the ideas Rollo May espoused in his book *Existence*, which we described in Chapter 4. But *Existence* was published ten years later, in 1958.

What is the dualism to which Perls refers, and how does it develop? Here is how Perls (1948: 570) outlines the development of neurotic behaviour:

> Difficult situations create wishful and magical thinking, scientific manipulation, propaganda, and the philosophy of the free will; in short, deliberateness in place of spontaneity. Human behaviour, as far as it was and is objectionable to a person or group, has to be changed, but the "goody-goody" behaviour is not replacing, it is only superseding the spontaneous attitude. Instincts as the source of unwanted behaviour cannot be eliminated, only their expressions can be modified or annihilated. Generally, it is the expression and execution of the organismic needs, of the biological, original personality which is scotomized and paralyzed. Consequently, the modern individual has to be resensitized and re-mobilized in order to achieve integration.

The dualism in personality, the split, occurs when the individual is *prevented* by the external environment from being inherently spontaneous and self-regulating. In the case of the infant and child, the emerging gestalt which reflects biological and sensory integration is refused expression. The child, in response to external, parental, or other demands, is trained to control her organic and sensory spontaneity cognitively. While *control* is achieved through cognition, the original biologically based emerging gestalt is not eliminated. It can only recede upon closure. Thus, the individual demonstrates control, or reflects certain deliberate behaviour, while at the same time remaining in a state of tension and organismic confusion as the unfinished gestalt presses for closure.

DEALING WITH CONFLICT

The internal conflict we experience in such situations may be dealt with through denial, disowning, repression, projection, or avoidance. It is a basic law of gestalt that only one figure, one item, can become foreground. We can basically only think of one thing at a time. When two competing opposites or two different figures, like spontaneity and control, attempt to emerge, closure does not occur. Rather we experience confusion, fragmentation, and loss of coordination, integration, and smooth functioning. If the opposites involve good and bad, the good may become part of the ego-boundary self, while the bad is disowned, rejected, repressed, projected, or avoided. This process of disowning to resolve the conflict of competing opposites enables us to remain intact, but at the cost of disowning a part of ourselves. In addition, we are required to expend energy continually to maintain the disowning process each time the disowned figure begins to emerge and produces organism confusion. Our ability to cope with the world becomes lessened as our energy and potential resources shrink and the ego boundary of what we are becomes smaller and smaller. We experience less than our full potential, become more and more rigid, and attempt to deal with life according to a preconceived pattern which is unreal. The result is neurosis: being what we are not, afraid to be what we are.

PROJECTION EQUALS INTROJECTION

Perls borrowed the concepts of projection and introjection from psychoanalytic theory and altered them in an intriguing and significant fashion. He claimed (1969a) that when we alienate or disown a part of ourselves, *part-projection* rather than projection results. Part-projection resembles the Freudian concept of projection, that is, it occurs as a result of what we *believe* we perceive in the world or other people. Part-projection occurs as a result of an *incomplete* situation or gestalt which is confusing to us and interferes with the emergence and closure of other gestalts. As well, since the part-projection reflects a disowning of a part of ourselves, it results in a loss of our potential to be, and is thus pathological. However, Perls discovered that this process of disowning, part-projection, and subsequent loss and pathology is *reversible*. That is, by *identification* with the previously disowned part, the part may be *re-owned*. This he called *total projection*. By identifying with the disowned part, we may re-own or regain it or *introject* it, thus completing the gestalt and satisfying our organismic need for closure. Thus,

Part-projection = alienation, disowning, and loss of potential.
Total projection = identification, introjection, closure, and regaining of potential.

The symbols of alienation are "it," "that."
The symbols of identification are "I," "me."

ANXIETY

No theory of neurosis and problem behaviour would be complete without some attention to the role of anxiety. Perls had an excellent grasp of this concept and a very simple definition: Anxiety is the gap between the *Now* and the *Then*. "Whenever you leave the sure basis of the *now*," he said (1969a: 30), "and become preoccupied with the future, you experience anxiety." He compares this experience to stage fright. As we become uncertain about whether we will receive accolades or brickbats for our performance, we become hesitant, our heart begins to pound, and our muscles tremble. The body energy becomes consumed in the anxiety response, and cannot be directed or employed fully in the activity of the performance. However, if we remain in the Now, we cannot become anxious because our body energy flows immediately into ongoing spontaneous activity. When we are in the Now, we are creative and inventive, we have access to our senses, our eyes and ears are operative, and we discover solutions.

The neurotic is essentially a future-oriented person, who lives a "what if" existence. Because she is primarily concerned about what *might* be, a fantasy, a cognitive exercise, she does not use her *senses* to respond to the existing internal and external environment. Since she does not pay attention to the sensory data which she must use in order to orient herself to the world, she cannot be *aware* of the present moment. She is poorly oriented to reality, and therefore unable to respond in the present creatively and spontaneously and to discover, learn, and grow. Her existence is characterized instead by sameness, conservatism, and maintenance of the status quo of existing values and conditions.

The overconcern with the future is part of the neurosis of our society and is reflected in the enormous amount of time devoted by both the private and public sector bureaucracies, in planning activities which for the most part reflect little creativity and, in the long run, prevent the natural evolution of a humanistically oriented social system.

SUMMARY

The development of neurotic and problem behaviour results from the dis-integration of personality which occurs in the infant and young child as she is trained to substitute spontaneous, innate, organismically self-regulated behaviour for deliberate, externally oriented, other-directed behaviour. Still further, as this substitution characterizes the early experience of all children, neurosis appears to be the norm of human development. Perls ponders, under these circumstances, whether there is a "market value" for the truly actualized individual and, if personality re-integration through therapy is possible, whether such a person can survive in our society.

The dis-integration of the original unity of the human person results from the persistence of the organically based gestalts to push for closure. Thus, our deliberate cognitive control brought about through training by parental and other social forces does not replace emerging organismic gestalts. What results is a conflict between sensory and cognitive aspects of the person with attendant confusion, disorientation, and loss of potential. The personality dis-integration prevents us from using our potential resources for personal growth and self-actualization. Our existence becomes past- or future-oriented, but we have little awareness of the present moment. Figure 6·1 contrasts and compares normal and neurotic behaviour in GT terms.

FIGURE 6·1
Normal and Neurotic Behaviour Viewed in GT Terms

Normal	Neurotic
Integration of feelings, thoughts, and actions	*Dis-integration* of feelings, thoughts, and actions
Mature • self-supporting, autonomous	*Immature* • dependent on environmental supports
Aware • experiences needs (emerging gestalts) and satisfies them (closure) • pays attention to bodily sensations and feelings • accepts self and reality • chooses between alternatives • risks • experiences hurt and pain • accepts responsibility for choices and behaviour • relaxed • Now-oriented • does not compute	*Not Aware* • does not experience needs, closure not attained • does not pay attention to bodily sensations and feelings • dislikes self and denies reality • unable to make choices • does not risk, seeks safety of routine • avoids any hurt and pain • avoids or denies responsibility • tense, anxious • Past- or future-oriented • computes
Spontaneous • creative, productive, joyful	*Deliberate* • depressed, angry, unhappy, unproductive, destructive

MAJOR DYNAMICS OF THE THERAPY PROCESS

A discussion of the major dynamics of the therapy process itself is of course essential in understanding what actually occurs during therapy. In addition, however, their examination will also clarify and elaborate on many of the ideas we have covered above when considering normal and neurotic development. Let's begin with the goal of GT.

The Goal of GT

The ultimate goal of any living organism is maturation. A living thing, be it a plant or animal, grows to maturity. The goal of GT is to facilitate the growth or maturation of the individual whose existence is viewed as in the process of development. Therapy is required to facilitate the growth process when the normal process of development has been inhibited and is stagnant, or is deteriorating and regressing in response to the parental or societal demands described above. It is important to note that GT does not aim to achieve total personality integration, but rather only as much integration as is required to initiate or regain for the individual the self-regulating growth process. Perls (1948: 572) described it as follows:

> The ultimate goal of the treatment can be formulated thus: We have to achieve that amount of integration which facilitates its own development. This is in accordance with the fact that the dissociated person is inhibited or even degenerating in his development. To repeat once more, the criterion of a successful treatment is: the achievement of that amount of integration which facilitates its own development.

The goal of GT, then, is to enable the *dis*-integrated person to become *re*-integrated and self-actualizing or mature. This process of re-integration is initiated in the patient through the development of patient *awareness*. Awareness per se is considered curative. Awareness enables the use of our full potential in satisfying the need for closure of emerging gestalts.

> If you become aware each time that you are entering a state of confusion, this is the therapeutic thing . . . If you understand this, and stay with confusion, *confusion will sort itself out by itself*. If you *try* to sort it out, *compute* how to do it, if you ask me for a *prescription* how to do it, you only add more confusion to your productions (Perls, 1969a: 24).

The therapeutic facilitation of the maturation or self-regulation of the patient requires the patient to give up her dependency on external or environmental supports and adopt a self-reliant, self-directing, autonomous stance. Thus, the therapist from the beginning *requires* the patient to discover for herself that she has the capacity of doing much more for herself than she believes she can. Since learning or discovery occurs only through *experiencing*, the emphasis in GT is on "manipulating" the patient into *producing behaviour* and in facilitating the *ownership* of that behaviour by the client. In GT the patient experientially discovers how she has been continuing to prevent her own growth and the realization of her potential. As she learns to cease inhibiting her growth, her life becomes richer and more enjoyable and her potential increases. As Perls (1948) suggested above, there is a Catch-22 for the person who is actualizing—who is living every minute afresh and reviewing it. The non-habituated person is also not predictable. Yet to be considered a good citizen in our society, one must be consistent and predictable. In this sense, our society seems to demand that we *not* grow and self-actualize. Perls's comments on this dilemma were even stronger twenty years later:

> If you don't adjust, you are either a criminal, or a psychopath or loony or a beatnik or something like that. Anyway you are undesirable and must be thrown out of the boundary of that society (Perls, 1969a: 30).

How then can we survive in our society? Must we all accept our neurosis as a condition of life? Perls suggested we had a choice. Either we "take risks and become healthy and perhaps also crucified" or we participate in our neurotic society. But if we take the risk and choose maturity and growth there is a reward:

> If you are centred in yourself, then you don't adjust any more—then, whatever happens becomes a passing parade and you assimilate, you understand, you are related, to whatever happens (Perls, 1969a: 30).

GT Dynamics

The Gestalt therapist concentrates his attention on a number of key aspects of the patient's experience and behaviour. We will first describe the therapist's general approach to the patient, and then discuss the specific focuses of GT.

THE THERAPIST'S APPROACH

The basic task of the therapist is to help the patient overcome barriers that block awareness, and let nature take its course so that the patient can function using all of her potential. The therapist does not help to solve the problems of the patient. Instead, he helps to reestablish the conditions under which the patient can best *use her own problem-solving abilities*. Thus the therapist does not assume a superior stance with the patient or facilitate or maintain dependency in the patient.

How does the therapist go about helping the patient to find her missing potential? Perls suggested (1969a) he do this by becoming a *projection screen*. The patient expects the therapist to demonstrate the very capacities she is unable to mobilize in herself. She therefore *projects* onto the therapist what Perls called the "*holes*" in her personality. The most important missing part or hole is the *centre*. Achieving or finding our centre means being grounded in our self, being autonomous, creative, inventive, spontaneous, productive and joyful—being aware.

The missing "holes" are always obvious in the patient's behaviour. So the first thing the therapist does is to provide an opportunity for the patient to *experience* what her needs are that are not being met. These needs are represented by the missing holes or parts she has alienated or disowned from inside her ego boundary or self. Once these holes are experienced, the therapist must create a situation in which the patient can begin to re-integrate them within her personality. To accomplish this, the therapist confronts her and frustrates her into discovering her own potential, and discovering as well that what she expects from the therapist she can do just as well for herself.

THE FOCAL POINTS OF GT

Filling in the Holes
All the needs the patient has disowned can be recovered through understanding or reexperiencing the disowned parts. This experiencing is achieved primarily through role-playing, through the patient *becoming* the disowned parts. By having the patient play/be these disowned "things," she discovers that in fact she already has what she thinks only others can give her. The result of this discovery is that she *re-owns* the disowned, projected parts of her personality, fills in the holes, and in so doing increases her potential. Therapy then gives the patient more and more power over herself, more experience and understanding until she is truly integrated and self-directing.

Avoidance, Symptoms, and Holes
The holes are always identified by symptoms and the symptoms of the holes are always indicated by avoidance. This is the reason we need a therapist, another person, to help us to discover ourselves. We cannot do it alone because we are not aware of what it is we are avoiding. The neurotic person does not see the obvious. The closer she gets to the hole, the more she avoids. Strangely enough, the neurotic, in her attempt to avoid the fantasied catastrophic future, or expectations, prevents herself from *being*. She chooses mediocrity and sameness rather than risking growth. And in so doing, she controls not only herself, but others around her. She'd rather manipulate others around her for her own support than risk learning to stand on her own. She does so by various devices such as playing stupid, helpless, tough, etc. But the paradox is that the person who attempts to control others always ends up being *controlled*.

> The crazy person says, "I am a Princess."
> The neurotic person says, "I wish I was a Princess."
> The healthy person says, "I am I and you are you."

Here and Now
Now is the present; it is what we are aware of, whether we remember or anticipate. We do it *now*. The past is no more, the future is not yet. If we say "I was," that's not now, that's the past. If we say "I want to," that's not now, that's the future. Perls (1969a) considered that the great error of psychoanalysis was in assuming that memory is reality. He claimed that this idea fostered infantile or irresponsible behaviour, because it suggested to the patient that the "cause" of her current illness was the past. If the past is still being carried around in the present, then there is an unfinished situation, or an incomplete gestalt. The patient must deal with the past as though it is *now*, and complete it. If the patient deals with the past *now*, she can take responsibility for her behaviour and re-integrate it or fill the "hole."

How and Why
The question of causality in GT is interesting. Perls believed "why" questions infer a linearity of events from start to finish, that is, cause and effect. Gestalt, on the other hand, assumes that life is a continuing process. So the important questions for GT are not cause and effect, S-R, "why" questions, but "how" questions. "How" infers *process*; therefore "how" questions are concerned with the *function* and *structure* of things. If we change the structure we change the function; if the function changes, the structure is altered. "Why" questions lead only to explanations, rationalizations, or interpretations and these impede the development of experiencing, discovery, learning (awareness), and growth. In GT, "why" questions are avoided by the therapist.

Questions and Statements
Perls (1969a) considered that all questions are *underdog* manipulations. They are attempts by the patient to retain her environmental, external support system by manipulating others into accepting her dependency. The underdog manipulator can be identified by her "crybaby" refusal to accept responsibility with comments such as:

> "I know I should have but . . ."
> "I couldn't because . . ."
> "I'm only . . .", "I can't . . ."
> "If you don't I'll ———"

on the one hand, and her manipulating questions on the other.

The question is the hook of a demand. The therapist needs to recognize these demands and refuse to be manipulated. The therapist does this by requesting the patient to change her question to a statement. When the questioner makes a statement out of her question, the background out of which the question arose opens up and the possible answers are discovered by the questioner herself. By refusing to answer questions the therapist helps the patient to discover and develop her own resources. "Learning," says Perls (1969a: 36), "is nothing but discovery that something is possible. To teach means to show a person that something is possible." The relevance of this concept for the classroom and work environment is obvious.

Attention and Phobic Pain
Attention is as significant as awareness in GT. The central concern of the Gestalt therapist is with what the patient *avoids* (phobic reactions) in contrast to the psychoanalyst's concern with what the patient *resists*. What Perls calls *phobic pain* is the patient's refusal to experience a small portion of suffering or discomfort. This phobic pain results in the patient's refusal to grow.

Pain is considered to be merely a signal to the organism for attention. In small amounts it is adaptive for the organism as an alert that there is a surplus or deficit (need) situation in cells, organs, or organ systems which is detrimental to optimal functioning of the whole organism. The organism is required to satisfy the need or seek closure of the incomplete gestalt. However, if even small amounts of pain or unpleasantness are experienced with avoidance or phobic pain, attention is withdrawn from the need source before the organism is able to respond. As with disowning, the failure of the organism to *pay attention* to the need reduces the organism's capacity or potential to be and become.

Again we have the justification for the therapist. The therapist's role, according to Perls (1969a), is to both provide situations in which a person can experience the unpleasantness associated with something being avoided, and to frustrate the patient's avoidance attempts, until she is willing to mobilize her own resources to deal with the experience. Once the patient begins to experience, *feel, sense* the unpleasantness, she is giving it her attention. If she can maintain this attention and experience the pain long enough, she will become *aware* of her need, her avoidance, her "holes," etc.

Paying Attention to the Obvious
GT requires the cooperation of the patient. With a skilled therapist and willing patient a successful experience seems inevitable.

> . . . any one who has a little bit of goodwill will benefit from the Gestalt approach because the simplicity of the Gestalt approach is that we pay attention to the obvious, to the utmost surface . . .
>
> So don't listen to the words, just listen to what the voice tells you, what the movements tell you, what the posture tells you, what the image tells you. If you have [eyes and] ears, then you know all about the other person. . . . What we say is mostly either lies or bullshit. But the voice is there, the gesture, the posture, the facial expression, the psychosomatic language (Perls 1969a: 53-54).

SUMMARY

The Gestalt therapist does not appear to resemble at all closely the Rogerian. While we have seen a number of similarities in their assumptions and concepts related to the normal and neurotic personality, and even in the general goal of therapy (self-actualization), their therapeutic approaches and focuses are very different. The Gestalt therapist approaches the patient as a mirror. The basic concern is with the patient's avoidance and refusal to be self-regulating and autonomous. The therapist confronts the patient with her avoidance or symptoms and frustrates her refusal to accept the discomfort which will arise with attention given to them. The patient is facilitated or manipulated by the therapist into producing behaviour which enables the avoidances or holes or needs to be *experienced*. The experiencing results in discovery and learning and the subsequent assimilation of disowned parts of the personality. The patient is required to focus attention on the present and to remain in the Here and Now. As the therapist manipulates the patient into filling the holes of her disintegrated personality, the patient discovers her own resources and potential and begins to re-integrate and self-actualize.

SOME METHODS AND TECHNIQUES OF GT

The Pseudo-Group

Perls conducted his therapy sessions as a cross between a small seminar demonstration and group therapy. His approach was to have eight or ten people as a group but to "work" with only one of them at a time. Thus the actual patient-therapist interaction was for the most part between the therapist and one member of the group, with the other members as observers. They might comment or react to the dyad exchange they were participant-observing, or Perls might speak to them directly at times, but the majority of his communication was focused on one person at a time who *chose* to "work" with him.

The Hot Seat and the Empty Chair

Perls used two props, the hot seat and the empty chair, as his primary tools. The hot seat was the chair the patient took if she chose to "work" and the empty chair was placed opposite and near. The empty chair is a significant prop for assisting the patient to *role-play*. Thus, in working on re-owning projected feelings, attitudes, or things, the patient is asked to *become* another person, object, or feeling, and to sit in the empty chair while doing so. The empty chair therefore facilitates an exchange between the patient and her projected avoidances. The patient, moving back and forth between the "hot seat" and the empty chair at the direction of the therapist, engages in talking to herself, really the two opposite poles of her personality, experiencing both and beginning to experience awareness of the polarities. Once awareness occurs, the disowned and projected holes can be re-owned and filled, and a measure of re-integration of her personality has been achieved by the patient. The conflicting polarities are integrated and the patient becomes more unified and centred.

The Five Questions

Perls claimed (1970) that if the therapist could ask only the following five questions in working with patients, he would eventually be successful with all but the most seriously disturbed:

> "What are you doing?"
> "What do you feel?"
> "What do you want?"
> "What do you avoid?"
> "What do you expect?"

The Therapist in Action

John Enright (1970: 108) described the therapist in action as follows:

When the patient is communicating well verbally, and his other ongoing activities are minimal or congruent, I listen. At those times, I assume his awareness to be integrated with his organismic attention, and thus he is doing nothing that I as a psychotherapist can help him with; his problems are his, and he is working in them effectively at the moment. . . . My task begins when these other "unconscious" activities begin to stand out in the total gestalt and vie with the verbal content.

The therapist then watches for *splits* in attention and awareness, that is, for evidence that the focused organismic attention is developing outside of awareness. For example, if the client expresses fear while smiling, the smile reflects a split between feeling, thinking, and external behaviour. Enright (1970: 108) continues:

I then encourage the patient to devote some attention to these other activities asking him to describe what he is doing, seeing, feeling. I make no interpretations but simply draw awareness to these phenomena and let him make of them what he will.

Gestalt therapy, then, consists of various interventions which the therapist makes in response to the patient's behaviour. It is primarily an active, confrontation, doing role in contrast to a passive, responsive, listening role. These interventions may be characterized as follows:

1. The intervention builds on actual present behaviour, even though neither the patient nor therapist may know the significance of the behaviour.
2. Interventions therefore are not interpreted by the therapist. He merely asks what is happening or what the patient is doing.
3. The intervention is intended to enhance or expand the patient's responsibility for her own behaviour.
4. Questions are "what" and "how" in nature, not "why" or "what for." Since most people don't know fully *what* they are doing, all therapy need do is enable them to achieve full awareness of the "what." Once this is achieved, concern about the "why" disappears.

The basic assumption here is that a patient can deal adequately with life's problems if she knows *what* the problems are and can fully use her own abilities to solve them.

GT Patient Guidelines

Six techniques of therapy are outlined by Enright (1970) for his patients. These are:

THE PRINCIPLE OF THE NOW
The patient is told that she is to remain in the now and to focus on the moment,

not on the past or on the future, but on what she is saying, feeling, thinking, sensing, doing, *now*.

I AND THOU COMMUNICATION
The concern here is to have the patient become aware of her interpersonal interactions and that true communication involves both sender and receiver. Is she making genuine contact with others? How can she do this better?

IT AND I LANGUAGE
The purpose of having the patient use "I" instead of "it" to describe her own behaviour is to increase the sense of responsibility for and involvement with her body. The object is to have her see herself as an active agent who *does* things rather than a passive creature to whom things *occur*.

Examples: T: "What are you doing with your eyes?" P: "They are crying."
T: "What are you doing with your eyes?" P: "My eyes are crying."
T: "What are you doing with your eyes?" P: "I am crying."

USE OF THE AWARENESS CONTINUUM
The basic attempt of Gestalt Therapy is to get at the *how* of experience. Use of the awareness continuum is the means through which Gestalt avoids endless patient verbalizations, explanations, and interpretations and leads the patient to confront the only reality she may be certain of, that is, her feelings, sensations, and perceptions of the moment.

NO GOSSIPING
Gossiping is defined as talking about an individual when she is actually present and could be just as easily addressed directly. The therapist would have the patient say what she wished directly to the other person. The object here is to have the patient learn to confront others directly.

ASKING QUESTIONS
While the patient may have a legitimate need to ask certain questions, the therapist must learn to recognize what questions are not intended so much to obtain information, as to have the therapist accept her dependency. If this is the case the therapist may ask the patient to change the question to a statement.

SUMMARY

Perls provided the following brief description and overview of Gestalt Therapy in his introduction to the film *Three Approaches to Psychotherapy*, Part Two (1967):

Gestalt therapy works on creating an awareness of certain kinds of reality. In contrast to depth psychology we try to get hold of the obvious, of the surface of the situation in which we find ourselves and to develop the emerging gestalt strictly in the I and Thou, and Here and Now basis. Any escape into the future or the past, is examined as a likely resistance to the ongoing encounter. Modern man has alienated and given up so much of his potential that his ability to cope with his existence becomes very impoverished. My aim is this. The patient should recover his lost potential. He should integrate the conflicting polarities; understand the difference between game playing, especially the playing of verbal games, on the one hand, and of genuine, authentic, confident behaviour, on the other. The upsetting work on inner conflict weakens the efficiency and comfort of the patient, but every bit of integration will strengthen him. Now, in the safe emergency of the therapeutic situation the patient begins to take risks and to transform his energies from manipulating the environmental supports, into developing greater and greater self-supports until relying on his own resources. This process is called *maturation*. Once the patient has learned to stand on his own feet, emotionally, intellectually and economically, his need for therapy will collapse. He will wake up from the nightmare of his ignorance.

The basic technique is this: Not to explain things to the patient, but to provide the patient with opportunities to understand and to discover himself. For this purpose I manipulate and frustrate the patient in such a way that he is confronting himself. In this process he identifies his lost potential through assimilating his projections by acting out. By acting out the alien parts of his self.

I consider any interpretation to be a therapeutic mistake as this would imply that the therapist understands the patient better than the patient himself. It takes away from the patient the chance of discovering himself by himself and prevents him from finding out his own values. On the other hand I disregard most of the content of what the patient says and concentrate most on the non-verbal level. On the non-verbal level, the resident gestalt can always emerge and be dealt with in the Here and Now.

7
Primal Therapy

> ... Primal Therapy as a psychophysiologic process is based on the concept that neurosis is a state of being. It is neither a "psychotherapy" nor a "body" therapy. It is both at once. It is based on the simple idea that what happens to us as children does not evaporate the moment the experience is over, but rather remains as part of our physiology. Pain is not simply an idea or an attitude. It is registered as an experience *and must be resolved experientially*. Thus, one must aim to achieve, through feeling, a thorough resolution and understanding of how those early events are laid down, where they are buried, and the process by which they are kept repressed.
>
> —Arthur Janov, 1980: 46

Arthur Janov's Primal Therapy has been included in the text primarily on the basis of the therapeutic technique involved, which is its distinguishing feature. Although Janov sees his approach as unique, Brown (1979) has pointed out a number of similarities shared by Primal Therapy and variants of direct body contact therapy, not the least of which are the "screams" emitted by patients involved. It is included as well because it shares many of the same theoretical assumptions regarding neurotic behaviour we have discovered in Rogerian and Gestalt Therapy. There are also close similarities in therapeutic goals. Janov would hotly contest such comparisons, of course, in light of his assertion that Primal Therapy is the only cure for neurosis, and cannot be integrated with other therapies (Janov, 1972). Compare this assertion with the following description of "holistic primal therapy" by the Centre for Holistic Primal Therapy, Toronto, Ontario (1978):

> Holistic primal therapy helps people free themselves of neurotic traits and symptoms by a gradual reliving of those early formative experiences of their lives which contributed to their present difficulties. As patients progress in therapy, their feelings become unblocked and they discover through their own inner experiences both the causes of their neuroses and the strength to change.
>
> Our therapy recognizes some of the important contributions to psychotherapy made by Freud, Reich and Perls, as well as the major advances instituted by Arthur Janov. Holistic primal therapy differs from Janov's approach in certain significant respects. Rather than dismantling defenses at a rate determined by the therapist, we provide a humanistic environment where people move at their own speed. We place emphasis on rediscovering primal joy as

well as primal pain. We also stress the need for the fully realized person to contact not only their emotions but also their thinking, sensing and intuitive faculties in order to develop a fuller awareness of their potential for experiencing life.

Obviously, the Centre for Holistic Primal Therapy *has* integrated Janov's Primal approach with several other therapies in eclectic fashion. But Janov has gone further than to suggest that his is the *only* effective therapy. He has also broadly criticized and condemned all other psychologists and therapists as narrow, stupid, and arrogant. In some ways, this is an intriguing projection. An analysis of Janov's work, however, suggests that he is not so much arrogant as ignorant. His understanding and conceptualization of psychological dynamics are at times brilliant. But his work reflects, at the same time, an almost total disregard, and at times disdain, for the field of psychotherapy and of other therapeutic approaches (Janov, 1980). And while there is some theoretical clarity to his work, his own writing is often alogical, suffers from over-generalizations, is poorly organized, inconsistent, idiosyncratic, and unclear.

Here are some examples of his ignorance of the field of psychotherapy and his own conceptual confusion:

In criticism of encounter groups he stated (1972: 231):

> One does not *disclose* oneself to others. One feels it, and that makes any disclosure unnecessary — particularly in reference to a contrived caring situation, like marathons and group psychotherapy. Feelings are not "revealed," they are experienced.

This is a typical unnecessary attack by Janov on another therapeutic method — unnecessary in the sense that his attack indicates ignorance of the dynamics involved in group therapy. An encounter facilitator or group psychotherapist would in fact be in agreement with his emphasis on "experiencing" feeling.

An example of an incomplete, and unclear statement:

> . . . psychotherapy is not a learning situation in which someone learns to cope in new ways. Everything he is ever going to experience is already there inside, lying in wait. He has only to experience it piece by piece (Janov, 1972: 32).

Even in context, it is not clear what Janov meant here. If he was referring to the potential of the person to self-actualize or become what he is, or to achieve full development, then why didn't he use such terms?

Here are three statements which refer to the present or here-and-now. In two of them, there is a strong admonition against having the patient assume a present orientation. In the third, there is a complete turnaround. The first two statements are incomplete and dogmatic; the third is a fuller explanation which is wholly compatible with both Rogerian and Gestalt approaches.

> We can see how useless the confrontation and encounter therapies are. While the therapist is operating in the present, the patient is living out his past. Though

the patient is expressing anger at his peers in group therapy, his real anger is toward his parents (Janov, 1972: 192).

Therefore, nothing which deals with the here-and-now, the presenting behaviour, or with symptoms can be a cure (Janov, 1972: 25).

Our early feelings are with us each minute, stored as memories exerting their force, and ready to emerge as soon as the unreal symbolic, grownup self is removed. It isn't as though we go back in time and become children. We go to what is real now in our systems—those little-child feelings (Janov, 1972: 193).

The following are examples of statements in Janov's work which contradict his assertion that Primal Therapy is unique. These excerpts reflect the same holistic, organismic, and gestalt concepts and therapeutic aims we have noted in both Perls's and Rogers's work.

All curing neurosis involves is bringing down the tension level through Primals to a level where the person is more feeling than defended; where his feelings are accessible to him; and where the initial automatic reflex to situations is not to repress (Janov, 1972: 25).

Fortunately we have within us at all times the means with which to cure ourselves (Janov, 1980: x).

But neurosis is not just an overt behavior. Each overt behavior is part of an organismic behavior pattern, which include what the blood vessels, muscles, and nerve cells are doing. To study social behavior alone is but one more fragmentation of the human being (Janov, 1972: 23).

[U]nfulfilled need is the fount from which spring all the varieties of mental aberration. . . . Lack of satisfaction of that need, or conditional satisfaction of need, provides the grounds for psychologic disease (Janov, 1972: 22).

If they [therapists] understood that there is no "better," only getting real, which means becoming you, then they would automatically be led to the kind of therapy that would lead the patient into himself. There is no "better" than you (Janov, 1972: 38).

The only proper cues for "better" are the internal ones; and, in truth, no one ever really gets "better," they just become themselves (Janov, 1980: 151).

These statements could in most instances have been made by either Rogerian or Gestalt therapists, and by contemporary helpers from various other specific or eclectic orientations.

The original or unique aspects of Janov's approach, then, rest primarily in his *method* or *technique* rather than in his theoretical assumptions regarding personality development, neurotic behaviour, and attendant therapeutic goals. His claim that his entire orientation is new and "revolutionary" cannot be substantiated or demonstrated, and the assertion that Primal Therapy is the only cure for neurosis is irresponsible if not patently dishonest. Thus, while he may be credited for his dogged attempts to continually refine and scientifically validate his ideas with research evidence of biochemical and physiological changes in his "cured" patients (Janov, 1976; 1980) his critics remain skeptical of both his research and therapeutic efforts (Torrey, 1976). The basic concepts of Primal Therapy, then, are all contained in existing Freudian, existential, gestalt, organismic, and learning psychology, and in the major contemporary helping strategies discussed in this text. To date there is no comparative evidence to suggest that any one therapy is better than any other. As we have discussed in Chapter 1, it would appear that more can be learned from observing what "works" among therapists of various approaches with clients than in trying to develop and demonstrate the one perfect system. Had Janov not initially adopted his self-aggrandizing, presumptuous, and unprofessional style, Primal Therapy might have received little attention. His most significant contribution to the field to date would appear to lie in the recent attention he has given to buttressing his theory with physiological evidence and the use of biochemical and physiological tests to evaluate the effectiveness and process of therapy. Whether or not Janov's efforts in this respect are credible, certainly he is to be applauded for his research imagination and originality.

ARTHUR JANOV (1924-   )

Born and raised in Los Angeles, California, in a working-class family, Janov served in the United States Navy in World War II, enlisting on graduation from high school in 1943. He saw combat in both the Pacific and Europe and was discharged in 1946.

He then enrolled at UCLA, majoring in social sciences, and obtained a bachelor's degree in 1949. He continued graduate study in social work at UCLA and completed research for his thesis at the Los Angeles Veterans' Hospital (cf. William Glasser, who completed his psychiatric residency there), receiving his M.S.W. in psychiatric work in 1951. Janov's promise as a therapist was recognized, and from 1950 to 1952 he was given the opportunity for advanced training in psychotherapy at the Hacker Psychiatric Clinic in Beverly Hills, and some involvement in research being conducted by Theodore Adorno. Between 1952 and 1955 he was a member of the social work staff of the Los Angeles Children's Hospital while at the same time developing his own private practice. He obtained a Ph.D. in clinical psychology with a specialization in neurophysiology from Claremont Graduate School in 1960.

Between 1955 and 1967, Janov maintained a private practice in traditional psychotherapy. Thus, he had been a practising therapist for fifteen years prior to his "discovery" and development of Primal Therapy. He had become dissatisfied with conventional methods and his effectiveness in helping his clients, and was thus ready for the discovery.

Since his discovery of Primal Therapy in 1967 and the success of his first book, *The Primal Scream*, in 1970, Janov has attracted considerable attention from professional colleagues, the media, and laypeople. Although Janov's unprofessional marketing of his ideas and methods has been much criticized, Primal Therapy has flourished. Janov himself seems to have emerged with his discovery. After a quiet initial fifteen years as a psychotherapist who devoted himself to seeing patients, Janov has in the past ten years written and published six books and countless articles on Primal Therapy; established the Primal Institute for training and treatment purposes; founded the Primal Research Laboratory, headed by a neurologist; established an affiliation with Antioch College such that the Institute may offer an M.A. degree in psychology; and acts as the editor-in-chief of the *Journal of Primal Therapy,* which he created.

Janov, who has undergone Primal Therapy himself, is described as "handsome and hawkish." He is separated from his wife Vivian, a psychologist who, with his son Richard, continues to assist in the administration of the Primal Institute. Janov's home is in Los Angeles. He continues to be in great demand as a lecturer and spends several months each year in Europe writing (*Current Biography,* 1980: 15-18, and personal correspondence).

Let's explore his approach further and determine for ourselves the significance of Primal Therapy in the field of helping.

ORIGIN AND DEVELOPMENT

Primal Therapy was developed by Janov following an incident which occurred during a therapy session with one of his patients.

> Some years ago, I heard something that was to change the course of my professional life and the lives of my patients. What I heard may change the nature of psychotherapy as it is now known—an eerie scream welling up from the depths of a young man lying on the floor during a therapy session. I can liken it only to what one might hear from a person about to be murdered. This book is about that scream and what it means in terms of unlocking the secrets of neurosis.
>
> The young man who emitted it will be called Danny Wilson, a twenty-two-year-old college student. He was not psychotic, nor was he what is termed hysteric; he was a poor student, withdrawn, sensitive, and quiet. During a lull in our group therapy session, he told us a story about a man named Ortiz who was currently doing an act on the London stage in which he paraded around in diapers drinking bottles of milk. Throughout his number, Ortiz is shouting, "Mommy! Daddy! Mommy! Daddy!" at the top of his lungs. At the end of his act he vomits. Plastic bags are passed out, and the audience is requested to follow suit.
>
> Danny's fascination with the act impelled me to try something elementary, but which previously had escaped my notice. I asked him to call out, "Mommy! Daddy!" Danny refused, saying that he couldn't see the sense in such a childish act, and frankly, neither could I. But I persisted, and finally, he gave in. As he

began, he became noticeably upset. Suddenly he was writhing on the floor in agony. His breathing was rapid, spasmodic; "Mommy! Daddy!" came out of his mouth almost involuntarily in loud screeches. He appeared to be in a coma or hypnotic state. The writhing gave way to small convulsions, and finally, he released a piercing, deathlike scream that rattled the walls of my office. The entire episode lasted only a few minutes, and neither Danny nor I had any idea what had happened. All he could say afterward was: "I made it! I don't know what, but I can *feel!*"

What happened to Danny baffled me for months. I had done standard insight therapy for seventeen years, both as a psychiatric social worker and as a psychologist. I was trained in a Freudian psychiatric clinic, as well as in a not-so-Freudian Veterans Administration department. For several years I had been on the staff of the psychiatric department of the Los Angeles Children's Hospital. At no time during that period had I witnessed anything comparable. Since I had taped the group session that night, I listened to the recording frequently over the next several months in an effort to understand what had happened. But to no avail.

Before long I had a chance to learn more about it.

A thirty-year-old man, whom I shall call Gary Hillard, was relating with great feeling how his parents had always criticized him, had never loved him, and had generally messed up his life. I urged him to call out for them; he demurred. He "knew" that they didn't love him, so what was the point? I asked him to indulge my whim. Half-heartedly, he started calling for Mommy and Daddy. Soon I noticed he was breathing faster and deeper. His calling turned into an involuntary act that led to writhing, near-convulsions, and finally to a scream.

Both of us were shocked. What I had believed was an accident, an idiosyncratic reaction of one patient, had just been repeated in almost identical fashion.

Afterward, when he quieted down, Gary was flooded with insights. He told me that his whole life seemed to have suddenly fallen into place. This ordinarily unsophisticated man began transforming himself in front of my eyes into what was virtually another human being. He became alert; his sensorium opened up; he seemed to understand himself.

Because of the similarities of the two reactions, I began listening even more carefully to the tapes I had made of Danny's and Gary's sessions. I tried to analyze what common factors or techniques produced the reactions. Slowly some meaning began to emerge. Over the next months I tried various modifications and approaches in asking the patient to call for his parents. Each time there occurred the same dramatic results.

I have come to regard that scream as the product of central and universal pains which reside in all neurotics. I call them Primal Pains because they are the original, early hurts upon which all later neurosis is built. It is my contention that these pains exist in every neurotic each minute of his later life, irrespective of the form of his neurosis. These pains often are not consciously felt because they are diffused throughout the entire system where they affect body organs, muscles, the blood and lymph system and, finally, the distorted way we behave.

Primal Therapy is aimed at eradicating these pains. It is revolutionary because it involves overthrowing the neurotic system by a forceful upheaval. Nothing short of that will eliminate neurosis, in my opinion.

Primal Theory is an outgrowth of my observations about why specific changes take place. Theory, I must emphasize, did not precede clinical experience. When I watched Danny and Gary writhing on the floor in the throes of Primal Pain, I had no idea what to call it. The theory has been expanded and deepened by the continuing reports of one patient after another who has been cured of neurosis.

This book is an invitation to explore the revolution they began (Janov, 1970: 9-11).

Thus, unlike Rogers and Perls, whose theory and approach developed and evolved over many years of therapeutic practice through a *deductive* procedure, Janov conceived Primal Therapy to explain a single therapeutic event. This is an *inductive* reasoning process: a general statement or prediction is made based on a single case or solitary event. In the natural sciences, which are governed by physical *laws,* an inductive theory, in which one moves from observation of a particular event to the development of a general principle which will pertain to all such future events given the same circumstances, is appropriate. If a specific physical event governed by the laws of nature occurred once, then one may safely assume that one has "discovered" a general principle which will always pertain given this situation. But in the social sciences, we do not yet have laws governing human behaviour, and therefore theories based on single observations are suspect. Even the deductively derived theories which characterize social science, and are based on repeated observations of events and then applied to particular situations or cases, are suspect. But they reflect at least a deliberate, planned, rational, and logical process of knowledge accumulation which lends to them credibility and a measure of reliability if not validity. Since Primal Therapy is now more than ten years old, we might conclude that Janov's theory must have been correct—or has Janov's strong personal bias and prejudice resulted in his interpretation of his clients' behaviour and response to therapy in terms of his preconceived ideas of neurotic behaviour and process?

AIMS, BASIC ASSUMPTIONS, AND MAJOR CONCEPTS

Absence of a Theory of Human Growth and Development

Primal Therapy is incomplete in the sense that while it is directed toward cure of neurosis, it does not describe or define the normal or non-neurotic person clearly. We are not told exactly what the characteristics of the healthy individual might be, or the specific behaviour which one might expect from a "normal" person. It is as if healthy or normal behaviour is what remains when one's neurosis is *cured,* without specifying what is left. If Janov had postulated an inherent drive to develop the individual's potential, then the absence of neurotic behaviour might be *replaced* by new growth. But no such life force is suggested. Janov gives little attention to "normal" behaviour, and his depiction of the "normal" person is that of an overly rational, cool, super-realist who is ultra-autonomous. When speaking of depression, for example, he suggested (1972: 167):

> A normal person is *never* depressed; he has no backlog of sadness lying unresolved inside. He is open to feel and does not repress unpleasantness. He will be sad when it is appropriate. But sadness is a "now" event, a real feeling related to real situations. Depression is a "then" event, unrelated to now insofar as a current situation triggers something from the past.

Brown (1979), took issue with the cynicism and austere outlook reflected in Janov's view of the normal character, considering it to be unrealistically pessimistic and severe. On the subject of sex and love, for example, Brown noted (1979: 79):

> In his written statements Janov finds nothing special about sex. The search for satisfying sex, like the search for love in general, he reduces to a neurotic search for parental affection which is invariably doomed to failure. As he says (Janov, 1970) "It is the Primal hypothesis that when needs are deprived and feelings are blocked early in life, they emerge in symbolic form. In sex this means that the act will be experienced (usually by way of the fantasy) as fulfilling the need (p. 281)." Or, "When a person has been loved early in life, he does not have to extract it from sex (p. 284)." Or again, "When a neurotic woman has suppressed her feelings, no matter what she thinks is going on in terms of a loving relationship, she is not likely to enjoy sex fully. But if she is normal she will not have to make something special out of sex. She won't be loyal to a concept such as love. She will not have to hear special words, 'I love you', in order to enjoy her physical self (p. 285)."
>
> What Janov is saying here about sex and love adds up to a consistently wholesale invalidation of the intrinsic values and virtues of both phenomena. The implication of his whole position is that no normal healthy person should ever take one or the other so seriously as to get emotionally wrought up about them. Sex is sex and nothing more. Love is an illusion created by those who still struggle and hope to find mommy's and daddy's love finally actualized in their adult lovers. There is no suggestion that the pursuit of both are authentically real and hence healthy needs in their own right.

To be fair, Janov did address himself in the last chapter of *The Primal Revolution* (1972), to a discussion of a "well" society and "real" people. Unfortunately he did not describe exactly what they would be like, other than "feeling" and "conscious." He did suggest a number of characteristics that such "Primal conscious" people would *not* have:

. . . there would be little of the allergies, asthmas, arthritis, headaches, stomach aches, etcetera, which plague all of us . . . .

Healthy parents will not flee from their children and will not be perpetually crabby and critical and tired . . . .

Healthy people would not have latent fears that would make them want to arm themselves against fantasied enemies. No one could make them give up their loved ones to go kill strangers. . . .

In a real world people would not pollute and destroy a nature they feel so much a part of. . . . There could be no false needs drummed into people to make their total aspiration one of consuming more (Janov, 1972: 282-83).

SUMMARY

The absence of a developmental theory or description of the normal or healthy person weakens Janov's approach. For even were we to agree that neurosis is "normal" in the statistical or cultural sense, as Perls suggested, without some concept of normality which is based on our assumptions about human nature, how could we define our therapeutic goals, and/or know when the client had achieved them? Let's look now at the primal theory of neurosis.

The Primal Theory of Neurosis

In this section we will outline Janov's basic assumptions regarding the development of neurosis, describe the process of neurotic development, and discuss the major concepts and terms involved in Primal Therapy.

BASIC ASSUMPTIONS REGARDING NEUROTIC DEVELOPMENT

1. Neurosis is considered a "disease of feeling," and therefore gaining insight or a cognitive appreciation of a problem will not alter neurotic behaviour. Therapy is directed at patient feelings in effecting behavioural change.
2. The basis of neurosis is seen as "suppression" of feelings. Janov appears to use the terms *suppression* and *repression* synonymously. Certainly the young preverbal infant could not consciously suppress, and in general since she is dealing with lost memory, the concept of *repression,* or preconscious blocking or forgetting, seems more appropriate.
3. All neurosis is viewed as having the same *specific* origin and therefore may be treated with the same specific procedures.
4. Primal Therapy believes that we are born neutral, not neurotic: we just *are*. While Janov considers the human person as mind and body, physical and psychological, he does not accept the existential view of neurosis as part of the human condition.

... Primal Therapy as a psychophysiologic process is based on the concept that neurosis is a state of being. It is neither a "psychotherapy" nor a "body" therapy. It is both at once. It is based on the simple idea that what happens to us as children does not evaporate the moment the experience is over, but rather *remains as a part of our physiology* (Janov, 1980: 46).

5. Primal Therapy assumes that "defenses" or neurotic symptoms may help the person to function better outwardly. However, this is accomplished at the expense of a continued state of internal tension.
6. The cure for neurosis is seen as the systematic and ordered dismantling of the causes of inner tension and defense systems and the expression of previously repressed feeling.
7. By understanding the origin of neurosis and neurotic defense systems, this behaviour may be predicted, controlled, and ultimately prevented.

THE PROCESS OF NEUROTIC DEVELOPMENT

The Primal Theory of neurosis is essentially a need-satisfaction theory. Basic needs such as food, warmth, touch, stimulation, etc. are considered to be "Primal" needs. Neurosis begins when any of these needs are unmet for any length of time. The important point is that *neurosis is viewed as beginning in infancy as a result of basic unmet needs, which are mainly physical*. If this situation persists into childhood, when love, affection, protection, and caring become equally important "survival" needs on a psychological or feeling basis, or if these basic needs of childhood are unmet, the neurotic process may *begin*, or be *finalized*, respectively.

Janov believed that neurotic behaviour patterns may be finalized in childhood at the point the child begins to realize that she is not unconditionally loved by her parents and that she never will be. This *realization* he called the "Primal Scene." It may result from some traumatic event with parent figures, or from the sheer weight of a series of minor situations or events which suddenly result in this conclusion. At this point, the hurt and pain of such an overwhelming realization cannot be tolerated. To protect herself from this developing awareness, she blocks the feeling of hurt and pain from consciousness and represses it. At this point Janov believed that the child, previously a *unified* person in the sense of integration of feeling and thought, "splits." The feeling part becomes blocked and the child begins to repress all feeling, attempting instead to operate as she *thinks* her parents want her to. From this point on she is no longer the integrated person, the "whole" being that she was at birth. Instead the cognitive part of her makeup predominates and feeling is suppressed. She must thereafter cease being the person she really is and become what her parents want her to be. The facade of pretending to be what she is not creates internal tension, and this tension requires the construction of an external defense system (neurotic behaviour) to keep the tension under control.

That's a very brief outline of Janov's theory of neurosis. We may note certain similarities to psychoanalysis, and to Rogers's and Perls's ideas. Now let's follow it through again in a little more detail.

Janov suggests (1980) that if the infant experiences needs which are unsatisfied and which over a period of time result in painful feelings which she cannot herself alleviate, the pain or need is eventually "suppressed" from consciousness and some suitable substitute source of gratification is sought. This substitute may be a *symbolic* gratification or satisfaction which does not completely satisfy the need and leaves the organism in a state of inner tension. For example, when we are dieting, substituting celery for chocolate leaves us craving for a sweet. Similarly, the soother substituted for the breast may leave us craving for the nipple, with the tension emerging in adult life via the symbolic satisfaction of "smoking." *The key to neurosis, according to Janov, is the pursuit of such "symbolic satisfactions" as a substitute for real needs and real satisfactions.*

Why are these satisfactions symbolic? Janov believes these symbolic satisfactions act as a defense against psychobiological pain, that is, Primal Pain. Neurosis is maladaptive because *symbolic* satisfactions can never fulfill *real* needs. As a result, the real unmet needs create a state of constant inner tension. Not being *aware* of the real needs, due to the process of repression we cannot satisfy them and eliminate the tension. The *only* means through which to satisfy real needs is by *recognizing* the need. That means being (1) aware of what it is, (2) feeling or experiencing it for what it is, and (3) by then seeking real satisfaction. This is the goal of therapy.

Janov considered the *loved* child to be one who has her basic needs met. *Unconditional* love prevents the occurrence of pain. When the child's needs are met she can feel; she can experience her body and environment. But when they are not met, the only sensory experience she may feel is tension. In an attempt to decrease uncomfortable tension, the child may try to *stop feeling*. As the child reacts to the tension of unmet needs by turning off, she relates to herself and the world in an unreal fashion. The neurotic parent who will not or cannot satisfy the child's needs reinforces the child's unreal behaviour. Often, the child from infancy merely adopts her parent's needs and defense system, and thereafter struggles within to become her real self.

The various parental actions which require the child to repress feeling and to deny primal needs results in what Janov called *Primal Pains*. Primal Pains are needs and feelings which are repressed or denied consciousness. These pains reflect a self-concept which might be expressed as "I am not loved and have no hope of love when I am really myself."

Again, we may observe the similarity here to Rogerian and Gestalt approaches. These Primal Pains originating in repressed needs and feelings are stored up by the infant and child in what Janov called the Primal Pool. "Each time a child is not held when he needs to be, each time he is shushed, ridiculed, ignored, or pushed beyond his limits, more weight will be added to his pool of hurts" (Janov, 1970: 25).

But in addition to this pool of hurts Janov posited a final blow to the child's self-concept which he described as the major *Primal Scene*. This refers to the event in the child's life which after numerous hurts finally weights the scale to alter the child's self-image such that she unconsciously accepts that "there is no hope of being loved for what I am," and defends against full conscious realization of this assessment by slipping quietly into neurosis. After she experiences the Primal Scene she alters her behaviour to conform to parental demands, becomes unreal, and in time her neurotic response becomes automatic.

Note the similarity between Janov and Perls in Janov's comment (1970: 26):

> Neurosis involves being what one is not in order to get what doesn't exist [love]. If love existed, the child would be what he is, for that is love—letting someone be what he or she is.

Thus, Janov points out that nothing wildly traumatic need occur to produce neurosis. The child becomes neurotic by being forced into behaviour which is unreal through inability to express real feeling and satisfy real needs.

Janov (1980: 225-26) sees the major reason for children becoming neurotic as their parents' struggle with their own unmet infantile needs:

> A parent who is critical *as a way of being* is so because he needs his children to be something else, because he, the parent, needs.

The attempts the child makes to please parents Janov called "the struggle." It begins with parents and later *generalizes* to the world:

> Parents can put their child into a neurotic struggle just by the way they are. If the parent is constantly sad, the child may spend a lifetime trying to cheer up his parent. Later being very funny with others is a way of cheering up his parents symbolically. If he has to be the clown to be liked, then that's the kind of personality he's going to develop (Janov, 1980: 223).

MAJOR CONCEPTS AND TERMS OF PRIMAL THERAPY
Now let's examine in slightly more detail some of the major concepts in Primal Therapy introduced above. These are: (1) Primal scenes (2) Primal pain (3) Primal memory (4) Tension and neurosis, and (5) Sensation and feeling.

Primal Scenes
Primal Scenes are described as minor and major. *Minor* Primal Scenes are all the countless experiences in which a child has been ridiculed, rejected, neglected, humiliated, and driven to perform. Eventually all of these events begin to make sense to the child until she adds them together and concludes "They don't like me as I am." This realization is the *major* primal scene and is catastrophic in implication and therefore repressed, denied, and buried. The child then begins "The Struggle" to cover the Primal Pain of lack of love by being unreal, so that she will not know when she is suffering. The major Primal Scene usually occurs between the ages of five and seven years and spells the end of the child as an integrated and connected human being. (In Transactional Analysis, Berne

refers to a similar phenomenon earlier in the child's development as "Days of Decision.")

The Primal Scene is an event which is *not* fully experienced. It is disconnected and unresolved. The full meaning is repressed or never experienced. What *is* experienced is tension and an altered, neurotic life course. It is a course which is not consciously selected or understood, nor is there awareness of the nature or origin or meaning of the neurotic behaviour. Most neurotics don't know they are neurotic.

The way out of the neurosis is to feel the Primal Pain which was never fully experienced. The feeling of the Primal Pain shatters the unreal self in the same way that denying the pain created it.

Primal Pain

Janov (1970) contended that the physical reaction to pain and awareness of pain may not be contiguous, but may occur independently. He referred to certain physiological evidence to support his contention, which is necessary to Primal theory. He suggested therefore that one can be unaware of the pain of primal events while at the same time acting to ensure the pain remains out of awareness. But the cost involved to the organism in suppressing this pain results in the dulling of all feeling responses such that we cease to feel much of anything. The neurosis then has the effect of not merely suppressing awareness of Primal Pain, as was the initial objective, but of suppressing the experiencing of nearly all feelings, pleasant and painful.

The relief or release of Primal Pain may be achieved only through "connection" of the pain to the original unmet need. While each incident related to minor and major Primal Pain need not be relived, the general feeling that accompanied many past experiences must be *felt* again.

The many Primal Pains are seen as filling a tank or pool. Therapy deals with emptying this pool of hurts and pain. When the pool is empty, the person is well.

What prevents people being comfortable in their neurosis is the natural tendency of the organism to be unified, or whole and real; for people to be "themselves."

What is striking about Primal Pain is that even when it is finally fully experienced years later by the adult, it seems to have the same force and intensity as it would have had at the time it originally occurred. The pain seems to live on unchanged or unaffected by time and life events.

The therapist must have the patient experience Primal Pain in order to cure neurosis. This requires the slow dismantling of the patient's defense system. Once the defense system is removed, the patient can begin to feel her own needs, wants, and hurts. This is the key to Primal Therapy: enabling the patient to *feel* deeply, to *recognize* the feeling and to be able to *experience* it fully. Once this has begun, and thought and feeling become re-integrated, feeling surfaces constantly and spontaneously and is experienced as such. Experiencing the hurt enables the patient to free herself from repression and neurotic behaviour, to regain integration of her being and to achieve a real identity. She can be the person she is. In Janov's recent work (1976; 1980), he has given exhaustive attention to developing biochemical and physiological measures of his clients in an attempt to note the changes in the "neurosis" before, during, and after therapy.

Primal Memory
In Primal Therapy the patient is supposed to have primal memory, that is, be capable of recalling actual details of Primal events, or at least of events leading to Primal Pain that were previously not experienced. Are there really such memory banks in the brain? Certainly there is physiological evidence of specific event storage from the work of people like Wilder Penfield. Studies in hypnosis also suggest quite exact recording of experienced events, even those which may be only at the preperceptual level. This view is further supported by Eric Berne and is the basis for Transactional Analysis theory as we will discuss in Part IV.

Perhaps more significant to Primal Theory than whether such memory exists physiologically is whether it is "repressed" and if so what effect this has on later behaviour. Janov obviously feels it is singularly important. Certainly pain either present or imminent does seem to affect memory and learning and it may well prevent or defend against recall or recognition of previously experienced events.

Tension and Neurosis
Janov's explanation and interpretation of the term "tension" is excellent from a clinical perspective. He claimed (1970) that the neurotic feels tension *rather than* real feeling. For the neurotic less tension feels good and more tension feels worse, so the neurotic merely tries to feel *better* or to lower her tension level. Thus, the neurotic has an extremely sterile emotional life both in terms of *breadth* and *intensity* of emotional experience.

Janov viewed tension as a survival mechanism which mobilizes the body either for need-satisfaction or for protection against overwhelming anxiety. But in the case of repressed needs and anxiety, as with Primal Pains, the need is unsatisfied and so the tension remains. The body is mobilized but is unable to act. Thus any suppressed or repressed behaviour results in a state of tension which cannot be expressed or resolved. The mechanism which triggers suppression of feeling of the need is fear. Fear or anxiety is aroused when the experience of Primal Pain is unchecked or when awareness of Primal Pain is about to occur.

Fear is viewed as an intrinsic and automatic response of the organism, part of its survival mechanism: it prepares the organism for attack. Anxiety is tension which is non-focused. For Janov the *basis* of anxiety is the fear of not being loved. The anxious person is reacting to the past as if it were the present. But the fearful person reacts to the present and is therefore more reality-oriented. Real fear occurs when one's life is threatened *now*.

Janov observed (1970) that it is not until the neurotic identifies her tension level as felt anxiety that she comes for therapy. This is most important because, as he stated previously, most neurotics don't recognize their own neurosis. When they do begin to connect their tension with *feeling* and that feeling with a vague *fear* (i.e., more than vague discomfort), and recognize that fear without a source is anxiety, then they may decide to seek help.

He considered the effects of Primal Pain to be permanent until *felt* and did not believe it could be eliminated through cognitive or behavioural approaches. Thus, he maintains that while one may alter the symptoms, Primal Pain will remain and other neurotic behaviours will be developed.

Sensation and Feeling

Janov (1970: 68) defined feeling nicely as "sensation conceptualized." When we attach a name to a sensation, it is conceptualized and can then be thought of or spoken of as "feeling." This is significant in that if we do not identify sensations correctly, we may not be able to satisfy them. That is, we must be able to connect properly the feeling and the need in order to obtain real satisfaction. Primal Pain is only the *sensation* of pain. It is not connected to the unmet need experienced due to the process of repression. In therapy, these *sensations* must become *feelings* by becoming *connected to the specific events or unmet needs which produced them originally*. By connecting the sensation to the previously repressed need, the patient can identify the feeling associated with it and experience it as such. When a pain sensation becomes identified as pain, the neurotic feels.

Until the sensation is properly connected, the neurotic may continue to attempt to meet incorrectly identified needs by behaviour which cannot satisfy the need. For example, we may identify a need as sexual, and attempt unsuccessfully to satisfy it with intercourse. The real need may be a need for being held, or for affection. Thus, many of the sensations or tensions we experience may be misidentified needs. The behaviour we initiate to "satisfy" what we sense to be needs may be inappropriate for this purpose and, rather than bringing us satisfaction, merely reduces our tension briefly. This is the sense in which we unconsciously substitute symbolic needs and satisfactions for the real satisfactions and needs which are repressed as a result of Primal Pain.

Janov (1970) spent considerable effort distinguishing between sensation and feeling. We have already used his definition. By feeling he meant *real* feeling and real feeling means *Primal* feeling. The neurotic, he said (1970), is sensation-bound until she *feels* (experiences Primal Pain and thus Primal feeling). The neurotic seeks to "exchange" painful sensations for pleasant sensations but doesn't feel *good* because all real (Primal) feelings are repressed, and repression is painful. So, no matter what the neurotic does—scuba diving, drinking, sex—her sensations are the same: all painful. Until she *connects* that tight sensation with real feelings, she will spend her life in sensation exchange.

Janov (1970: 72) considered feelings to be all or none:

> Feelings follow the all-or-none principle, in my view. Anything that evokes feeling will cause it to be felt all over the body. To a neurotic however, eroticism will often provide localized sensations in the genitalia, rather than full bodily sexual feelings which are felt from the head to the toes. The fragmentation of the neurotic accounts for his choked laughter, his suppressed sneezes, and speech which seems to ooze out of the mouth without any relation to the rest of the face.

Janov (1970: 74) believed as well that we cannot feel fully if we are cut off from our infant and childhood feelings:

> [T]o feel really rejected means to be writhing in pain during a Primal—to feel utterly alone and unwanted as that child. Once that is felt, there are no more feelings of "rejection"—only feelings about what is going on in the current moment.

SUMMARY

Janov's theory of neurosis has been described as a need-satisfaction theory in which basic survival needs in infancy, and later psychological needs for approval and recognition in childhood, are unfilled. The experience of the child that she is not "loved" for what she is results in what Janov called *Primal Pains*. The child represses or denies conscious awareness of these feelings, and in so doing she begins to lose the natural integration of thought and feeling. As the process of repression continues, a point is reached at around seven or eight years of age when the child develops preconscious awareness that she will never be accepted and loved by her parents for the person she is and must become the person her parents wish. This preconscious realization is called the *Primal Scene*. The repression of real felt needs from this point on in the child's life results in a generalized tension rather than the experience of the Primal Pain which is the feeling of hurt and disappointment at not being loved for what she is. The tension blocks real feelings, and emerges as neurotic symptoms or her attempts at satisfaction of the Primal needs through substitutes.

Since neurosis develops from repression of Primal needs resulting in Primal Pain and grief at not being accepted and loved, Primal Therapy is directed at enabling the patient to feel and experience the original Primal Pain so as to free the patient to feel again. In order to enable the patient to feel, the neurotic defenses of the patient must be eliminated. Once the patient connects her feeling to the original pain and then experiences it fully, she becomes re-integrated in thought and feeling and can begin to live and experience spontaneously in the present. Since patients amass countless Primal Pains over time in what Janov calls their *Primal Pool,* therapy involves the reexperiencing of all Primal Pains, until the pool is empty and the patient is fully re-integrated. Let's consider next the therapeutic techniques employed for this purpose.

GOALS AND TECHNIQUES

Goals

Janov does not outline clearly the goal or aim of Primal Therapy. In *The Primal Scream* (1970), for example, he merely alludes to certain goals or aims in various parts of the text.

> The point of Primal Therapy is to connect the body's needs with the stored and unconscious memories and so unify the person (Janov, 1970: 62).

> Whatever form it takes, the therapy is aimed at old unresolved feelings (Janov, 1970: 89).

In his most recent work, *Prisoners of Pain* (1980), we find a similar handling of therapeutic aims or goals but a change in content. Thus he now seems to focus more on the concept of pain and the experiencing of feeling.

> Pain is not simply an idea or attitude. It is registered as an experience and must be resolved experientially. Thus, one must aim to achieve *through feeling*, a thorough resolution and understanding of how those early events are laid down, where they are buried, and the processes by which they are kept repressed (Janov, 1980: 46).

However, perhaps the best description of the goal is the one already identified in our discussion of neurosis. Here we defined the goal as:

1. Recognizing or becoming aware of our real needs
2. Feeling or experiencing them for what they are
3. Seeking real satisfaction.

Therapeutic Techniques

The technique of Primal Therapy differs significantly in a number of ways from those approaches we have considered thus far. We will look at the first three days of therapy in some detail and then end with a brief look at Primal Groups and the effectiveness of the approach according to Janov. Unfortunately, although the technique of Primal Therapy has reportedly undergone refinement since Janov's description in 1970, he has not indicated these refinements in his later work.

INITIAL CONTACT
The initial contact with the therapist is generally via telephone. In a telephone interview the therapist listens to the patient's description of her problem, warns the patient that Primal is an unusual therapy, and asks her to obtain a thorough physical examination and to send in a letter outlining her life history, problems, previous therapy, and why she wants Primal Therapy. In most cases a personal

interview is unnecessary as the referral is from a physician or a friend familiar with the technique. If psychosis is suspected an interview is requested.

PREPARATION FOR THERAPY

Following the telephone interview and receipt of the patient's letter and medical report and upon decision to admit the patient for therapy, a list of instructions is forwarded to the patient.

The instructions specify that she must give up all alcohol, cigarettes, and drugs for the duration of Primal Therapy—a period of several months. She is told she will have three weeks of individual treatment where she is seen daily followed by several months of group sessions. She is asked not to work or go to school during her first three weeks. She will need all her energy for therapy. She will also be too upset to work even if she wanted to.

The new patient is the only person seen for individual therapy by the therapist during this initial three weeks. She is given all the time she needs each day. Only her feelings will determine when the session ends. Generally sessions last two to three hours.

THE NIGHT BEFORE

Twenty-four hours before beginning therapy the patient is isolated in a hotel room and asked not to leave the room until her therapy hour the following day. She may not read, watch television, or make phone calls. She is permitted to write. If it is believed that this is a well-defended patient she is asked to stay up all night. This procedure may be used occasionally during the first two weeks of individual therapy.

The isolation and sleeplessness are important techniques and often bring a patient close to a Primal. The isolation blocks outlets for tension and the sleeplessness weakens defenses. The aim is to force the patient to be concerned only with herself and her feelings or sensations.

THE FIRST HOUR

The patient arises suffering. She is tired and anxious. She may be kept waiting to build additional tension. The office is semi-dark and the phone off the hook. The patient lies on the couch. She is asked to be spread-eagled, to be in as defenseless a position as possible. What occurs after this depends on the patient.

The patient usually begins to discuss her tensions, problems, etc. If the patient is very tense and afraid the therapist asks the patient to let these feelings overtake her. If she gets panicked the therapist encourages her to call one of her parents for help. This will sometimes produce painful feeling within fifteen minutes. The patient is asked to discuss her early life, and usually states that she cannot remember much. The therapist pushes her to remember what she can. She then begins to speak about her early life. As the patient speaks, the therapist gathers information about the patient's defense system in two ways. First, she observes the *way* the patient talks, and second, *how* she handled situations at home. For example, what does her personal style of telling a story tell about her and what responses did she *learn to make* as a child in interacting with her parents?

The patient then may be asked to "sink" into an early situation that seems to have evoked considerable feeling. As the patient describes a scene vividly she may stop and relate painful bodily sensations. She is encouraged to "stay with it," "feel that." But the feeling usually disappears. This type of reaction may occur repeatedly over several hours or days but eventually the patient is able to maintain the feeling and report for example, "I feel tight all over."

At this point when the therapist sees that the patient is *into* the feeling and holding tight she asks the patient to breathe deeply and hard from the belly and to pull the feeling out. When the patient is breathing deeply and hard, shaking, and writhing, and her breathing is automatic, the therapist urges the patient to express this feeling to the parent in the scenes she has been describing. But as easy as that task seems, most patients are unable to say it. If it is screamed out, it will bring a flood of tears, and stomach-wrenching gasps.

This initial reaction is called a pre-Primal. These may occur for several days or even a week. It is basically a wearing-down process in which the defense system of the patient is being dismantled. It is not done easily after years of reinforcement and nurturing of the system by the patient.

After fifteen minutes or so, the patient usually regains calm and may begin talking with the therapist on a non-feeling level. The therapist then leads her back to a painful situation in childhood. The therapist also continues to *confront* other aspects of the patient's defenses. For example, if the patient is speaking softly, the therapist tells her to speak up. If she is intellectualizing, it is pointed out.

Primal Therapy or its validity is not discussed, since this is seen as diversion from the patient's speaking about herself. Whatever her mask, it is pointed out by the therapist in an effort to get beyond defense to feeling. As a new early situation is described the therapist watches for signs of feeling. When this is noted she again urges the patient to breathe and feel. Finally, the patient becomes shaken. The therapist does not know what feeling is being experienced, nor does the patient. As the patient tenses against the feeling the therapist starts the pulling and breathing exercise. The patient may begin to gag. Again she is urged to say the feeling, that is, *label* it, even though she may not know what she is feeling. She may begin to form a word and thrash about in pain. She is urged to let it come out. Then finally, it will come. A scream, "Daddy be nice," "Mommy, Mommy, help," or just a word, "hate" or "I hate you!"

> This is the Primal Scream. It comes out in shuddering gasps, pushed out by the force of years of suppressions and denials of that feeling (Janov, 1970: 83).

The scream is both a scream caused by the pain being experienced, and a release from it—a *liberating* event in which the patient's defense system is dramatically exposed. It is largely an involuntary act. It is both cause and result of a crumbling defense system.

After the first session the patient returns to her hotel room. The therapist is on constant call should she be needed. The patient still may not watch TV or go to the movies.

THE SECOND SESSION
The patient is usually overwhelmed with insights and arrives anxious to share all of her thoughts. She starts right in, relating memories forgotten the previous day. She may begin weeping within ten minutes. But still she will hide behind masks and continue to maintain her defense system. Then she again strikes a painful memory and the process begins. This time a more violent expression may take place, with writhing and screaming. At the end, the session is terminated and the patient leaves, exhausted.

THE THIRD SESSION
The patient is gradually becoming defenseless. Sometimes she begins crying as soon as she walks into the office. Or she may be found sobbing on the floor in the waiting room. Again a painful memory is described and explored. The patient may now relive completely the past experience with tears, sweating, gasps, retching, tremors, and screams. She talks automatically to her parents and expresses the feelings she has. This is a "Primal," a total feeling-thought experience from the past. The patient is not *discussing* her feelings, she is *feeling* them.

AFTER THE THIRD DAY
The treatment process continues in much the same fashion as described above for the next three weeks. With each new day of therapy further defenses are stripped away, with the process gaining momentum as the patient learns to feel additional pain. Each new "Primal" seems to break loose new hidden memories which lead to additional "Primals."

Although the "Primals" increase in their encompassing intensity, involving more and more of the total organism, there seems too to be a natural pace at which the organism tolerates pain. Therefore, the patient is not hurried, and "Primals" are allowed to occur in an ordered and safe sequence.

This sequence is the tendency for the patient to uncover painful memories further back into her childhood as her treatment progresses. This is often accompanied by the exact voice quality and grammatical structure of that age, regressing eventually to the infantile cry. In respect to the natural sequencing, there is a significant comment made by Janov (1970: 88), about infantile hurts.

> This indicates that even in a preverbal state, trauma exists. It isn't just how the mother or father screamed at the child which produces neurosis; trauma seems to be laid down in the nervous system and remembered *organismically*. The physical system "knows" it is being traumatized even when there is no accompanying consciousness.

After a while there is little for the therapist to do except to remain silent. There is no discussion of pain by the patient, only experiencing.

PRIMAL GROUP

By the end of the third week the major work of dismantling the defense system is done. The patient is not yet well, but it is not necessary to keep her in individual therapy. She may require an individual hour periodically, but the major work can now be done in group therapy.

Post-primal groups meet several times each week for three to four hours. The group is composed of patients who have gone through the three weeks of individual therapy. Its major function is to stimulate group members into new "primals." One person's "primal" may be the stimulus for "primals" by other group members. When many "primals" occur at once the scene is bedlam. But because the "primal" is unsettling, the group also has the purpose of providing comfort and support to group members.

However, the *dynamics* of a primal group differ from most other therapy groups. There is very little interaction of group members with one another—none of the here-and-now, give-and-take characteristic of most groups; no questioning of one another, or display of anger, or fear, to one another. The focus is intrapersonal rather than interpersonal. Group members understand that whatever inordinate reactions do occur in the group, they relate to *old* experiences. And lastly, the primal group time is "defenseless" with people having "primals" immediately in the group since they can no longer hold back repressed feelings.

While the sessions may last two to three hours, the first hour is devoted to "primals," the second to quiet individual reflections and "coming down," and the third to sharing the experience with other group members.

After a year or more of group therapy patients may continue to require primal experience to "empty the tank" but can do so at home and without the aid of a therapist.

EFFECTIVENESS OF PRIMAL THERAPY

In reporting the results of a questionnaire study of 200 post-Primal patients Janov (1980: 169) notes that:

> More than 90 percent felt that Primal Therapy had changed their lives and that they were more in control of their lives. Some 94 percent had not engaged in another form of therapy since Primal Therapy. Over 90 percent felt that Primal Therapy held up over time.

SUMMARY

We might summarize our exploration of Primal Therapy as follows:

1. It was "discovered" and developed as a result of a single accidental clinical event.
2. It is described not as a therapy, but *the* cure for neurosis.

3. Its basic assumptions and major concepts are derived from existing schools of psychology and contemporary helping strategies, and are not "revolutionary" as Janov claimed.
4. It is concerned with internal, not external, events.
5. It is past-oriented.
6. It focuses on childhood and infancy events.
7. It is concerned with identity and self-concept, though these terms are not employed.
8. The concepts of repression and suppression are central to the theory.
9. The concept of love is central to the therapy but is not fully explained.
10. The origin of neurosis is believed to be found in parent-child relationships.
11. The technique does not closely resemble other therapeutic approaches.
12. Both individual and group therapy are employed.
13. The focus in therapy is on the patient's experiencing of feeling.
14. Therapy focuses only on painful experience and feeling.
15. The therapist is directive.
16. It emphasizes the need to evaluate the process and effects of therapy in terms of the biochemical and physiological condition of the patient.

IV

Cognitive Therapies

In Part III, we examined three helping methods which might be said to have as a central focus the *emotional/feeling/sensation* aspect of the client's behaviour. We noted that this was a somewhat arbitrary categorization, and that these approaches, particularly Gestalt Therapy, also included cognitive, social/environmental, and motoric/behavioural aspects. In Part IV we find a similar situation. And so although the three methods included here might be said to reflect an emphasis on the *cognitive/intellectual* and *social/environmental* aspects of client problem behaviour, they also take into account the emotional/sensory and motoric/action components. In this regard, it should be pointed out that what is referred to as "classical" Transactional Analysis (TA) is described here. This is in keeping with the presentation of therapeutic approaches in their "pure" form as originally developed by their founders. Thus Eric Berne's largely cognitive approach to TA now represents only one of the three major schools of TA which have emerged in the past decade. We will look at the development of TA in Chapter 10. Suffice to say at this point that TA has been grouped with the more cognitively oriented approaches because that was Berne's (the founder's) emphasis.

Here are some of the similarities and differences in basic assumptions, concepts, aims, and methods we may anticipate encountering in Rational-Emotive Therapy (RET), Reality Therapy (RT), and TA.

SIMILARITIES
- All three emphasize the importance of early childhood and infancy experience on the later development of neurotic behaviour.
- All three are ex post facto theories resulting from the clinical experience of the originator.
- All three are non-medical approaches which do not consider neurosis or problem behaviour as "illness."

- All three are present- and future-oriented although they do consider the significance of past events as they are experienced now.
- All three have as their aim the increased autonomy, independence, self-fulfillment, and happiness of clients.
- All three focus on developing increased awareness of current behaviour and thought processes.
- All three focus on clients' beliefs about themselves and others.
- All three perceive clients' behaviour as attempts to meet their basic needs.
- All three perceive the client's problem behaviour as involving client choices or decisions which require reexamination.
- All three recognize the importance of the patient-therapist relationship although RT has emphasized this aspect more than RET and TA.
- All three claim to be jargon-free, but use their own unique terminology.
- All three emphasize the importance of praise, attention, and recognition in personality development.
- All three are directive and concrete with the therapist assuming the role of teacher/friend.
- All three require the construction of specific patient contracts or plans which require the patient to do "homework" and report to the therapist on the results.
- All three employ both group and individual therapy sessions.
- All three originators have expressed a social action orientation.

DIFFERENCES
- TA includes a complete theory of personality development and human communication. RET and RT do not have fully developed personality theories and are largely theories of neurosis and/or problem behaviour.
- Language and terminology differ considerably from one approach to the other; TA has the largest esoteric vocabulary.
- RT and TA have an organismic base, the latter being more fully developed, but only TA accepts the concept of self-actualization and a single primary drive to explain human motivation.
- RT and RET have based their motivation theory on three primary needs, with love and happiness being common to both.
- RT and TA include defense mechanisms to explain patient behaviour, RET does not.
- RT and TA were originated by psychiatrists and RET by a psychologist.
- RT and RET deal explicitly with client and societal value and belief systems and their impact on client behaviour.
- RT and TA require the patient to evaluate and assess his behaviour while RET attempts to have the patient cease self-rating behaviour.
- RET focuses on changing patient thinking and beliefs in order to alter the way the patient feels and bring about a change in behaviour. Specific behaviour changes may also be initiated by the RET therapist at the same time. RT, on the other hand, directs its attention to changing the problem behaviour first,

with the expectation that improvements in the client's feeling and thinking will occur subsequently. TA concentrates on increasing awareness of existing beliefs, values, and communication patterns and their relationship to client problem behaviour, so that the client may choose a more appropriate course of action.

Again, as in Part III, there appear to be more similarities than differences in the basic assumptions and treatment philosophies of the therapies in Part IV. It is the therapeutic methods which appear to distinguish each from the other in a significant sense, although even in methods used, we will note some overlap.

8
Rational-Emotive Therapy

Men are disturbed not by things, but by the view which they take of them.

—Epictetus, 500 B.C.

Albert Ellis is recognized as a leading sexologist and sex therapist, as well as being responsible for founding a unique therapeutic approach appropriate for the treatment of a broad range of neurotic behaviour disturbances. Ellis's major contribution to the field of psychotherapy first appeared in 1956, when he revealed his "rational" theory of neurotic disturbance in a paper presented to the American Psychological Association annual meeting. This paper showed Ellis's genius in approaching the problem of the origin of neurosis from the exact opposite position from that which all helpers had until then considered neurotic behaviour. Neurosis had, from the time of Freud, been viewed as a disturbance of *feeling*, usually resulting from repression or suppression of emotion or instinctual urges. The resulting overabundance of bodily tension and anxiety was considered to interfere with normal intellectual functioning, resulting in intellectual confusion, problems in concentration, and/or intellectual rigidity or defensiveness. Thus, the treatment of neurosis was to facilitate emotional expression, reduce the tension level, and enable the client to gain *insight* or a cognitive appreciation of his problem or discomfort.

Ellis demonstrated that neurosis, instead of being viewed as originating in repressed feelings, resulted from *illogical or irrational thinking* on the part of the client. The inappropriate ideas, beliefs, or thoughts of the client, he said, *produce* inappropriate feelings, tension, or emotion, as well as other behaviours, which in turn produce responses from the external world of people and things to confirm the original irrational belief. Thus, treatment of neurosis would require the therapist to concentrate on the client's belief system, values, and thought processes, which initially led to the problem behaviour or distress. While Ellis's early work (1962) seemed to focus almost exclusively on helping the client to gain insight into how his value system and thought processes produced his own problems and misery, Ellis in recent years (1976a, b) has adapted various behaviour therapy techniques (see Part V) to RET, giving it increased potency and applicability.

ALBERT ELLIS (1913-   )

I do not believe that the events of my early childhood greatly influenced my becoming a psychotherapist, nor oriented me to becoming the kind of individual and the type of therapist that I now am. . . . I now believe that children bring to their early environments (and to their benighted and entrapped parents) their own powerful innate predispositions to act in highly individualized ways (Ellis, 1972: 103-4).

Thus Ellis began the autobiographical statement included in Arthur Burton's *Twelve Therapists* (1972). It is an adamant renunciation of the developmental and environmental theory which has been universally accepted as a basic principle in psychology and human behaviour. As an extreme "heredity first and last" position, it is no more acceptable than the opposite orthodox psychoanalytic position of developmental determinism, to which it is a reaction. Certainly, the theory and method for Ellis's approach could incorporate a developmental component without significantly affecting his basic tenets. We must conclude, then, that his extreme anti-environmental stance is taken in a conscious attempt to focus attention on what he believes is unique and essential in RET which distinguishes it from other helping methods. On the other hand, perhaps Ellis's obstreperous personal style and character, rather than information about RET, is the real element revealed by such statements. As we shall see below, Ellis's beliefs about the greater importance of hereditarily determined personality predispositions vis-à-vis early environment influences are reflected in his own childhood experience.

Albert Ellis was born in Pittsburgh, Pennsylvania in 1913, and has lived in New York City almost all of his life. His focus on the rational and cognitive aspect of human behaviour appears to reflect something of his own attempts to deal with early need satisfaction. As a child, Ellis was disabled by a serious kidney disorder and a negative family environment culminating in his parents' divorce when he was twelve. In response to his physical condition, Ellis turned from sports to books, and he learned to cope with the family strife by increasing his awareness and understanding of others' needs and behaviour (Gregg, 1973).

Despite all this, I somehow refused to be miserable. I took my father's absence and my mother's neglect in stride—and even felt good about being allowed so much autonomy and independence (Ellis, 1972: 105).

Ellis's early career choice and careful planning again suggest a personal style which is concrete and goal-oriented. He had decided by the time he reached junior high school that he wanted to become a novelist. However, realizing that this was not a lucrative field, particularly for the novice, he planned to obtain a degree in accounting first. Accounting, he felt, would logically lead to the greatest opportunity for early financial success. With his "fortune" made by the time he was thirty, he could "retire" and carry on his writing with financial security.

The Depression prevented these plans from materializing, but he did complete a degree in Business Administration at the City College of New York in 1934 at the age of 21. His first business venture was unsuccessful and after a series of minor jobs, he became the personnel manager for a gift and novelty firm in 1938.

During these years, Ellis spent most of his spare time writing short stories, plays, novels, essays, and non-fiction books. By the time he was 28, he had completed twenty full-length manuscripts but had not been able to get them published. Ellis finally realized that he was not to be the successful fiction writer he had hoped, and turned his attention instead to non-fiction.

He had become interested in changing values regarding the family and sexuality. If we recall the events described in Chapter 3, this pre-war era saw the world in turmoil. The Depression had shaken the economic and social fabric of America. The "Roaring Twenties" in the U.S.A. had been a time of both license and constraint. On the European scene was the decline of monarchies, social and economic unrest, the new Freudian psychology, existential philosophy, and the rise of Fascism, Nazism, and the persecution of the Jews.

As Ellis amassed more information for a book he was to call *The Case for Sexual Liberty,* his friends began to see him as an expert in this field and to seek him out for advice. Ellis discovered that he enjoyed the role of personal counsellor and decided to pursue further training in the field.

In 1942 Ellis entered the clinical psychology program at Columbia University, and received his master's degree the following year. He began a private practice in family and sex counselling while continuing to work part-time for the novelty and gift firm.

Having continued doctoral studies at Columbia, Ellis received his Ph.D. in 1947. By this time Ellis was steeped in the new psychoanalysis and believed it to be the most effective form of psychotherapy. He was determined to become a psychoanalyst himself. Although psychoanalytic institutes had by this time refused to admit trainees without M.D. degrees, Ellis found an analyst who agreed to work with him. He completed his own analysis and began to practice classical psychoanalysis under his analyst's supervision.

During this time, he held various teaching and clinical positions in the New York area. But he soon discovered his faith in psychoanalysis waning. In particular, he noted that the patients he saw once a week or every other week seemed to progress just as well as the patients he saw daily. When he began to take a more active role in therapy than is appropriate in orthodox psychoanalysis, his clients seemed to improve more quickly. More and more he found himself reverting to his old role of sex and family counsellor in which he gave advice and made direct interpretations of behaviour and events. He recalled that, prior to his own analysis, he had relied on the philosophies of people like Epictetus, Marcus Aurelius, Spinoza, and Bertrand Russell to help him sort out his problems. He began to teach his clients these principles that had worked for him.

By 1955 Ellis had given up psychoanalysis completely and had begun to evolve his own unique approach of confronting people with their irrational beliefs and persuading them to give them up in favour of a more rational value system. He found this role to be one that enabled him to be more genuine, and from which he received greater personal satisfaction.

In 1956 Ellis presented his new *Rational Psychotherapy* to the American Psychological Association annual meeting. His first book on Rational-Emotive Therapy, *How to Live With a Neurotic,* was published in 1957, and two years later he founded his Institute for Rational Living in New York City.

Ellis's Institute is a thriving centre with a staff involved in preparing print, videotape and film materials on RET and designing courses, seminars, and workshops for professionals and laypeople throughout the U.S.A. and Canada. Since 1957 he has published more than thirty books and more than four hundred articles on RET, sex, and marriage.

AIMS, BASIC ASSUMPTIONS, AND MAJOR CONCEPTS

Undeveloped Theory of Normal Human Behaviour

As was the case with Perls and Janov, Ellis has not presented a theory of normal human growth and development or personality. Like them, he has concentrated on describing the development and maintenance of the *neurotic* personality and made only cursory comments in passing with regard to the normal. While psychoanalytic concepts and dynamics are not evident in his approach, he does utilize social learning theory to explain the development of neurotic behaviour in much the same way as did Rogers, Perls, and Janov. Thus, he too holds that the "normal," in the sense of the average, is the neurotic in our society, with the true normal being the exception. While Ellis has recently begun to employ some of the operant conditioning principles of the behaviour therapies (1976a, b) as a therapeutic adjunct, he considers his approach to be essentially humanistic, phenomenological, and holistic in character (Ellis, 1979b: 90):

> It particularly focuses upon and employs people's experiences and values; it accepts all individuals with their human limitations; it emphasizes their ability to create and direct their own destinies; and it views them as holistic, goal-directed, self-actualizing people who are important in their own right, just because they are alive, and (together with their fellow humans) have the right to continue to exist and enjoy and fulfill themselves.

This is a very important statement of Ellis's own value system and is worth examining briefly. Note first that he states that RET focuses on people's "experiences and values." Thus, there is a concern with both past and present experience, or with both social learning and phenomenology or our subjective perception of our internal and external environments. The interest in client values is significant in RET since it leads to an appreciation of client motivation and the importance of having the client become aware of needs, goals, options, and choices.

Second, Ellis claims that RET "accepts all individuals with their human limitations." This is an unusually explicit statement of the concept of positive regard or acceptance underlying RET. It reflects Ellis's disregard of a social or external value system which imposes expectations and standards as ideals for which to strive, or with which to gauge our success or "goodness." As he said later, "people are important in their own right, just because they are alive."

Third, he points out the importance of men's and women's unique ability "to create and direct their own destinies." Ellis seems to suggest here that in RET individuals are viewed as essentially creative dynamic organisms who not only have the potential for self-direction, but also the *right* to choose their own fate.

Fourth, RET views individuals holistically as functioning and acting as integrated organic wholes, such that any dysfunction will affect all other aspects.

Fifth, RET considers individuals to be goal-directed and self-actualizing. The concept of goals is particularly significant for RET, as we shall see below in discussing some differences Ellis has with existential psychology. The perception of people as naturally goal-directed, however, does imply self-control and the processes of choosing, planning, and organizing behaviour for goal pursuit and attainment. Ellis's use of the term "self-actualization" appears to be synonymous with self-fulfillment and does not include the motivational single drive component originally intended by Goldstein. In RET, self-actualization seems to mean the development of an individual's potential such that he or she is able to satisfy intrinsic needs and goals and experience a sense of personal enjoyment and happiness. It does *not* mean *being* the person that one truly *is*.

Sixth, RET, while sanctifying individual autonomy, also appears to recognize the significance of social responsibility as a natural consequence of the human condition in the statement that individuals ". . . (together with their fellow humans) have the right to continue to exist and enjoy and fulfill themselves."

Contained in this statement of RET's essential humanistic bias is an implied acceptance of the unique human attributes with which we identified normal human behaviour in Chapter 1: positive self-regard, self-control, personal responsibility, social responsibility, competence, and personal ideals, values, or goals. But while Ellis's RET seems wholly humanistic, it is not entirely existential.

In particular, Ellis believes the existential concepts of "being" and "essence" and the corresponding single drive theory of "self-actualization" place both restrictive and proscriptive demands on individuals, which are essentially negative in effect. Ellis feels that the concepts of "being" and "essence" promote perfectionistic values which are translated into self-rating ideas such as self-esteem or self-confidence. Ellis believes self-rating to be destructive because it promotes an unrealistic goal of perfection which, because it is unattainable, can only lead to self-depreciation. Ellis promotes instead the idea of our fallibility and *im*perfection in an effort to increase individual self-acceptance. Further, while Ellis accepts the importance of the concept of "choice" or "choosing," he refuses to align this process with the concept of "being," since it leads ultimately to ontological guilt, another destructive self-rating outcome. In fact,

Ellis (1976a), in his attempt to avoid what he feels are negative aspects of self-rating, even though they are holistically oriented, allows a logical inconsistency in conceiving of behaviour in terms of external traits and characteristics. Thus, one's "essence" or "being" or identity, according to Ellis, is not determined or expressed by one's behaviour or actions. This suggests that somehow one's behaviour may be dissociated with one's self.

What, then, are we if we are not what we do? Do we not define our nature and establish our identity on the basis of our behaviour? Ellis would refuse to answer the first question, since by its very phrasing it implies an existential answer. But he could easily deal with the second without referring to human essence or being. He does this by identifying three basic human goals and values which reflect his motivation theory. Thus, instead of concerning himself with what humans are or might be, Ellis looks instead at three basic human goals or values: survival, absence of pain, and happiness. Survival and absence of pain reflect physical need satisfaction while happiness is a psychological need. The first two are self-explanatory. The third, happiness, would obviously be wholly subjective in definition and reflect the individual's personal values. It would necessarily include the additional elements of self-direction, social relationships, and self-fulfillment.

In summary, then, Ellis, like Perls and Janov, has not articulated a theory of normal human growth and development against which to consider his theory and treatment of neurotic behaviour. The underlying value system for RET, however, does suggest a perception of essential normal human attributes which is consistent and compatible with the model developed in Chapter 1. Ellis's refusal to adopt or to deal with the existential concepts of "essence" and "being" creates a logical flaw in his claim that RET is holistic. This may be scientifically objectionable, but Ellis appears to sacrifice his scientific principles on humanistic grounds. At least in this sense he acts consistently in terms of his own values. He rejects the existential concepts of essence and being, which promote a perfectionistic ideal, because perfectionism underlies much neurotic behaviour. He does so with apparent ease because he is more interested in therapeutic effectiveness than in theoretical perfection. In 1958 he wrote:

> In consequence, the therapist who *only* employs logical reconstruction in his therapeutic armamentarium is not likely to get too far with many of those who seek his help. It is vitally important, therefore, that any therapist who has a basically rational approach to the problem of helping his clients overcome their neuroses also be quite eclectic in his use of supplementary, less direct, and somewhat less rational techniques (Ellis, 1958: 49).

Ellis appears to have retained this openness about his methods which is reflected in the changes and inclusions made over time, and while his writing and speaking style may at times convey the impression of arrogance or certitude, his recent (1979b) defense against such allegations suggests otherwise:

> . . . I merely claim to "know" about my clients on probabilistic grounds since both my clinical experience and literally hundreds of controlled psychological

experiments have now shown that many of the basic theories of RET are backed by observable data (Ellis, 1977). RET claims no complete or absolutist knowledge of anything, and doubts whether such knowledge exists (Ellis, 1979b: 91).

Let's turn now to Ellis's theory of neurotic disturbance.

The Rational-Emotive Theory of Neurosis

AN OVERVIEW

The following basic assumptions underly Ellis's theory of neurotic behaviour and therapeutic approach:

1. Thoughts produce feelings and emotions. "Thoughts" may include beliefs, values, ideas, attitudes, and assumptions.
2. Emotions produce positive and/or negative behaviour. Positive behaviour is behaviour which fulfills the basic goals set by the person. Negative behaviour is behaviour which does not lead to basic goal fulfillment. (Remember that the basic goals are (1) survival, (2) freedom from pain, and (3) happiness.)
3. Illogical or irrational thoughts or beliefs produce inappropriate feelings and emotions. Inappropriate emotions may be emotions which are unwarranted given the real situation, or feelings which are exaggerated or too intense for the real stimulus situation.
4. Inappropriate emotions, that is, emotions which are unwarranted and/or exaggerated given the actual situation, result in negative behaviour.
5. Negative behaviour results in the individual's failure or inability to fulfill his basic goals and values.
6. When the individual is able to change his illogical and irrational thoughts and ideas to logical, rational beliefs, he will change his emotions from inappropriate to appropriate, and in turn, his behaviour from negative to positive, such that his basic goals will be fulfilled rather than unfulfilled. Thus, we can make ourselves feel bad and behave in such a way as to prevent the satisfaction of our chosen goals by the kinds of thoughts and ideas we have. However, by changing our ideas and beliefs, we can begin to feel good, which results in behaviour that leads to our self-fulfillment.

Let's examine Ellis's basic assumptions more closely now with an exploration of his use of the major concepts involved: (1) emotion, (2) reason and rationality, and (3) neurosis.

DEFINITIONS OF KEY CONCEPTS

Emotion
Emotion is very broadly defined by Ellis as indicated in his use of Stanley Cobb's (1950) definition:

> ... (1) an introspectively given affective state, usually mediated by acts of interpretation; (2) the whole set of internal physiological changes, which help (ideally) the return to normal equilibrium between the organism and its environment; and (3) the various patterns of overt behaviour, stimulated by the environment and implying constant interaction with it, expressive of the stirred-up physiological state (2) and also the more or less agitated psychological state (1).... An emotion [constitutes] rather, an acute disturbance, involving marked somatic changes, experienced as a more or less agitated feeling.... Thus an emotion [remains] at once physiological, psychological, and social since other persons usually [emerge as] the most highly emotogenic stimuli in our civilized environment (Ellis, 1976a: 18-19).

Emotion, then, does not occur by itself, in isolation from the organism or its environment. In fact, none of the basic life processes essential for the basic goals of survival, freedom from pain, and happiness exist autonomously. Perception, emotion, movement, and thinking are seen to be interrelated. As Ellis says (1976a: 16):

> We function, then holistically—perceiving, moving, thinking and emoting simultaneously. Our four basic modes of relating to the world do *not* work separately each beginning where the others leave off. They all significantly overlap and denote different aspects of the same life processes.

However, *intense* emotion, while having survival value at times, is generally seen as *interfering* with the integration of these processes, particularly in the attainment of the third basic life goal, happiness. The focus of attention in therapeutic psychology has therefore been on helping people to change or control intense (inappropriate) emotion which is disruptive to the other three life processes. Ellis (1976a) noted that the therapist may use three approaches to effect change or control of debilitating emotion: (1) physical means (drugs), (2) motoric or emotive means (catharsis, role-playing, screaming), and (3) rational means (reason, values, ideas, reality). (As has been indicated earlier, Ellis has also employed certain behaviour therapy techniques to support RET methods.) He suggests that while physical and motoric or emotive techniques may bring temporary relief or control, philosophic and rational changes are necessary for producing substantive and permanent change and control. Does this concentration on reason and rationality mean that one is expected to behave as a machine, a human computer, a Mr. Spock? How then does Ellis define reason and rationality?

Reason and Rationality
Ellis (1976a: 23) quotes Dr. Maxie Maultsby, one of his disciples, as follows:

> Rational thinking has the following four characteristics: (1) It [bases itself] primarily on objective fact as opposed to subjective opinion. (2) If acted upon, it most likely will result in the preservation of your life and limb rather than your premature death or injury. (3) If acted upon, it produces your personally defined

life's goals most quickly. (4) If acted upon, it prevents undesirable personal and/or environmental conflict.

Ellis suggests, however, that thinking and emoting are not discrete processes but rather are closely interrelated. They can be distinguished from one another when externally observed in this way: *Thinking* behaviour is characterized by tranquility, low level of activity, and an objective response to the environment. *Emotional* behaviour is characterized by less tranquil, more somatically involved, activity-directed, vigorous behaviour, and a subjective response to the environment.

Although it is *possible* to think without emoting, or to experience emotion in the absence of thought, typically there is an interrelationship between the two. Thus, as Ellis points out (1976a: 22):

> You do not *merely* feel; nor do you *just* (for no reason) feel. You feel, rather because you *evaluate* things as good or bad, favourable or disadvantageous to your chosen goals. And your feelings motivate—move—you to survive and feel happy (or unhappy) while surviving.

Thinking or reasoning, then, is involved first in assessing or evaluating things in the environment as *good* or *bad*. The evaluation of these "things" as good/positive, or bad/negative, is what produces this *feeling*/behaviour of attraction to, or repulsion from, these "things."

When these feelings help a person to achieve survival and happiness goals, they are viewed as *appropriate*. When they block basic goal attainment they are viewed as *inappropriate*. Rational thinking as described above normally leads to appropriate, and irrational thinking to inappropriate, emoting or feeling.

Although emotion *may* exist without thought, it does not do so for any sustained period of time. We cannot sustain emotion (or have awareness of it) for any period without thinking about it. And in this context thinking consists for Ellis of self-talk, self-verbalizations, or internalized sentences. What we say to ourselves, then—our thoughts, ideas, attitudes, and values—precede, accompany, and subsequently sustain, our feelings and emotions. Thus if we are telling ourselves irrational or illogical ideas or beliefs, we will create inappropriate feelings which will produce behaviour which cannot be directed at attaining basic survival and happiness goals. If such thinking characterizes our behaviour, we are neurotic.

Neurosis

Ellis defines neurosis as stupid behaviour by non-stupid people. Neurosis is characterized by inappropriate, self-destructive emotion, such as severe anger, depression, guilt, or anxiety, resulting from consciously or unconsciously held prejudiced, childish, irrational ideas which lead to inefficient, self-sabotaging behaviour and the lack of fulfillment of personal goals. He is in agreement with Carkhuff and Berenson, Rogers, Perls, and Janov that the neurotic personality is the norm in our society, not because we did not experience unconditional positive regard as infants and children, which is in itself a value, but rather because the overall values of our society are themselves irrational and illogical. We don't make up crazy things to believe and revere all by ourselves; we have a lot of help. If we briefly reflect, we could not conceive of a more irrational world than the one in which we now live. We come by our confusion of values, our conflicting ideas, and our illogical belief systems honestly. While we have certainly made amazing technical advancements in the past century, which would permit sharing in peace and prosperity the world's resources, we find ourselves instead closer than ever before to nuclear annihilation and locked in conflict in almost every facet of modern living. We have waste and greed side by side. The poverty gap between the haves and the have-nots grows. Political leadership has become synonymous with stupidity and corruption. Power struggles are no longer confined to the powerful versus the powerful but include the weak versus the weak. Business is viewed with distrust and seems characterized by fraud. Labour has adopted the style of management. The church, if not seen as ridiculous, is considered ineffectual. On a personal level we daily interact with friends, colleagues, and family members who behave irritatingly, ignorantly, provocatively, insensitively, callously, ineffectually, even viciously. Modern life, says Ellis (1976a), rather than a bowl of cherries, resembles a barrel of prune pits. But he does not despair. The solution is in learning to cope. And learning to cope means learning to live rationally, learning to give up the irrational values and beliefs which characterize the world today and impede the attainment of the basic human goals for survival, absence from pain, and happiness. How can we do this? Let's first look at how we develop and maintain our emotional disturbance. Since we all have our share of irrational ideas and beliefs, we are all to some extent at least neurotic in the sense that we all at times permit these beliefs to impede or defeat our goal of attaining happiness and self-fulfillment.

THE PROCESS OF NEUROTIC DEVELOPMENT

Ellis utilizes a simple paradigm to describe what he calls the ABC theory of emotional disturbance, in which:

>   A = an Activating experience or event,
>   B = a Belief system (iB irrational belief)
>   (RB rational belief), and
>   C = an emotional Consequence (iC inappropriate C)
>   (AC appropriate C).

When an emotional response occurs at point C, it is not the activating event at point A which results in C, but rather the belief system we hold about A. B, our beliefs (what we say to ourselves), creates C, the emotional response, not A. Thus, if an inappropriate emotional response (iC), results following an activating event (A), it occurs in response not to (A) directly, but in response to the irrational beliefs (iB) we hold about (A). The equation then would be:

> If A leads to → iB, the iC will occur which will
> deny basic goal attainment and self-fulfillment.

If, on the other hand, the emotional response to A is appropriate, AC resulting from a rational belief about A, then basic goal attainment is assured. In this case the equation would be:

If $A \rightarrow RB \rightarrow AC$ = goal attainment

For example, let's suppose that after experiencing some loss (A) we could identify feelings such as disappointment or sorrow which were considered appropriate to the situation (AC). In expressing our values or beliefs about the loss or in simply thinking about it, we might say, "I think it is unfortunate I lost this thing." If this statement was based on rational and logical grounds (RB), then we would need to be able to logically or empirically confirm this statement that in fact some disadvantage is experienced in terms of our own value system and life goals as related to the loss.

If, however, we felt anxiety and depression which were considered inappropriate emotions, as a result of the loss, we would have had to have held certain irrational beliefs about the loss. This would in effect be saying to ourselves, "I find it *awful* or *terrible* that I have lost this thing." Why should this be an irrational belief and produce an inappropriate emotional response? Because, as Ellis says (1976a: 77-78):

> No matter how very, very unfortunate you find it to have lost your mate or your job, it still emerges only as unfortunate. Even when you deem it extremely, exceptionally, or outstandingly unfortunate, it still cannot rate as *more* than that. And the term *awful*, when it leads to panic or depression, really means—think of it now; do not merely take our word for it!—infinitely more than unfortunate. It has a magical, surplus meaning, which has no empirical referent. . . .
>
> Your seeing any Activating Experience or Event as *awful, horrible, terrible* gives the illusion that you absolutely cannot control it and that you must remain too weak to cope with the *awful* essence of the universe that creates such horror and insists on plaguing you with it.

Thus if this is our belief system (B) then such emotional responses as panic, anxiety, and depression may be *logical*.

But if our belief system is not true, cannot be proven, defended, or given consensual validity, then it is *irrational* and the resulting emotional responses it creates, such as panic, anxiety, and depression, are inappropriate and therefore indicate emotional disturbance or neuroticism.

"Well," one might say, "OK, Ellis has indicated *where* our irrational beliefs come from and *how* they result in emotional disturbance or neurotic self-defeating behaviour. But surely we recognize our failures to attain the goals we want. Why don't we learn what it is we need to alter, and change our beliefs? What prevents us from thinking clearly and feeling appropriately?"

Ellis suggests that, while we may indeed be aware of being unhappy and/or unsuccessful in getting what we want out of life, and even recognize that many of our difficulties are related to our own behaviour, we are in fact *not* able to change this behaviour on our own. The reason we are unable to change is that we do not understand why we behave the way we do in the first place. In brief, we lack insight and awareness of our own motives and behaviour in three ways:

1. We fail to recognize the relationship of current problems to earlier events involving certain ideas, beliefs, or values learned in childhood.
2. We fail to appreciate that irrational ideas that we created or acquired in our early lives still continue to direct our behaviour, and that they largely continue to do so because we habitually reindoctrinate ourselves with such ideas and work hard, consciously and unconsciously, to retain them.
3. We fail to accept personal responsibility for our problems continuing and to realize that only if we *actively work* to change our current beliefs and values will our problems be eliminated.

In summary, then, we maintain our neurotic behaviour because we (1) inadequately understand the connection between past events (beliefs and values) and our present behaviour, (2) fail to appreciate that these past influences are maintained in the present by what we ourselves continue to tell ourselves, and (3) do not know that we can eliminate our problem behaviour only by working at changing our irrational ideas and beliefs and by beginning to tell ourselves things which make sense in the present. Only in this way can we attain more of the things we want such as love, recognition, and comfort, or the basic human goals of survival, freedom from pain, and happiness.

DEVICES FOR MAINTAINING
EMOTIONALLY DISTURBING BEHAVIOUR

Ellis (1976a) describes four major activities through which we reindoctrinate ourselves with emotionally disturbing ideas: (1) overgeneralizing, (2) confusing past and present, (3) using words inaccurately or incorrectly, and (4) self-rating. Let's examine each of them carefully and discover how powerfully and negatively our own thoughts can determine our behaviour.

Overgeneralizing

Ellis points out (1976a) that self-deprecating beliefs and emotions often stem from unrealistic overgeneralizations that have no scientific validity. They contain magical formulations that remain subjective and unprovable. For example we might say, "I have failed at this task and I find that disadvantageous or unfortunate." This can be objectively tested, that is, we can prove whether or not we failed and what goals the failure affects for us. If, however, we say "I have failed at this task and I find it *awful* and it proves I'm a *failure*," we make two statements that cannot be tested empirically. First, we cannot really define "awfulness" since it seems to suggest something more than 100 per cent disadvantageous, obnoxious, or inconvenient. It is difficult to conceive of just what "awful" would be in that sense. What it suggests is that we *can't stand* failing and we *should not* fail. But in fact we *can* stand failing and it is not written anywhere in the universe that we should or must not fail. The second hypothesis that failing makes us *a failure* means (1) that unfortunately we have in fact failed, (2) that since we have failed we have essential and intrinsic *failingness* and we will therefore *always* and *only* fail, and that (3) one who always fails, "a failure," is bad and punishable. The only part of this hypothesis that can in fact be confirmed, however, is the *failing*. It is obvious that we cannot confirm what is yet to happen nor would this likely be possible even by examining all past behaviour. Thus a label of "failure" cannot be proven. It is an overgeneralization based on insufficient fact.

Confusing Past and Present
We maintain our disturbances as well by continuing to hold on to irrational ideas and beliefs from the past. The importance of these ideas to our present behaviour, however, is not merely that they originated in the past, nor even what our ideas and attitudes were about these events, but that we *still now*, in the present, believe them. It does not matter whether we accurately recall the events, or even whether or not the events actually occurred. What is important is what we *believe* about these events *now*. Maternal rejection in childhood, for example, is considered by many to be a serious event which leads to neurotic behaviour. However, as we know, it is not merely the past event, rejection, whch is important but, as well, (1) what the child thought or believed then about the rejection and (2) what the adult thinks about it now. If we are able to consider the idea of maternal rejection rationally and wholly objectively, we might possibly conclude that our cultural ideas and attitudes about maternal rejection are themselves so powerful that *they*, rather than the behaviour itself, produce the negative feelings and responses we make to this behaviour. The child's experience of maternal rejection without awareness of such ideas may not be too devastating.

On the other hand, ideas and beliefs which may have been appropriate or significant at an earlier time may on careful examination no longer be significant in the present. Thus, while one may have been justifiably angry at parental neglect as a child, such anger maintained in later life would be logical only on the grounds that parental dependence is still required by the now adult child. In fact, the adult does not require his parents to be dependable or nourishing any longer. To continue to maintain his anger (emotion) in the present, based on conditions (beliefs) experienced in the past, is therefore inappropriate and self-defeating. His only rational course is to begin to concentrate on changing his own ideas and beliefs and to cease trying to change his parents'.

Using Words Inaccurately or Incorrectly
As simplistic as it may at first appear, Ellis points out that neurotic and disturbed individuals maintain their disturbance through a number of semantic mistakes. They incorrectly substitute or exchange certain words and concepts for one another which are not identical or interchangeable. The following are

typical semantic mistakes made by neurotic and disturbed individuals which maintain inappropriate feelings and problem behaviour.

"Thinking & believing = feeling"

A casual use of language, perhaps reflecting an over-emotionalizing in our culture, involves the exchange of the two very different processes of thinking and feeling. Thus one finds people saying things like:

"How do you *feel* about inviting Mary to dinner?"

when what is meant is:

"What do you *think* about inviting Mary to dinner?" or
"I *feel* that we have made a good decision in this case."

when what is meant is:

"I *believe* that we have made a good decision."

Thoughts, attitudes, beliefs, ideas, and assumptions are not emotions, sensations, and feelings, and vice versa. It is important then to note this confusion and the way in which the semantic mistakes of the neurotic *impede* clear thinking and *prevent* rational behaviour.

"Wants = needs; wishes = demands"

A *need* means necessity, compulsion, obligation; something required for life and happiness. In our culture we often confuse the *needs* of children with the *wants* of adults. The term "need" is used by the neurotic or disturbed individual when what is really meant is "prefer," "desire," or "want." Thus when the term "need" is used, what is usually meant is "strongly desire" or "like" something that brings pleasure. But while we may *like* to have all desires and wants fulfilled and would be temporarily disappointed or inconvenienced if they are not, most desires and wants are *not essential* for survival or happiness. To assume or believe that satisfaction of wants and desires is necessary for survival is irrational and will produce inappropriate emotion and problem behaviour.

In the same way, the neurotic translates what are initially healthy *wishes* into unhealthy *demands* while personally refusing to help satisfy the demand. Ellis (1976a) gives the example of a person, fearing that a maid will not carry out household responsibilities satisfactorily, demanding that she have a Ph.D. in home economics before hiring her. Thus, his healthy desire or wish for domestic competence becomes an unhealthy demand which cannot be attained.

"Unfortunate, inconvenient, disadvantageous = awful, horrible, terrible;
Prefer = must, should, ought."

While Ellis contends that RET will not make people happy, he does claim that RET will enable people to be free from severe *un*happiness which is the mark of the neurotic and disturbed person. In this context he gives a cogent definition of *un*happiness or misery and shows the distinction between rational and neurotic thinking and the resulting appropriate and inappropriate emotion:

> Misery . . . consists of two fairly distinct parts: (1) desiring, wishing, or preferring that you achieve some goal or purpose and feeling disappointed and irritated when you do not achieve it [rational thinking and appropriate feeling]; and (2) demanding, insisting, commanding, and gently necessitating that you achieve this goal or purpose and feeling bitter, enraged, anxious, despairing, and self-downing when you do not [irrational thinking and inappropriate emotion]. We distinguish, in consequence, between healthy feelings of sorrow or irritation when you lose something you clearly desire; and unhealthy feelings of depression or rage stemming from your childish refusal to *accept* a world with frustrations and losses, and from your *whining* that such things absolutely *must* not exist (Ellis, 1976a: 77).
>
> Unhappiness [then] actually seems to consist of at least two distinct elements: (1) a feeling of sadness, sorrow, irritation, annoyance, or regret at your not getting what you want or at your getting what you do not want; and (2) a second and quite different feeling of anxiety, depression, shame, or rage because (a) you see yourself as deprived or balked and (b) foolishly convince yourself that you should not, *must* not, suffer frustration and that things remain *horrible*, and *awful* because you have suffered (Ellis, 1976a: 76).

As Ellis points out, there is an important semantic difference between saying and believing that something is unfortunate, and believing that it is awful or horrible. We can do something about misfortune, but turning it into catastrophe in the "terrible" or "awful" belief category results in: *thoughts* that we are powerless to do anything about it; *demands* that someone do something; *predictions* that no solution is possible; and self-deprecating statements that "prove" one deserves such misfortunes.

By "horriblizing" and "awfulizing" misfortune and loss, we are really saying that *because* one finds it exceptionally disadvantageous, it *should* not, *must* not, *ought* not to exist.

Ellis demonstrates the illogical character of such thinking as follows:

> Something "horrible" or "awful" . . . really means something that you see as (a) unusually obnoxious and (b) absolutely should or must not exist *because* you find it obnoxious. Although you can fairly easily prove the first part of this belief—that you find the thing or act uncommonly obnoxious—you cannot prove the second part: that it *therefore* must not exist. Indeed, if a law of the universe held that Activity Events (at point A) that you find extremely unpleasant (at point B) must not exist (at point C), A and C could not possibly coexist. So when you dogmatically contend (a) that such events must not prevail and (b) that they distinctly (and horribly!) *do* you patently believe in the impossible. If

you accept reality—and stop making up immutable laws of the universe in your silly head—you can accept the obvious fact that whatever exists exists—no matter how unpleasant and inconvenient you find its existence. Consequently, nothing truly winds up as "awful," "horrible," or "terrible" (1976a: 146-47).

Self-Rating
A fourth means by which the neurotic maintains emotionally disturbing ideas and values is self-rating. As we discussed earlier, Ellis does not agree with the validity of the concept of personal or intrinsic worth since it leads to self-rating, which he considers dangerous. He suggests (1976a: 98) that if one insists on maintaining such intrinsic values, ". . . you'd better claim to have it by virtue of your mere existence, your aliveness, your essence—and not because of anything you do to 'earn' it." The reason for this is that obviously no one can give or award this to us. Others can only give us *ex*trinsic value—worth to them. If *in*trinsic value exists, one has it because one chooses or decides to have it. It exists through personal definition only; we are "good" if we think we are.

This is considered by Ellis to be a highly significant truth, since if we do not rate but rather consider ourselves intrinsically worthwhile by choosing to do so, there is no *need* for the approval of others. This does not mean that we should attempt to rate ourselves, however. Ellis cautions that we should avoid in particular attempting to determine our intrinsic value on the basis of our behaviour or deeds. This is self-rating and is as pernicious as leaving our personal value to be determined by others. If we say, "I like myself because of *this*," we can just as easily say, "I don't like myself because of *that*." The danger of self-rating our worth or value based on our behaviour leads to establishing perfectionistic goals and setting ourselves up for failure. Subsequent failure brings guilt, self-disrespect, self-blame, shame, anger, hostility, etc. Instead, Ellis suggests avoiding the establishment of both "worth" based on effectiveness or "goodness," and worthlessness based on ineffectiveness or "badness," by acknowledging only that one *exists*.

The term "self-acceptance," on the other hand, is considered to be an important and positive concept:

> . . . self-acceptance means fully accepting yourself, your existence, and your right to live and to devise as happy a life as you can for yourself—no matter what traits you have or performances you do. It does not mean self-esteem, self-confidence, self-respect, or self-regard. For all these terms imply that you can accept yourself *because* you do something well or because other people like you. Self-acceptance, however, merely means that you accept yourself because you remain alive and have *decided* to accept yourself. Only a relatively limited number of talented, intelligent, competent, or well-loved people can gain self-esteem or self-confidence. But anyone, merely because he chooses to have it, can gain self-acceptance (Ellis, 1976a: 100).

We have examined four commonly used devices for maintaining emotionally disturbing and self-defeating behaviour and have noted they are characterized by absolutistic and perfectionistic thinking. Let's look now at some common irrational beliefs and values themselves which Ellis claims result in and maintain emotional disturbance.

TEN COMMON IRRATIONAL BELIEFS

1. ". . . the idea that you *must have love or approval from all the people you find significant*" (Ellis, 1976a: 88).

The assumption that people *need* approval is incorrect. While we in fact *desire* or prefer approval, we don't need it. That is to say, our survival does not depend on the approval of others. Thus, the adult may, as Ellis says (1976a: 90), ". . . accept the disapproval of others, make allowances for it, do something about it, and come off relatively unscathed. He may never learn to *like* disapprobation or negative criticism; but he may definitely learn to *tolerate* it and to *use* it for his own good."

2. "The idea that you must prove thoroughly competent, adequate, and achieving . . ." (Ellis, 1976a: 102).

Again, as was indicated above, this idea involves the assumption that people are only valued in proportion to their accomplishments and that lack of competence or adequacy is cause for scorn, exile, and death. This idea includes the following irrational notions: that human perfection is possible; that achievement is an indicator of personal worth; that some aspect of one's behaviour is equal in value to one's total being; that recognized accomplishment brings happiness; that accomplishment makes one *better* than others. In fact inordinate striving leads inevitably to failure and, even worse, fear of failure.

3. "The idea that when people act obnoxiously and unfairly, you should blame and damn them, and see them as bad, wicked, or rotten individuals" (Ellis, 1976a: 113).

Ellis finds this irrational belief to be the very essence of emotional disturbance. He says (1976a) it is invalid for the following reasons:

a. Much of human behaviour in fact is not rationally determined as we have shown, but results from the "programming" of parents, media, societal values, and habits.
b. The concept of goodness and badness is not universal, but is a "relative" depending on societal or cultural definitions.
c. Even if the standards of good and bad are agreed upon, blaming wrongdoers does little since it does not teach them to *do* good, it simply says they *are* bad.

Once people accept the concept of blame and devaluate themselves as human beings for having done a wrong act, they will tend either to consider themselves worthless and inadequate (instead of merely mistaken or unethical) or will (rather than devaluate themselves) refuse to admit that they committed errors in this act; or they may even refuse to admit that they committed the act at all. . . . They don't get around to the relatively simple act of correcting their behaviour, because (due to self-blame) they feel preoccupied either with punishing themselves or with refusing to admit that they did wrong in the first place. Blame or guilt, then, instead of alleviating wrongdoing, often leads to further immorality, hypocrisy, and even evasion of responsibility (Ellis, 1976a: 114).

d. "Blaming people" he claims (1976a: 115) "confuses wrong acts with their sinful *essence*." This is the same dilemma as was discussed above with self-rating. One is not one's acts in the sense that this does not define or limit what one *is*.
e. Blaming others results in the production of angry feelings towards them. The angry or hostile feelings reflect a superiority which might be articulated as "because I do not like your behaviour you *should* not do it."
f. Blaming oneself or others does not change the disliked behaviour but in fact, due to the arousal of angry and hostile feelings, may provoke inhuman behaviour in the "saviour/blamer." "I'll teach you to behave that way!"
g. Lack of forgiveness toward others promotes lack of forgiveness toward oneself and the setting up of perfectionistic attitudes for one's own failings. The failure to achieve one's own unrealistic goals leads to self-deprecation and neuroticism.

4. "The idea that you have to view things as awful, terrible, horrible and catastrophic when you get seriously frustrated, treated unfairly, or rejected" (Ellis, 1976a: 124).

This is erroneous for several reasons:

a. While it is unpleasant not to attain one's goals, it is not catastrophic unless one believes it to be.
b. Adults can and do tolerate considerable frustration philosophically.
c. Reality exists. Even when fate deals unkind blows, if one cannot change it, one might just as well accept it, because no amount of wailing, wishing, or demanding will alter it.

5. "The idea that emotional misery comes from external pressures and that you have little ability to control or change your feelings" (Ellis, 1976a: 138).

Not true, says Ellis. The worst that can happen to us is some physical harm or deprivation. Most of the discomfort stems from what we bring on ourselves by taking the actions or statements of others too seriously. It *is* possible for us to bring our feelings under control even when a sudden event sets off automatic responses, by talking to ourselves.

6. "The idea that if something seems dangerous or fearsome, you must preoccupy yourself with, and make yourself anxious about, it" (Ellis, 1976a: 145).

Ellis says this is a self-defeating stance for the following reasons:

a. If there is a real danger, one should assess its actual implications and prepare to cope with it. To whine about its horror will not alter the danger or facilitate coping with it.
b. While certain accidents may happen to us, the most we can do is to take reasonable preventive measures and hope for the best. Worry will not ensure their absence.
c. Fantasy is worse than reality.
d. Intense anxiety and worry itself is one of the most painful life experiences. One might well prefer to experience the condition or event producing the anxiety than to live in the throes of panic.

7. "The idea that you can more easily avoid facing many life difficulties and self-responsibilities than undertake more rewarding forms of self-discipline (Ellis, 1976a: 158).

Basically the idea that the easiest way is the best way is untrue. No one ever said that life was or should be easy. To obtain what we want out of life demands some discipline and effort on our part.

8. "The idea that your past remains all-important and that because something once strongly influenced your life, it has to keep determining your feelings and behaviour today" (Ellis, 1976a: 168).

This assumption is untrue for the following reasons:

a. A belief that an event in the past must always *be*, that is, exist, now and in the future is an overgeneralization. What was true in the past does not necessarily hold true for all time. Thus statements like "I've always felt like that" or "I've always done that" suggest a belief that one must go on feeling or doing "that" forever.
b. The above statement (belief) reduces the actual options available for the individual in coping with novel situations.
c. Behaviour that is appropriate for satisfying needs or attaining goals in the past may not be appropriate in the present or future.

9. "The idea that people and things should turn out better than they do and

that you must view it as awful and horrible if you do not find good solutions to life's grim realities" (Ellis, 1976a: 177).

This is an unfounded belief for the following reasons:

a. The fact that one would like people to behave differently, or for things to happen differently, does not mean that they *should* or *must*. Such beliefs are grandiose and irrational.
b. Even when people or things turn out differently than we expect or might like, they usually do not affect us as seriously as we might fear.
c. Should people actually harm us or events affect us significantly, responding with excess emotionality will not help the situation and may exacerbate it.
d. Overconcern about other people and events sidetrack us from our main concern: ourselves, the way we behave, and what we do.

10. "The idea that you can achieve maximum human happiness by inertia and inaction or by passively and uncommittedly 'enjoying ourself'" (Ellis, 1976a: 186).

There are several reasons why this belief is invalid:

a. While normal human behaviour includes periods of rest and inertia between activity, a continual state of inaction is contrary to the human tendency to arousal and activation.
b. Most intelligent people require some type of absorbing creative activity in order to remain alive and happy.
c. Living, conceived as doing, acting, loving, creating, thinking, is negated by prolonged inertia and inactivity.
d. Action is required to undo the effects of habit and self-defeating behaviour and enable change.

SUMMARY
Although Ellis did not develop a theory of normal personality development per se, it is possible to identify in his work the elements of normal human behaviour which were outlined in Chapter 1. These were self-regard (or self-acceptance), self-control, personal responsibility, social responsibility, competence, and personal ideals and values. Although RET is humanistic, it differs in some ways from existentially oriented approaches. In particular, RET rejects the existential concern with "being" and "essence" because these concepts appear to involve perfectionistic, self-rating ideas, which ultimately lead to neurotic behaviour. For similar reasons, the single-drive theory of self-actualization, which underlies the therapies in Part III, is rejected and replaced by a motivational theory which includes the pursuit of three basic human goals: survival, freedom from pain, and happiness or self-fulfillment.

Neurosis, or problem behaviour which impedes or denies the attainment of the three basic human goals, is conceived as originating from illogical or irrational beliefs, ideas, and thoughts which produce inappropriate emotional responses. The emotional response is inappropriate if it prevents or interferes with personal goal attainment. It may be inappropriate to the situation, that is, the wrong emotion, or it may be too intense an emotional response, and interfere with adaptive behaviour. Neurotic and problem behaviour stemming from illogical beliefs and values occurs in all members of our society, largely due to our contemporary beliefs and value system. Ten such beliefs were discussed as well as four common intellectual activities which ensure the maintenance of these beliefs. Resolution of behaviour problems that deny self-fulfillment requires insight into the role played by one's ideas and beliefs in the origin and maintenance of those problems. Figure 8·1 presents the RET paradigm of neurotic behaviour.

FIGURE 8·1
The RET Paradigm of Neurotic Behaviour

Typical Belief	Feelings Produced	Behaviour Resulting
"*I* must be perfect" and when *I* fail →	I feel: anxious, depressed, bad about myself →	and I: prattle, cry, volunteer, eat and/or sleep more, worry, make mistakes, drink and/or take drugs.
"*You** must be perfect" but when *you* fail →	I feel: anger, bitterness, hostility →	and I: lash out, blame, damn, destroy, hurt others, don't volunteer, and behave cynically.
"*It*† must be perfect" but when *it* fails →	I feel: apathy, self-pity →	and I: cop out, withdraw, whine, regress, despair.

* You = others: boss, friends, children, spouse, parent.
† It = society, institutions, things.

GOALS AND TECHNIQUES

Therapeutic Goals

While the general purpose or aim of RET may be stated quite simply in much the same terms today as it was in Ellis's original paper in 1956, we will go further and look at its several objectives as well. Briefly, RET aims at helping people to live self-fulfilling, creative, and emotionally satisfying lives by teaching them to discipline their thinking. The following therapeutic goals are identified:

1. RET aims to help people uncover the basic unrealistic ideas and beliefs with which they disturb themselves; to see clearly the misinformation and irrationality behind these ideas; and, on the basis of better information and clearer thinking, to change the beliefs which underlie and maintain their problems.
2. RET aims to help people to more fully and openly observe their feelings, determine their inappropriateness, choose to feel what they want to feel, and behave in ways which enable their self-fulfillment.
3. RET aims to help people evolve a highly personal, and to a great extent individualistic, philosophy of life which provides the principles necessary to determine what they want and the behavioural direction required for attainment of these wants.
4. RET aims to help people, while ensuring that they do not needlessly and gratuitously hurt others, to consistently do those things that bring them the most personal satisfaction and to absorb themselves in people and things outside themselves because they truly enjoy them.

It is important to note here that while RET aims to enable the individual to focus on the satisfaction of his own needs and wants, and personal self-fulfillment, that this must occur within the context of a morality of enlightened self-interest. Enlightened self-interest includes or assumes social interest or the concept of social responsibility which we discussed in Chapter 1. Thus, because we exist within a social group, consideration of others' wants and needs involves not only the reciprocity required in attaining one's own goals, but as well the personal satisfaction which results from meeting the needs of others in the process of helping, caring, and loving.

The Process of Therapy

Ellis (1976b) describes RET as a *comprehensive* form of treatment which involves all three aspects of client functioning: cognitive, emotive, and behavioural. The various approaches employed fall relatively neatly into these three categories, and provide a multi-faceted attack on the client's problem as he experiences it in these three areas. The three approaches (shown in Figure 8·2) are integrated, and therapy includes utilizing the approaches concomitantly, if not simultaneously.

Let's consider the therapeutic process from the perspective of these three approaches.

COGNITIVE

Individual Client-Therapist Sessions
The initial interview would require the client to describe and discuss the problem issue or behaviour. It is during this phase that the RET therapist would attempt to establish the necessary client-therapist relationship and begin to

FIGURE 8·2
Therapeutic Approaches in Three Areas of Client Functioning

	Aspect of Client Functioning Involved Approach, Technique, or Method Employed
Cognitive	Individual Client-Therapist Sessions • Insight by the patient into problem • Education and information • Assignment of cognitive and behavioural homework; Client Homework • Sensory imagery • Rational-emotive imagery
Emotive	Group Therapy Sessions • Education • Personal awareness through feedback from others • Confronting feelings • Emotional support of group
Behavioural	Client Homework • Desensitization • Self-reinforcement

understand the nature of the client's difficulty. The following questions might be introduced for purposes of clarification. These questions would not necessarily be phrased in exactly this way and would, of course, be introduced skillfully into the conversation in an appropriate manner.

1. What is the issue or problem?
   (In not more than 3-5 sentences—if this is not possible then the client doesn't know what the problem is.)
2. What is the impact of this issue or problem on you?
3. Perspective: past—present—future
   What led to it?
   What is happening now?
   What is likely going to happen?
4. What have you done about it, and what were the results?
   and/or
5. What have you thought about it?
   and/or
   What prevented you and what do you think would have happened if you had?

6. In what way do you believe I might be of some assistance?

Once the therapist has begun to build a relationship and has some understanding of the nature of the problem, he begins to work on helping the client to develop insight into his difficulties.

In practice, development of insight and the homework carried out by the client go hand in hand. That is, while the direct interaction between the client and therapist is focused on developing insight into the problem, the therapist would at these times set homework assignments for the patient to carry out in the interval between their sessions and discuss these assignments in the following session. While it may be somewhat artificial to divide the therapy into three functions, it does assist in describing the process.

The development of insight function, then, might be described as part of the process which focuses on changing the "thinking" (ideas, assumptions, beliefs, attitudes) of the client, and the homework function as the part of the therapy process which reinforces new thought processes and beliefs and at the same time enables the client to practice changing his external behaviour and actions.

We described earlier the significance of developing insight. This involves teaching the client how to observe his own feelings and actions and how to evaluate them objectively instead of moralistically or grandiosely. You may recall that Ellis described three insights:

Insight No. 1 is the identification by the client that a problem exists and that the problem has developed through a series of prior events.

Insight No. 2 is the full awareness that irrational ideas (beliefs) related to these antecedent or prior events are still believed and in fact continue to exist because of what the client keeps telling himself.

Insight No. 3 is total acceptance or belief by the client that he has created his own problem by maintaining irrational beliefs and that the only way of eliminating the problem is by his working to change his beliefs.

During this aspect of therapy the therapist is highly directive and is involved in what appears to be a "battle of wits" with the client. His principal goal is to continually and consistently reveal to the client his past and current illogical and self-defeating verbalizations and beliefs by:

1. Bringing them to the client's attention or consciousness.
2. Showing the client *how* they are causing and maintaining disturbance and unhappiness.
3. Demonstrating exactly what the illogical links in the client's internalized sentences are.
4. Teaching the client how to rethink and reverbalize these and other similar sentences in a more logical, self-helping way.

In addition, the therapist attempts to educate and inform the client by pointing out the non-unique character of the client's values and problems by revealing the main irrational ideas and beliefs existent in our society and suggesting more rational philosophies of living which might be substituted. The following brief extract of an RET session reported by Ellis (1976b: 26-27)* illustrates this insight development process:

Therapist: You seem to be terribly afraid that you will fail at making good initial contacts with a woman and also at succeeding sexually.

Client: Hell, yes! To say the least, I'm scared shitless in both these areas.

Therapist: Because if you fail in either area, what—?

Client: If I fail, I'll be an utter slob!

Therapist: Prove it!

Client: Isn't it obvious?

Therapist: Not for me! It's fairly obvious that if a woman rejects you, socially or sexually, it'll hardly be a great thing. But how will that prove that *you*, a total person, will be no good?

Client: I still think it's obvious. Would this same woman reject *anyone?*

Therapist: No, probably not. Let's suppose that she accepts many men, but not you. Let's also suppose that she rejects you because she finds that, first, you're not terribly good at conversation and, second, you come quickly in intercourse. So she finds you doubly deficient. Now, how does that still prove that you're no good?

Client: It certainly proves that I'm no good for *her*.

Therapist: Yes, in a way. You're no good for her conversationally and sexually. You have two rotten *traits*.

Client: And she doesn't want *me*, for having those traits.

Therapist: Right. In the case we're assuming, she rejects *you* for having those two traits. But all we've proved is that one woman despises two of your characteristics; and that this woman therefore rejects you as a lover or a husband. Even she, mind you, might well accept you as a nonsexual friend. For you have, don't forget, many other traits—such as intelligence, artistic talent, reliability, etc.

Client: But not the traits she *most* wants!

Therapist: Maybe. But how does this prove that *all* women, like her, would find you equally wanting? Some, actually, might like you *because* you are shy and *because* you come quickly sex-

---

*From the book *Modern Therapies*, edited by Virginia Binder, Arnold Binder, and Bernard Rimland. © 1976 by Prentice-Hall, Inc. Published by Prentice-Hall, Inc., Englewood Cliffs, NJ 07632.

	ually—when they don't happen to like intercourse, and therefore want to get it over rapidly!
Client:	Fat chance!
Therapist:	Yes, statistically. For *most* women, presumably, will tend to reject you if you're shy or sexually inadequate, in their eyes. But a few, at least, will accept you for the very reasons that most refuse you; and many more, normally, will accept you in spite of your deficiencies, because they nonetheless become attached to you.
Client:	Who the devil wants *that*!
Therapist:	Most of us do, actually, if we're sane. For since we're all highly imperfect, we're happy that some people accept us *with* these imperfections. But let's even suppose the worst—just to show how crooked your thinking is. Let's suppose that, because of your shyness and fast ejaculation, *all* women rejected you for *all* time. Would you still be a worthless slob?
Client:	I wouldn't exactly be a great guy!
Therapist:	No, you wouldn't be Jesus Christ, or Napoleon, or certainly, Casanova! But many women, remember, wouldn't want you if you were one of them. Jesus, if he ever really existed, seems to have been pretty shy with women; and Napoleon may well have come quickly. As for Casanova, most women, at least today, wouldn't want him just *because* he was so sexy. Anyway, we're evading the question; *would* you be a total slob?
Client:	Well, uh, I—no, I guess not.
Therapist:	Because?
Client:	Well, because I'd still have other, uh, good traits. Is that what you're getting at?
Therapist:	Yes, partly. You'd still have other good traits. And *you*, if you were ratable at all, would equal *all* your traits and not merely two of them, such as shyness and sexual prematurity.

Cognitive Client Homework

RET has always included a "homework" element, since it held that people must not only change their irrational thoughts but *act* against such ideas. While not identified as such in the earlier stages, some of this homework actually involves what has since been described as behaviour therapy. In particular RET uses the operant conditioning principles involved in self-reward and self-reinforcement. (Elements of both Wolpe's systematic desensitization and Stampfl's Implosive Therapy may be noted as well.) These specific behavioural approaches will be examined in Part V, but it is important to note here their inclusion within the context of RET.

Ellis utilizes two types of homework assignments, one which involves the use of cognitive imagery, and another which requires the client to act in certain ways. Ellis describes two types of imagery exercises: rational-emotive imagery

(REI), and sensory imagery. The idea here is that one may practice acting against one's irrational ideas, beliefs, anxieties, obsessions, compulsions, and inhibitions by *fantasizing* as well as by actually behaving in or *experiencing* a certain situation.

An example of sensory imagery homework. The client might be requested to spend ten minutes a day in negative imagery. He would be instructed to select something which would produce anxiety, depression, shame, and hostility. He would be asked to think of this event or situation and to concentrate on how he feels as he imagines it and to deeply experience it. Then while he is strongly experiencing this feeling he is instructed to change his feeling—his bodily sensations—to those related only to disappointment, regret, annoyance, and irritation—not anxiety, depression, and anger. Then when these new feelings are being experienced he is told to observe what he has done to his thoughts in order to bring the emotional change about. He is told to pay careful attention to exactly *how* he altered his belief system about the fantasized event or situation to produce an alteration in his bodily state (emotions). He is directed to keep working at the feelings to alter them while fantasizing the upsetting event *until they change,* and not to give up. Eventually, with practice, the client when either fantasizing or actually experiencing the originally upsetting event, will find that the event or situation does not produce emotionally upsetting feelings.

An Example of rational-emotive imagery homework. Using positive imagery, the client may be requested again as homework to fantasize as vividly and intensely as possible an unpleasant event. He is told again to get fully into this emotion and experience it for a brief period. Then he is requested to notice what he says to himself in order to originate and maintain this feeling. When these statements are fully understood, then he is told to *dispute* them as he learns to do in the therapy session with the therapist, acting himself as the therapist does with him. Then, as he disputes his irrational beliefs, he is instructed to fantasize about how he would feel and behave after he started giving them up and started instead to have rational beliefs about these events, feeling appropriately displeased or disappointed rather than inappropriately depressed or hostile, and acting in a concerned rather than upset manner. Again the client is instructed to practise this procedure, including starting with mildly unfortunate events and creating inappropriately severe emotion, next observing what irrational statements are required to accomplish this, then strongly imagining the disputing of these statements and feelings and acting in accordance with new rational philosophies such that the concluding feeling is one of concern, not overconcern.

EMOTIVE

The emotive approach described by Ellis involves the use of group therapy. Within the group environment, the basic dynamics described in Appendix A of Chapter 5, Intensive Group Experience, would operate. In the group, the client would gain in personal awareness through the process of the feedback obtained from others, would be required to confront and deal with his feelings, and would receive the emotional support and caring of group members.

BEHAVIOURAL

The behavioural approaches employed both involve client homework exercises. Ellis describes the first as a "desensitization" method and the second as self-reinforcement.

Desensitization (Risk-Taking)

In some ways the desensitization procedure resembles Stampfl's Implosive Therapy. The patient is encouraged to approach rather than avoid anxiety-producing situations. While concentrating on avoiding self-defeating, irrational verbalizations and defeatist self-talk, the client is directed to try to do the things he fears most. This might be done in a series of steps to ease the client gradually toward the feared behaviour. Although it is described as "desensitization," it does not follow the principles set down by Wolpe (1973) for this purpose. It would appear to be more closely related to either Stampfl's approach (1967) or simple behaviour modification. Nonetheless, it is an effective means of involving the client in the change process in a specific and ongoing manner in which his own efforts at change are rewarded.

Self-Reinforcement

This is an effective means of ensuring that the homework assignments the client commits himself to are carried out. The client selects something which is very enjoyable and which he does almost daily—reading, eating, television viewing, masturbation, etc. This activity is used as a self-reward or reinforcer by having the client agree to engage in it only *after* the homework exercise has been completed for that day. In the same way the patient may select a penalty for not doing his homework—having to do something he dislikes for a period of time. Thus, he can increase his tendency to carry out the commitment by having both a positive (attraction/pull) reinforcement, and a negative (repulsion/push) penalty.

In developing either cognitive or behavioural homework assignments it is important to make them very simple and non-demanding in the beginning. This will ensure first that they are carried out, and second that the client achieves success rather than failure when he does them. As therapy proceeds the difficulty of the assignments may be increased gradually. Thus, if studying is a problem, a student might be encouraged to begin by studying fifteen minutes a day at first. While this may seem to be of little value in itself, in fact it's fifteen minutes more than may be occurring at present, and its initial purpose is primarily in establishing a new routine and attitudinal change. In time, the rewards in achievement and goal attainment will be powerful self-reinforcers in themselves.

Therapy Summary

Rational-Emotive Therapy employs a multifaceted approach to behaviour change. All aspects of client behaviour are involved—cognitive, emotive, and behavioural—and specific techniques are applied to each. The client participates in both individual and group therapy and is expected to engage in homework assignments. The initial phases of therapy deal with identifying the problem areas in the client's life, and in the development of insight by the client into the role played by his ideas and beliefs in the production and maintenance of his problem behaviour. In his individual work with the therapist, the client learns to dispute his irrational beliefs and is given exercises in sensory imagery and rational-emotive imagery through which he can practice gaining conscious control over his emotions and changing his belief system. In group therapy, he becomes more aware of his behaviour through feedback from group members, is challenged to deal with his feelings and gains support and caring in his struggle to change. He learns through his behavioural homework exercises to seek out the satisfactions he wants but fears to approach, and to reinforce his own homework behaviour positively and negatively as appropriate.

SUMMARY

Ellis (1976b: 32-33) provides this capsule summary of RET:

> Rational-emotive therapy (RET) consists of a comprehensive form of treatment that heavily stresses the cognitive, philosophic, value-oriented aspects of human personality. It holds that people largely manufacture their own psychological symptoms and have the ability, with consistent work and effort at changing basic attitudes, to eliminate or minimize these symptoms and make themselves much less disturbable. It does not strive for symptom removal so much as for a worthwhile philosophic solution to people's fundamental "emotional" problems. It keeps gaining support through controlled clinical and experimental studies;* and it thrives as an intrinsic and vital part of the newly developing field of cognitive-behaviour therapy. Although hardly a panacea for all ills, RET provides an important part of today's psychotherapeutic methods.

---

* In the introduction to *Growth Through Reason* (1971), Ellis lists an impressive number of studies by independent researchers which are claimed to confirm or support the major principles and assumptions of RET, as well as many others which have demonstrated RET's effectiveness with specific client groups and in summary stated:

> I could present a great deal more evidence that cognitive-behaviour therapy, in general, and rational-emotive therapy, in particular, not only works but is probably more effective than any other major system of therapy thus far devised (Ellis, 1971: 13).

9

Reality Therapy

> *Once involvement is gained and reality is faced, therapy becomes a special kind of education, a learning to live more effectively, that is better and more quickly achieved if the therapist accepts the role of teacher.*
>
> —William Glasser, 1975a:60

In this chapter considerably more space is devoted to examining the evolution and development of the theory and principles of Reality Therapy (RT) than has been given to the actual therapeutic method. There are several reasons for this:

1. It provides us with an opportunity to examine a therapy in the process of development.
2. It enables us to consider the relationship of theory to methods and techniques.
3. It is appropriate since the RT therapeutic process and dynamics have remained essentially unchanged while the theoretical base and focus have been continually expanded.

Reality Therapy is the only approach included in the text which appears to be in its developmental phase. Rogerian Therapy, in contrast, while still evolving, is mature in theory and technique. This is also true for Gestalt Therapy. Primal, we have been led to believe by Janov, is perfect as it is, and so little improvement may be anticipated. Rational-Emotive too appears to be in a mature stage, now reflecting theory and principles involved in the five major schools of psychology. And Transactional Analysis, which we will discover in Chapter 10, while continuing to increase in its complexity, appears to have achieved a firm theoretical and dynamic base. This leaves the behaviour therapies, which are soundly supported by the psychology of learning and their well-established methods.

RT, on the other hand, while demonstrating considerable stability as well as effectiveness in terms of *methods,* has at the same time been characterized by an absence of theoretical rigour and consistency. Since RT is a more recent addition to the therapeutic milieu and as its founder, William Glasser, has continued to share his developing ideas, it seems opportune that we explore RT in this way.

We have been examining each therapy in terms of its theory, and the technique or methods employed by the therapist which follow logically from that theory. Obviously the two, theory and method, should be directly related, as in the case, for example, of a client-centred approach following upon the principle of self-actualization or self-regulation. If *method* is not directly related to theory, then we would have to question why the therapist employed a certain technique with a patient. If *theory* is not related to technique, then we would question why the assumption is made in the first place if it makes no difference to what the therapist and/or patient do.

Reality Therapy is interesting because the theory appears to be changing and evolving more rapidly than the technique at this point. This appears to be occurring because the initial theoretical base did not provide the total rationale for Glasser's method. His approach was *stimulated* by his rejection of traditional psychiatric methods, but was *developed* largely as a result of his remarkable intuitive sense of what was required to help his patients. The loose theoretical framework was initially sufficient to "explain" why he did what he did, but this occurred after the fact. It seemed logical enough and provided a working rationale, but it was not definitive or comprehensive. It was an intellectual exercise and as such incomplete. Thus, RT *worked,* but *why* it worked could not be totally explained or understood according to RT theory. Since 1965 Glasser's work has reflected a constant exploration of new ideas and a readiness to adapt these where possible to RT. Thus, his theoretical base continues to expand, deepen, and become more comprehensive. It is noteworthy that his most recent work, *Positive Addiction* (1976), explores the significance of our "intuitive" capacity for the attainment of self-fulfillment. Perhaps Glasser's search for a deeper understanding of the human condition will lead him back to using the same intuitive capacity to round out his theory as he used in finding his method.

WILLIAM GLASSER (1925-   )

Genial, warm, gentle, quiet, down-to-earth, imaginative, creative, hardworking, self-made, pragmatic, rebellious—these are some of the adjectives used to describe William Glasser in one of the few articles (Reilly, 1973) written about the man behind Reality Therapy. Glasser was born in Cleveland, Ohio in 1925 to Jewish parents, the last of three children. His early life appears to have been nurturing and satisfying: his parents were loving and appreciative. Although shy as a child, Glasser made friends easily, achieved good grades in school, played in the school band, and was interested in sports.

His intellectual prowess and drive is reflected in his graduation from Case Institute of Technology with a degree in chemical engineering at only nineteen years of age. An interest in psychology led to his return to complete a master's degree in clinical psychology in 1948, and shortly thereafter, he entered Western Reserve University School of Medicine where he completed his M.D. in

1953. He married a distant cousin, Naomi, after beginning his medical training, and their first son, Joseph, was born in 1951.

Glasser undertook his psychiatric training at UCLA and began to question the effectiveness of traditional psychiatric methods while finishing his last year of residency in 1957. His criticisms of current psychiatric practices, his heretical ideas, and his search for better techniques to help patients did not endear him to his superiors and colleagues. Thus on graduation his new private practice suffered from lack of referrals. When the opportunity to take a position as head psychiatrist with the Ventura School for Girls presented itself, he accepted gladly.

Over the next twelve years, during which he was associated with the Ventura School as a consultant, Glasser's ideas about therapy were organized into a theory and method called Reality Therapy (RT). His first book, *Mental Health or Mental Illness* (1961), outlined his concerns with the mental health system and went largely unnoticed. But with his second book, *Reality Therapy* (1965), he began to receive wide recognition and attention from the helping professions. The success of *Reality Therapy* brought requests for Glasser to give workshops and seminars on RT all over the U.S.A. and in major Canadian cities. Soon after, he began his Institute for Reality Therapy in Los Angeles to help teach the concepts and principles of RT to professional psychologists, social workers, teachers, clergy, correctional workers, and to laypeople and parents. This acclaim brought an invitation to consult with a local school board on the handling of "difficult" students in the classroom. The work with this school board opened up a new avenue for Glasser's RT with teachers and students, which he described in his next book, *Schools Without Failure* (1969). In anticipation of the requests for information and courses which would be stimulated by *Schools Without Failure,* the Educator Training Centre (ETC) was opened shortly after the book went on sale. The ETC is now a large, well-staffed organization which produces film, videotapes, and course materials, and conducts training seminars and workshops for thousands of teachers annually.

Since the success of *Schools Without Failure,* Glasser has written two more major works, each reflecting further refinement in his ideas and approach: *The Identity Society* (1975), and *Positive Addiction* (1976a), but his basic methods appear unchanged.

Glasser's family now includes two sons and a daughter, and reflects the comfortable closely knit unit that he experienced with his own parents. Fame and fortune, rather than disorienting and confusing him as they do so many, seem to have enabled Glasser to be even more himself, to reinforce a basic value system he finds meaningful, and to bring him and his family great personal satisfaction and reward.

ORIGINS AND DEVELOPMENT

All of the therapies considered thus far have been strongly influenced by Freudian psychology and psychoanalysis in that the early education and training of all the founders of the various approaches included Freudian theory and practice. Glasser was no different. Trained as a psychiatrist in the late 1950s, he would have been a Freudian or neo-Freudian by definition, since there was no alternative. Carl Rogers, as we have seen, had published by then, but he was a psychologist and would not have been widely known among the medical profession. Fritz Perls did not arrive in the United States until 1946, did not publish until 1947, and received little recognition from psychiatric colleagues until well into the 1960s. The various other humanists did not begin to emerge as such until the 1950s and did not begin to have a substantive impact upon psychiatry for another decade. Ellis's RET, as we have seen in Chapter 8, was first described in 1956, and both Transactional Analysis and the behaviour therapies, as we shall see, did not receive the attention of psychiatric trainers until the mid-1960s. So Glasser, a product of his time, was trained as a psychoanalytically oriented psychiatrist.

Two things are significant, then: first, that Glasser's early rejection of some of the basic ideas of the psychiatry of the 1950s required a novel response on his part, and second, that while his initial ideas do not appear to have been fully developed as RT until after he began his work at the Ventura School in 1958, and were not articulated formally until 1965, he described the time of their origin as 1957, his *final year of psychiatric training* (Glasser, 1975a). While some of the differences he had with the psychiatry of the day, and which still characterize RT, may now appear mundane, they reflect astonishing insight and sensitivity for that period. When we consider that these insights appear to have been gained and developed largely *independently* of other approaches under development at the same time, Glasser's contributions to the helping field are a most remarkable achievement.

Since RT was a direct consequence of Glasser's dissatisfaction with a number of the basic concepts and practices employed by conventional psychiatrists at the time, it is important to consider first just what his concerns were, and how RT attempted to deal with them. What was the therapeutic alternative which Glasser attempted to create?

Let's consider first, then, some of the differences between Glasser's approach and conventional psychiatry as they were understood by Glasser during the late 1950s and early 1960s, before examining in some detail the evolution of RT concepts and principles between 1965 and 1978.

BASIC ASSUMPTIONS, MAJOR CONCEPTS, AND PRINCIPLES

Differences Between RT and Traditional Psychiatry

In *Reality Therapy* (1965), Glasser outlined six ways in which he believed RT differed positively from conventional psychiatry. These six basic assumptions continue to provide the foundation for RT theory and practice. But although they continue to distinguish RT from psychoanalytically based therapeutic approaches, we will notice an affinity between several of the basic tenets of RT and those of other contemporary helping methods discussed in the text thus far. The six basic assumptions are as follows: (1) mental illness vs. irresponsibility, (2) delving into the past vs. carefully examining the present, (3) achieving "insight" vs. changing external behaviour, (4) therapist objectivity vs. therapist involvement, (5) freedom from values vs. value emphasis, and (6) non-directive vs. directive (teacher/educator) therapist.

MENTAL ILLNESS VS. IRRESPONSIBILITY

Glasser does not believe in the concept of "mental illness" or "sickness," because it suggests that something over which the patient has no control has happened *to* her, and that the helper's job is to do something *to* her to cure her. It implies a passive, dependent role on the part of the patient. Instead, the assumption in RT is that the patient only requires help in satisfying her own *needs*. When unable to satisfy her own needs the patient does not demonstrate "illness" but rather "weakness." The role of the RT helper is not to accept the dependency and weakness of the patient, but rather to help the patient help herself to become stronger and again satisfy her needs on her own regardless of what has happened to her in the past. The term "irresponsible" is used in RT to refer to a person *unable to satisfy her own needs*. Using this definition, in RT there is no difference in the treatment of various psychological problems. The only diagnosis necessary is to determine whether or not the patient is able to satisfy her own needs, regardless of the actual behaviour involved.

DELVING INTO THE PAST VS. EXAMINING THE PRESENT

Glasser does not believe that delving into the patient's past is of any benefit. All that is required for RT is knowledge of the patient's life *now*, and how she is unable to satisfy her own needs.

ACHIEVING "INSIGHT" VS. CHANGING EXTERNAL BEHAVIOUR

RT, rather than looking into the past for causes of the patient's problems, with the hope that the patient will gain "insight" which will ultimately result in a change in the problem behaviour, emphasizes the patient's *behaviour* itself. RT concentrates on changing the patient's behaviour first, and, contrary to Ellis, maintains that changing the patient's behaviour will subsequently change the way the patient thinks and feels.

Glasser further believes that emphasizing or delving into the patient's "unconscious" behaviour is detrimental to the patient. Again, acknowledgment of unconscious motivation or behaviour is similar to concern with the patient's past by the therapist, and is considered to be another suggestion to the patient by the therapist that the patient is not responsible for her behaviour or that there are "forces" over which she has no control. Instead RT, like Gestalt Therapy, holds that what is below the level of the patient's consciousness is *full awareness of what she is doing now*. The RT therapist concentrates on having the patient become fully aware of her present conscious behaviour which is not fulfilling her needs.

THERAPIST OBJECTIVITY VS. THERAPIST INVOLVEMENT

Glasser does not believe in transference or in the maintenance of the traditional "distance," objectivity, or impersonality of the therapist. RT emphasizes instead the significance of the "involvement" of the therapist with the patient. The definition of RT "involvement" will be discussed later. Suffice to say at this time that it includes the Rogerian concept of "relationship" with some added features.

FREEDOM FROM VALUES VS. VALUE EMPHASIS

In RT it is considered necessary to include in therapy the morality of the patient's behaviour. Glasser contends that if the therapist is to avoid promoting the patient's dependency and irresponsible, weak behaviour, the patient must evaluate her present behaviour in terms of its success in fulfilling her own needs, but also in terms of the standards of the community in which she lives. He asserts that standards of right and wrong behaviour do in fact exist in the patient's community, and should therefore not be ignored by the therapist or patient.

This is a very interesting point, and the one on which Glasser has been criticized perhaps most unfairly. The charge has been made that RT is "moralistic" and that the RT therapist therefore imposes his values on the patient. Certainly the question of values—patient's and therapist's—cannot be honestly avoided. The therapist's values are likely to be communicated to the patient in some manner or another. Perhaps Glasser is correct in saying they should be communicated *explicitly* rather than *covertly*. This might at least enable the patient to explore and adopt her own values, rather than those of the therapist, if there exists within the therapy a mechanism through which this value exploration may occur. Again, because of its significance to RT, the process through which the patient's behaviour is considered in terms of "right and wrong" will be further explained later in the chapter.

THE NON-DIRECTIVE VS. THE DIRECTIVE THERAPIST

RT, unlike conventional psychiatry, emphasizes the therapist's role as a teacher. In RT the therapist does not concentrate on patient insight and awareness with the assumption that once certain "understanding" occurs, appropriate behaviour will naturally emerge. Instead, RT therapists are directive in questioning the patient, confronting the patient with her behaviour, answering patient questions, and suggesting ways to solve problems and become involved with people. This active, enabling, teaching role of the therapist will be considered in some detail under "The Process of Therapy."

Evolution and Development of RT Concepts and Principles (1958-78)

The theoretical base for RT was developed ex post facto on the basis of Glasser's clinical experience and observations. It has been developed to explain and support Glasser's therapeutic procedures and technique. Its focus therefore has been more on the personality dynamics underlying the development and maintenance of problem behaviour than on the normal person. Perhaps it would be more accurate to say that RT theory appears to have originated with hypotheses about patients demonstrating problem behaviour. Of course, since there is an implicit polarity in concepts like weakness-strength, involvement-uninvolvement, responsible-irresponsible, or abnormal-normal, the exploration of one pole results in statements and conclusions regarding the other. In this sense, Glasser's theoretical development parallels that of Perls. Thus, while we find in Glasser's work an explicit theory of the origins and maintenance of problem behaviour, his concept of "normal" human behaviour and development appears more implicit and less well-defined.

We do not find in his approach the theoretical sophistication of Carl Rogers, in which terms are carefully defined and basic assumptions are developed and presented in a logical and ordered fashion, each one following from or building upon the other, culminating in a comprehensive base for understanding all human behaviour. We do not find the attention to research investigation of RT concepts and principles that we found in both Rogerian Therapy and RET. And, in general, we do not find in Glasser's work attempts to relate his ideas and methods to other contemporary therapeutic approaches.

We might perhaps note here the major schools of psychology which *are* evident in RT. We have described above Glasser's rejection of some basic ideas of Freudian psychology and psychoanalysis. With respect to organismic psychology, it is interesting that Glasser's medical training is not in evidence in his early work and that RT had no specific organismic base until 1976. We do see in RT strong affinities with existential and humanistic psychology and with theories of learning and the behaviour therapies. Thus, we will note similarities between RT and certain concepts and procedures of Rogerian Therapy, Gestalt Therapy, RET, TA, and the behaviour therapies.

Glasser's personality theory, then, includes influences from Freudian psychology, and embodies basic existential, humanistic, and learning theory principles. It is not a comprehensive theory of personality development and, as we shall see, is not wholly consistent and logical in its organization and presentation. It does, however, appear to provide a sufficient base for the rationalization of his therapeutic procedures, for which he has claimed excellent results (Glasser, 1965, 1975, 1978). Finally, we will note below some major changes in RT concepts and procedures bewteen 1965 and 1978 which suggest that RT is not yet a "mature" approach and that further refinement and elaboration of RT principles may be anticipated.

The "Normal" Person

1965

Motivation Theory
In *Reality Therapy: A New Approach to Psychiatry* (1965), Glasser posited three

basic needs which must be satisfied if suffering is to be avoided, and the process through which this must occur. The three basic needs were:

1. Survival needs (food, warmth, rest, etc.)
2. The need to love and be loved
3. The need to feel worthwhile to ourselves and others.

Thus, we find a similarity in the motivation theories of Ellis and Glasser. Ellis suggested that satisfaction of the basic needs of survival, absence from pain, and happiness, could explain all human behaviour. Neither Ellis nor Glasser appear to agree with the concept of self-actualization.

Glasser suggested further that the satisfaction of these three basic needs required involvement with other people. Obviously, the survival needs of the infant would require satisfaction through another person capable of accepting the dependency of the young. But in addition, the satisfaction of the need to love and be loved and to feel worthwhile would also require involvement with other people. There is, then, in Glasser's theory of normal development, a strong social orientation. About the need for love he stated:

> In all its forms, ranging from friendship through mother love, family love, and conjugal love, this need drives us to continuous activity in search of satisfaction (1975a: 9-10).

This strong social orientation is further reinforced by the third need, that of feeling worthwhile to oneself and others. The satisfaction of the need to feel personally worthwhile requires self-evaluation of behaviour in terms of both personal and social morality, and the satisfaction of the need to feel worthwhile to others entails both receiving love from them as well as approval and acceptance of our behaviour by others. Thus Glasser stated:

> Certainly the child should be loved, but love need not mean a blanket approval of everything he does. . . .
> But, whether we are loved or not, *to be worthwhile we must maintain a satisfactory standard of behaviour* (1975a: 10).

We might note here that while Glasser does not appear to agree with Rogers's concept of *unconditional* positive regard, there are close parallels between Glasser's, Rogers's and Perls's theories of personality development in terms of the importance of concepts like love, approval, worth, recognition, and identity. Similarly, while Ellis would agree with Glasser that love may exist without acceptance of the total person in the sense of disapproval of some specific disliked behaviour, he would not agree with the self-rating involved in self-evaluation which Glasser suggests is required for determining personal worth.

Responsibility
In addition to the three primary needs listed above, Glasser (1975a) included in

his theory of normal behaviour the concept of *responsibility*. He defined responsibility as:

> the ability to fulfill one's needs and to do so *in a way that does not deprive others of the ability to fulfill their needs* (Glasser, 1975a: 13).

Responsibility is learned through the child's relationship with parents and other significant adults who demonstrate to the child both love and discipline. Glasser considered that teaching children how to fulfill their three basic needs themselves was the primary task of parents, and the most difficult to accomplish.

> Children do not know that what seems easy to them will not fulfill their needs, so almost from infancy they struggle against the reality that they must learn from their parents how to fulfill their needs. . . . Through discipline tempered with love, parents must teach their children to behave better. The child learns thereby that the parents care (Glasser, 1975a: 17).

We may note here the absence of the concept of self-actualization in Glasser's theory. He would appear to view the child in a Freudian context as in need of external *control* rather than guidance. His many references to "discipline" tempered with "love" give an authoritarian slant to his approach to child development and suggest a somewhat negative view of human nature. Lastly, his references to "correct" behaviour, "better" behaviour, or the "right" way indicate the value-judgmental elements in Glasser's approach, which continue to distinguish it from all others.

The dilemma involved in Glasser's early view of normal human development may be best illustrated by examining his summary statement on the learning of responsibility, which, remember, is the ability to satisfy our needs without preventing others from satisfying theirs.

> . . . we learn responsibility through involvements with responsible fellow human beings, preferably loving parents who will love and discipline us properly, who are intelligent enough to allow us freedom to try out our newly acquired responsibility as soon as we show readiness to do so (Glasser, 1975a: 19).

Learning responsibility then assumes: (1) adult behaviour, (2) love—which in this case is conditional, (3) "proper" discipline—which is not defined, (4) intelligence—which is not defined, (5) permission—which suggests dependency and inferiority, and (6) "readiness"—as interpreted by the adult.

Finally, it is worth noting that while Glasser's therapeutic procedures based on such ideas might be effective with patients experiencing problems in living, his concept of "responsible" parenting would, according to Rogers, Perls, Janov, and Ellis, result in unfulfilled *individual* needs and neurotic behaviour. On the other hand, perhaps Glasser was right, for his view of both parenting and education does appear to more closely reflect societal norms. And if this is the case, then his approach, which is based upon the "reality" of what has been called by others a *neurotic society* may, in "reality," be effective in enabling patients to exchange their individual neurosis for a more comfortable or "acceptable" collective one.

1968

Motivation

By 1968 Glasser's theory of motivation had changed. The three basic needs of security or survival, love, and self-worth had been reduced to two, *security* and *identity*. Since basic security needs were not considered to be of primary significance to North American society, the concern for *identity* was now considered to be the basic motivating human need. Love and self-worth were now viewed not as *needs* but as *means* through which one's identity was established and maintained. Thus the concept of identity as the central motivating force for Glasser may be likened to the concept of self-actualization which underlies Rogers's, Perls's, and Janov's work.

The Concept of Identity

The introduction of the concept of identity into RT represented a major development in Glasser's thinking. It suggested a shift away from his earlier, more authoritarian, attitudes and his concern with teaching acceptance of an external value system, to a greater concern for the *individual* in society and existential-humanistic values. The content, style, and use of language found in *Identity and Society* (1972) clearly reflect this change. Consider, for example, the following statements:

> It is my argument that today almost everyone is personally engaged in a search for acceptance as a person . . . (Glasser, 1975b: 2).

> As a society we can no longer afford to ignore this new priority in human motivation. . . . schools and families that function as if this new motivational sequence did not exist are in serious trouble (Glasser, 1975b: 2).

Glasser did not specifically define identity, but seemed to use the term conventionally to mean our sense of self or who we are. Giving and receiving love was still important, but was seen as a means of both developing our identity and of maintaining it. Thus, involvement with others who we care about and respect, and from whom we receive caring and respect, was considered essential. No specific mention was made of conditional love, but neither was love said to be unconditional.

Worth

The concept of personal worth which previously required self-evaluation in terms of our ability to meet both personally set and socially imposed standards, remained much the same. However, worth was now viewed primarily in terms of a person's *work*. Thus Glasser stated:

> A person may labor alone as an artist or scientist for years, but eventually what

he produces must be recognized by others or he will not gain a successful identity (1975b: 24).

Glasser's introduction of the concept of work or labour into the previous concept of worth was also a significant addition to RT, for it emphasized creative and/or productive activity as an essential element in establishing and maintaining personal identity. Our worth then is determined by our own and others' recognition and appreciation of what we *do,* that is, what we create, produce, or contribute for ourselves and others.

The nature and extent of our *involvement* with others, that is, our experience of giving and receiving love, caring, and respect, combined with our *worth,* determined by our own and others' assessment of our *work,* then establishes and maintains our *identity*.

1976

Motivation
Glasser's most recent book, *Positive Addiction* (1976a), reflects further changes in his ideas. The earlier concept of identity as the primary motivating force seems to have been replaced by "happiness":

> To begin let's examine what happens when we don't have enough strength to find the happiness that I believe most of us want more than anything else from our lives (Glasser, 1976a: 2).

And while happiness is not defined, Glasser seems to include in this concept the following elements, which he called "the facts of life":

- fulfillment
- pleasure
- recognition
- the enjoyment of loving and being loved
- a sense of personal value

We may note in the latter three the theme of his earlier work.

Love and Worth
Love and worth remain as the primary avenues through which to attain happiness, but Glasser's concept of worth has been altered somewhat from that expressed in his earlier work. Worth is not determined solely by a person's labour or work, but on the basis of her *accomplishments*. Glasser described how the young child begins with external evaluations of her behaviour in terms of what is right and wrong, but eventually learns to judge for herself what is worthwhile. He noted that the differences that may occur between what we believe to be worthwhile and what others believe to be worthwhile require *compromises:*

> Most of us spend our lives in a series of compromises between doing what we believe in and doing what will please those who are important to us. Happiness

depends a great deal on gaining enough strentgh to live with a minimum of these compromises (Glasser, 1976a: 3).

Accomplishment, then, which gains recognition from others, and may require compromise, was considered by Glasser to result in pleasure. It would appear from the treatment of this concept that we might substitute "accomplishment" for worth and consider the dual route to happiness to be through our *accomplishments* and *involvements* (love).

Strength

The terms "strength" and "weakness" used throughout his work appear to take on greater significance in Glasser's latest book, *Positive Addiction* (1976). While he used these terms to reflect the style of behaviour, or the characteristic quality of the individual's approach to life, they are also used to describe the internal drive state and potential of the individual. In this sense strength is both cause and effect: a person is strong because she has strength, or she demonstrates her weakness by her irresponsible behaviour and her irresponsible behaviour shows how weak she is.

In 1965, for example, in rejecting the concept of mental illness in favour of the term "weakness," he said:

> If there is a medical analogy which applies to psychiatric problems, it is not illness but weakness. While illness can be cured by removing the causative agent, weakness can be cured only by strengthening the existing body . . . .
>
> . . . Regardless of past circumstances, the psychiatric patient must develop the strength to take responsibility to fulfill his needs satisfactorily (Glasser, 1975a: 46).

In the latter sentence we could substitute the following terms for the word "strength," and the statement would read equally well: "capacity," "potential," "ability," "will," "desire," "drive," "determination," "courage," "confidence," or "power." These words all suggest a force which exists naturally within the individual. And in this sense "strength" or "weakness" would appear to refer to an innate drive or motivation. The primary role of the RT therapist, then, would be to teach the patient how to develop her own innate capacity for self-fulfillment.

> Our job is to help the patient help himself to fulfill his needs right now (Glasser, 1975a: 46).

In *Positive Addiction* (1976), Glasser again uses the concept of strength as a quality and drive, but the drive aspect is now explicitly described and becomes one of the most important concepts in RT. "Strength" is now uniquely defined by Glasser in a way which distinguishes its use in RT from common parlance. Strength, says Glasser (1976a), is the real key to happiness.

> To find the happiness we all desire we have to figure out: (1) what to do, (2) how to do it, and (3) *where to get the strength to get it done*. In the struggle for love

and worth, what to do and how to do it are rarely difficult. . . . The problem is we don't have the *strength* to do what will make us happy (Glasser, 1976a: 4).

Strength is now identified as an *intrinsic, organically based* and *cognitive* capacity. That it is an intrinsic capacity is reflected in statements such as the following:

> . . . it is most characteristic of the very strong that they also have the strength to take care of themselves in situations where they have neither experience nor support. It almost seems that they are *endowed* with strength . . . (Glasser, 1976a: 63, italics added).

That it is organically based is suggested by Glasser's comment:

> I believe that within the brains of the strong the ten billion neurons that we all have available to us are interconnected into many more pathways than most of us have (Glasser, 1976a: 64).

That it is a cognitive capacity is indicated in Glasser's assertion that:

> They [very strong people] have learned to rely on this complex thinking organ to solve hard problems, even problems for which there is no precedent. They may be helped by experience *but they don't depend on it and in many cases they don't seem to need it* (1976a: 63).

Between 1965 and 1976, then, Glasser's understanding and definition of the concept of strength as a drive and motivating force appears to have become much more sophisticated. But it represents more than a refinement in his terminology; it suggests as well a major shift in his perception of human behaviour and development. There are several implications for RT theory which follow logically from Glasser's newly altered concept of strength through *increasing self-acceptance* and *decreasing cognitive control:*

> . . . the key to the whole process of gaining mental strength through positive addiction is self-acceptance to the point where you are able to leave your brain alone long enough to experience the PA state (Glasser, 1976a: 80).

In contrast to Glasser's earlier emphasis on externally imposed standards, control, and discipline, we find suddenly an expression of confidence in the possibility of organismic self-regulation or self-actualization. Still further, Glasser believes that this positive and intrinsic growth quality, which is expressed spontaneously by the child, becomes extinguished during the process of socialization:

> He is bombarded too much with the standard admonitions of our culture. He is told to stop daydreaming, get on the ball, not to waste time, to buckle down, all of which tell him the payoff is to pay attention and keep his mind occupied. He soon learns to abort these natural PA-state experiences and once he gets the knack of preventing their occurrence, a knack almost all of us develop at an early age, he successfully stops them for good. One way to recapture them as an

adult is to develop a positive addiction. This is the only way most of us can overcome the barrier of self-criticism that our culture has inculcated into all of us, a barrier that keeps the PA-state away (Glasser, 1976a: 142).

There is, then, a new acknowledgment by Glasser of the negative effects on human development which not only *may* occur from too much societal control, external competition, and self-evaluation, but which *do* result from these cultural values and standards. In recognition of the importance of this innate capacity he calls "strength," which facilitates our ability to fulfill our needs and achieve happiness, Glasser suggested three activities which he felt would develop our brains such that we could be aware of more options available to us. These were: (1) having more fun, (2) positive addiction, and (3) being less self-critical. By "having more fun," Glasser meant having more time for relaxation and personal enjoyment; more time for freeing our brains from routine and "work" so that new neural pathways might be established. By "positive addiction" (PA), Glasser meant an activity which we engage in simply for the pleasure we gain from it. It must be non-competitive, and enable total involvement without any self-evaluation. It must be done every day. After a time, the individual experiences during such activity a feeling of pleasure from within that is not a part of the activity. The activity is continued thereafter for the express purpose of feeling that pleasant sensation. Glasser believed that PA also frees the brain from its routine activity, and during PA-states, new neural pathways are developed such that the brain becomes more powerful. By "being less self-critical," Glasser again referred to the need to develop new approaches. If we decrease our self-criticism and free our brain, we experience new ideas and feelings and our brains develop further.

We find in *Positive Addiction*, then, several new ideas which give to his theory an explicit humanistic-existential and organismic quality. His emphasis on rationality, which underlay his earlier work, is made much more explicit and given greater significance. His perception of self-rating as potentially negative reflects a change—perhaps only a refinement in his earlier ideas, but an important one. Most surprising, however, is Glasser the realist's bold speculative leap into neurophysiology to explain strength, and his acceptance and promotion of the phenomenon he called positive addiction. This is an unexpected development in view of Glasser's earlier work, and seems to confirm a substantially altered perception of human behaviour.

In a 1978 VTR production on RT, we find Glasser having incorporated his new and older concepts into a description of the *Rational Person*, which he claimed paralleled Maslow's self-actualizing individual. The Rational Person was characterized as: (1) strong, (2) involved, in the sense of giving and receiving love and compassion, (3) successful, in the sense of gaining worth and recognition, (4) self-disciplined, (5) positively addicted, (6) intuitive and creative, (7) having fun, (8) developing, and (9) future-oriented.

As Glasser did not begin with a comprehensive theory of personality, we have had to read between the lines in our attempt to pull together his ideas with respect to normal human behaviour. Since he did not initially believe that the patient's past was significant for the therapist, it is understandable that he saw no need to determine the origin of the patient's problem. There was therefore no theory of normal development. But while we can help patients with problems to change without an understanding of problem development, we cannot *prevent* problem behaviour from occurring unless we know the *conditions* under which the initial problems arose so that we can change those conditions. Consideration of the "kind" of person the therapist would like to see develop can be avoided because the adult patient can choose for herself what or who she wants to be. But the infant and child cannot choose. Therefore we require some preconceived notion of the principles of human behaviour and development which, if followed, facilitate the growth of a psychologically normal person.

Glasser's early work reflected more a rejection of psychoanalytically oriented concepts than acceptance of ideas from other schools of thought. RT did not closely resemble any other approach. But as his theory and practice has evolved, we have seen RT develop a definite humanistic bias. While this move toward a more normal psychology may have occurred by chance, it would appear more likely that it resulted from Glasser's own strong social conscience and his recognition of the need for prevention and intervention (Glasser, 1975b; 1976a). Thus it is not enough to help the weak, it is imperative that we also develop and maintain the strong, lest they too become weak.

> My job as a psychiatrist and educator, is to try to help the weak grow stronger regardless of their situation. As a citizen I try to make the world better—that is my ongoing responsibility (it's yours too) (Glasser, 1976a: 11).

The "Neurotic" Person

As with normal behaviour, Glasser did not present a comprehensive theory to describe the origin and development of "irresponsible," "unsuccessful," and unfulfilling behaviour. He had found from experience that knowledge of the patient's past didn't seem to be of much help to him or the patient in dealing with the problem *now*, nor did the psychiatric labels and psychological terminology used to describe the patient's problem. What was left after the past was eliminated and the learned language removed was *the patient with a problem now*.

Once he had dispensed with labelling patients and worrying about how they became patients in the first place, Glasser became struck by the similarity of his patients' behaviour and what seemed to him to be a *common problem*. Not that his patients all did the same things, but rather that they seemed to approach life with a similar attitude. Over a twenty-year period Glasser altered and refined his analysis of the person who needs help, and established a patient classification system of his own, but he maintained his treatment procedure almost wholly intact. Let's conclude this section on basic concepts in RT by exploring briefly Glasser's approach to patient problem behaviour as it has evolved between 1962 and 1978.

1965

The Basic Problem of the Psychiatric Patient
Glasser rejected psychiatric classification, labelling, and diagnosis because they gave the false impression of understanding of the patient's problem. He suggested instead that the patient's behaviour, no matter what it was, merely indicated an inability of the patient to satisfy certain essential needs. As Goldstein had observed with his brain-damaged patients in the First World War, no matter how bizarre or unusual the patient's behaviour appeared, it could only be understood as the patient's attempt, however irrational, inappropriate, or unsuccessful, to satisfy her needs.

Behavioural Characteristics of People Unable to Satisfy Basic Needs
Glasser observed that the behaviour of individuals with unfulfilled basic needs had three common features: denial of reality, lack of involvement, and irresponsibility.

Denial of reality. The person unable to satisfy basic needs appears to be unaware of the real world around her, and when challenged with reality, denies it. Glasser described the appearance of patient denial of reality in behaviour such as lawbreaking, lying, projecting, fantasizing, and rationalizing. He found that while the extent as well as the nature of the denial differed greatly from one patient to the other, all refused to deal with the real world. The denial of reality occurred in the patient's behaviour when she was unsuccessful in having her needs met, and resorted to attempting to meet them by behaving as though the world were different than it is. Her behaviour thus became inappropriate, ensuring that her needs would not be met. Therapy was required, then, not only to enable the patient to accept reality, but also to help her to fulfill her needs in the real world so that she would not need to deny reality now or in the future.

Lack of involvement. As was pointed out in the section on normal development, basic need satisfaction requires the involvement of other people. Glasser emphasized this concept over all others. Both the infant and adult must be intimately involved with at least one other person in order to survive and to satisfy one essential human need: the need for love, caring, and respect. Thus involvement, which is required for the physical survival of the human infant, also establishes a psychological need, whose satisfaction is strongly reinforced during infancy and childhood. In the process we are rewarded for giving our love, and both giving and receiving of caring, love, and respect are satisfying and pleasurable. But love is not unconditional. It is tied to approval of one's behaviour, and approval from others shapes the individual's identity and feelings of worth.

The two basic psychological needs of love and worth, then, require involvement with others for their satisfaction. Glasser believed that if these needs were not satisfied the individual would experience pain. The experience of pain would then act as a stimulus to some form of activity by the individual which would eliminate the pain. In the case of experiencing the pain of being rejected or disapproved of by others, the behaviour of the individual to eliminate the pain may result in denial of the need itself. Since the need *is* real, denying it results in inappropriate behaviour which brings further rejection and disapproval. Thus, the individual must be helped in therapy to examine her behaviour that is not meeting her needs, and to change it to more appropriate behaviour that will.

The involvement with the therapist is critical, because without involvement with at least one other person, the patient cannot begin to learn to satisfy her own basic needs of love and worth, through accepting reality and involving herself with other people.

Irresponsibility. Glasser described as "irresponsible" those who had failed to learn, or had lost the ability, to satisfy their own needs. He considered need satisfaction to be a lifelong process, but one which is learned initially in childhood and the teaching of which is the major responsibility of parents. Glasser believed that people who behave irresponsibly later in life do so either because they were not exposed to love and discipline as infants and children, or because they were unable to respond appropriately to a crisis situation in which they experienced severe stress.

1968

Identity

By 1968, as we have discussed above, Glasser had begun to revise and expand some of his earlier ideas. Love and worth, rather than being considered basic needs, were instead now viewed as means through which one developed a personal identity or sense of self. With the focus of RT now turning to the patient's identity, the dynamics and process of the patient's problem behaviour became clearer. At this time Glasser made one of his significant contributions to the field: his appreciation and description of the dynamics involved in the *maintenance* of problem behaviour by the patient, and her *resistance* to therapy or change. Thus, although we have seen how important a part the concept of identity or self-concept has played in the understanding of the origin and development of problem behaviour in the therapies of Rogers, Perls, Janov, and Ellis, Glasser is the first to describe how the patient's identity is also involved in maintaining the problem behaviour and why she is reluctant to change it even though she is in pain and misery.

In his book, *The Identity Society* (1972), Glasser developed the thesis that, with the basic survival needs of the Western world assured of satisfaction, we have turned to primary concern with psychological need satisfaction. Personal fulfillment, or the attainment of a "successful identity," as he called it, was considered to be the goal of those living in the new "identity society." A successful identity required involvement with people, and work which was personally satisfying as well as socially significant. Those who were not involved with people and whose work or activity was not socially significant were described as having a "failure identity." The behaviour of people with failure identities was characterized by: emotional distress, loneliness, and choosing symptom companions.

Emotional distress. Glasser described people with failure identities as seeing themselves as inadequate and inferior to everyone else. Feeling and believing themselves to be "no good," and unable to obtain basic need satisfaction, they deny reality and withdraw from social contact. This denial and withdrawal further isolate them, such that emotional pain is the only feeling they experience —no pleasure, no joy. Glasser believed (1975) that the inappropriate emotional behaviour of "failures" demonstrated their inability to learn, as children, to respond to the pain of anger, frustration, and disappointment in ways which would increase involvement with others and decrease their pain. Instead, they seemed to learn to behave impulsively, demandingly, and aggressively, thereby *decreasing* their experience of love, caring, and approval.

While the pain of anger is reduced by immediate emotional expression, or better still is given "relief" (Glasser's term) a new pain is experienced: the pain of rejection or loneliness, which may occur in response to their acting out angry behaviour.

When the person cannot express anger directly, containing it may result in depression, tension, anxiety, fatigue, boredom, and psychosomatic symptoms. But while all of us experience these responses from contained anger at times, and on occasion express anger directly, the "failure person" is seen as doing so typically. At the same time she does appear to learn that these responses do not bring satisfaction of her basic needs. To demonstrate the difference between the successful and "failure" identity person's response to frustration and anger, Glasser (1975) provided this description:

> Successful people characteristically learn to suppress the immediate, angry emotion. Although they know when to be assertive and aggressive, they do so without the anger that may reduce or destroy needed involvement. They can stand up for their rights without getting into an irrational argument because they have learned that as long as they stay involved, the painful feelings will dissipate. When attacked or rejected, they usually respond with consideration, thus blunting the attack and making themselves harder to reject. Successful people learn to cope with anger or its civilized derivatives, such as depression and anxiety, quickly and effectively by working to turn the situation toward involvement. Knowing from experience that good feelings are possible, they learn behavior that creates pleasure rather than pain (Glasser, 1975b: 29).

Glasser viewed "failure" people, then, as behaving impulsively. Their impulsive behaviour tends to alienate them from others' love and approval, which in turn further decreases their sense of personal worth. If they do manage to suppress their anger, they seem unable to alleviate their depression, anxiety, and tension by seeking involvement which will satisfy their basic need and dispel the depression, anxiety, and tension. Thus they remain in pain and distress.

Loneliness. If it is true that the failure person is lonely and in pain, one would expect her to welcome the involvement of the therapist and the chance to change. Not so, said Glasser (1975b: 43-44):

> Despite all the people helping to relieve pain, many of whom understand that the pain, whatever its form, is a result of loneliness and failure to gain a successful identity, we are making little headway in reaching the many people who need help. Even under the best conditions, with a good therapist who knows how to get involved and a motivated client who understands the need to change his behavior toward more involvement, changing from failure to success is very hard.

Why? Glasser (1975b) eloquently offers four reasons which provide the underlying dynamic of the "failure" person. First, "failure" people do not believe that the pleasure of mature involvement is possible for them. So strong are their own feelings of worthlessness and self-hate that, not recognizing in themselves any qualities that someone else would like or admire, they cannot contemplate *being loved* and accepted, nor imagine themselves *giving love*. Second, they are therefore afraid to risk even trying to change, because this would require them to begin to change the way they think of themselves. They know *who* they are now: they are "no good." As painful as a "no-good" failure identity is, it is better than having no identity at all. "Failure" people cling in fear to their inadequate self-image because it offers them a kind of security. Third, and most important, "failure" people resist change to success and pleasure because it requires real involvement. They have learned to replace their need for real involvement by withdrawal from others into themselves. This does not eliminate the pain of loneliness, and so must be supported by various activities which enable "failure" people to avoid the realization of pain by focusing attention outside of themselves. Fourth, the pain of depression, anxiety, tension, and loneliness is at least strongly experienced *feeling*, however unpleasant, and so has a bittersweet quality. Feeling pain is better than feeling nothing, and may provide a locus for the "failure" person's attention. At times, it may almost be enjoyed in the sense that strongly felt emotion may define and increase our sense of self and our uniqueness. Consider, for example, how we all sometimes wallow in our own depression or loneliness because it provides an opportunity to deeply experience feeling. The "failure" person may refuse to give up feeling bad because she cannot imagine that feeling good can be experienced in the same intense and encompassing way.

The activities or symptoms which become the focus of attention in the "failure" person, then, appear as the patient's problems. They serve to disguise the real problem: the unsatisfied need for involvement with others in which love and worth may be experienced. The "failure" person characterized by emotional pain and distress appears reluctant to exchange her pain for pleasure, however. Even when she recognizes her own problem behaviour and is given the opportunity for therapy she resists change because:

1. She feels she is a "no-good" person, and she cannot believe it is possible that other people can love her and meet her needs.
2. She has a strong self-concept as a "no-good" person and knows who she is now, and she is afraid to risk giving up this identity for an unknown "good" one.
3. Change and therapy require her to become involved with another person. She has, however, both denied her need for involvement and withdrawn into herself in order to relieve the pain of loneliness. Risking involvement in therapy may increase her pain temporarily, and if it is unsuccessful she may feel even worse.
4. The experience of emotional pain, while unpleasant, is a real sensation which verifies her existence and humanity. She cannot imagine pleasant sensations doing the same thing.

(We may note in these dynamics underlying patient resistance to therapy a patient belief system which is one of the cornerstones of Ellis's RET.)

Choosing symptom companions. Glasser also believed that "failure" people *choose* their particular form of inappropriate or aberrant behaviour, beliefs, emotions, or psychosomatic illness.

> Obsessions, compulsions, psychoses, and most long-term symptomatic illnesses that have no presently known medical cause all serve the same purpose as depression. They act as companions that lonely people *choose* because they are unable to tolerate the knowledge that they have only themselves with whom to become involved, knowledge that might lead to suicide if a symptom companion cannot be developed or relief be obtained for the pain (Glasser, 1975b: 55).

Glasser suggested that the symptoms are not picked at random, but develop slowly through a process of learning. The symptoms the patient *decides* to use as a substitute for the involvement she really wants and needs emerge suddenly when she experiences unusual stress or slowly when she experiences long-term loneliness and failure. The implication for treatment is significant: if we believe the patient *chooses* her symptoms as "companions" out of despairing loneliness, we cannot cure her as though she had a physical illness. The initial step in helping must be for the therapist to try to become involved with the patient and get her to choose the therapist's companionship over her symptom companions.

1978

We have outlined above Glasser's recent elaboration of the concept of *strength*. We noted several important changes in this concept from its use in 1965, and in particular, its implications for normal human growth and behaviour. In a similar fashion, the concept of *weakness*, which you may recall Glasser (1975a) earlier substituted for *mental illness*, has been refined and expanded to include three basic response patterns on a continuum. The weak person, feeling pain and in distress, unable to attain happiness (love and worth) due to her undeveloped neural capacity to perceive options (Glasser, 1976a), proceeds to make the following three choices: to give up, to adopt a symptom companion, and to adopt a negative addiction. The weak person always begins with the first and, depending on the circumstances, may move on to the second and then the third. Let's examine these three response patterns of what Glasser described as the "give-up person," the "symptom person," and the "negatively addicted person."

The "Give-up person." Glasser described the "give-up person" as one who, after repeated unsuccessful attempts to obtain the love and worth she wants and needs, stops trying. She stops trying because failure is painful. She decides that if she settles for less, she can reduce her pain and misery. She cannot eliminate her pain completely, because love and worth are essential needs, but she can at least reduce the pain of continued failure and disappointment if she accepts the fact that she will never be happy. The weak person finally gives up trying when she becomes convinced that no matter how hard she tries she will not be successful because she just doesn't have "it." The "it" may be intelligence, luck, appearance, skill, money, or personality. Glasser called "it" *strength*, and strength was described as an innate intellectual capacity for problem solving involving the spontaneous emergence of goal-oriented behavioural options. The weak become stymied and frustrated and fail to satisfy their basic needs for love and worth. The strong explore a continuing array of options until they succeed. While we may all "give up" at times—according to Glasser, there are varying degrees of "give-up people,"—the "give-up person" may, after a time, make the second choice: to become a "symptom person."

The Symptom person. Glasser (1976a) described the dynamics behind the "symptom person" in this way: the "give-up person," in pain and distress, decides to give up in order to reduce the pain of repeated failure. For a while, this works; she feels less pain initially when she stops trying and stops failing. But before long not trying at all makes her feel even more inadequate, and the old pain returns. The "give-up person" accepts responsibility for failure, decides she simply doesn't have "it," and stops trying. But as the pain returns, and her personal inadequacy becomes more evident, she chooses a *symptom* as a means to avoid recognizing this inadequacy, by suggesting that she is not responsible for her failure because "sickness" has descended upon her. The symptom enables her to feel better about herself and obtain from other people some of the love and attention which she could not get by giving up. Glasser (1976a) described four common symptom categories:

Symptom Categories	Typical Behaviours
1. Acting out	tantrums, aggression, destruction, fighting, lying, cheating, breaking laws, rules, and norms
2. Neurotic	depression, irrational fears, phobias, tension, anxiety, dejection, irritation, complaining, anger, deceit, hypocrisy, prejudice, blaming, desire to punish, withdrawal, denial
3. Crazy (psychotic)	paranoia, hallucinations, delusions
4. Psychosomatic	headache, backache, migraine, hypertension, heart disease, asthma, allergies, colitis, ulcers, skin disorders

The Negatively addicted person. Unlike the first two choices, addiction does reduce the pain of failure to obtain love and worth. Not only does it completely relieve the pain, it provides, as well, a brief period of intense pleasure. The combination of pain reduction and the experience of pleasure make addiction very resistant to therapeutic intervention. Glasser described the dynamic of the addict in this way:

> The obvious problem of addiction is that the addict, through his addiction, is able to live with little love or worth, without having to suffer the pain of failing to get it. In fact, he enjoys his life if his addiction is satisfied, and has no need for anything else. His credo is why search for something as tenuous, in his experience, as love and worth when his addiction is sure. It goes without saying that the pleasure of addiction depends on a regular supply (love and worth do too) of whatever you are addicted to. If deprived of your addiction you must return not only to the pain and misery of your previous second-choice symptoms but to the additional pain, mental and physical, that comes with withdrawal. In alcohol and heroin and food the addiction is both physical and mental, in gambling it's all mental, but for practical purposes they all hurt when they are stopped. You miss what you have got used to having and you suffer (Glasser, 1976a: 34).

In summary, Glasser's ideas about the origin and development of problem behaviour reflect a gradual change in emphasis and greater elaboration and refinement between 1962 and 1976. While some of his original ideas and assumptions remain unchanged, such as the belief in the importance of involvement, they have been incorporated with others that have been altered, like the concept of worth, and those that appear to be new, like negative addiction. Glasser's theory of problem behaviour centres around the individual's unsatisfied basic need for love and worth, or happiness. The failure to satisfy this need

9: Reality Therapy 297

FIGURE 9-1
The Basic Concepts of Reality Therapy

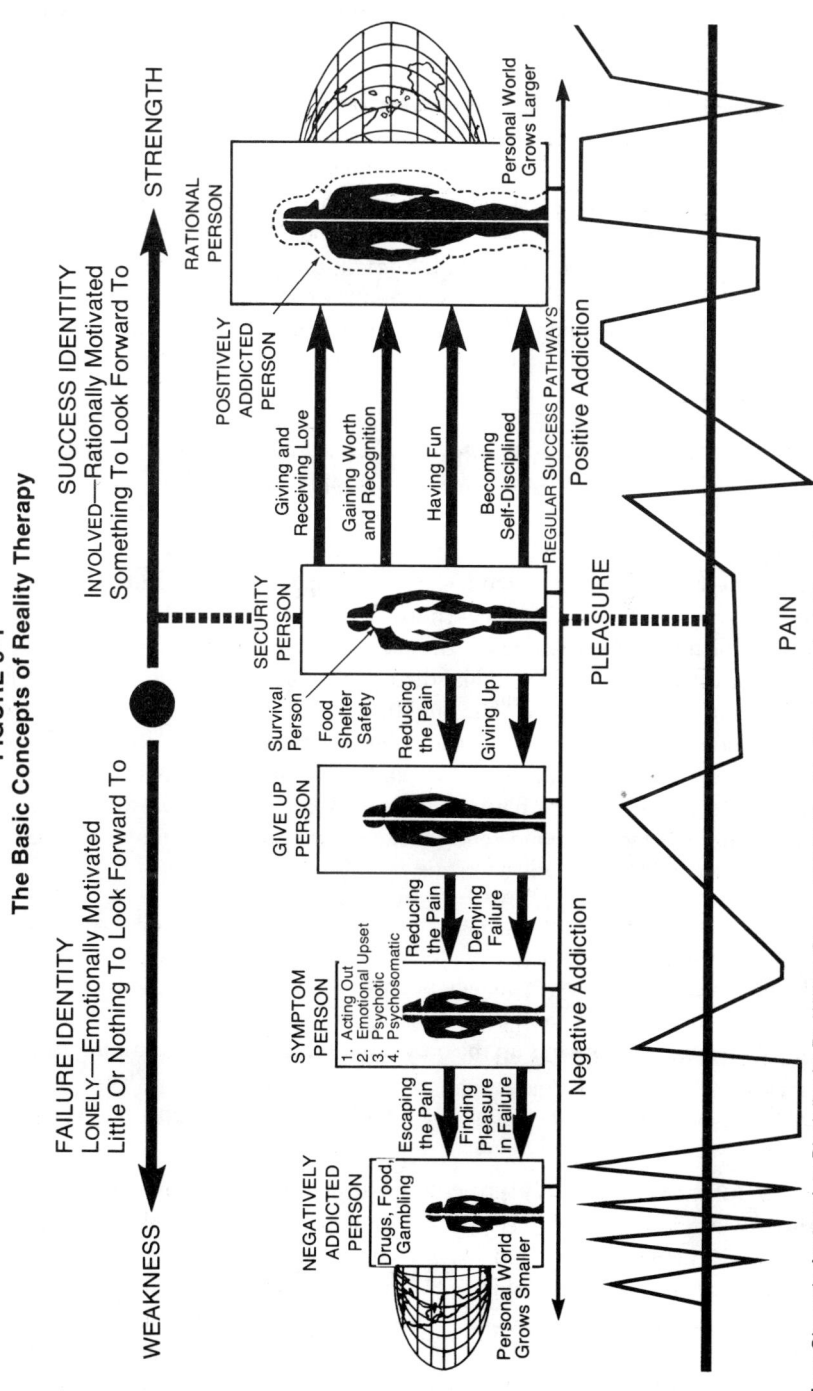

From *Glasser's Approach to Discipline* by Dr. William Glasser (1978). Reprinted by permission of the author.

results in the development of a failure identity or negative self-image on a cognitive level, and the experience of pain and distress on an emotional level. The failure person responds to the pain of lack of involvement with others, which she requires to experience love and worth, by denying pain and withdrawing into herself. The failure person's unsuccessful attempts to satisfy basic needs are the result of weakness, which Glasser recently described as an organically determined capacity. This is a cognitive capacity involving the spontaneous emergence of options through which to explore problem situations. This capacity, he believes, can be facilitated through learning and practice. After repeated failure to obtain happiness, the failure person may choose to give in in an attempt to relieve the accompanying pain and distress. But giving up brings only temporary relief. Soon the old pain returns, and with it the further pain of realizing the inadequacy of giving up. At this point, the failure person may choose to adopt a symptom through which she can avoid responsibility for her failure identity. The symptom enables her to deny responsibility for her behaviour, feel less inadequate, and at the same time obtain from others a little of the love and attention she needs. Glasser describes four common symptom patterns: acting out, neurotic, crazy, and psychosomatic. If the second choice is unsuccessful in relieving the pain, and if she is not helped to change and to learn how to satisfy her own needs, she may choose to become negatively addicted. Negative addiction is the last choice, the final attempt at relief of pain. It is very resistant to change because, unlike the other choices, it brings not only relief from pain, but also pleasure. The only help for the failure person who is negatively addicted appears to be anti-addiction organizations like Alcoholics Anonymous which provide an intensive and comprehensive approach through which the addict may be able to experience some love and worth. All failure people are reluctant to change and resistant to therapy, even though distressed and in pain, for the following reasons:

1. They do not believe there is anything about them that other people might truly value or desire.
2. They are afraid to try to change because failure after trying will make them feel even less worthy and even greater pain.
3. Changing means giving up the only thing which provides meaning for their lives—their symptoms.
4. They cannot imagine the feeling of pleasure that therapy may provide, because they know only pain.

Figure 9·1 graphically presents most of the major concepts described thus far.

GOALS AND TECHNIQUES

Therapeutic Goals

Although we have noted significant changes in RT concepts and emphasis in the previous section, the goal of RT has changed little during the past fifteen years. In 1965 Glasser stated the goal as follows:

Psychiatry must be concerned with two basic psychological needs: *The need to love and be loved and the need to feel that we are worthwhile to ourselves and to others.* Helping patients fulfill these two needs is the basis of Reality Therapy. . . .

The proper role of psychiatry will always be to help people to help themselves to fulfill their needs, given a reasonable opportunity to do so (Glasser, 1975a: 9).

By 1972, Glasser had begun to emphasize the concept of identity, and in his goal statement at that time we find that RT is no longer reserved for psychiatric patients alone:

Reality Therapy is not exclusively for the "mentally ill," incompetent, disturbed, or emotionally upset. It is a system of ideas designed to help those who identify with failure learn to gain a successful identity and to help those already successful to maintain their competence and help others become successful (Glasser, 1975b: 73).

Still later, Glasser wrote:

Reality Therapy is designed to help people I call irresponsible or failing people become involved and to gain and then maintain a successful identity (1976b: 52).

The reference to psychiatry had disappeared altogether in this latter statement of aim, reflecting Glasser's increased involvement in non-clinical settings such as schools, and his own developing identity as an educator of educators.

His most recent book, *Positive Addiction* (1976), does not deal directly with Reality Therapy, but does utilize the basic concepts and assumptions of RT. It introduces into Glasser's work the two new concepts of *strength* and *positive addiction* (PA). Since strength, an innate capacity, is critical to the achievement of happiness, that is, love and worth, and requires an absence of self-criticism or competition, we might anticipate in the future some further changes in RT goals. Glasser appears to have altered his earlier blanket endorsement of self-evaluation, for example. On the other hand, we might expect an emphasis to be made on therapeutic activities which, like PA, may facilitate the development of strength.

For the moment however, RT remains concerned with enabling people to fulfill their basic needs for love and worth themselves through involvement with others. It is important to remember that, while Glasser (1972) claimed to have eliminated jargon from his approach, as we have seen above, terms like "love," "worth," "involvement," "strength," and "positive addiction" are all RT concepts and as such are uniquely used and defined by Glasser.

The Process of Therapy

WHAT IS "THERAPY" AND WHO SHOULD DO IT?
Glasser takes the position throughout his work that "therapy" is not the prerogative of the professional.

... we must remember that many other people do therapy—at least in the sense of helping people better fulfill their needs. Anyone using the general principles of Reality Therapy who attempts to help a person help himself toward more responsible behaviour does nothing basically different from psychiatrists or for that matter different from parents who try to the best of their ability to raise a child to be a responsible citizen . . . . the major difference between therapy and common guidance that is effective is in intensity, not in kind (Glasser, 1975a: 20).

This view of therapy parallels that which was outlined in Chapter 1. An interesting implication of Glasser's method is that *anyone* can employ the basic techniques. Thus, therapy is defined by Glasser as "a special kind of teaching or training which attempts to accomplish in a relatively short, intense period what should have been established during normal growing up" (1975a: 20).

Again, we find Glasser demystifying and deprofessionalizing the helping process by relating it to commonly held values and practices underlying child care and human relations. These ideas were welcomed by many non-medical professional helpers, such as psychologists and social workers, whose legitimate role in the therapeutic milieu was often questioned and diminished by the more politically powerful psychiatrists. Glasser also gave credibility to non-professional helpers, such as counsellors, teachers, clergy, volunteers, and friends, and provided them with some very simple procedures which they could quickly learn to increase their effectiveness in helping others to meet their needs more ably.

THE EIGHT STEPS OF RT

While we have seen considerable change and development in the concepts underlying RT in the previous sections, the actual method employed by Glasser appears to have changed very little since 1965. At that time Glasser described his technique as composed of three separate procedures: (1) involvement, (2) rejection of unrealistic patient behaviour, and (3) teaching the patient better ways to satisfy needs.

The process of establishing involvement with the patient was described at length, but the latter two procedures were not. By 1972, Glasser had further elaborated and refined the second and third procedures while retaining the first, thereby articulating seven therapeutic principles: (1) involvement, (2) current behaviour, (3) evaluating behaviour, (4) planning responsible behaviour, (5) commitment, (6) accept no excuses, and (7) no punishment. An eighth principle "never give up," has appeared in Glasser's workshops and reports.

These principles occur during the course of therapy in the order they are listed above.

Involvement

Glasser's principle of *involvement* refers to the patient-therapist relationship and includes what Rogers has termed the core conditions of a therapeutic relationship, and what we defined in Chapter 1 as essential therapist qualities. Helping cannot begin until involvement with the patient is established. We have earlier defined involvement with others as the process through which one learns to give and receive love and worth, that is, the process through which one learns to fulfill basic needs. For the patient whose problems reflect her inability to fulfill her needs, involvement has not occurred. The therapist's first task, then, is to become involved with the patient. He does this by demonstrating certain personal qualities, and by talking with the patient. Between 1965 and 1976, Glasser identified a number of therapist qualities which must be communicated to the patient: warmth, friendship, emotional involvement, caring, understanding, honesty, sharing, reassurance, acceptance, sincerity, responsibility, interest, strength, and empathy.

There are, of course, limitations to the involvement possible within the structure imposed by the therapy situation, but as Glasser pointed out (1976a), this does not mean that the patient will consider the involvement artificial or unreal.

> The deliberate involvement of the professional therapist may seem to make therapy artificial, but to someone who is lonely, warm and friendly acceptance is not artificial. The therapist's problem is to provide enough involvement to help the patient develop confidence to make new, deep, lasting involvement on his own (Glasser, 1976b: 53-54).

The RT therapist does not talk to the patient about her problems, but instead directs the patient's attention away from a discussion of problems, because dwelling on problems reinforces the patient's self-image of failure. Any other subject is appropriate. The conversation with the therapist then resembles that which might ensue with a friend or family member. The therapist wants the patient to focus on positive topics which are interesting and involving and which enable therapist and patient to share equally in the discussion.

> In the therapy relationship anything is open for discussion. This is a difficult concept for patients and beginning therapists to understand, but it is natural and easy for friends or family to accept. Current events, movies, books, plays, goals, and personal and family relations are all good grist for positive involvement. The patient's problems often do not enter many of the therapy hours [at this stage]. Interesting non-problem discussions are valuable in therapy because they develop the intellectual sharing that is important in Reality Therapy. They should be stimulating, with values, opinions, and beliefs brought out and some emotion experienced (Glasser, 1976b: 54).

Glasser nicely summarized the principle of involvement this way:

> Involvement is the foundation of therapy. All other principles build on and add to it. As soon as possible, the person being helped must begin to understand that there is more to life than being involved with his misery, symptoms, obsessive thoughts, or irresponsible behavior. He must see that another human being

cares for him and is willing to discuss his life and talk about anything both consider worthwhile and interesting. In this relationship any subject of mutual interest can serve as a bridge to build involvement. Any subject can provide the warmth and give-and-take that help a failing person learn that he can be accepted by and accepting of another human being (Glasser, 1975b: 78).

Current Behaviour
If we have recognized in the principle of *involvement* some close parallels to Rogerian Therapy, we will see in the second and third principles—*current behaviour* and *evaluating behaviour*, some dynamics also identified with Gestalt and Rational-Emotive approaches. Once the RT therapist has established involvement, he may, while continuing to maintain this relationship, begin to draw the patient's attention to her behaviour. This principle would include what Perls referred to as *awareness* and *attention*. Glasser maintained (1975b, 1976b) that the rationale for this principle lay in the fact that patients often seem to be unaware of their present behaviour and cannot develop a successful identity without awareness of what they are doing that prevents their success. While he does not indicate specifically, it would also appear to be essential for the client to begin to accept *ownership* of her own behaviour before she can accept responsibility for it or consider her behaviour as something she chooses and therefore over which she has control.

What Glasser does identify (1975b, 1976a) is the significance of RT's focus on current behaviour over feelings. While Ellis's approach is founded on the principle that beliefs and ideas *produce* inappropriate emotions which lead to inappropriate behaviour, and therefore one should focus on changing the patient's beliefs and ideas, Glasser's RT adopts the premise that inappropriate feelings are the *result* of inappropriate behaviour, and therefore to change feelings one should first change behaviour.

The emphasis on current behaviour, then, follows involvement, and facilitates the patient's awareness of what she is doing, so that she may accept *ownership* of the behaviour, and begin to recognize that it involves a *choice* on her part. The therapist draws the patient's attention to her behaviour by carefully asking questions such as: "What are you doing?" "What are you doing now?" "What did you do yesterday?" "Do you think you are doing ____?" If this were Gestalt, the therapist might stop here, with the expectation that once the patient establishes sufficient awareness, she will again become self-regulating and self-actualizing. But in RT and in RET, the patient, once aware of her behaviour, is expected to *evaluate* it in terms of personal needs and societal expectations.

Evaluating Behaviour
The principle of evaluating behaviour has often been misunderstood by professional helpers and has led to the charge that RT is *moralistic*. This misperception of RT, we have suggested above, may have resulted from Glasser's initial failure to clarify and explain this concept fully. Certainly as it is more recently

described (Glasser, 1975b, 1976b), there appears to be no imposition of the therapist's value system on the patient. The therapist requests that the patient examine the outcome of her behaviour. Once the patient is aware of what she is doing, the therapist asks whether this behaviour is satisfying. Is it the best the patient can do toward helping herself get what she wants out of life? The therapist also asks the patient to assess the effect of what she is doing on her family and friends, and lastly, if applicable, on the community in which she lives.

This concern with the effect of the client's behaviour on others and the community reflects the RT value judgment that one cannot satisfy one's own needs at the expense of others. This distinguishes it from therapies based on the principle of self-actualization, such as those of Rogers, Perls, Ellis, and Janov, in which there is an implied belief that once the blocks to personal fulfillment are removed in therapy and the patient returns to an integrated, self-directed condition, she will automatically also experience the caring and compassion for others which is intrinsic to human behaviour. However, since this assumption is not made by RT, it is dealt with explicitly by the therapist. Evaluating one's behaviour, then, in RT, is primarily directed toward meeting one's own needs and attaining happiness, but the patient must recognize that meeting her own needs requires involvement with others who also seek happiness and fulfillment. Thus RT is not merely moralistic, but rather is realistically concerned with having patients examine their own goals and behaviour in terms of the mutual and reciprocal nature of human social organization.

In some ways Glasser's rationale for requiring patients to evaluate their behaviour may be more adaptive and realistic. Certainly it does provide a mechanism through which to explore other options, if the outcomes or implications of the patient's behaviour are not what the patient wants. It is also true that other people she wishes to love and be loved by have their own values, and that there are real rules, regulations, laws, and standards in the community and society in which she lives. The RT therapist does not impose his own or the community's values and standards on the patient's behaviour, but he does require the patient to take them into consideration when evaluating what she is doing. Through this process, should the patient decide to reject certain societal values, she will at least have become aware of her behaviour, have considered her goals, have explored the options possible, have made a choice, and be prepared to risk and accept the possible consequences of her actions. This process would appear to facilitate the development of at least the first three attributes of the normal person outlined in Chapter 1: self-control, personal responsibility, and social responsibility.

At the same time, it seems fair to identify in RT a philosophic and behavioural emphasis on social conformity, compromise, and adaptation, in contrast to the self-actualizing therapies' focus on client independence, uniqueness, and individuality. But this emphasis, in view of Glasser's own social action orientation and concern with social change, would appear to reflect, not so much Glasser's own values, but more his view of what is most likely to assist his patients as they attempt to re-involve themselves with others. Glasser's professional training and background and subsequent theoretical position has shown him to be a rebel with a cause. That Glasser's position on morality represents his attempt at a more practical, common-sense approach appears to be supported by the following comment:

> Whatever the morality or the laws of the society, we can rarely excuse our behavior because we do not agree with them. We must understand that we have to accept the consequences of our behavior if we defy the existing morality or existing laws. Guidance by a concerned person able to point out the realities of the society helps us recognize what we are doing. If a young man wanted to protest the Vietnam war by failing to report for induction, he knew his behavior was cause for arrest. It was his decision, and he should have prepared himself for jail. The same risk applies to smoking marijuana openly.
>
> In my experience, most individuals who feel failure gain strength more readily by conforming to the ongoing morality and laws of society; later, when they are stronger and more successful they may wish to defy them. The job of the Reality Therapist, when discussing morality and law and the patient's role in society, is to bring out everything that he can about them relevant to the decision the patient must make. Then, if the patient chooses an action to protest the war that leads to jail, he has made a rational, not an emotional, decision (Glasser, 1975b: 92-93).

Planning Responsible Behaviour
When the patient has become *involved* with the therapist, has begun to become *aware* of her behaviour, has begun to *assess* her behaviour as "good" or "bad" *for her* in achieving her goals or satisfying her needs and wishes, she is ready to develop and explore what she might *do* to alter or replace her "bad" ineffective behaviour for that which appears more likely to bring her the results she wants. Although many people may know that what they are doing is not making them happy, they may not know how to change their behaviour. This change requires planning. The RT therapist's experience in speaking with many people about their problems and plans gives him a broader base of information from which to draw than is available to the average person, and he may be more knowledgeable as well about community resources and programs which may be utilized by the patient. The therapist's role, then, in assisting with a plan, is to act as an information resource. The therapist's skill level is reflected in his ability and effectiveness in having the patient make her own realistic plan. The plan must be reasonable or possible and the patient must *experience* the plan as hers and not that of the therapist. Even if reasonable, if the plan is to work, it must be *owned* by the patient. This does not mean that the RT therapist is non-directive; he must be very actively involved in the patient's plan. The therapist therefore may ask questions, make comments on the patient's ideas, offer suggestions, give direct information, express concerns, and ask the patient to describe outcomes expected or anticipated from certain actions.

The therapist, then, acts as an information resource, but also plays the role of devil's advocate; acts as a mirror, giving feedback to the client about her own feelings, ideas and behaviour as they are experienced by the therapist; and confronts the patient with her inconsistencies, flaws in logic, irrational ideas or beliefs, and overgeneralizations. The therapist, then, is actively involved with the patient, both initiating and responding to patient behaviour. The therapist's goal at this stage is to enable the patient ultimately to make a plan that will work, that is reasonable, and that will succeed. It is *successful* goal attainment that the therapist wishes to ensure for the patient. Thus the patient will be cautioned not to attempt too much, and to begin with very short-term goals. At the same time, the plan must be that of the patient, and the therapist must be willing to go along with the patient's plan if the patient insists, even though the therapist may disagree with it or feel that it will not succeed. So long as the therapist has thoroughly explored with the patient the possible outcomes of her behaviour, and the patient is prepared to accept responsibility for the plan, the therapist has done the best he can. Once a plan is decided on by the patient, the therapist then assists the patient in every way possible to ensure its success.

Commitment

Because RT holds that patients with failing identities believe that other people don't care about them or what they do, once a plan is made by the patient, she is required to make a commitment to carry it out. The commitment is often made in writing, since this increases its concreteness and makes it seem more binding; and it is made to *another person* as well as herself. The commitment to carry out her plan is made to a person she believes does care about her. This means that she also commits herself to involvement since she is promising to do something for someone else—to give something of herself to someone else who cares about her. The person she makes the commitment to may be the therapist, or a spouse, parent, teacher, child, or friend—but it must be someone with whom the patient is *involved*.

Accept No Excuse

If the patient fails to keep her commitment or the plan fails, which is likely to occur, the therapist does not accept excuses or reasons nor does he ask *why* or express disapproval. It does not matter why the commitment was not kept or the plan failed, and the therapist's expression of anger or disappointment with the patient's failure would only serve to destroy their involvement. Instead, the therapist merely acknowledges the fact that the commitment was not kept or the plan failed and proceeds to reexamine with the patient the original assessment which the patient made of her behaviour to determine whether the evaluation remains valid. If the evaluation is the same, the patient reassesses her plan. If the plan still seems to be reasonable, then the patient must renew her commitment to complete it. If she does not wish to do so, she must say so to the therapist. If the patient does renew her commitment, the therapist again holds her responsible for the plan. If the patient decides she cannot carry out a particular plan and keep her commitment, the therapist helps the patient to formulate another plan that she can commit herself to and carry out.

The therapist cannot help unless he and the patient are both willing to re-examine the plan continually and make a mutual decision either to renew the commitment, if the plan is a good one or to give it up, if it is not. The therapist must say to the patient, "If you are not going to do it, say so, but don't say you are and then give excuses when you fail" . . . .

To do Reality Therapy well requires the ability not to accept excuses, not to probe for fault, not to be a detective to find out *why* (Glasser, 1976b: 61).

No Punishment
Glasser's position is that punishment—physical or mental pain—is destructive to involvement and therefore leads to, or reinforces, failure. It is therefore as important not to punish people for failing to keep commitments as it is to not accept excuses. It is paradoxical that successful people, who have many options open to them, respond to the threat of punishment by selecting other options and are rarely punished, whereas "failure" people, who lack options, are continually punished for their irresponsible behaviour. *Punishment therefore merely maintains and reinforces the failure identity of irresponsible and lonely people.* The application of punishment in child-rearing and pedagogy is considered particularly dangerous since it *creates* a failure identity by preventing involvement and by denying the child the opportunity to evaluate her own behaviour and develop internalized controls.

This is not to suggest that the child or patient should have free rein. The parent, guardian, or therapist is responsible for identifying with the growing individual the structure within which she may act. The behaviour of the child or patient must be considered in the light of specific family mores, institutional norms, community standards, societal laws, and the natural environment. Within this context, the child or patient needs to understand and agree upon *in advance* the likely consequences of her irresponsible behaviour. But learning new and appropriate behaviour implies the risk of failure, and when failure occurs, the child and patient require involvement, that is, continued love, caring, and respect. The role of the parent or therapist is to remain consistent and responsible in the presence of failure in his child or patient. Even though the child or patient didn't keep her part of the bargain—commitment—the parent or therapist does keep his, including holding the child or patient to her commitment. It is not necessary to punish the child or patient for failure; the experience of failure is punishment enough. But it *is* necessary for the patient or child to examine the commitment with the therapist or parent and make a plan which can be successful.

Never Give Up
Glasser's eighth treatment principle—*never give up*—is not identified in his books, but is part of his seminar and workshop presentations. He emphasizes the need for the therapist to persevere. At first the patient will fail to keep commitments, will attempt more than she can reasonably achieve. She will test the therapist to see whether he will accept her when she fails, or whether he will

reject and punish her as others have done. She may try to manipulate the therapist as she has manipulated others. Because change is very difficult for the patient, she may try to find a way out of therapy by frustrating the therapist so that the therapist will give up. There are many reasons why the patient will fail and why she will attempt to destroy the involvement with the therapist. It is important for the therapist to anticipate these responses, to accept no excuses, to not punish, to maintain involvement, and to consistently require the patient to reassess, replan, and recommit herself. Glasser (1978: 5) did not suggest a specific length of time for which the therapist should persevere:

> Each of us must define "never" for ourselves but a good basic rule of thumb is to hang in there longer than the student thinks you will.

THERAPY SUMMARY

We have in RT technique the basic Rogerian requirement, common to all effective therapies, of involvement, or the establishment and maintenance of a therapeutic relationship. In addition, RT includes the Gestalt emphasis on achieving patient *awareness* of present behaviour. It involves a behaviouristic element by requiring the patient to change her *behaviour first* in order that she may begin to *feel* better. It employs certain RET and social work methods by attempting to *teach* the patient to improve her use of *cognitive* skills so that she may meet her needs and solve her problems more effectively.

The apparent simplicity of RT technique, with its eight steps and everyday language, is perhaps its most attractive feature. Practical and action-oriented, it appeals to the layperson as well as the professional and is readily understood by the patient. It gives immediacy to the helping process and offers the patient hope of rapid goal attainment. Glasser has claimed impressive results from the use of RT principles in both group and individual therapy, with a wide range of patients with problem behaviour: acting-out, hostile, severely disturbed adolescents, long-term hospitalized adult patients diagnosed as schizophrenic, or children with classroom behaviour and learning difficulties. Glasser claims that RT is effective in helping 80 to 90 per cent of these patients to learn to live responsibly, autonomously, and happily (Glasser, 1975a, 1975b, 1978).

SUMMARY

We might summarize what we have learned about RT as follows:

1. RT has a deductively determined ex post facto theoretical base, as do Rogerian Therapy, GT, and RET.
2. Glasser's work is particularly noteworthy in that it reflects an early (1950s) rejection of several key traditional psychiatric concepts and principles which appeared unresponsive to patient needs.
3. Glasser demystified therapy and aimed his approach at the mass of

"natural" and non-medical helpers such as psychologists, social workers, teachers, counsellors, parents, clergy, nurses, and institutional staff.
4. RT has been described as a "developing" approach. Its as yet incomplete theoretical base has potential implications for further elaboration and refinement in RT techniques and methods.
5. RT is present- and future-oriented.
6. RT considers that all patient behaviour reflects attempts to satisfy needs.
7. The basic needs of all individuals are considered to be "love" and "worth"; satisfaction of these needs results in happiness and self-fulfillment.
8. Basic need satisfaction can only be achieved through "involvement" with others.
9. RT terms such as "love," "worth," "responsibility," "involvement," and "strength" are used uniquely in RT and reflect more than their normal meanings. Thus RT is not entirely jargon-free, but the terminology is not "foreign" or esoteric to the initiate.
10. Neurotic or problem behaviour results when the individual's basic needs (love and worth) are not satisfied and the pain of rejection, loneliness, and inadequacy results in withdrawal from, and/or denial of, reality.
11. Inability to satisfy basic needs results in the establishment, in time, of a negative "failure identity."
12. The neurotic person is resistant to change even while in pain because she cannot believe real involvement with others is possible for her, and because she fears further failure experiences which may make her feel worse.
13. The neurotic person chooses symptoms to avoid responsibility for behaving irresponsibly or inadequately, and to gain attention and caring from others.
14. The key to helping a person with problems to live more successfully or to satisfy her needs herself is to become genuinely involved with that person as a friend.
15. Involvement with at least one other person is required for basic need satisfaction.
16. RT therapy involves eight steps:
    - Involvement
    - Focusing patient attention on, and achieving full awareness of, her current behaviour
    - Requiring the patient to evaluate her behaviour in terms of its potential for helping her get what she wants out of life, taking into consideration the norms of the social group and community in which she resides and belongs or wishes to belong
    - Helping the patient to make a short-term written plan to do something to achieve her goals
    - Obtaining from the patient a commitment to the therapist that she will follow the plan
    - Following up on the plan of action and its outcomes, supporting the patient and acknowledging failure, but not accepting excuses

- Not punishing failure, but rather reviewing the behaviour evaluation, goals, and plan and renewing a commitment to try again
- Perseverance.

17. RT believes that the patient must *act* first in order to change her beliefs and feelings. By doing things and achieving success the patient will begin to think and feel better.
18. The concept of strength, while new, appears to reflect a shift to a more organismic/existential approach while at the same time focusing on cognitive/rational skills as central to successful need satisfaction.
19. RT is directive; the primary role of the therapist is that of a friend-teacher.
20. The key to successful, rewarding, and self-fulfilling behaviour, or happiness, appears to lie in our ability to be "involved" with others, to receive social recognition and personal satisfaction from our work, and to have cognitive skills which enable exploration of an infinite number of options when we are faced with problems, such that we may attain our goals.

10
Transactional Analysis

We are more aware of ourselves than apes are, but not really very much.

—Eric Berne, 1972: 244

Let's begin our examination of Transactional Analysis (TA) with a brief look at its development since 1955 and the characteristics of the three major TA schools or focuses which have evolved to date.

The Four Stages of TA Development

Dusay (1977) described the four stages of TA development as: (1) ego states (1955-62), (2) transactions and games (1962-66), (3) script analysis (1966-70), and (4) action (1970-present).

EGO STATES

TA began in 1955 with Eric Berne's observation of what appeared to be different personalities existing within a single patient. It is noteworthy that, like Janov's, this "discovery" began with his experience with one patient. Berne observed in this patient two types of thinking: one logical and objective, and the other alogical, subjective, and magical. The former, logical thought processes seemed to dominate the patient's working life, while the latter, alogical approach was evident in the patient's fantasy and social life. Both Berne and his patient were able to identify these two separate behaviour patterns, which were distinguished as well by facial expressions and vocal tone and quality, in his therapy sessions.

These two distinct behaviour patterns Berne subsequently called "ego states," and he viewed them as real and consistent patient approaches to thinking, feeling, and acting. The logical, rational pattern Berne saw as mature and called it the Adult ego state. The alogical, magical, subjective, creative personality aspects he viewed as more childlike, and called this the Child ego state.

Later, he observed patient behaviour which suggested the incorporation, or in Freudian terms, "introjection," of parental attitudes and values, which suggested a third ego state—the Parent. Together, Child, Adult, and Parent made up the total personality configuration. This personality theory was represented by the now familiar three joined circles:

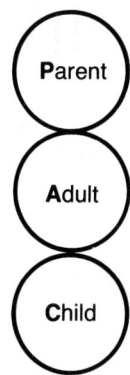

At this first stage (1955-62) TA focused on the *structure* of the personality, and therapy was largely an intellectual, cognitive exercise. The patient was assisted by the therapist to achieve awareness of the various personality aspects —ego states—involved in his behaviour, to recognize the behavioural options which therefore existed for him, and to begin to choose which ego state he wished to govern his behaviour, depending on the situation and his needs and goals at the time.

TRANSACTIONS AND GAMES
The second stage (1962-66) in the development of TA added a *communication* theory and a theory of *motivation*. The development and incorporation of a communication theory in a therapeutic approach is unique to TA, and one of Berne's most significant contributions. Basically, Berne observed two kinds of patient communications: manifest and latent. *Manifest* communication was direct verbal or non-verbal communication in which the patient directly indicated a need, desire, expectation, idea, etc. *Latent* communication was an indirect verbal or non-verbal message in which the patient covertly expressed a hidden, possibly unconscious, need, demand, desire, expectation, or idea. The latent communications were viewed as patients' attempts to manipulate and exploit themselves and others, and were called "games." Games insulated the patient from authentic involvement with others and were used to maintain neurotic behaviour. Berne combined his personality theory with his communication theory in such a way that patient communications could be analyzed in terms of what ego states were involved.

At this point, TA therapy involved both enabling the patient to become *aware* of his various ego states or personality structure (structural analysis), and also to *analyze* his communications (transactions) with others (transactional analysis). Therapy was still a largely cognitive process in which the patient's insights about his personality structure and his game-playing enabled him to choose more personally rewarding behaviour. It was during this period that Berne and his associates concentrated their efforts on identifying, labelling, and categorizing a host of typical games. In 1964, Berne and TA suddenly achieved world-wide recognition through Berne's best-selling book *Games People Play*.

SCRIPT ANALYSIS

The third stage of TA's development occurred between 1966 and 1970, "when transactional analysts began to explore why different persons choose various games to play, and why they exhibit specific types of personalities" (Dusay, 1977: 38). This concern with the origin and development of problem behaviour led to the concept of "scripts." A script was the unconscious life plan of the individual which determined his present behaviour. The script was developed by the child in response to parental messages. These script messages were of three kinds called "values," "don'ts," and "here's how." *Values* were parental messages about how we *should* behave. *Don'ts* were parental messages about how we should *not* behave. *Here's how* were parental messages gained from the parents' example.

A questionnaire called a "script matrix" was developed for plotting individual personality structure in terms of the values, don'ts and "here's how" messages experienced and recalled by the patient. With the script matrix, both therapist and patient could identify the source of the patient's typical behaviour and communication patterns.

With the introduction of script analysis, however, the TA focus changed from cognitive behaviour to patient feelings. It was no longer enough for patients to develop insight into script behaviour. To change scripts required reexperiencing the Child ego state in which the original messages were received. It was assumed that even though the Child part of the person may have been "overwhelmed" with Parental values and injunctions in his early development, he accepted only some of these messages while rejecting others. Even the "weak" Child, then, had *some* responsibility for choosing to accept certain Parental messages. Thus, changing the Child aspect of the personality required a reexperiencing of Parental messages in order to enable the Child to accept responsibility *now* for choosing to unlearn or redecide what had earlier been learned or decided. The reexperiencing of childhood required the reexperiencing of the whole range of childhood feelings as well as thoughts. TA was no longer only an intellectual approach, but now focused on both the thoughts and feelings of the whole person.

ACTION

TA is presently in its fourth stage, which began around 1970, although there is no consensus among TA practitioners as to its current focus (Barnes, 1977). This is probably because sufficient time has not yet elapsed to enable us to gain a clear perspective on the evolution of TA. Dusay's (1977) comments in this regard, then, may be somewhat biased by his own work. He has suggested, for example, that the fourth phase is identified by an interest in the *energy* exuded by an individual in each of his ego states at any one time. This energy level is represented by the "egogram," a device of his making. The egogram enables both the patient and therapist to work out a contract for raising and/or lowering the energy level in the various ego states to the patient's satisfaction. Dusay (1977) claimed that various techniques have been developed for this purpose.

In summary, the development of TA between 1955 and 1970 appears to have occurred in three distinct phases. The fourth phase of development is now underway and is less well-defined. Each of the first three phases is identified by a specific focus, with all three now contributing to TA theory and practice. The first phase involved the discovery of ego states and structural analysis of the personality. The second phase occurred with the development of TA communication and motivation theory and the analysis of overt and covert patient communications or transactions. The third phase began with the search for the origin of the pattern of patient thought processes and communication and the development of the script concept. During this phase, TA began to focus on patient feelings, as well as thoughts.

The Three Schools of TA

Barnes (1977), in describing the development of TA, identifies the emergence of three "schools," each with distinguishing characteristics: the Classical school, the Cathexis school, and the Redecision school. Let's consider briefly the major assumptions and resulting therapeutic focus and practices of each.

THE CLASSICAL SCHOOL

Basic Assumptions
- We are born in a state of mutual trust: "You're OK, I'm OK." Parenting results in a breach of this trust and the conclusion by the child that he is not OK, or they (others) are not OK, or both he and others are not OK.
- We are at least partially responsible for our own decisions and for choosing our life script.
- Anything that is decided can be redecided.
- Problem behaviour occurs as a result of the Child ego state response to covert parental messages.

Therapy
- Therapist and patient are each responsible for their own behaviour.
- The therapist's responsibility is to cure the patient.
- The patient is required to make a contract with the therapist for behaviour change.
- Group treatment is preferred.
- Therapists tell their patients what they observe them doing in TA terms.
- Therapists share their thinking and TA theory with their patients.
- Patients are not rewarded for game-playing.
- Therapy begins with structural analysis, proceeds to analysis of transactions —particularly games—and ends with analysis of scripts.

- Primary attention in treatment groups is focused on the units of communication (transactions) occurring among group members.
- The goal of therapy is achievement of autonomy by the patient, or the effective use of the Adult ego state in which the harmful script programming of the patient is overcome.

THE CATHEXIS SCHOOL

Basic Assumptions
- Whether or not we are OK when we are born is irrelevant. What is important is the self-concept which emerges through the feedback received from others between the ages of two and three. OKness, then, is relative to the social and cultural conditions within which people live. OKness depends on what is considered to be developmentally appropriate in the particular culture, and it changes as the values of the culture change and as the individual grows older.
- Scripts, as life plans, may be either satisfactory or unsatisfactory.
- Games reflect the individual's early failure to obtain nurturing and his inability to alter his inappropriate current behaviour through which he continues to attempt to elicit nurturing from others.
- The Parent ego state is not viewed as fixed, but as a part of the personality that grows and alters in response to new values and information.
- Very regressive and incapacitated patients are considered to be amenable to the Cathexis approach.

Therapy
- Clients are primarily young people diagnosed as schizophrenic.
- The therapist adopts an eclectic attitude to therapy and is open to any approach which will help the patient.
- The therapeutic environment is structured to resemble the family.
- The therapist focuses attention on accepting the patient's needs for nurturing and provides this experience for the patient. The therapist-patient relationship is described as symbiotic.
- The patient is seen as developmentally delayed due to interference in basic early need satisfaction.
- The therapist essentially attempts to be the "good," nurturing parent with the patient. When the patient is unable to assume responsibility for his behaviour, the therapist does.
- The goal of therapy is "to rear oversized infants into healthy adults."

THE REDECISION SCHOOL

Basic Assumptions
- Early script decisions by the child are made for survival reasons and out of fear.

- Games and rackets are used to maintain the self, and other behaviour and responses are determined by these early decisions.
- The focus of attention in therapy is on the Adult and the Parent ego states, and thus on the autonomy and power of the patient.
- Phobias are viewed as responses to early parental injunctions.
- The logical, cognitive, objective aspects of the personality are not ignored, but are considered to be later developments and thus subordinate to the more basic and dominant emotional, intuitive, and subjective elements.
- Intrapsychic activity is the focus.
- Heredity or biological or environmental influences do not excuse the individual from responsibility.
- Autonomy can be achieved by all.

Therapy
- Begins with a contract between patient and therapist to work on the problems the patient is experiencing *now*.
- The patient's power is emphasized and the therapist's diminished.
- The patient is challenged to face choices, make decisions and accept responsibility for them.
- The therapist rarely makes suggestions.
- The therapist confronts the patient with his games and rackets and works with him to reexperience the "bad" feelings which resulted in early pathological decisions. Once the early decisions are understood and experienced, work is focused on having the patient make a new and better decision.
- The goal of therapy is to help people become what they really are.

In the course of the development of TA, three "schools" have emerged, each with distinguishing characteristics and practices. The first, called the Classical school, follows Berne's ideas most closely. The second, called the Cathexis school, has emphasized the reexperiencing of feeling and emotion. The third, called the Redecision school, combines certain Gestalt Therapy techniques with TA concepts. In keeping with our attempt to present each therapy from the perspective of the originator or founder, the remainder of the chapter will examine TA in terms of the Classical approach. Let's turn now to a brief look at Eric Berne.

ERIC BERNE (1910-70)

Born Eric Leonard Bernstein on May 10, 1910 in Montreal, Berne was the only son of Jewish parents. His father, a dedicated physician, died at thirty-eight when Berne was only nine years old, leaving his mother to support the family. His mother appears to have been a strong, well-educated woman, ambitious for Berne's success (Gardner, 1975). She supported the family by working as a writer and editor following his father's death, and even had Berne writing for her when he was only eleven years old. At his mother's urging Berne, like his father, pursued a career in medicine and graduated with his M.D. degree from McGill University in 1935.

He moved to the United States in 1936 and completed his psychiatric residency at the Yale University School of Medicine. Around 1939 he became an American citizen and shortly thereafter changed his name to Eric Berne. The reasons for the name change are not known, for Berne appears to have been very secretive about such details of his private life.

He was first married in 1940 and through this union fathered two children. In 1941 he began training as a psychoanalyst with Paul Federn and later with Erik Erikson. During the Second World War he served as a psychiatrist in the Medical Corps, and discovered his gift for clinical intuition and observation. He had a peculiar capacity for correctly assessing patient personality dynamics after brief contact with the patients and without knowledge of their social or psychiatric history.

Following the war, Berne appears to have undergone some major personality changes himself. He left his first wife, moved to the West Coast where new developments in psychotherapeutic activity were concentrated, and began to make his own unique contribution to the field with the publishing of his first book, *The Mind In Action* (1947), written during his army service.

In 1947 Berne met his second wife, but at the insistence of his analyst waited two years before marrying her. His second wife had three children of her own, and so with Berne's own two as frequent visitors, and the two to be born from this second union, Berne became a loving and loved father to seven children. For almost ten years, Berne worked hard, carrying on several consultantships concurrently, engaging in private practice and writing for various journals. During the later part of this period he prepared himself to qualify for entry into the Psychoanalytic Society, only to have his application in 1956 denied. Berne was apparently crushed by this rejection, and while he appeared already to be moving away from traditional psychoanalytic methods, this professional rebuff hastened his withdrawal.

In 1957 Berne published a revised second edition of *The Mind in Action*, retitled *A Layman's Guide to Psychiatry and Psychoanalysis*. As the new title conveys, this second book discussed basic Freudian theory and concepts in an informal and conversational style. It did not, however, contain any material which reflects Berne's own emerging therapeutic theory and practice. This is interesting, in that in this same year, 1957, he published an article in the *American Journal of Psychotherapy* on ego states, demonstrating that this central TA concept was already well-developed even then. It was not until 1961, with his third book, *Transactional Analysis in Psychotherapy*, therefore, that Berne outlined his new approach for the first time. These works attracted some professional interest, but it was not until 1964, with the best-seller *Games People Play*, that Berne achieved real acclaim.

But although fame and fortune had descended upon him, Berne's personal life had not fared so well. At the peak of his professional success and recognition, his second marriage ended in divorce. A third marriage, to a much younger woman, was also short-lived.

On June 30, 1970, at sixty years of age, Eric Berne suffered a heart attack. On July 15, 1970, while he was recuperating in hospital, a second coronary attack killed him.

Claude Steiner, friend, colleague, and follower of Eric Berne for twelve years prior to his death, wrote that Berne lived out a script of his own. Berne's script appears evident in two areas: in his inability to achieve one of the four TA goals, intimacy, and in his approach to his work.

> One of the brilliant ideas that Berne introduced is that people's lives are preordained from early in life by a script which they then follow faithfully. I believe that Eric was himself under the influence of a life script that called for an early death of a broken heart. This tragic ending was the result of very strong injunctions against loving others and accepting others' love on the one hand, and equally strong attributions to be an independent and detached individual on the other (Steiner, 1974: 16).

But while Berne's intuitive genius and disciplined character gave him fresh insights into the personality structures and behaviour of others and enabled him to develop a dynamic treatment method, he was unable to help himself.

> It is my opinion that, as is the case with every great innovator, Eric Berne's personal life script set a limitation to his life and to the full exploration of the phenomena that he was interested in. In his case, the fact that he had a life-limited script, based on injunctions that stood in the way of obtaining strokes, prevented him from fully exploring scripts and strokes theoretically and caused him to throw up subtle barriers for his followers. These barriers had eventual consequences for him; his own script was unclear to him and hence unavailable for change. The injunctions concerning strokes which kept his script operative and his heart aching went unchallenged. The distance he kept from those who loved him, and whom he loved, including myself, prevented us from comforting him; he slipped out of our lives. I still feel the gap he left—he could have lived to be ninety-nine years old on the sunny beaches of Carmel (Steiner, 1974: 19).

Let's turn now to TA theory.

BASIC ASSUMPTIONS AND MAJOR CONCEPTS

TA, as noted above, comprises four interrelated yet discrete components: structural analysis, analysis of transactions, game analysis, and script analysis.

The first two components provide a basis for examining TA principles related to normal growth and development. More specifically, structural analysis provides the basis for TA personality theory, and analysis of transactions reflects Berne's insightful communication and motivation theory. The last two deal with neurotic and problem behaviour and TA treatment dynamics.

We will first explore TA in terms of normal behaviour, then consider the TA conception of abnormal behavioural development, and finally discuss the therapeutic method.

TA Concepts and Principles
Related to "Normal" Human Growth and Development

STRUCTURAL ANALYSIS

Ego States
The term "ego states" describes a state of mind and related behaviour patterns. There are three basic patterns which together make up the total personality: Parent, Adult, and Child. The Parent aspect reflects actual parent behaviour and attitudes we have experienced in childhood. The Child aspect of our personality reflects our actual childhood experiences, perceptions, and behaviour. And the Adult aspect reflects our rational, objective behaviour which is unique to ourselves as individuals in the sense that it does not reflect either parental or childhood influences. The original discovery of the ego states occurred through Berne's clinical observation of patient behaviour. However, he later postulated an organic origin for them (Berne, 1966). Thus, the here-and-now, phenomenological behaviour defined in terms of ego states is considered to reflect *actual physiological correlates* in brain tissue. When we experience the Parent ego state, for example, our behaviour is being influenced by the actual stored memory experience of the parenting we received, which we retrieve and play back to ourselves like a videotape recording.

The three ego states act like relatively consistent unique mini-personalities which we may recognize by their different qualities when they emerge in our behaviour. Here is a brief description of each:

The Parent ego state is the incorporation of the attitudes and behaviour of all emotionally significant people who served as parent figures for us as children. Our own subsequent prejudicial, critical, and nurturing behaviour results from our prior experiences with these parent figures. The Parent ego state has two major behaviour aspects: the Nurturing Parent who is loving, warm, protective, soft, competent, helpful, yielding, supportive, respectful, empathic, encouraging; and the Critical Parent who is restrictive, authoritarian, controlling, withholding, punishing, conditional, condemning. Our Parent ego state may reflect either parental influence or actual parental behaviour and experience, which is wholly incorporated and becomes part of us. Our Parent ego state then includes bipolar behaviour which either nurtures or disparages others.

The Adult ego state is not determined by age, but rather refers to behaviour which is principally concerned with transforming sensory stimuli into pieces of information which may be processed and analyzed in terms of our previous experience. It includes reality-testing behaviour: separating fact from fantasy, traditions, opinions, and archaic feelings; and perceiving and evaluating our current situation and relating that data to past knowledge and experience. Reality testing allows us to figure out alternative solutions. We can then estimate the probable consequences of our various potential courses of action in order to minimize the possibility of failure and regret, and therefore increase the possibility of creative success (James and Jongeward, 1971).

The Child ego state includes all behaviour patterns established and experienced in childhood involving our own feelings, thoughts, and activities at the time. Thus James and Jongeward (1971) say that when we are feeling and acting as we did when we were children, we are in our Child ego state. The Child ego state is further divided into three parts or aspects, each with special characteristics. The Natural Child is the very young child who is impulsive, expressive, self-centred, pleasure seeking, curious, aggressive, and rebellious. The Little Professor is the naturally wise child who has not yet experienced formal education or socialization, but who responds to non-verbal communication, and is insightful, creative, and intuitive. The Adapted Child is the socialized child reflecting the influence of parent figures. He is complying, withdrawing, procrastinating. This is very often the primary ego state experienced by the neurotic or unhappy person.

Berne (1964) saw each ego state as having a vital function for the human organism. The Child reflects some of the most interesting aspects of personality, and is responsible for our creative, intuitive, and spontaneous behaviour related both to productive endeavours like work (research, invention, discovery, arts, etc.) and to less obviously fulfilling behaviour such as play and recreation.

The Adult is the survival-oriented aspect of our personality which processes data, computes possibilities, and suggests alternatives. It has a self-rewarding feature: we experience intrinsic satisfaction as a result of developing skills and performing successfully. The Adult is also involved in regulating the behaviour of our Child and Parent and mediates between them when necessary.

The Parent has two main functions: it enables us to assume a parent role with actual children, and it is responsible for automatic or habit responses in routine situations where Adult data processing is necessary but the creative Child is not required.

In *balance,* our three ego states each play an important part in normal personality functioning and it is only when one or other of them becomes *predominant* or *confused* or *absent* that personality analysis and reorganization (therapy) is required.

Recognizing Ego States
There are basically five ways in which we can recognize our own and others' ego states, that is, the predominant ego state at any point in time. We may do

so through phenomenological observation of our own and others' behaviour. It is similar to the observation or awareness involved in Gestalt Therapy and includes observing words or language used, facial expressions, vocal tones, gestures, and posture. Figure 10·1 indicates some typical behaviour patterns associated with each of the three ego states.

FIGURE 10·1
Types of Behaviour Associated With Specific Ego State Experience

Behaviour	Ego States		
	Critical Parent	**Adult**	**Natural Child**
Words	should, ought must, never	believe, might, seems, suggest, appears, consider	won't, can't, need, want
Facial Expression	furrowed brow, frown, raised eyebrow, clenched jaw, raised eyes	thoughtful, pensive	smile, laughing, pouting, pursed lips, eyes down
Vocal Tones	harsh, loud, sharp, quick	modulated	loud, high, sharp
Gestures	pointing finger, outstretched arm, raised arms, arms on hips, "listen to me!"	explanatory	pleading, crouching, folded up, head down, hands held
Posture	upright, open-legged, head high, back straight, walk brisk, stiff	natural, relaxed	tense, slouched, stooped, slow

SUMMARY

Perhaps the most significant of Berne's contributions to the field of psychotherapy was his discovery of ego states. This simple construct provides a unique means for understanding personality structure and functioning using layperson's language and simple pictures. It has as well a strong common-sense appeal and face validity. Lastly, it has direct behavioural correlates which can be easily observed and experienced and consensually confirmed. It is therefore an excellent tool for increasing awareness of our own and others' behaviour and for developing insight into how we typically think, feel, and act. And while ego states provide the basis for the first step in TA therapy, structural analysis, they may be employed with other therapeutic approaches as well, as a simple means by which to discuss personality structure and development with the patient. Later, we will discuss the implications of ego states in structural analysis. Let's now complete our consideration of TA concepts related to normal human growth and behaviour by considering transactions.

ANALYSIS OF TRANSACTIONS

While Berne did not use the term "self-actualization," he did appear to hold a view of human nature which suggested a single primary drive to growth and maturing and fulfillment of organismic potential. Pathology, or abnormal behaviour, indicated that some type of trauma or injury had been or was being experienced by the otherwise "normal" organism; normal behaviour would occur spontaneously and automatically. The potentially intact organism would grow and develop "normally" unless some experience or event prevented this unfolding. The mature stage of development Berne called "autonomy," which he said (1964: 178) was achieved through "the release or recovery of three capacities: awareness, spontaneity and intimacy." The words "release" and "recovery" identify his conception of a primary drive, like self-actualization, which results in the automatic unfolding of human potential.

Using this general primary drive as a base, Berne then developed an ingenious theory of human motivation as expressed through verbal and non-verbal communications which he called *transactions*.

Transactions

Probably as a result of his early medical training, Berne sought to link the psychological events observed as "personality" and "motivation" to the biological or physiological state of the organism. If such a direct association could be found or at least proposed as a strong possibility, the existence of the psychological events themselves might be better substantiated, and therefore more easily explained and understood. We may recall in this regard that the ego states too were considered to have actual physiological correlates in nerve cell tissue such that our current behaviour was considered to be represented neurologically by engrams, or memory traces. If so, the experience of the Child or Parent ego states is not role-playing, but more like neurological tape-playing of actual earlier parent or child behaviour which has become a part of us. But while the physiological basis for Berne's personality theory of ego states is not strong, the same is not true for his theory of motivation and communication, which are combined in his concept of transactions.

Berne pointed out (1964) that there was considerable research in the areas of emotional and sensory deprivation to support the notion that "stimulus hunger" was a characteristic of the human animal. Human beings appear to require a certain minimum level of sensory stimulation and input in order for normal infant development to occur, and for the maintenance of appropriate adult behaviour. The physically and/or emotionally deprived or unstimulated infant fails to develop normally, and the sensorily deprived adult soon experiences difficulty in reality-testing.

Berne suggested that this stimulus requirement demonstrated the human organism's physiological *need* for external stimulation. At first this need is partially satisfied by the parent's handling of the infant. As the child grows, however, the tactile responses of the parent decrease and are gradually replaced, first by signs and signals (gestures, body language) to the child, and later by arbitrary symbols (language). Thus, communication between the infant and parent begins as a largely tactile, physical experience, with holding, cuddling, nursing, feeding, bathing, changing, dressing, etc., and moves gradually to the stage where the infant-parent communication becomes less physical. As the child achieves greater physical autonomy, communication with the parent is characterized more by parental body language, facial expressions, and voice tone and quality (signs and symbols). Child-parent communication becomes primarily psychological when the child develops language. Although the parent continues to meet certain physical needs of the child and communicates tactually to some extent, as time goes by the child (and adult) tends to be touched less by other people, and language becomes the primary means for communication. Thus, the adult squeezes or nuzzles the infant to convey love, but smiles or pats the young child. Soon the smile is accompanied by words of affection and/or praise, until words alone, spoken or written, can meet the need for "love" stimulation.

Berne believed that this latter stage in stimulus-hunger satisfaction involved the conversion of originally non-specific tactile and/or physical stimulation to specific psychological stimulation. He called this new, specific, psychological need "recognition-hunger." It is *recognition* by and from others that serves as the prime motivating force for the adult. The adult need for psychological recognition takes the place of the infant need for physical stimulation. All of our interactions with other people may be analyzed on the basis of our attempts to satisfy our need for recognition from others. Consistent with this concept of motivation, Berne labelled recognition-satisfaction as "stroking."

Strokes. A stroke is ". . . any act implying recognition of another's presence" (Berne, 1964: 15).

Strokes satisfy our need for recognition or affection from others. They may take the form of physical contacts, symbolic gestures, or words. They may be positive, being expressions of understanding, affection, appreciation, praise, respect, and caring which convey the message "You're OK." Healthy development and growth cannot occur or be maintained without positive strokes. If we fail to get enough positive strokes we may provoke negative strokes, feeling that some kind of recognition or acknowledgment by others of our existence is better than none at all. To be ignored, that is, to receive no response from others, is to be made to feel insignificant and alienated and leads to apathy. We may note here the similarity to some of Glasser's ideas.

Negative strokes are responses from other people which say "You're not OK." When we are ignored, teased, humiliated, diminished, physically degraded, laughed at, called names, or ridiculed, we are in some way treated as though we are inferior. In TA this is called being "discounted." Being discounted is always painful. Parents who discount their children induce personality pathology and make their children "losers." Discounting between grownups leads to unhappy human relationships or feeds into destructive "scripts." We will discuss the concepts of "losers" and "scripts" in the next section. Because positive strokes are essential for achieving autonomy, which is the goal of TA, those involved in TA learn how to give and receive strokes through touch, gestures, signs, and symbols. Strokes, then, are really only interpersonal communications. But by using Berne's term "strokes," we are reminded of the real significance and purpose of our communication with others.

It is important to remember that, in TA terms, our communications to others are not random expressions, nor are others' communications to us. There is an implied *request* by the sender or transmitter of the stroke for a *specific* response or *expected* response from the *receiver*. This is one of Berne's most cogent discoveries. He has added a significant element to communication theory by going beyond the simple notion of "sender" and "receiver" to point out that the sender, when he communicates, has a definite *expectation* that a specific response will be returned by the other person. In a sense, all interpersonal communication says, "I have a certain need I want satisfied; this is it." The receiver has to first recognize the need and then respond, indicating this awareness, in an appropriate manner. But Berne noted that this may not always occur, and that in fact there were three basic kinds of communication patterns, or transactions: complementary, crossed, and ulterior.

Complementary transactions are those which originate in one of the three ego states of one person and produce the expected or desired response from the appropriate ego state in the other person. These are communications which Berne called normal, appropriate, or expected, in healthy, human relationships.

They are diagrammed thus:

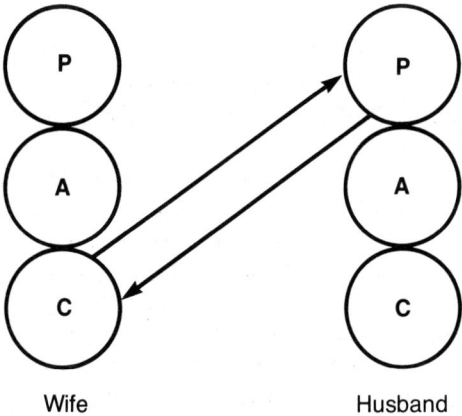

In this example, the wife might demonstrate an affectional need to her husband by moving close to him and touching him gently. If they were alone, the husband might respond by holding her. If they were at a cocktail party, he might take her hand and squeeze it gently. The husband recognizes the wife's need and wishes to satisfy it. Communication between them is taking place and may continue. The sender's (the wife's) message was understood and responded to as the sender desired and in a manner appropriate to the situation.

In other words, we don't communicate with people at random. All our communicative responses are, or should be, *purposive*. We make assumptions about the effect our communications will have on others, and about what the nature of their feedback will be. If we communicate with others keeping in mind what our purpose is, or what kind of reaction or response we would like or expect, and we obtain this response, then in TA terms a *complementary* transaction has occurred.

Crossed transactions occur when an unexpected response is made to a sender's communication or message, that is, the response does not come from the ego state for which the message was intended. This may occur because the sender has not determined the purpose of, or is unaware of, the message sent or because the receiver interprets the message incorrectly or does not wish, or is unable, to meet the expectations of the sender. The surprise response cuts off communication and results in the sender feeling puzzled or threatened, such that he responds by changing the nature or direction of the original message by withdrawing or retreating, or by avoiding a response. The crossed transaction is diagrammed thus:

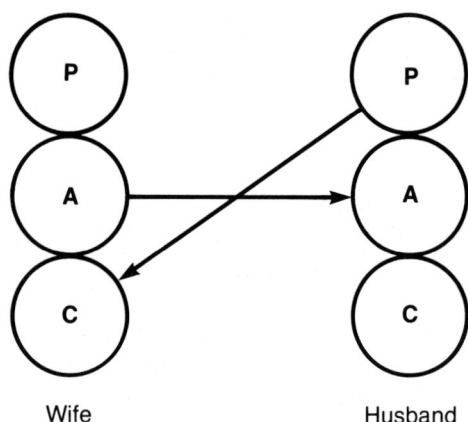

Crossed transactions indicate failure to communicate or to receive the positive recognition or stimulation required, and result in negative feelings about ourselves.

Ulterior transactions are those which involve more than one of the sender's ego states. When an ulterior message is sent, it is disguised or hidden in the form of some other message, trapping the receiver into making an inappropriate response or responding with another ulterior message. Ulterior transactions are not authentic communications but rather "games" which attempt to manipulate rather than encounter. They are diagrammed thus:

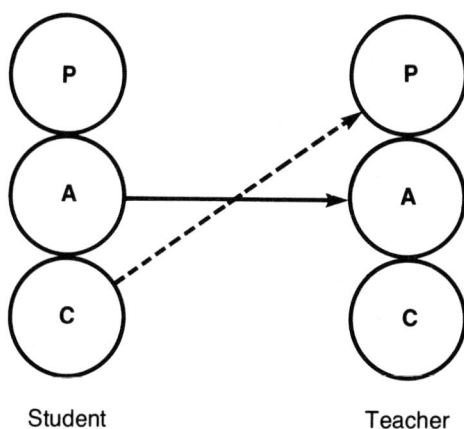

Since ulterior transactions reflect neurotic or problem behaviour, a more in-depth discussion will follow in the next section.

Time Structures
In addition to the concept of transactions, Berne's theory of motivation and communication attempted to place all human behaviour into six broad categories for the purpose of analysis. He suggested that these six behaviour patterns could identify how we spend our time. With an appreciation of time structuring, we can begin to appreciate what kinds of options we have for spending our time, how much time we actually spend now in various behaviour patterns, and then decide whether we would like to change the way we structure our time. The six patterns he identified are: withdrawal, rituals, pastimes, activities, intimacy, and games.

Withdrawal refers to removing ourselves either physically or psychologically from others. It may take place as a result of behaviour originating in any of the three ego states: in the Parent state, we may copy our parents; in the Adult state, we may make a rational decision to be alone to reflect; in the Child state, we may retreat into fantasy after being hurt.

Rituals are simple and stereotyped complementary transactions such as greetings, ceremonies, and formalities.

Pastimes are those transactions in which we pass time with one another in small talk, or in passive recreation and leisure activity which demands little involvement, such as TV, cocktail parties, or play. Both pastimes and games are considered substitutes for real living and intimacy.

Activities are the things we do to accomplish some specific goal. Activities are what we want to do, need to do, or have to do, such as work or hobbies.

Intimacy occurs in those rare moments of human contact that arouse feelings of tenderness, empathy, and affection. It involves genuine caring or encounter in Rogerian terms. "Intimacy begins when individual (usually instinctual) programing becomes more intense, and both social patterning and ulterior restrictions and motives begin to give way. It is the only completely satisfying answer to stimulus-hunger, recognition-hunger and structure-hunger" (Berne, 1964: 18).

Games differ from all other interactions or transactions in two important respects. First, there is an ulterior, *hidden* motivation and, second, there is a specific psychological payoff or gain to those involved, particularly the originator, but also for the respondent if there is an ulterior transactional response. Games are dishonest communications often resulting from unconscious motivations. Berne describes a game as

> . . . an ongoing series of complementary ulterior transactions progressing to a well-defined predictable outcome. Descriptively, it is a recurring set of transactions, often repetitious, superficially plausible, with a concealed motivation; or, more colloquially, a series of moves with a snare, or "gimmick" (Berne, 1964: 48).

Withdrawal (for the purpose of reflection and inner growth), activities, and intimacy are all viewed as positive behaviour patterns reflecting a psychologically healthy position. Rituals and pastimes, while not particularly growth-inducing, are not harmful unless they represent a major time commitment in our lives. But games reflect problem behaviour and a position of unsatisfactory and inappropriate goal attainment. Game behaviour, then, is a focus of TA therapy.

SUMMARY

Berne evolved a personality theory based on the concept of ego states. The adult personality is a combination of three ego states referred to as Parent, Adult, and Child, each of which has specific functional importance for the healthy integrated human organism. While each ego state may be identified or recognized phenomenologically by external behaviour such as body language, voice tone and quality, and facial expression, Berne conceived of the ego states as having physiological correlates in the brain in the form of engrams, or memory traces.

In addition to Berne's contribution to the field of psychotherapy of a simple means for discussing personality factors and dynamics, his concept of transactions brilliantly demonstrates the direct relationship between human communications and motivation. Here, too, his theory is supported by biological evidence and research. Transactions and ego states together form a framework within which to investigate, analyze, or explore specific individual behaviour patterns. Time structures provide a means for identifying how we spend our time and how much time we spend in various types of activity. This information may enable us to determine whether or not we are using our time in a manner which is most likely to enhance our self-fulfillment and happiness.

TA Concepts and Principles Related to Neurotic or Problem Behaviour

DEVELOPMENT OF NEUROTIC BEHAVIOUR
Berne, like Rogers, Perls, Janov, and Ellis, believed in the initial integration of the human infant and the principle of self-regulation within the human organism, which, he felt, would lead to actualization of potential. And like them, he saw this natural unfolding of human potential thwarted primarily through parental influence. Of course, since parents merely live out the values and imperatives of the larger society, they should not be viewed as villains. In fact, as each of the theorists presented thus far has maintained, it is likely that even when infants, children, and adolescents are handled "well" by current standards, pathology is likely to occur. The continual acquiescence of the infant, child, and adolescent to external parental or other demands produces neurotic or disturbed behaviour. This aspect of personality was described above as the *adapted child* ego state. There is an element of the adapted child in all of us, but when this ego state predominates, neurotic and problem behaviour follows. The severely neurotic person may reflect a basic "no growth" behaviour pattern in which he directs his efforts at maintaining his current status rather than seeking new opportunities for development of his potential. His goal is not self-actualization, but survival. The less disturbed individual may demonstrate inappropriate behaviour only in certain situations. In general, however, his lack of wholeness and his resistance to growth and change impede his overall development and the realization of his specific potential. The saving grace for all of us is that we can undo our early influences, decisions, and choices through therapy and thus trade neurotic survival for autonomous being. Let's look now at the two TA concepts which best describe the origin and maintenance of neurotic and problem behaviour: life positions and scripts.

Life Positions
Life positions are basic decisions we make about ourselves in childhood. Harris (1976) contends that these decisions occur as early as age two or three and form the basis for our self-concept, sense of self-esteem, and identity. Whether or not we agree with this idea of such very early self-appraisal by children and the spe-

cific conclusions reached regarding their self-worth, it is generally held that the development of identity does begin very early and is relatively well-defined between five and eight years of age. As well, during the time that the child is developing his *own* sense of self he is also formulating ideas about *others* and their worth and value. Our subjective and selective perceptions of the world, then, are influenced at a very early age by our own self-appraisal as well as by our evaluation of significant others.

There is, however, the obvious problem of the validity of such early appraisal activity. These judgments and impressions are based on the perception, awareness, and intellect of the child and his brief, limited life experience, and are subject to considerable error. Nevertheless, it is on the basis of these judgments of self and others that we adopt our life positions. Berne outlined four possible life positions which we can take in our relationship to ourselves and others. The latter three reflect behaviour originating in the Child ego state, while the first position reflects a balanced personality involving all three ego states. The four positions are:

1. I'm OK, You're OK
2. I'm OK, You're Not OK
3. I'm Not OK, You're OK
4. I'm Not OK, You're Not OK

I'm OK, You're OK is potentially a healthy position. If it is realistic, a person with this position about himself and others can solve his problems constructively. His expectations are likely to be valid.

I'm OK, You're Not OK is the position of persons who feel victimized or persecuted. They blame others for their problems.

I'm Not OK, You're OK is a common position of persons who feel powerless when they compare themselves to others. This position leads them to withdraw, to experience depression, and, in severe cases, to become suicidal.

I'm Not OK, You're Not OK is the position of those who lose interest in living, exhibit schizoid behaviour, and, in extreme cases, commit suicide or homicide.

Harris (1976: 49), pointed out that the significant feature of these life positions is that the latter three (2, 3, and 4) are in the Child ego state and are

> the result of the accumulation of impressions from the significant early experiences in the life of the individual in his first five years.

The first position, "I'm OK, You're OK, he maintained, could be achieved

> . . . only by the Adult through the application of new data and in the examina-

tion of archaic data in the Parent and Child which hampers the function of the Adult in establishing reality-based data and achieving freedom of choice and the development of new options for decision making in the present (Harris, 1976: 49).

The suggestion made here is that *none of us* can achieve the first life position without some effort, that is, some form of therapy or educational process, which will enable us to reexamine the decisions we made about ourselves and others as children which form the basis of our existing adult self-concept and world view. Without such a concerted effort we will continue to govern our adult lives on the basis of judgments we made about ourselves and others when we were children. It is very unlikely that our original assessments reflect current reality. They are therefore an inappropriate and inadequate basis for our behaviour now.

Figure 10·2 presents the four life positions diagrammatically.

FIGURE 10·2
The Four Psychological Life Positions

	I'm Not OK	I'm OK	
You're OK	**3** FACADE DEPRESSIVE INSECURE POWERLESS "*My* life is no good."	**1** HEALTHY GROWING REALISTIC "Life is good." (Winner)	**You're OK**
You're Not OK	**4** FUTILE DEPENDENT HOPELESS SIT AND WAIT "Life is no good." (Loser)	**2** PARANOID CRUSADER PERSECUTED DELINQUENT "*Your* life is no good."	**You're Not OK**
	I'm Not OK	I'm OK	

Scripts
Having decided on and taken one of the above identity positions, we attempt to maintain this identity by initiating behaviour which both ensures and reinforces our chosen identity. The stronger our need to maintain a particular identity, that is, the more rigid and irrational we are, the more concertedly we behave in

ways which ensure that the responses we get from others and the world around us confirm and reinforce our early appraisal of self and others. These attempts to ensure consistency of our identity, of our perception of the world outside ourselves, and of confirming responses from others are called *scripts*.

> A psychological script is a person's ongoing program for his life drama which dictates where he is going with his life and how he got there. It is a drama he compulsively acts out, though his awareness of his script may be vague (James and Jongeward, 1971: 69).

Thus, a script becomes a trap or self-fulfilling prophecy. Early experiences in childhood lead to appraisal decisions. These decisions lead to adopting a certain life position. Adopting the life position leads to the creation of a script for behaviour. The script reinforces and maintains itself.

Woolams and Brown (1979: 191) provide this excellent description of the life script and its dynamics:

> Once a person has decided upon a life script, she tends to live out the most important aspects of her life based on these preconceived notions. Her script influences how she will lead her life in two ways, providing both an overall *life plan* and a *life style* for carrying it out. A person's life plan is similar to a theatrical play and requires other persons to play specific roles within the context of a complete drama. This play has a beginning, a middle, and a climax, furnishing the *content* of a complete life story which outlines her destiny. A person's life style, or process of living, includes patterned behaviors that are consistent with her overall life plan, that reinforce it, and that provide subplots which help the life drama to unfold. She repeats these behaviors on a minute-by-minute basis in order to get strokes. These strokes, in turn, reinforce her beliefs, perceptions, feelings, and behaviors. Thus, a life script is both ongoing and repetitive. Certain messages are particularly significant to the formation of certain parts of the script. A person's life plan or content is mostly influenced by her injunctions, while her life style or process is mostly influenced by her drivers. The script program provides information in both areas: "how to" reach a final destiny as well as "how to" lead a life style.
>
> Script content refers to messages, decisions, and payoffs, and can be uncovered by asking the question *"What?"* *"What* is missing from the person's life?" *"What* is the person's life plan?" *"What* is her goal in life?" *"What* is her chosen final payoff (including how tragic will it be)?"
>
> Script process can best be determined by asking the question *"How?"* *"How* does the person set up her life to reach her goals?"

"The ultimate goal of transactional analysis" wrote Berne (Steiner, 1977: 52) "is the analysis of scripts, since the script determines the destiny and identity of the individual!!"

Winners and Losers
Life positions 1 and 4 are opposites and lead to the development of what are called *winner* and *loser* scripts.

Although people are born to win, they are also born helpless and totally dependent on their environment. Winners successfully make the transition from total helplessness to independence and then to interdependence [*autonomy*]. Losers do not. Somewhere along the line they begin to avoid becoming self-responsible (James and Jongeward, 1971: 3).

Here are some distinguishing features which James and Jongeward (1971) suggest characterize winners:

- Winners *are* themselves, not trying to be what they think they *should* be.
- Winners recognize the difference between *being* stupid and *acting* stupid. They do not need to hide behind a mask.
- Winners are not afraid to do their own thinking. They can separate facts from opinion and don't pretend to have all the answers.
- Winners listen to others and evaluate what they say, but come to their own conclusions.
- While winners can admire and respect other people, they are not totally defined, demolished, bound, or awed by them.
- Winners assume responsibility for their own lives.
- Winners are their own bosses and know it.
- Winners respond appropriately to the situation. Their response is related to the message sent and preserves the significance, worth, well-being, and dignity of the people involved.
- Winners' timing is right. They know that for everything there is a season and for every activity a time.
- To a winner time is precious: he doesn't kill it, he lives it here and now. He knows his past, is aware and alive in the present and looks forward to the future.
- Winners know their feelings and limitations. They can give and receive affection, love and be loved.
- Winners enjoy their own accomplishments without guilt and the accomplishments of others without envy.
- Winners can enjoy themselves freely or postpone enjoyment. They can discipline themselves in the present to enhance their enjoyment in the future.
- Winners do not get their security by controlling others.
- Winners care about the world and its people. They are concerned, compassionate, and committed to improving the quality of life.

And here are some features which James and Jongeward suggest characterize losers:

- Losers may say they are successful, but are really anxious, trapped, or unhappy.
- Some losers say they are beaten or that they are bored and without purpose.
- Losers seldom live in the present. They occupy their minds either with memories or with future expectations.

- Losers speak of their bad luck.
- Losers blame others for their misfortunes.
- Losers who live in the past use "if only":
    "If only I had married someone else."
    "If only I had a different job."
    "If only I had finished school."
    "If only I had been born rich."
- Losers who live in the future wait for a rescue:
    "When school is over. . ."
    "When the kids grow up. . ."
    "When my ship comes in. . ."
- Some losers live under the dread of catastrophes:
    "What if I lose my job?"
    "What if I fail the course?"
    "What if they don't like me?"
    "What if I make a mistake?"
- Losers who live in the future experience continual anxiety in the present over real or imagined future events such as tests, loves, illnesses, weather, etc. Being so occupied with the future, these people let the present possibilities slip away.
- Losers' anxieties block out current reality so that they do not hear, see, feel, taste, touch, or think for themselves.
- Without the total use of their perceptual apparatus, losers' perceptions are incorrect or incomplete or distorted and therefore their ability to make appropriate responses to reality is hampered.
- Losers spend much of their time play-acting. They pretend, manipulate, and perpetuate old roles from childhood.
- Losers repress their capacity to express spontaneously and appropriately their full range of possible behaviour.
- Losers do not enter into intimate, honest, direct relationships with others. Rather, they try to manipulate others into living up to their expectations, and themselves into living up to others'.
- Losers misuse their intellect in rationalizing. They make excuses for their actions in an attempt to make them sound plausible, and by intellectualizing or attempting to "snow" people through verbiage.

We have examined the two major TA concepts related to the development of problem behaviour: *life positions* and *scripts*. In doing so we have noted that the TA theory of neurosis is similar to the theories of neurosis in the other therapies discussed thus far. In particular, TA holds that the human infant begins life as a potentially autonomous, self-directing organism. The achievement of autonomy and the unfolding of potential is thwarted by the conditions of normal parenting. In order to survive, the infant or child must acquiesce to external demands. In TA terms, the child *chooses* or *decides* to conform and meet the expectations of others. This involves the development of the ego state known as the *Adapted Child*. The young child gradually develops a sense of self or personal identity. Beginning at two or three years of age, he establishes a relatively fixed notion of his own self-esteem. Between five and eight years of age the child learns to value and appreciate others. It is at this point that the young child takes one of four life positions. The child really has only three choices, since the first position, representing psychological health and maturity, can be achieved only through some form of therapeutic intervention in adult life, because typical parenting prevents our choosing the first position of autonomy and self-direction. Once his life position and identity is determined, the child constructs a *script* which ensures and reinforces it. Both the choice of life position and the subsequent script, based as they are on the subjective perceptions, awareness, and intellect of a child with limited life experience, are considered to offer an inadequate, inappropriate, and inaccurate framework for achieving individual self-fulfillment and actualization of potential. Some characteristic behaviour following from the contrasting first and fourth life positions was presented under the terms *winners* and *losers*.

GIVING AND RECEIVING NEUROTIC MESSAGES
Neurotic messages are involved in both the origin and maintenance of neurotic behaviour. These neurotic messages include negative strokes, rackets, stamps, stamp collecting, trading stamps, or playing games.

When transactions involve negative strokes, the person on the receiving end of such communication feels hurt and fearful. Some examples of negative strokes are criticism, belittling, scorn, ridicule, rebuke, or displays of anger and hostility. Since negative strokes from adults are particularly significant to children, whose existence may be seriously threatened by the hostile adult who is bigger and more powerful than the child, the child learns that the best response to negative strokes is a survival response: he withdraws in order to avoid conflict. But the child's denial of the hurt and his inability to express hurt feelings directly establishes a pattern for later life. The unexpressed hurt is not dissipated, but is merely retained or held until it can be expressed in a safe situation.

TA calls the holding in of hurt feelings a *racket*. Rackets are masks which we use to cover up, deny, or avoid expressing our real feelings. When we are disappointed at the actual response we obtain from a transaction, we may cover up our disappointment with silence, a smile, a laugh. But the feeling of disappointment remains and is saved. In TA, these saved or unexpressed feelings of hurt are called *stamps*.

This buildup of hurt feelings creates pressure for their expression or release in a "safe" situation. The suppressed person may look for, or suddenly find, a transaction in which he can release these feelings, or in TA terms, "trade in his stamps." The result, of course, is that he gives negative strokes to someone else, usually in the form of an outburst. This attempt to eliminate hurt feelings at someone else's expense may be either conscious or unconscious.

In therapy, the patient comes to recognize the pattern of his own responses to the negative strokes or hurts received from others and the games he typically plays to cash in his stamps. He discovers that not only can he refuse to accept the hurts or stamps others try to give him, he can also refuse to trade stamps or play games with people. In order to stop receiving or giving stamps, he must unlearn his childhood responses of avoidance, denial, and withdrawal in the face of negative strokes from others. Since his "survival" as an adult is no longer contingent upon responses he learned as a child, he can begin to respond with more appropriate behaviour in those situations. In fact, to achieve individual growth and self-fulfillment, he must give up his rackets and masks and game-playing in favour of the immediate discrete expression of his real feelings.

SUMMARY

Berne, like Rogers, Perls, Janov, and Ellis, viewed the development of neurotic or problem behaviour as the "norm" in our society. Under typical parental influence, the natural drive of the infant and child to autonomy and self-fulfillment of potential is thwarted. As the young child grows, he learns to acquiesce to external demands and gradually gains an appreciation of his own and others' worth. By the age of eight, his own identity or sense of self and his perception of the value of other people are well established. It is at this point that he takes one of the three neurotic life positions: "I'm OK, You're Not OK"; "I'm Not OK, You're OK"; or "I'm Not OK, You're Not OK." These neurotic life positions result from the child's inability to evaluate realistically himself, others, and the world around him. Once he has taken one of these life positions, the child establishes a script, a programmed behaviour pattern which both ensures and reinforces this identity position.

The transactions in which the individual is involved are the means through which he achieves both his life position and his script. In particular, negative strokes and ulterior transactions (games) result in withdrawal, denial, and avoidance behaviour and feelings of hurt and unhappiness. Game-playing prevents authentic, spontaneous, creative, intimate behaviour and reinforces a "loser" script. Therapy is the only means through which the adult, neurotic "loser," whose inappropriate, child-programmed, script-patterned behaviour prevents his growth, can discover his self-defeating behaviour and achieve adult autonomy and self-fulfillment.

AIMS, DYNAMICS, AND TECHNIQUES OF TA THERAPY

Goals and Aims of TA

AUTONOMY: "I'M OK, YOU'RE OK"
We have already made reference to the ultimate goal of TA—autonomy. James and Jongeward accurately restate Berne's meaning of this concept and its three

aspects, and embellish it with their own definition of Adult ethics and courage:

> Being autonomous means being self-governing, determining one's destiny, taking responsibility for one's own actions and feelings, and throwing off patterns that are irrelevant and inappropriate to living in the here and now (1971: 263).

Autonomy includes three capacities: awareness, spontaneity, and intimacy.

> Awareness is knowing what is happening now . . . to hear, see, smell, touch, taste, study and evaluate for himself. . . . He perceives the world through his own personal encounter rather than the way he was taught to see it. Knowing that he is a temporal being, an aware person appreciates nature now. He experiences himself as part of the universe he knows, and is part of the mystery of those universes yet to be discovered (1971: 264).

An aware person listens to the messages of his own body, and knows when he is tensing himself, relaxing himself, opening himself, closing himself. He knows his inner world of feelings and fantasies and is not afraid or ashamed of them. An aware person also hears other people. When they talk, he listens and responds actively.

Spontaneity is the freedom to choose from the full range of Parent, Adult, and Child behaviour and feelings.

The spontaneous person is flexible, not foolishly impulsive. He sees the many options open to him and uses what behaviour he judges to be appropriate to his situation and to his goals. He makes and accepts responsibility for his own choices. He learns to face new situations and explore new ways of thinking, feeling, and responding. He constantly increases and reevaluates his repertoire of possible behaviour.

Intimacy is the expression of the natural child feelings of warmth, tenderness, and closeness to others. An autonomous person risks friendships and intimacy when he decides it is appropriate. Berne (1961: 24) observed that integrated, autonomous persons ". . . have a charm and openness of nature which is reminiscent of that exhibited by children."

James and Jongeward (1971) also speak of *adult ethics,* a kind of TA philosophy. (While this concept is not one of the three primary capacities identified by Berne, it seems to nicely round out the concept of the "whole person" being described.) James and Jongeward claim that to achieve autonomy we must reevaluate our present value system and design our own ethical code. We examine the values transmitted by our parents and society, discard those we find to be arbitrary, irrelevant, or destructive, and retain those which are conducive to our growth.

> The protection, enhancement, and well-being of people, and the . . . inanimate and animate world are fundamentals on which Adult ethics are based. . . .

> A decision is ethical if it enhances self-respect, develops personal integrity and integrity in relationships, dissolves unreal barriers between people, building a core of genuine confidence in self and others and facilitates the actualizing of human potentials without bringing harm to others. . . .
>
> An ethical person does not discount problems or the significance of them. Instead he assumes that he and others working together can solve them. He works on his own personal problems, community problems, and such worldwide problems as those caused by rats and disease that eat away at babies, and over-population and wars that bring death and hopelessness to millions of people. He can crusade as Berne suggests against the Four Horsemen—War, Pestilence, Famine and Death whose innocent victims are the infants of nations. . . . He recognizes that apathy is consent in matters such as infant mortality, child beatings, urban deterioration, and unfair employment, education and housing practices. He is indignant over the injuries and injustices suffered by mankind and tries to change them. He is aware of and responsive to all creation (James and Jongeward, 1971: 273-74).

They speak, too, of *courage*:

> It takes courage to experience the freedom that comes with autonomy, courage to accept intimacy and directly encounter other persons, courage to take a stand in an unpopular cause, courage to choose authenticity over approval and to choose it again and again, courage to accept the responsibility for your own choices, and, indeed courage to be the very unique person you really are (1971: 274).

We may note considerable similarities between the goals and aims of TA and those outlined by Rogers, Perls, Ellis, and Glasser. The addition of adult ethics to the concept of autonomy emphasizes the need for acceptance of social responsibility and provides a rationale for involvement in social action endeavours in fields such as environmental protection, children's rights, poverty, and conservation. Autonomy means more than *personal* fulfillment—it includes our creative, active participation in and commitment to helping to improve the quality of life for all people of the world of which we are a part.

The Four Elements of TA Therapy

As was noted earlier, TA has four distinct therapeutic components, each with its own aims and dynamics. We have discussed these four components in terms of their contribution to the theory and basic assumptions underlying TA. They are: (1) structural analysis, (2) analysis of transactions, (3) game analysis, and (4) script analysis.

Let's consider first the therapeutic goals of each component, and then discuss the actual therapy process. The end result of the integration of the four components is autonomy.

STRUCTURAL ANALYSIS

By introducing the patient to the concept of ego states, the therapist assists him to:

- Learn the origins of his behaviour
- Learn to categorize his behaviour according to ego states
- Learn that there are at least three main ego state options open regarding possible behaviour patterns
- Learn that changing typical patterns is possible
- Learn to recognize which ego state is dominant at any one time
- Learn to shift from one ego state to another
- Learn to decide which ego state is most appropriate to a given situation.

Berne described the focus of therapy at the point of structural analysis as the struggle between the infant who once was and the parents who once were. The problem for the neurotic is that this struggle, once carried on between two different people, is now going on within *one* person, the patient, who is behaving alternately as Parent and Child. The patient is unhappy because the Child continues to frustrate and anger the Parent and the Parent continues to condemn and anger the Child.

The aim of structural analysis is to master internal conflicts through the diagnosis of ego states. The therapeutic goal is to achieve a balance between the ego states and maintain Adult control when the individual is under stress. Thus the objectives are (1) elimination of exclusions, and decontamination, (2) the achievement of stability of ego states, and (3) the maintenance of Adult control under stress.

ANALYSIS OF TRANSACTIONS

The aim of the analysis of transactions, including game analysis, is *social control*. An individual who decides not to proceed to transactional analysis might still benefit from structural analysis. Analysis of transactions, however, enables the person to assume greater self-control and therefore increase his freedom and flexibility to act. Attaining social control means that the Adult is in charge in social interaction and decides when and where to release the Child or Parent, so that we cannot be manipulated by people who try to activate our Child or Parent. Social control means being able to refuse to play others' games.

The key question in analysis of transactions is "What did you expect the response to your communication would be?" In other words, what need, what "gain," in the sense of recognition or stroking, did you want? From structural analysis, the next question would be "what part of you (i.e., what ego state) initiated or received the transaction or communication, and to or from what part of the other person was it directed or received?"

GAME ANALYSIS

Games involve ulterior transactions and as such, suggest that the individual may be unconsciously motivated and have little control over his behaviour.

Since games prevent growth and change, they are a major focus in therapy. Games originate from the life position and subsequent script which the person has created for himself. The actual reasons for such behaviour, emanating from childhood decisions and evaluations, may be unknown, but games are learned in childhood and become set patterns of behavioural response yielding specific gains or satisfactions.

Functions of Games
- Games help to maintain biological homeostasis because they involve stroking. That is, they, like all transactions, provide the organism with stimulation and satisfaction, since the organism has converted stimulus-hunger to recognition-hunger.
- Games promote psychological stability through reconfirming and reinforcing the person's adopted life position or script. That is, they satisfy the individual's need for internal consistency and maintenance of identity.
- Games are a substitute for intimacy—real human encounter—which many persons are unable to experience. Yet they give the illusion of significant social interaction and emotional expression.
- Games maintain the illusion of "health" or satisfactory human functioning and enable the individual to avoid questioning his life position and script.

Thus game analysis must be carefully handled, because depriving an individual of his games may produce despair and apathy.

Berne (1964) described eight steps in game analysis: (1) thesis, (2) antithesis, (3) aim, (4) roles, (5) dynamics, (6) transactional paradigm, (7) moves, and (8) advantages.

Thesis. The thesis involves the general description of a game based on the therapist's observations. It includes the immediate sequence of events in the particular interaction leading to game behaviour as well as the known information about the patient from history and structural analysis.

Antithesis. To determine whether a set of interactions involves a game, the therapist must do some testing. If the therapist or others in a group refuse to play the game, one form of validating evidence would be an increase in the individual's efforts to continue the game. If those present continue to refuse to play, or if they expose the individual's behaviour for what it is, the person may lapse into "despair." His despair resembles depression but is more severe and accompanied by frustration and confusion, demonstrated by tears, silence, or withdrawal.

If the intervention succeeds, despair will suddenly change to laughter or surprise as the person spontaneously achieves insight into his behaviour and responds with Adult awareness.

Aim. The aim is simply the purpose for the game. What gain does the person hope to obtain—reassurance, support, sympathy, respect, vindication?

Roles. Ego states are not roles, but roles are involved in games and may or may not reflect the ego state of the person at the time. While the person may be aware that he is role-playing he will not be aware of his motivation for doing so or the payoffs these games have for him.

Dynamics. Dynamics are the motivation for the game: fear, disappointment, frustration, avoidance, anger, punishment, etc.

Transactional paradigm. A transactional paradigm is a drawing of a transaction, showing the social and psychological levels and indicating the ulterior transaction, as shown in Figure 10·3.

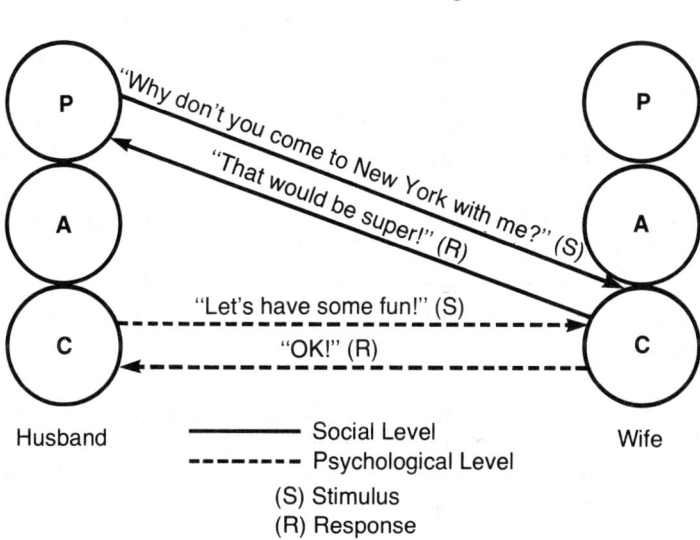

**FIGURE 10·3
Transactional Paradigm**

Moves. The moves in a game are like strokes in a ritual. They are learned and perfected so that there is an economy of moves (transactions), and the maximum payoff is achieved with a minimum of effort.

Advantages. In general, games are played in order to maintain a comfortable, though ultimately unsatisfying, self-perception and response from others. Games are therefore homeostatic mechanisms which reduce, or permit avoidance of, risk, change, novelty, and spontaneity. They therefore prevent the tension and anxiety necessary for normal growth experience. But while they protect the individual from potentially painful experience, they also remove the potential for personal growth, authenticity, and the joy of genuine human encounter. The game-player trades the tension which accompanies the attainment of the jewels of life, as small and rare as they may sometimes be, for a lifetime of mediocre crumbs.

Classification of Games

Berne identified a number of commonly experienced games and categorized them for analysis in the book *Games People Play* (1964). These are but a sample of those possible, for new games are formulated all the time, and variations on old ones are established to suit the needs of particular individuals with specific life positions and scripts, in unique social and environmental situations.

> Games prevent honest, intimate and open relationships between the players. Yet people play them because they fill up time, provoke attention, reinforce early attitudes about self and others and fulfill a sense of destiny (James and Jongeward, 1971: 33).

Can we avoid "games"? Yes, but first we have to recognize ulterior transactions, avoid using them ourselves, and refuse to get "sucked in" when someone gives us an ulterior message. We can do this by remaining in the Adult ego state.

SCRIPT ANALYSIS

The aim of script analysis, said Berne (1961: 119) is to "close the show and put a better one on the road." While the aim of the analysis of transactions is freedom from manipulation by others, the aim of script analysis might be said to be freedom from manipulation by *oneself* and others, for although this may be partly achieved in games analysis, it is script analysis which enables a person to discover the meaning of his games pattern from a historical and life position perspective. He can then begin to recognize the ways in which he manipulates people around him in order to obtain the gains associated with maintaining the life position he adopted as a child. Script analysis is currently the major focus of TA.

THE PROCESS OF TA THERAPY

THE INITIAL INTERVIEW

TA begins with an initial diagnostic interview in which the therapist attempts to understand the problem with which the patient is seeking help. During the course of this interview the therapist will ascertain, carefully and without standardized format, but in response to the patient's responses and conversation, general information about the patient which might be obtained in a social history. The object here is to place the patient in some historical, geographical, social, and cultural perspective so that his current behaviour may be more easily understood. Thus the patient would not only give details about specific current behavioural difficulties and their onset, but also include information about his family, work, friends, hobbies and activities, schooling, and the attitudes and values of people who are significant to him. On the basis of this information the therapist decides whether she believes she can help the patient. If she believes she can, she describes briefly the format of therapy and indicates the nature of the contract she wishes to set up with the patient. The contract would relate to the payment of fees, the frequency, length, and setting of sessions, and the expectations of the patient regarding significant decisions, attendance, honesty, homework, etc. while in therapy. The therapist would also explain her own role, what she does and is prepared to do, what she will not do or cannot do and the approximate time she feels is required for significant improvement or elimination of the patient's problem. If the patient agrees to the contract, therapy may proceed. Part of this contract would be the agreement of the patient to have a general physical examination and have the physician's report forwarded to the therapist to ensure that there are no physical indications against therapy.

THE TA CONTRACT

The treatment contract is a special feature of TA. Like a legal contract it has the following four features (Steiner, 1974: 243-50): (1) mutual consent, (2) consideration, (3) competency, and (4) lawful object.

Mutual Consent

Mutual consent means that the therapist, after hearing the client's problem and request for help, offers that help under certain conditions, and the client accepts the offer and conditions. It is essential that the client understand the contract. If the therapist believes that the client is disturbed enough to have difficulty in understanding it, a short-term contract may be arranged to give the client time to gain a better understanding of the treatment process. At the end of the short-term contract, another contract may be made. Steiner (1974) emphasizes the need for a clear understanding by the client at this stage that acceptance of the therapist's offer to help means that the client must commit himself to doing everything in his power to help himself. Failure of the client to be fully involved in helping himself results in a game of Rescue, in which the client assumes the role of the passive victim who waits for the therapist to fail at singlehandedly attempting to "rescue" him from his problems. The client's acceptance of the offer of help should mean that he will attend sessions regularly and on time, that he will be involved and participate in the group, that he will do whatever homework may be assigned, and in general follow whatever rules or conditions are established for his treatment. Mutual consent means that the client must do more than cooperate with the therapist; he must invest all the effort he can in the process—after all, he expects no less of his therapist!

Consideration

Consideration is the benefit to parties involved in the contract. In therapy, the benefit to the client should be effective treatment of problem behaviour. The benefit to the therapist typically is a fee, but may entail other rewards both tangible and intangible. In order to ensure that the client indeed benefits from the contract, it is important to describe in the contract in detail exactly what behavioural change or outcome constitutes "effective treatment" or satisfactory resolution of the client's difficulty.

Competency
Competency means that those making the treatment contract are fit to do so. Contracts cannot be made by those who are so severely disturbed that they do not understand the implications of such an agreement, nor by those who are under the influence of toxic drugs. In addition, certain problems may be encountered in contracts involving minors. To avoid having a contract with a minor broken by his legal guardian, it is best to arrange the contract with the legal guardian and minor client such that the legal guardian cannot terminate the contract without the minor client's consent.

Lawful Object
While not usually pertinent in therapy, this feature holds that "[t]he contract cannot be in violation of the law or against public policy or morals, nor should the consideration be of such nature" (Steiner, 1974: 250).

Steiner (1974: 247) provides the following example of a condensed request for therapy, offer of therapy, and acceptance:

THERAPIST: What brings you here, Mr. Jones?

MR. JONES: I'm drinking too much, I have made myself physically sick, I am losing my wife, and I am in trouble with the law. I want to stop drinking so I am here for treatment. (Request)

THERAPIST: O.K., Mr. Jones, I think we can work together on your problem. While you are in therapy you'll attend group therapy once a week, and perhaps an occasional individual session. I'll expect you to stop drinking entirely as soon as possible and to continue to abstain for at least one year, since it is my experience that individuals who do not abstain for at least a year tend not to recover from alcoholism. If you remain abstinent for a year while in therapy, you will probably gain control over your drinking to the point that drinking will no longer be of concern to you. This contract implies that you will be actively pursuing not only sobriety but any number of other things which might be helpful to you. I, as the therapist, will be guiding and working with you as long as you want to work on your problem. I will be able to see you on Monday at 10:00 A.M. (Offer)

MR. JONES: O.K., I'll see you next Monday. (Acceptance)

MAJOR TA TREATMENT STRATEGIES

Once the treatment contract has been established, the patient enters a treatment group and begins the therapy process with structural analysis. While structural analysis may occur with only the patient and therapist present, analysis of transactions, games, and scripts requires a group setting in order to expand the potential number of transactional stimuli and responses and to minimize the chance of transference and countertransference between patient and therapist.

At the same time it enables the therapist to act as an objective observer and analyst. This increases her opportunity for "thinking," since she does not have to be continually responding, but can make cogent "interventions" when necessary. Since one of the functions of group therapy is patient self-revelation based on the feedback of others and development of the patient's potential for responding effectively and appropriately, the therapist need not intervene if this process is taking place, but only when she feels she can make a significant addition to what is already happening.

Steiner (1974) described seven basic kinds of interventions used by the TA therapist: work, command, fun, permission, protection, potency, and unloading negative feelings.

Work

"Work" refers to the typical transaction employed by insight therapists which represents Adult-to-Adult communication. In the group, a member may present a problem. During a *clarification* phase the group considers whether in fact a problem really exists, or whether this problem is a device to avoid dealing with a more important but more difficult problem. If it appears that there is a real problem worthy of "working on," the group then moves to the next stage of the work process: *challenge*. At this point someone in the group raises the question "Now that you know the problem, what are you going to do about it?" This puts the person with the problem on the spot. As Steiner (1974: 253) says, "A cherished old pattern of behaviour is being re-examined, a parental injunction is being challenged, and the person's Adapted Child is expected to balk." This is called an *impasse*.

The typical insight therapist would have to wait for one of the other members of the group to put pressure on the member who is at impasse from his Child or Parent. The TA therapist, on the other hand, could use the *permission* transaction. Permission is an Adult rational reason for acting which the therapist directs at the patient's Child. If the group member accepts the permission of the therapist, the group as a whole experiences well-being and closure. Once this piece of "work" is finished, there may be a short silence, after which the process begins anew. If the group member becomes upset while working and gets into difficulty, the therapist may intervene with nurturing, support, and protection. While some therapists may wish to continue to confront the defensive, resistant group member to break down his defense system, Steiner believes this approach to be destructive. Steiner would respond instead by breaking off the work of the group and responding with *protection* to the distraught group member.

Command

A command is an emergency transaction from the Parent ego state of the therapist to the Child ego state of the patient. It is used to disrupt or stop transactional sequences which the therapist feels are dangerous. It is apparently effective in dealing with self-destructive and violent patients. Thus, a suicidal patient may be told by the therapist not to kill himself. Verbal attacks by one member on another may be responded to by the therapist's Parent command to stop.

Fun
"Fun is a transaction in which the Childs of the group's members are able to experience joy together" (Steiner, 1974: 257). Fun is believed not only to speed therapeutic work, but also to make it more enjoyable. The effect on the therapist who continually deals with problem behaviour and human misery and tragedy is considered to be important. Steiner (1974) suggests that, since fun is best recognized by hearty laughter, any therapist who does not find herself laughing at least once per treatment session should consider whether or not she is being unduly serious and perhaps adopting a rescue position.

Permission
Permission is a transaction used by the therapist to counteract a previous parental injunction which remains in the patient's Child. It is both a confirmation of a Parent-to-Child command and an Adult-to-Adult communication of information needed for a rational decision and behaviour.

Protection
The protection transaction is closely linked to permission. When the therapist gives permission, she countermands a parental injunction. If the patient takes the permission and acts against the injunction, he may lose parental protection and as a result experience fear and anxiety. The therapist may be required to supply the lost protection. If she does not, or cannot, the patient will return to his script behaviour. It is important, then, that the therapist offer permission only when she is able to provide the protection that may subsequently be required. (In order to ensure that his patients have protection when they need it, Steiner gives them his home phone number.) While there is a risk that the patient may manipulate the therapist into being a *rescuer* and refuse to accept personal responsibility, such manipulations are easily recognized by the skilled therapist.

Potency
Potency is the effectiveness of the TA therapist. Steiner suggests that the TA therapist is more potent as a result of adding the command, protection, permission, and fun transactions to the basic Adult-to-Adult work strategy. The transactional therapist will consider using any technique which may increase her therapeutic effectiveness (potency) and speed the patient's cure. Some activities which may increase therapeutic effectiveness or speed patient progress are permission classes,* marathons, and homework.

---

* Permission classes are group sessions in which selected clients make a contract with the therapist to practice specific behaviours currently being inhibited by previous parental injunctions against such behaviour. Examples of "permissions" might be "permission to dance," "permission to be assertive," or "permission to touch others."

Unloading Negative Feelings
Steiner (1974: 268) describes two further techniques aimed at increasing potency by enabling group members at the beginning of each session to get rid of negative feelings carried over from the previous session: *held resentments* and *paranoid fantasies*. Held resentments are stamps collected from the previous session. Rather than trading them in a game, the member with the stamp asks the member he wishes to give the stamp to if he will accept a stamp. If the member agrees, the stamp collector expresses his hurt. The person receiving the stamp does not respond to the stamp but merely acknowledges his understanding. Paranoid fantasies are irrational beliefs about another group member which prevent trust and open communication. These fantasies are based on something, so when the fantasy is expressed, the person accepting it must be prepared to offer a rational response which might justify the existence of such a belief. By getting rid of unexpressed resentments and paranoias, group members can more easily become involved in the real work of the group.

SUMMARY OF TRANSACTIONAL THERAPY
We have discovered TA's aim of autonomous, authentic, game and script-free behaviour to be similar to the aims of Rogerian, Gestalt, Primal, Rational-Emotive, and Reality Therapy. The process of TA therapy, while having many distinguishing features, also shares much in common with these therapies.

- It employs group process, though the role of the therapist and the focus of the group members is unique.
- TA, like Gestalt Therapy, directs specific attention to the patient's observable behaviour, in the form of various body movements, facial expressions, voice quality, and use of language, to increase and improve patient awareness.
- Feedback from TA group members is as essential as it is for encounter, Rational-Emotive, and post-Primal groups.
- As is the case in Gestalt, Rational-Emotive, Primal, and Reality Therapy, the TA therapist intervenes actively to initiate, rather than to merely respond to, patient behaviour.
- TA therapy, like Rational-Emotive and Reality Therapy, is highly cognitive, requiring the patient to evaluate, to accept responsibility, to find alternatives, to become aware of options, and to make contracts and commitments.
- The TA therapist considers the patient-therapist relationship to be essentially that of a student and teacher, and explains the basic assumptions and therapeutic process to the patient.
- The TA therapist shares openly her own values and beliefs and assists the patient to confront and explore his own and society's value systems.
- The TA therapist views the patient as someone who has made a choice to act self-destructively, with therapy designed to demonstrate that this is so, and that the patient can now choose to behave differently.

Thanks to Eric Berne's intuitive genius, his creative fantasy, his penchant for logical, rational thought, and his commitment to help his patients get better as quickly as possible, TA was born. Theoretically sound and offering a number of exciting new perspectives from which to consider personality development and problem behaviour, TA continues to evolve and to provide the stimulus for a growing number of effective therapeutic techniques.

V
The Behaviour Therapies

Learning is behaviour change.

11
The Behaviour Therapies

You may recall that in Chapter 2 we noted that there were five major approaches, or schools, of psychology which had been significant contributors to the helping field. They were: Freudian psychology, Gestalt psychology, organismic psychology, existential-humanistic psychology, and the psychology of learning. We have examined in some detail the specific concepts and principles involved in the first four schools, but have not yet considered the psychology of learning and the important therapeutic contributions made by the behaviourists. This chapter will focus on learning-theory-based therapies.

The three behaviour therapies are presented in a single chapter instead of devoting a chapter to each. They are powerful helping methods and as such are essential to a discussion of contemporary therapy. We have already seen the introduction of learning principles and techniques into the psychodynamically based approaches described in Part IV, particularly Rational-Emotive Therapy, and there is increasing evidence (Thoresen and Coates, 1978; Goldfrid, 1978; Strupp, 1979; McNamara, 1980) that behaviouristic and psychodynamic therapists are relinquishing their traditional animosities and becoming more open to one another's ideas and methods. For example, Wolpe's and Stampfl's therapeutic techniques, although based on learning theory, do not ignore the psychodynamics involved in the therapist-patient relationship, and make specific use of unobservable psychic activity such as fantasy.

Let's begin our exploration of the behaviour therapies by considering first the learning theory from which they are derived; second, some of the basic assumptions of the behaviourists regarding human growth and development; and third, the principles and methods involved in each of the three behaviour therapies, Behaviour Modification, Reciprocal Inhibition, and Implosive Therapy.

LEARNING THEORY AND BEHAVIOUR THERAPY

The Psychology of Learning

Although the impact on helping methods by learning theorists is recent (for example, Wolpe's interest in applying learning theory in psychotherapy did not occur until the late 1940s; Skinner coined the term Behaviour Therapy in 1954), we might call these approaches "traditional" (Carkhuff and Berenson, 1967). Learning was a central concern to the (then) new science of psychology at the turn of the century, has been responsible for some of the most sophisticated psychological theorizing and research between 1920 and 1960, and continues to occupy a major portion of, if not dominate, the activities of contemporary academic psychologists. Not until the 1960s did behaviour therapy become a force within the helping field (Harper, 1975), and until recently it has been viewed negatively by the older analytically based and newer existential-humanistic approaches. The antagonism of the insight-analytic camp toward the behaviourist school has been heightened by the behaviourists' claims of therapeutic success after brief treatment with clients similar to those who had improved only slightly after lengthy treatment by insight-analytic methods. Wolpe (1973: 9) for example, has claimed that,

> Statistical studies of the effects of behavior therapy by competent therapists have shown that almost 90 percent recovery or marked improvement may be expected among patients who have had a reasonable amount of exposure to behavioral methods.

Kisch and Kroll (1980) suggest that the claims made by Wolpe and others have not been borne out by research, and conclude that since such research is methodologically impossible, empirical proof of the effectiveness of therapy may be unattainable.

Had the claims of the behaviour therapists been correct, we might rightly have asked first why these methods had been so long in coming and, second, why they had not been welcomed after their arrival. The answer to both questions is complex and would require a more comprehensive discussion of the field of learning than is intended here. Suffice to say in answer to the first question that the practical application of learning theory principles has not been unduly delayed, but has followed a relatively "normal" path of a discipline characterized by a laboratory research methodology. The implications of learning theory for psychotherapy were considered by Pavlov as early as 1903 and by Hull in 1935 (Hilgard and Bower, 1966). Watson is described (Wolpe, 1973) as the *first* behaviour therapist because of his use of learning theory to deal with the famous case of Little Albert's conditioned fear of furry objects. But it is B.F. Skinner's dramatic work in operant conditioning that has done the most to move learning theory out of the laboratory. Beginning with dramatic live demonstrations of the operant conditioning of pigeons, Skinner increasingly sought practical applications for his ideas in human behaviour. In 1954 he introduced his teaching machine, an instrument designed to increase the efficiency of teaching arithmetic, spelling, reading, and other school subjects. Its success is shown by the prevalence of programmed learning in contemporary education (Hilgard and Bower, 1966).

The growth of and interest in learning-based therapies was, however, only indirectly related to learning theorists themselves. Even Skinner, whose learning principles and techniques form the basis of behaviour modification therapy, did not develop a therapeutic method as such. Rather, the behaviour therapies have been created, developed and/or practised either by older, disenchanted, analytically oriented therapists like Wolpe, who has developed a systematic therapeutic approach based on learning principles, or by the new post-1960 psychologists academically trained in learning theory.

The lack of welcome for the new behaviour therapists from the old guard is understandable, but does appear to be changing. The animosity appears to be historically rooted in an initial attack on the traditional therapists by Eysenck in 1952. But there are also major differences in theory, technique, and values, which foster, interestingly among therapists, professional paranoia and the attendant behaviours associated with an "I'm OK, You're Not OK" position.

Let's briefly consider next the specific *learning principles* involved in the behaviour therapies before turning to look at the assumptions about human behaviour with which these approaches are identified.

Stimulus-Response Theory and Behaviour Therapy

Learning theories fall into two major categories: *stimulus-response* (S-R) theories and *cognitive* theories. Thorndike, Pavlov, Guthrie, Hull, and Skinner belong to the S-R group, while people like Tolman and the classical Gestalt psychologists belong to the cognitive group. Behaviour therapies are derived from the former S-R theories. S-R or conditioning theories in turn are divided into *classical conditioning* theories such as those of Pavlov, Guthrie, and Hull, and *instrumental conditioning* theories, of which Skinner's *operant conditioning* is one.

In what is termed *classical* conditioning, the conditioned and unconditioned responses are of the same kind. No new response is learned; rather, the goal is to achieve an existing response or demonstrated behaviour under different stimulus conditions. Thus classical conditioning may be employed in toilet training, where the goal is not to change elimination per se, but to change the stimulus conditions under which elimination occurs—that is, not at the moment of felt need, but rather while sitting on the potty. Any reinforcement, whether positive or negative, of the desired response occurring, is controlled by the experimenter/therapist/trainer.

In *instrumental* conditioning, on the other hand, the conditioned and unconditioned responses are not of the same kind, and the goal is to achieve a new type of behaviour which is "instrumental" or causally related to the reward or reinforcement, which is also controlled by the responding organism. The child client who receives tokens for completion of units of work in school which later may be cashed in for food treats is learning by instrumental conditioning. The schoolwork in this case is the conditioned response being reinforced by tokens. The unconditioned response, of the eating of the unconditioned stimulus, treats, is unlike the conditioned response of doing schoolwork. In this case, the child determines the reinforcement since the tokens are obtained only through her conditioned response of completing units of schoolwork.

In operant conditioning, the principles of rewarding or reinforcing the conditioned response following its occurrence, and the control of reinforcement by the responding organism remain, although the method for applying these principles is different. Skinner's operant conditioning or shaping is described below.

In summary, then, it may be said that the learning principles which underlie various forms of classical and instrumental conditioning appear to be similar, with only the experimental conditions involved in each appearing to define them (Hilgard, 1956; Hilgard and Bower, 1966). The two learning principles involved which form the basis for all behaviour therapy are:

1. *Reinforcement* (positive and negative), that is, any event which increases the occurrence of a conditioned response, and
2. *Extinction,* the process of removing or eliminating reinforcement for a previously conditioned response.

The principles of reinforcement and extinction are both employed in Behaviour Modification therapy, while the principle of extinction underlies both the Reciprocal Inhibition and Implosive Therapy methods.

Basic Assumptions of Behaviour Therapists

ABSENCE OF A THEORY OF "NORMAL" BEHAVIOUR

The behaviour therapies have not articulated a set of characteristics or qualities to describe the "normal" human person, nor have they provided a general theory of human growth and development. They do not subscribe to a personality theory which concerns itself with internal events like cognition and emotion; the behaviour therapist concentrates on *external* events, like client actions, reactions, and responses. Unlike the therapies presented in Parts III and IV, the behaviour therapies do not present a social value system or philosophy. The human person is not viewed as initially good or integrated, or bad and uncontrolled, but primarily as a biological organism whose behaviour is governed by certain general laws of learning and the physical environment. Human behaviour is explored and considered in terms of animal learning principles based on laboratory research.

THEORY OF NEUROTIC OR PROBLEM BEHAVIOUR

Wolpe's and Stampfl's methods are specifically directed to alleviate neurotic, maladaptive behaviour which is personally distressing, and are based on well articulated theory supported by considerable research evidence (Wolpe, 1958, 1973). Behaviour modification, on the other hand, which employs classical and instrumental conditioning principles, is not specifically directed at alleviating neurosis, which is accompanied by maladaptive anxiety, but more to altering patient behaviour to reflect social expectations. As a result, Behaviour Modification therapy does not involve a specific theory of the origin or development of problem behaviour, but considers problem behaviour to reflect basic learning principles.

In very general terms, the behaviour therapies view problem behaviour simply as "bad" habits which have been acquired by the patient as a result of past learning experiences. These habits, bad in the sense that they prevent the satisfaction of basic needs, and/or result in high levels of anxiety which disrupt physical, intellectual, and motor behaviour, are maintained or *reinforced* by the patient's own behaviour, and through events occurring in her social and physical environment.

Therapeutic Goals of Behaviour Therapies

With almost every therapy we have seen thus far the therapeutic goals include improved or increased productivity, creativity, self-fulfillment, joy, interpersonal satisfaction, and self-worth. In behaviour therapies, however, the goals are, by nature of the theory and approach, restricted to specific, definable, measurable behavioural responses: either symptomatic relief or the evocation or improvement of new and more adaptive responses. To evoke new, lost, or more adaptive responses, Behaviour Modification may best be employed using reinforcement principles underlying classical and instrumental conditioning. This approach is most commonly used with severely regressed psychotics, with mentally retarded children and adults, and with acting-out children and adolescents. To obtain symptomatic relief when functioning is being *inhibited* by inappropriate responses, and a *restoration* of performance or the *elimination* of the inappropriate response is desired, either Reciprocal Inhibition Therapy or Implosive Therapy may be more useful. Behaviour Modification with its emphasis on reinforcement principles, then, may be most appropriate for eliciting or evoking socially desirable behaviour, while extinction therapies such as Reciprocal Inhibition and Implosive Therapy are aimed at the *elimination* of responses (neurotic behaviour) which are painful and restrictive to the patient.

BEHAVIOUR MODIFICATION
USING OPERANT CONDITIONING OR SHAPING

Four operant conditioning principles form the basis of the behaviour modification approach: (1) the free operant, (2) specificity of response and stimulus, (3) response frequency, and (4) shaping.

The Free Operant

The principle of the free operant distinguishes operant conditioning from classical or respondent conditioning. It means that the organism is theoretically free to respond or not to respond under certain conditions. The apparatus used *generates a response* which takes a short time to occur and leaves the organism in the same place ready to respond again. Thus, when the organism is *free* to respond, its behaviour can be *shaped*, beginning perhaps with diffuse or exploratory responding.

Specificity of Response and Stimulus

Essential to any behaviouristic approach is the identification of specific behaviours for study and control. This is one of the difficulties with psychodynamic approaches where response expectations are unclear, terminology is abstract and esoteric, and behavioural descriptions and observations are often vague and subjective. The behaviourist experimenter/therapist must determine in advance specifically what she wishes the individual whose behaviour she is manipulating to do. Indicating what response or behaviour is desired by the therapist is relatively easy. What is difficult is determining the *stimulus* which will evoke that response or behaviour. Thus, the behaviour therapist using operant conditioning principles does not randomly attempt to discover what specific stimuli might produce the desired behaviour, but instead concentrates on evoking the response she wants and observing when it occurs and under what conditions. *The basic rule in operant conditioning is that the response must occur before it can be reinforced.* Positive reinforcement (reward) is any event likely to increase the probability that the response will recur; *negative* reinforcement (punishment) is any event likely to decrease that probability.

Response Frequency

The frequency of certain behavioural responses we observe in others and ourselves gives rise to our labelling people as hostile, aggressive, or happy. These labels really only refer to the frequency of our observations of that behaviour.

Shaping

When the behaviour therapist can specify the response she desires from the patient and the frequency with which she wishes it expressed, she is in a position to *shape* the patient's behaviour.

Shaping is defined by Sidman (Bacharach, 1965: 68) as follows:

> Shaping is accomplished by reinforcing successively closer approximations to the behavior with which the experimenter [therapist] ultimately wants to work. The experimental situation, for example, may be one in which a monkey is to be reinforced with food for pressing a lever. If the monkey just sits quietly at first, the experimenter will wait until the animal moves and will then immediately deliver the food. By continuing to reinforce all movements, the experimenter will soon have an active animal with which to work. He then reinforces only those responses which bring the animal closer to the lever, as if drawn by an invisible string. The experimenter now directs his attention to the animal's hand. He delivers the food whenever the hand moves closer to the lever, and it is not long before the animal places its hand on the lever and depresses it. The

experimenter can then turn the rest of the job over to his automatic apparatus which will deliver the food only when the animal actually depresses the lever.

Bacharach (1965) then develops from Sidman's description the following shaping "rules":

1. Reinforce desired behaviour *immediately* so as not to confuse reinforcement with some other response.
2. Reinforcement during shaping should be *neither too frequent nor infrequent* since during the shaping process, responses must be extinguished which were initially reinforced as the organism moves closer to the end response or desired goal. There are real parallels here in therapy for the therapist who moves too quickly and loses "ground" with her patient.
3. As the shaping process proceeds each successive step requires careful *specification of the response* to be reinforced. This needs to be rigorously adhered to in order to ensure reinforcement of the desired response.

The excellent film *Reinforcement Therapy* provides a classic demonstration of behaviour modification using operant conditioning.

RECIPROCAL INHIBITION THERAPY (RIT) OR SYSTEMATIC DESENSITIZATION

The Theory of Competing Antagonistic Responses

The underlying hypothesis involved in Wolpe's RIT is stated this way:

> If a response antagonistic to anxiety can be made to occur in the presence of anxiety-evoking stimuli so that it is accompanied by a complete or partial suppression of the anxiety responses, the bond between these stimuli and anxiety responses will be weakened (Wolpe, 1958: 71).

Wolpe's approach is derived from the classical conditioning principles of Hull and the physiology involved in the condition of anxiety. Wolpe, an analytically trained psychiatrist, encountered the work of the learning theorists by chance, and being disenchanted with his own therapeutic effectiveness, saw in learning theory a potential new means for treating neurotic disorders. He observed that experimentally induced neurotic anxiety in cats could be eliminated by the gradual presentation of the anxiety-producing stimuli while they were eating. This led to the hypothesis that the previously conditioned responses in the cats were *inhibited* by the new conditioned eating responses occurring at the same time. He then investigated the *types* of responses which might be effective in the inhibition of anxiety, and concluded that, since anxiety responses or behaviour primarily involved the sympathetic nervous system, indicated by sweating palms, increase in blood pressure, rapid breathing, and increased heart rate and muscular tension, responses opposite or antagonistic to anxiety would involve the parasympathetic nervous system. These latter responses would include muscle relaxation, feelings of calmness and control, and physical pleasure, such as sexual activity. Research evidence indicated that parasympathetic responses might *inhibit* sympathetic responses occurring at the same time—that is, the parasympathetic nervous system was not only opposed to, but also dominant over the sympathetic system. For example, normal anxiety and/or guilt associated with being "discovered" in sexual activity is almost absent at the height of sexual arousal, but returns immediately following orgasm. Various animal experiments confirmed the hypothesis of reciprocal inhibition; the clinical evidence, as we have noted above, is quite overwhelming.

In simple terms, RIT is based on the principle that we cannot feel "good," relaxed, and contented, and at the same moment anxious, uptight, and concerned. *The RI therapist's task is to induce responses in the neurotically anxious patient which are antagonistic to her anxiety.* Wolpe has found three major types of responses to be useful in this regard: assertive responses, sexual responses, and relaxation responses.

Assertiveness training is used to decondition patients' unadaptive anxiety habits which occur in response to the people with whom they interact. Wolpe (1973: 81) defines assertive behaviour as ". . . the proper expression of any emotion other than anxiety towards another person." Assertiveness training usually precedes systematic desensitization because the patient can do homework on it between sessions. With such a broad definition of "assertiveness," it is likely that some aspect of a patient's interpersonal relations would benefit from assertiveness training.

Sexual responses of course would be initiated only for those patients who are experiencing some problem in sexual activity. The therapist's role here is to determine what conditions result in the antagonistic anxiety responses which interfere in sexual activity, and to instruct the patient how to structure the conditions under which sexual activity occurs so that anxiety is reduced and sexual response becomes dominant.

Relaxation responses are used for the inhibition of all other anxiety-related behaviour and form the basis for systematic desensitization. The basic desensitization technique is to teach the patient to relax and then remain relaxed in the presence of mildly anxiety-evoking stimuli. After this is accomplished, the patient gradually learns to remain relaxed in the presence of increasingly stronger anxiety-evoking stimuli until no stimuli produce anxiety responses. The fact that the treatment works in the therapist's office with imaginary stimuli, (although the patient may also do homework in real situations) suggests that the fantasized learning transfers to the real world. This transfer occurs because the stimuli presented by the therapist in word-pictures are capable of evoking real anxiety responses in the patient.

The Aim of RIT

The task of RIT is the elimination of specific neurotic behaviour and the relief of the pain and distress which accompany this behaviour. RIT does not aim to help patients grow and mature, to become self-actualizing or self-directed, to improve their feelings of self-worth, or to become more socially responsible, ethical, or competent. It only claims to bring relief from specific neurotic symptoms and maladaptive anxiety. Although the patient may benefit from the caring and concern shown by the therapist, and may achieve insight and understanding about the development and maintenance of her problem behaviour, these are not goals of RIT, nor are they given specific consideration in the therapeutic process. The patient is not considered to be responsible for her behaviour or to have chosen it. The therapist is responsible for eliminating the undesirable or unwanted behaviour and failure to do so reflects the incompetence of the therapist, not a lack of cooperation by the patient.

According to Wolpe (1973: 270), elimination of specific neurotic behaviour has rarely resulted in the recurrence or substitution of neurotic symptoms in RIT patients.

The RI Therapeutic Technique

RIT includes the following ten steps: (1) initial interview, (2) patient history, (3) patient orientation to therapy, (4) assertiveness training, (5) construction of an extinction hierarchy, (6) relaxation training, (7) establishment of a scale of subjective anxiety, (8) presentation of scenes from the hierarchy while relaxed, (9) homework, and (10) termination.

INITIAL INTERVIEWS
The therapist concentrates on obtaining as much information as possible in the initial interviews about the patient's specific problem behaviour. In particular, she attempts to discover the nature of the situations in which the behaviour occurs in order to later construct, or determine the pattern of, events which precede the onset of the problem behaviour. The usual supports of therapist-client relationship and intimacy are included, although they are not the focus. The therapist explains that she is more concerned with current problem behaviour and situations than with the past. The therapist concentrates on asking what events, situations, and activities the patient avoids because she finds them too painful to experience, what feelings she wishes to eliminate, and/or what behaviour she wants to change. The patient is asked what she wants to accomplish in therapy and the therapist indicates whether or not she believes she can help her achieve her goals.

PATIENT HISTORY
Once the therapist has a full understanding of the nature and frequency of the problem and the events and conditions under which it occurs, she obtains information about the patient's past and present life. Five basic areas are explored in depth: early family life, education and school experience, employment history, sex life, and social relationships.

PATIENT ORIENTATION

This is an interesting aspect of RIT. After her history has been taken, the patient is interviewed and oriented regarding common misconceptions she may have about her problems or symptoms and their treatment. The therapist tries to allay any of the patient's fears and anxieties based on insufficient or incorrect information by sharing openly her knowledge, values, and beliefs and the RI theory and technique with the patient. Thus "superior therapist-inferior patient" role behaviour is avoided.

The patient is encouraged to discuss her anxiety reactions and bodily sensations so that the therapist may better assist her in coping with them. Tranquilizers and/or muscle relaxants may be prescribed. If the drug decreases the patient's painful anxiety and enables her to experience a situation more easily and appropriately, it also helps extinguish higher-level, debilitating anxiety. The patient may be taught self-help techniques for reducing anxiety, or for preventing anxiety or panic reactions from getting out of hand, for example, preventing or decreasing hyperventilation by deep breathing, breathing into a paper bag, talking, and self-distraction.

The patient may also be taught methods for preventing anxiety responses from becoming uncontrollable. For example, in "thought-stopping," when the patient becomes aware of anxiety-producing thoughts she says to herself, or out loud, "Stop." This technique does alter for an instant the existing thought process. Used repeatedly, it can bring a chain of compulsive thought behaviour under control. Another technique for thought-stopping is snapping an elastic band worn around the wrist. The motor behaviour and the brief pain help to intercept the neurotic thought process and enable the patient to better control anxiety in the early stages of therapy.

ASSERTIVENESS TRAINING

Wolpe routinely explores the need for assertiveness training. If he discovers patient anxiety in relationships with other people which interfere with the patient's ability to satisfy her own needs, then assertiveness training begins. It may be required in situations in which the patient's behaviour is impulsive or inappropriate, as well as inhibited, by interpersonal anxiety. Thus the patient who always volunteers and cannot say no needs just as much help in being assertive as does the patient who is afraid to speak up with authority figures.

CONSTRUCTION OF AN ANXIETY HIERARCHY

Construction of an anxiety hierarchy is the ranking of a list of stimuli on the basis of the amount of anxiety each evokes. The list is developed by the therapist about the same time as relaxation training begins. It is based on the earlier interviews, and items are checked out with the patient prior to the actual beginning of the relaxation sessions. The following hierarchy, reconstructed from an example described by Wolpe (1973: 116), deals with examination anxiety:

1. In the process of answering an examination paper.

2. The examination paper lies face down before her.
3. Awaiting the distribution of examination papers.
4. Standing before the unopened doors of the examination room.
5. On the way to the university on the day of an examination.
6. The night before an examination.
7. One day before an examination.
8. Two days before an examination.
9. Three days before an examination.
10. Four days before an examination.
11. Five days before an examination.
12. A week before an examination.
13. Two weeks before an examination.
14. A month before an examination.

RELAXATION TRAINING
Deep muscle relaxation, like assertiveness training, is a critical aspect of RIT technique. The therapist teaches the patient to relax by having her stretch out comfortably in a large reclining chair, close her eyes, and listen to the therapist's verbal directions. The therapist speaks slowly and soothingly, and repetitively alternates between urging and persuasive suggestion that the patient relax, beginning with the head, face, and eye muscles, followed by each area of her body in turn, until the patient is completely relaxed. This is not easy, especially for patients with high general levels of anxiety, and it requires several sessions before they are able to experience total relaxation. However, once she has learned the technique, the patient can on subsequent sessions sink within seconds into deep total relaxation, first at the request or with the assistance of the therapist, and then at will under her own volition. Total relaxation is another tool which the patient can apply to her life outside of therapy.

ESTABLISHMENT OF A SCALE OF SUBJECTIVE ANXIETY
In order to gauge the anxiety level of the patient at the beginning of actual desensitization sessions, and to rank the scenes in the hierarchy so that they are relatively evenly spaced in terms of the incremental amounts of anxiety which may be evoked by each, a subjective scale is used. The patient is asked to consider the most anxiety-producing stimulus or situation she can think of and imagine herself in it. She is then told that this degree of anxiety represents 100. Then she is told to imagine being absolutely calm. This level is zero.

PRESENTATION OF SCENES FROM THE HIERARCHY
The patient is now ready to begin systematic desensitization. First the patient must become totally relaxed. She is told by the therapist that a scene will be described and the patient is to imagine the scene as the therapist presents it. The moment the patient experiences *any change* from her relaxed state she is to signal awareness, not by talking, but merely by raising the index finger of her right hand. Note that the patient is *not* told to wait until she experiences discomfort or anxiety.

Then the therapist describes the lowest scene on the patient's anxiety hierarchy, presenting it graphically and in detail. If this scene produces no change in the patient's bodily sensations, the therapist moves up to the next scene. When the patient does experience a change in her bodily state, she raises her finger, and the therapist stops the presentation of the scene abruptly, tells the patient to stop imagining the scene, and calms her until she indicates by a finger movement that she is re-relaxed. (Wolpe reported a modification of the signal aspect of RIT in 1973: instead of the non-verbal indicator of the raised finger, the patient verbally reports the level of anxiety being experienced.)

At this point the therapist starts again at the bottom of the hierarchy and begins the presentation of scenes until again the patient signals a change and the therapist stops and re-relaxes the patient.

This is continued until gradually scenes presented over and over lose their ability to elicit anxiety responses and to disturb the relaxed state of the patient. As the therapist moves up the hierarchy, she shortens and finally leaves out the early scenes so that the range of scenes being worked on is always about the same.

HOMEWORK

As the patient moves up the hierarchy during therapy sessions in the office, the therapist encourages the patient to approach low-level anxiety-provoking stimuli in real life, and to use the techniques learned in therapy to handle the anxiety evoked.

TERMINATION

When the last, most anxiety-provoking scene in the hierarchy can be imagined without undue anxiety, the patient is ready to terminate treatment. Termination may involve several evaluation sessions in which the patient's improvement is assessed and the success of the therapy evaluated.

Summary of RIT

Developed by Joseph Wolpe, a psychiatrist, RIT is based on the classical conditioning principles of the learning theorist Clark Hull and the physiology of anxiety. While it uses some reinforcement principles, it is primarily aimed at the extinction of unwanted behaviour, specifically neurotic anxiety responses. The method involves the gradual presentation of anxiety-evoking stimuli in the presence of inhibiting relaxed behaviour. Wolpe claims 90 per cent effectiveness in eliminating or substantially improving patients' neurotic behaviour. The goal of RIT is the symptomatic relief of patient pain and distress, not general personality or behavioural change.

RIT has the following characteristics:

- It is "now"-oriented, although the therapist takes the patient's history in order to understand her past learning events and circumstances.
- It has no specific life-philosophy.

- Like most therapies, it values the establishment of a relationship of acceptance, trust, warmth, and respect between client and therapist.
- It is directive in nature; the therapist is in control but moves at a pace appropriate for the patient.
- It is non-psychodynamic, avoiding traditional psychoanalytically based concepts, terminology, interpretations, assumptions, and techniques.
- It is a rational/objective, non-mystical approach in which the therapist explains exactly what she is doing in simple terms to the patient.
- It involves a verbal contract, with the patient determining what behaviour she wants to change and the therapist setting certain expectations and limits.
- It is short-term and specific, oriented to altering definable behaviour.

IMPLOSIVE THERAPY (IT)

Implosive Therapy is the creation of an American psychologist, Thomas Stampfl. As a method in which the therapist evokes strong anxiety or fear responses in the patient, it resembles "flooding," a method first used by E.R. Guthrie prior to 1935 (Wolpe, 1973: 193). Although at first glance we might question such behaviour by a therapist, Wolpe (1973) notes that the analytic process called "abreaction" in which patients are encouraged to experience and express strong emotion in therapy, has long been considered a helpful, if not a necessary, part of the typical insight-relationship therapies.

Stampfl's work was first described in 1964, but it was not until 1966 that articles began to appear in the literature regarding the effectiveness of IT (Storms, 1976). Stampfl himself appears to have co-authored with Donald Levis only one article on IT, which appeared in the *Journal of Abnormal Psychology* in 1967. But while there appears to be continuing interest expressed in the technique and increasing evidence of its effectiveness, it is still not widely used (Shipley, 1979). Wolpe, who originally (1958) voiced strong concerns about "flooding" techniques, has softened his views in his more recent work (1973). This may relate partly to research evidence which has shown flooding to be more effective in some cases than RIT. Still Wolpe's (1973) caution appears to be valid, since the experimental learning principles on which IT are based cannot, in themselves, explain its success:

> So far, nobody has cured an experimental neurosis simply by exposing the animal for long periods (hours or days) to the stimuli to which anxiety has been maximally conditioned . . . (Wolpe, 1973: 195).

Let's consider briefly the learning theory principles and basic assumptions that are involved in IT.

The Theory and Assumptions Behind IT

THEORY OF NEUROSIS
The development of neurosis may be understood through putting together both classical conditioning and operant conditioning learning principles.

Stampfl and Wolpe would agree on this point. The experience of neurotic anxiety is seen as a product of numerous conditioning experiences in life which can easily be understood in terms of laboratory models.

Past specific experiences of punishment and pain confer strong anxiety reactions to initially neutral stimuli. These experiences are represented neurally, and the neural engram (memory, image) may be considered as possessing the potential to function as a stimulus (Stampfl and Levis, 1967: 497).

These thoughts, images, and memories will tend to be avoided because they are associated with pain and anxiety. So will specific events or situations in the real world which may act as stimuli. This is simple classical conditioning as practised by Pavlov. However, the avoidance behaviour, *because* it brings relief from anxiety, fear, or pain, acts as a positive *reinforcer* in operant conditioning terms. Avoidance behaviour is thus strengthened and maintained. The fear or anxiety is neurotic because objectively and rationally the situation or object or event is not in itself harmful to the patient. An uncomfortable feeling resulting from some experience related to the feared situation did initially occur. Fear or discomfort becomes associated with this originally identified situation or object and the patient subsequently *learns* to avoid these situations because by doing so she avoids the anxiety feelings. In time, she may not know *why* she feels discomfort or anxiety in such situations. But, worse, she finds her life narrowed by her avoidance behaviour and at times made very uncomfortable when avoidance is impossible. Consider, for example, the person who has a fear of elevators. This person may be inconvenienced daily by this fear, but periodically also experiences embarrassment and shame when having to admit this fear publicly. Attempts to avoid the embarrassment may require the person to further structure her life, and her neurotic behaviour is in this way expanded.

THEORY OF EXTINCTION
The principle of extinction is expressed by Stampfl in this way (1967: 498-99):

... a sufficient condition for the extinction of anxiety is to re-present, reinstate, or symbolically reproduce the stimuli (cues) to which the anxiety response has been conditioned, in the absence of primary reinforcement.

In other words, a conditioned stimulus followed by repeated non-reinforcement eventually leads to extinction of the conditioned response. Non-reinforcement means that the patient is unable to respond to the conditioned stimulus with avoidance. There is therefore no immediate reduction in anxiety. While the experience of anxiety itself is not pleasant, the patient eventually discovers that it can be experienced without anything unpleasant happening. In time, after repeatedly responding with anxiety to the conditioned stimuli when positive reinforcement of avoidance is impossible, the anxiety response begins to weaken in the absence of reinforcement and finally disappears. This very principle is considered by many learning theorists to offer the explanation for what happens in traditional psychotherapy. The therapist constitutes a non-punishing audience so that emotional responses evoked in the patient are *extinguished* by the therapist's non-reinforcement (acceptance, respect, empathy), and desired new behaviour is the result of the therapist's positive reinforcement (praise, support, encouragement, direction, suggestion).

The Dynamics and Technique of IT

Shipley (1979) divides IT into three major activities: therapist-client relationship, detective work, and scene presentation.

THERAPIST-CLIENT RELATIONSHIP
Several of the elements described in RIT, and others common to all therapies, are also emphasized in IT. One is the establishment of a warm, empathic, and supportive relationship which conveys to the client the empathic appreciation of her problem and distress. At the same time, during the actual presentation of IT scenes, the therapist may often assume a very harsh, directive, and non-empathic stance, recognizing that her role in this aspect of the procedure is to *evoke painful experiences* in the client. The therapist therefore must alternate between being "soft" and "hard." Before and after scene presentation, the therapist's behaviour resembles that considered appropriate in all helping situations. But during scene presentation, the therapist's task is to evoke high levels of anxiety and distress in the client.

Since this is an unusual technique, it is important that the client understand the theoretical basis for it and agree in advance to its use. This information and agreement is communicated in the initial interview.

DETECTIVE WORK
As in RIT, the initial two or three interviews with the client are used to gather information about the client's present problem. In particular, the therapist explores all aspects of the problem behaviour in an effort to discover the kinds of internal (thoughts, sensations) and external (events, objects, people) stimuli which produce the negative emotions (fear, anger) and avoidance behaviour. She also obtains social history details to further investigate and identify possible past experiences which may be associated with current behaviour problems. This process of identifying all stimuli which can cue either the negative emotion or the avoidance reaction continues throughout each IT session. Thus each session begins with reports by the client of any new symptoms or experience of current symptoms and the stimuli present at their occurrence. These reports, as well as the responses of the client during the session itself, provide the therapist with additional material from which to construct scenes.

SCENE PRESENTATION
Once the initial interviews have yielded sufficient information about the stimuli which produce the patient's negative emotion and avoidance behaviour to

enable the therapist to determine a pattern, and perhaps to hypothesize the existence of certain psychodynamic elements which may also be involved, she may begin to construct "scenes."

The work with scenes resembles the "imagery" method of RIT. IT, however, begins with a neutral scene. The neutral scene enables the therapist to test the client's ability to fantasize and become involved in imagery, to establish the role of the therapist and client in the process, and to confirm for the client that she *can* imagine things that have not or could not in reality occur.

At the beginning of the implosive scene presentation the client is instructed to become as involved as possible in the scenes presented. She is requested to try to experience the scene as though it were happening to her now, and to respond to it as though it were real.

The therapist prepares for the scene by writing an outline to a story. The story involves an event or situation (stimulus) which evokes the negative emotions and avoidance behaviour of the patient. The therapist may begin the story by gradually building up to the fear situation or object and then concentrate on it as graphically as possible, including in the story the various anxiety-producing stimuli. She may shout, use sound effects, and pound the desk. She may direct the client to touch the feared object or stimulus, to approach it, to speak, to make appropriate sounds or body movements. Her basic task is to get the client as involved as possible in experiencing the negative feelings and to prevent her from avoiding or escaping them.

If a scene does not elicit negative feelings it is passed over. If it does, it is re-presented over and over again until the client ceases to experience negative feeling or the desire to avoid it. As the scene is re-presented, it is elaborated on to cover a larger and larger range of possible stimuli. Homework is assigned, and is considered an important part of the therapy. The client is required to spend some time twice a day in imagining the implosive scene worked on in the session that week.

Therapy is terminated when the client's symptoms decline to her satisfaction. For neurotic problems Shipley (1974) claimed that significant improvement may be achieved in eight to fifteen sessions.

Summary of IT

IT is a behaviour therapy based on the learning principle of extinction. It is effectively employed with neurotic symptoms. According to IT, neurotic symptoms may be explained in terms of classical and operant conditioning. The neurotic symptom, such as unrealistic anxiety, is a conditioned response to a conditioned stimulus (e.g., elevators). The avoidance of the conditioned stimulus by the client gives positive reinforcement to this behaviour, because it lowers the negative feeling (conditioned response) which the conditioned stimulus evokes. By continually following the conditioned stimulus with avoidance, the conditioned response (anxiety and avoidance) is strengthened and maintained. The principle of extinction is used in IT to non-reinforce the conditioned response by forcing the client to experience the conditioned response (fear) in the absence of positive reinforcement (avoidance and decrease in fear). Therapy involves enabling the client through imagery to become actively involved in the experiencing of the negative emotions she is avoiding. This is done through the graphic presentation of scenes by the therapist which are constructed of stimuli which evoke negative emotion in the client. These scenes are re-presented repeatedly, until they no longer evoke negative emotion and the symptom behaviour is extinguished or decreased to the satisfaction of the client and therapist.

SUMMARY

In this chapter we have briefly discussed the contributions made to the helping field by the psychology of learning. Learning theories are of two basic types: *stimulus-response* (S-R) and *cognitive;* the behaviour therapies have been derived from the S-R theories. More specifically, the learning principles derived from Pavlov's *classical conditioning* and Skinner's *operant conditioning* form the basis for the three primary behaviour therapies: Behaviour Modification, Reciprocal Inhibition, and Implosive Therapy. Behaviour Modification, or the evocation or shaping of *new* behaviour, uses the *reinforcement* principles of operant conditioning; while Reciprocal Inhibition and Implosive Therapy rely primarily on the principle of *extinction,* and are directed at the elimination or reduction of *existent* undesirable behaviour.

Since their emergence in the early 1960s, the behaviour therapies, although relative newcomers to the field of psychotherapy, have become a potent force. They have offered techniques for behaviour change, particularly with clients whose problem behaviour had been resistant to other methods, which have relieved or significantly reduced human misery and suffering after relatively brief periods of treatment. In other cases, behaviour therapy has been successful in stimulating the development of new adaptive and autonomous behaviour in clients who appeared to be stuck in rigid patterns of infantile, regressive, or self-destructive behaviour. Thus, while they may not be "humanistic" methods, in the sense of the earlier definition of this term, they are to be carefully explored for their contributions to the armament of the humanistic helper.

Resources

CHAPTER 1

Books

Burton, Arthur, et al. *Twelve Therapists*. San Francisco: Jossey-Bass, 1972.
Carkhuff, Robert. *The Art of Helping III*. Amherst: Human Resource Development Press, 1977.
Carkhuff, Robert, and Bernard Berenson. *Beyond Counseling and Therapy*. Toronto: Holt, Rinehart & Winston, 1967.
Carkhuff, Robert, and Bernard Berenson. *Teaching as Treatment*. Amherst: Human Resource Development Press, 1976.
Coopersmith, Stanley. *The Antecedents of Self-Esteem*. San Francisco: W.H. Freeman, 1967.
Ellis, Albert, and R.A. Harper. *A New Guide to Rational Living*. New York: McGraw-Hill, 1978.
Fischer, Joel. *Effective Casework Practice: An Eclectic Approach*. New York: McGraw-Hill, 1978.
Frank, Jerome D. *Persuasion and Healing*. New York: Schocken, 1963.
Gaylin, Willard, Ira Glasser, Steven Marcus, and David J. Rothman. *Doing Good: The Limits of Benevolence*. New York: Pantheon, 1978.
Glasser, William. *Reality Therapy*. New York: Harper & Row, 1965.
Glasser, William. *Schools Without Failure*. New York: Harper & Row, 1969.
Janov, Arthur. *Prisoners of Pain*. New York: Anchor Press/Doubleday, 1980.

Articles

Alger, Ian. "Accountability: Human and Political Dimensions." *American Journal of Orthopsychiatry* 50 (1980): 388-93.
Ansell, Charles. "Counter-Transference: A Story." *Psychotherapy: Theory, Research and Practice* 16 (1979): 261-68.
Beutler, Larry E. "Values, Beliefs, Religion and the Persuasive Influence of Psychotherapy." *Psychotherapy: Theory, Research and Practice* 16 (1979): 432-40.
Ellis, Albert. "My Philosophy of Psychotherapy." *Journal of Contemporary Psychotherapy* 6 (1973): 13-18.
England, Mary Jane. "Children's Services in Massachusetts: '—and the First Will Come Last.' " *American Journal of Orthopsychiatry* 50 (1980): 205-10.

Foley, Henry A., and I. Schneider. "The Small-Is-Beautiful Approach to Resource Allocation." *American Journal of Orthopsychiatry* 50 (1980): 211-14.

Frank, Jerome D. "Mental Health in a Fragmented Society: The Shattered Crystal Ball." *American Journal of Orthopsychiatry* 49 (1979): 397-408.

Greben, Stanley E. "On Being Therapeutic." *Canadian Psychiatric Association Journal* 22 (1977): 371-80.

Greben, Stanley E. "The Influence of The Supervision of Psychotherapy Upon Being Therapeutic." *Canadian Journal of Psychiatry* 24 (1979): 499-513.

Heller, Liane, and Ellie Tesher. "16 Years Locked in Mental Wards." *Toronto Star*, December 22, 23, 1980.

"The Implications of Cost-Effectiveness Analysis of Medical Technology," Background Paper #3: "The Efficacy and Cost-Effectiveness of Psychotherapy." Washington, D.C.: Office of Technology Assessment, Congress of the United States, October 1980.

Kisch, Jeremy, and Jerome Kroll. "Meaningfulness Versus Effectiveness: Paradoxical Implications In The Evaluation of Psychotherapy."*Psychotherapy: Theory, Research and Practice* 17 (1980): 401-13.

Larson, Dale. "Therapeutic Schools, Styles, and Schoolism: A National Survey." *Journal of Humanistic Psychology* 20 (1980): 3-20.

Millington, Gordon. "Conflict in Social Work Education." *Journal of Further and High Education* 5 (1981): 17-23.

Morrison, James K. "A Consumer-Oriented Approach to Psychotherapy." *Psychotherapy: Theory, Research and Practice* 16 (1979): 381-84.

Peebles, Mary Jo. "Personal Therapy and Ability to Display Empathy, Warmth and Genuineness in Psychotherapy." *Psychotherapy: Theory, Research and Practice* 17 (1980): 258-62.

Pilisuk, Marc. "The Future of Human Services Without Funding." *American Journal of Orthopsychiatry* 50 (1980): 200-204.

Schwartz, B.D. "The Initial Versus Subsequent Theoretical Positions: Does the Psychotherapist's Personality Make a Difference?" *Psychotherapy: Theory, Research and Practice* 15 (1978): 344-49.

Shane, Paul. "Shame and Learning." *American Journal of Orthopsychiatry* 50 (1980): 348-55.

Shoben, E.J. "Towards a Concept of the Normal Personality." *American Psychologist* 12 (1957): 183-89.

Singer, Jerome. "The Scientific Basis of Psychotherapeutic Practice: A Question of Values and Ethics." *Psychotherapy: Theory, Research and Practice* 17 (1980): 372-83.

Sluger, Dan, and Jim Bebout. "Contracts in Gestalt and Analytic Therapy." *Journal of Humanistic Psychology* 20 (1980): 21-40.

Spielberg, Gil. "Graduate Training in Helpful Relationships: Helpful or Harmful?" *Journal of Humanistic Psychology* 20 (1980): 57-70.

"A Statement on Contemporary Familial Lifestyles." Ottawa: The Vanier Institute of the Family, 1977.

Strupp, Hans H. "The Therapist's Theoretical Orientation: An Overrated Variable." *Psychotherapy: Theory, Research and Practice* 15 (1978): 314-17.
Strupp, Hans H. "Humanism and Psychotherapy: A Personal Statement of the Therapist's Essential Values." *Psychotherapy: Theory, Research and Practice* 17 (1980): 396-400.
Towbin, A.P. "The Confiding Relationship: A New Paradigm." *Psychotherapy: Theory, Research and Practice* 15 (1978): 333-43.
Troemel-Ploetz, Senta. " 'I'd Come to You For Therapy': Interpretation Redefinition and Paradox in Rogerian Therapy." *Psychotherapy: Theory, Research and Practice* 17 (1980): 246-51.
Ulrich, Roger E. "Some Thoughts On Human Nature And Its Control: I Am My Neighbor and My Neighbor Is Me." *Journal of Humanistic Psychology* 19 (1979): 29-44.
Wachtel, Paul. "What Should We Say to Our Patients?: On the Wording of Therapists' Comments." *Psychotherapy: Theory, Research and Practice* 7 (1980): 183-88.
White, Robert W. "Motivation Reconsidered: The Concept of Competence." *Psychological Review* 66 (1959): 297-333.

Films

Hurry Tomorrow. 60-min. B & W. Demonstrates psychic assault by irresponsible use of drugs within a locked ward of the State Hospital at Los Angeles, California. Halfway House Productions, 1975. Distributed by Halfway House Films, Box 22251, San Francisco, California 94122.

Videotapes

The Myth of Psychotherapy. 30-min. col. Ontario Educational Communications Authority (OECA) Mike McManus Interview Program in which Dr. Thomas Szasz discusses his views regarding psychotherapy. OECA, Channel 19, 1978.
The Right To Be Mad. 30-min. col. Ontario Educational Communications Authority (OECA) Mike McManus Interview Program in which Dr. Thomas Szasz discusses his views on the contemporary concepts of mental illness, psychiatry, insanity, and therapy, contrasted with his model of what the helper-helpee relationship should be. OECA, Channel 19, 1976.

CHAPTER 2

Books

Ford, Donald H., and Hugh B. Urban. *Systems of Psychotherapy.* New York: Wiley, 1964.
Hall, Calvin S., and Gardner Lindzey. *Theories of Personality.* New York: Wiley, 1957.

McCary, J.L., *Psychology of Personality: Six Modern Approaches*. New York: Grove, 1956.
Munroe, Ruth L. *Schools of Psychoanalytic Thought*. New York: Holt, Rinehart & Winston, 1955.
Nordby, Vernon J., and Calvin S. Hall. *A Guide to Psychologists and Their Concepts*. San Francisco: W.H. Freeman, 1974.
Sarason, Irwin G., and Barbara R. Sarason. *Abnormal Psychology*. Englewood Cliffs, N.J.: Prentice-Hall, 1980.
Thompson, Clara, Milton Mazer, and Earl Witenberg, eds. *An Outline of Psychoanalysis*. New York: Modern Library, 1955.
Wolman, Benjamin B. *Contemporary Theories and Systems in Psychology*. New York: Harper & Row, 1960.

Articles

Bernstein, Arnold. "The Psychoanalytic Technique." In *Handbook of Clinical Psychology*, edited by Benjamin B. Wolman, pp. 1168-99. New York: McGraw-Hill, 1965.
Brill, Henry. "Psychiatric Diagnosis, Nomenclature and Classification." In *Handbook of Clinical Psychology*, edited by Benjamin B. Wolman, pp. 639-50. New York: McGraw-Hill, 1965.
Cohen, Mabel Blake. "Countertransference and Anxiety." In *An Outline of Psychoanalysis*, edited by Clara Thompson, Milton Mazer, and Earl Witenberg. New York: Modern Library, 1955.
Greenblatt, Milton, and David J. Levinson. "Mental Hospitals." In *Handbook of Clinical Psychology*, edited by Benjamin B. Wolman, pp. 1343-59. New York: McGraw-Hill, 1965.
Lewis, Nolan. "American Psychiatry From Its Beginnings to World War II." In *American Handbook of Psychiatry*, Vol. 1, edited by Silvano Arieti, pp. 3-17. New York: Basic Books, 1959.
Mora, George. "Recent American Psychiatric Developments (Since 1939)." In *American Handbook of Psychiatry*, Vol. 1, edited by Silvano Arieti. New York: Basic Books, 1959.
Morrison, James. "A Reappraisal of Mental Health Education: A Humanistic Approach." *Journal of Humanistic Psychology* 19 (1979): 34-51.
Polier, Justine Wise. "Law and Mental Health: Distrust, Excessive Expectations, and the Battle for Human Welfare." *American Journal of Orthopsychiatry* 50 (1980): 394-402.
Singer, Jerome L. "The Scientific Basis of Psychotherapeutic Practice: A Question of Values and Ethics." *Psychotherapy: Theory, Research and Practice* 17 (1980): 372-83.
Stevenson, Ian. "The Psychiatric Interview." In *Handbook of American Psychiatry*, Vol. I, edited by Silvano Arieti, pp. 197-214. New York: Basic Books, 1959.
Talbot, John A. "Toward a Public Policy On The Chronic Mentally Ill Patient." *American Journal of Orthopsychiatry* 50 (1980): 43-53.

Whitmer, Gary E. "From Hospitals to Jails: The Fate of California's Deinstitutionalized Mentally Ill." *American Journal of Orthopsychiatry* 50 (1980): 65-75.

Williams, Donald H., Elizabeth C. Bellis, and Sheila W. Wellington. "Deinstitutionalization and Social Policy: Historical Perspectives and Present Dilemmas." *American Journal of Orthopsychiatry* 50 (1980): 54-64.

Videotapes

This Is Psychiatry. A series of thirteen 30-min. videotapes produced by Dr. Stuart Smith, McMaster Medical School, Hamilton. Distributed by Conven Corporation, Hamilton, 1976.

CHAPTER 3

Books

Ford, Donald H., and Hugh B. Urban. *Systems of Psychotherapy.* New York: Wiley, 1964.

Gardner, Helen. *Art Through the Ages.* New York: Harcourt Brace & Co., 1959.

Goldstein, Kurt. *The Organism.* New York: American Book Co., 1939.

Goldstein, Kurt. *Human Nature In The Light of Psychopathology.* Cambridge, Mass.: Harvard University Press, 1940.

Hall, Calvin S., and Gardner Lindzey. *Theories of Personality.* New York: Wiley, 1962.

Josephson, Eric, and Mary Josephson, eds. *Man Alone: Alienation in Modern Society.* New York: Dell, 1962.

Kaufmann, Walter, ed. *Existentialism From Dostoevsky to Sartre.* New York: Meridian, 1956.

Lo, Samuel. *Tillichian Theology and Educational Philosophy.* New York: Philosophical Library, 1970.

McConnell, James V. *Understanding Human Behavior.* New York: Holt, Rinehart and Winston, 1974.

MacLeod, Alistair. *Paul Tillich: An Essay on the Role of Ontology in His Philosophical Theology.* London: Allen & Unwin, 1973.

May, Rollo, Ernest Angel, and Henri Ellenberger, eds. *Existence: A New Dimension in Psychiatry and Psychology.* New York: Basic Books, 1958.

Stein, Maurice, Arthur Vidich, and David White, eds. *Identity and Anxiety: Survival of the Person in Mass Society.* Glencoe, N.Y.: Free Press, 1960.

Wilson, Colin. *New Pathways in Psychology: Maslow and the Post-Freudian Revolution.* London: Victor Gollancz, 1972.

Wolman, Benjamin. *Contemporary Theories and Systems in Psychology.* New York: Harper & Row, 1960.

Woodworth, Robert, and Harold Schlosberg. *Experimental Psychology*. New York: Henry Holt and Co., 1960.

Articles

Goldstein, Kurt. "Functional Disturbances in Brain Damage." In *American Handbook of Psychiatry*, Vol. 1, edited by Silvano Arieti, pp. 770-94. New York: Basic Books, 1959.
Goldstein, Kurt. "The Organismic Approach." In *American Handbook of Psychiatry* Vol. 2, edited by Silvano Arieti, pp. 1333-47. New York: Basic Books, 1959.

Films

Maslow and Self-Actualization. 60-min., col. Psychological Films Inc., 110 N. Wheeler St., Orange, California, 92669.
Rollo May and Human Encounter. 60-min., col. Psychological Films Inc., 110 N. Wheeler St., Orange, California 92669.
The Humanistic Revolution: Pioneers in Perspective. 32-min., B & W. Psychological Films Inc., 110 N. Wheeler St., Orange, California 92669.

Videotapes

The Doctor and The Soul. 30-min. col. Interview of Victor Frankl by Roy Bonisteel, from The Best of Man Alive, Canadian Broadcasting Corporation, CBLT, Channel 5, Toronto, 1979.

CHAPTER 4

Books

Armitage, Andrew. *Social Welfare in Canada*. Toronto: McClelland and Stewart, 1975.
Fischer, Joel. *Effective Casework Practice: An Eclectic Approach*. New York: McGraw-Hill, 1978.
Hamilton, Gordon. *Principles of Social Case Recording*. New York: Columbia University Press, 1946.

Articles

Dwyer, Margaret, and Martha Urbanowski. "Student Process Recording: A Plea for Structure." *Social Casework*, May 1975.
Urbanowski, Martha. "Recording to Measure Effectiveness." *Social Casework*, November 1974.

CHAPTER 5

Books

Hart, J.T., and T.M. Tomlinson. *New Directions In Client-Centred Therapy.* Boston: Houghton Mifflin, 1970.
Kirschenbaum, H. *On Becoming Carl Rogers.* New York: Delacorte, 1979.
Rogers, Carl R. *Counseling and Psychotherapy.* Boston: Houghton Mifflin, 1942.
Rogers, Carl R. *Client-Centred Therapy: Its Current Practice, Implications, and Theory.* Boston: Houghton Mifflin, 1951.
Rogers, Carl R. *On Becoming A Person.* Boston: Houghton Mifflin, 1961.
Rogers, Carl R. *Carl Rogers on Encounter Groups.* New York: Harper & Row, 1970.
Rogers, Carl R. *Carl Rogers on Personal Power.* New York: Delacorte, 1977.
Rogers, Carl R. *A Way of Being.* Boston: Houghton Mifflin, 1980c.
Rogers, Carl R., and Rosalind F. Dymond, eds. *Psychotherapy and Personality Change.* Chicago: University of Chicago Press, 1978.

Articles

"Carl Rogers." *Current Biography,* 23rd Annual Accumulation (1962): 357-59.
Rogers, Carl R. "A Theory of Therapy, Personality and Interpersonal Relationships as Developed in the Client-Centred Framework." In *Psychology: A Study of a Science,* Vol. 3 (Formulations of the Person and the Social Context), edited by S. Koch, pp. 184-256. New York: McGraw-Hill, 1959.
Rogers, Carl R. "My Personal Growth." In *Twelve Therapists,* edited by Arthur Burton et al., pp. 28-77. San Francisco: Jossey-Bass, 1972.
Rogers, Carl R. "In Retrospect: Forty-Six Years." *American Psychologist* 29 (1974): 115-23.
Rogers, Carl R. "The Person." *Association for Humanistic Psychology Newsletter,* May 1980a: 8-9.
Rogers, Carl R. "Growing Old—Or Older and Growing." *Journal of Humanistic Psychology* 20 (1980b): 5-16.
Wood, John. "Carl Rogers, Gardener." *Human Behaviour,* November 1972, 17-22.

Films

Three Approaches to Psychotherapy, Film No. 1. 48-min, B & W. Carl Rogers briefly describes his therapeutic approach, demonstrates the approach with a real client, "Gloria," and later discusses his impressions of the interview. 1966. Available through Psychological Films Inc., 110 N. Wheeler St. Orange, California 92669.

Journey Into Self. 45-min., B & W. Depicts sixteen hours of encounter group process with Carl Rogers as group facilitator. Available through Marlin Motion Pictures, Lakeshore Road, Toronto, Ontario. 1968.

A Conversation with Carl Rogers. 60-min., B & W. Film taken from a videotape made at KCET TV, Los Angeles. Rogers is interviewed, discusses his life and work, and speaks out on social issues important to him. Available through Psychological Films Inc., 110 N. Wheeler St., Orange, California 92669. 1969.

The Steel Shutter. Depicts sixteen hours of group encounter between Northern Ireland Protestants and Catholics with Carl Rogers as a group facilitator. Available from the Centre for Studies of The Person, 1125 Torry Pines Road, La Jolla, California 92037. 1972.

Training

Center for Studies of the Person
1125 Torry Pines Road
La Jolla, California 92037

CHAPTER 6

Books

Perls, Frederick S., Ralph F. Hefferline, and Paul Goodman. *Gestalt Therapy: Excitement and Growth in the Human Personality.* New York: Dell, 1951.

Perls, Frederick S. *Ego, Hunger and Aggression.* New York: Random House, 1968.

Perls, Frederick S. *Gestalt Therapy Verbatim.* Lafayette, Calif.: Real People Press, 1969a.

Perls, Frederick S. *In and Out of the Garbage Pail.* Lafayette, Calif.: Real People Press, 1969b.

Perls, Frederick S. *The Gestalt Approach & Eye Witness to Therapy.* New York: Bantam, 1976.

Shepard, Martin. *Fritz: An Intimate Portrait of Fritz Perls and Gestalt Therapy.* New York: Bantam, 1976.

Articles

Anderson, Walt. "Fritz Perls Revisited." *Human Behaviour,* April 1973: 17-23.

Enright, John. "An Introduction to Gestalt Techniques." In *Gestalt Therapy Now,* edited by Joan Fagan and Irma Shepherd. Toronto: Fitzhenry and Whiteside, 1970.

Perls, Frederick S. "Theory and Technique of Personality Integration." *American Journal of Psychotherapy* 2 (1948): 565-86.

Yontef, G. "Gestalt Therapy." In *Modern Therapies,* edited by Virginia Binder,

Arnold Binder, and Bernard Rimland. Englewood Cliffs, N.J.: Prentice-Hall, 1976.

Films

Three Approaches to Psychotherapy. Film No. 2. 32-min., B & W. Frederick Perls describes his approach, demonstrates his therapy with a female patient, "Gloria," and later reviews his impressions of the effectiveness of the interview. Available from Psychological Films, 110 N. Wheeler St., Orange, California 92669. 1967.

Frederick Perls and Gestalt Therapy. Two parts. 60-min., B & W. Perls describes his theory, then demonstrates his approach with a group of patients. Several techniques are demonstrated, including work with a patient's dream. Available from Psychological Films, 110 N. Wheeler St., Orange, California 92669. 1968.

Training

The Gestalt Institute of Toronto, 395 Markham St., Toronto, Ontario.

CHAPTER 7

Books

Janov, Arthur. *The Primal Scream.* New York: Dell, 1970.
Janov, Arthur. *The Anatomy of Mental Illness.* New York: Putnam, 1971.
Janov, Arthur. *The Primal Revolution.* New York: Simon and Schuster, 1972.
Janov, Arthur. *The Feeling Child: Preventing Neurosis in Children.* New York: Simon and Schuster, 1972.
Janov, Arthur. *Primal Man: The New Consciousness.* New York: T.Y. Crowell, 1976.
Janov, Arthur. *Prisoners of Pain.* New York: Anchor/Doubleday, 1980.

Articles

Brown, Malcolm. "Beyond Janov: The Healing Touch." *Journal of Humanistic Psychology* 19 (1979): 69-89.
"Arthur Janov." *Current Biography* 41 (1980): 15-18.
Torrey, E. Fuller. "The Primal Therapy Trip: Medicine or Religion?" *Psychology Today* 10 (1976): 62-68.

Films

Primal Therapy. 10 min., col. Introduction to the principles and methods of Primal Therapy. Produced and distributed by the Centre for Holistic Primal Therapy, 93 Harbord St., Toronto, M5S 1G4.

Training

The Primal Institute
2155 Colby Ave.
Los Angeles, California 90064

The Centre for Holistic Primal Therapy
93 Harbord St., Toronto, Ontario
M5S 1G4

CHAPTER 8

Books

Cobb, Stanley. *Emotions and Clinical Medicine*. New York: Norton, 1950.
Ellis, Albert. *Reason and Emotion in Psychotherapy*. New York: Lyle Stuart, 1962.
Ellis, Albert. *Growth Through Reason: Verbatim Cases in Rational-Emotive Therapy*. Palo Alto, Calif.: Science and Behavior Books, 1971.
Ellis, Albert, and R.A. Harper. *A New Guide to Rational Living*. Hollywood: Wilshire Book Co., 1976a.
Ellis, Albert, and John M. Whitely. *Theoretical and Empirical Foundations of Rational-Emotive Therapy*. Monterey, Calif.: Brooks/Cole, 1979a.
Wolpe, Joseph. *The Practice of Behavior Therapy*. Toronto: Pergamon, 1973.

Articles

Ellis, Albert. "Rational Psychotherapy." *The Journal of General Psychology* 59 (1958): 35-49.
Ellis, Albert. "Psychotherapy Without Tears." In *Twelve Therapists*, edited by Arthur Burton et al. San Francisco: Jossey-Bass, 1972.
Ellis, Albert. "My Philosophy of Psychotherapy." *Journal of Contemporary Psychotherapy* 6 (1973): 13-18.
Ellis, Albert. "Is Rational-Emotive Therapy Stoical, Humanistic, or Spiritual?" *Journal of Humanistic Psychology* 19 (1979): 89-92.
Ellis, Albert. "The Essence of Rational Psychotherapy: A Comprehensive Approach to Treatment." New York: Institute for Rational Living, n.d.
Ellis, Albert. "Rational-Emotive Therapy." In *Modern Therapies*, edited by Virginia Binder, Arnold Binder, and Bernard Rimland. Englewood Cliffs, N.J.: Prentice-Hall, 1976b.
Gregg, Gary. "The Rational Therapist: Epictetus, Not Freud. A Sketch of Albert Ellis." *Psychology Today*, July 1973.
Stampfl, Thomas G., and Donald J. Levis. "Essentials of Implosive Therapy." *Journal of Abnormal Psychology* 72 (1967): 496-503.

Films and Videotapes

Three Approaches to Psychotherapy. Film No. 3. 22 min., B & W. Albert Ellis describes his approach, demonstrates his therapy with a female patient,

"Gloria," and later reviews his impressions of the effectiveness of the interview. Available from Psychological Films, 110 N. Wheeler St., Orange, California 92669. 1967.

Other films are available through the Institute for Advanced Study in Rational Psychotherapy.

Training

The Institute for Advanced Study in Rational Psychotherapy, 45 East 65th Street, New York, N.Y. 10021

CHAPTER 9

Books

Glasser, William. *Mental Health or Mental Illness?* New York: Harper & Row, 1961.

Glasser, William. *Reality Therapy: A New Approach to Psychiatry.* New York: Harper Colophon Books/Harper & Row, 1975a.

Glasser, William. *The Identity Society.* New York: Harper & Row, 1975b.

Glasser, William. *Positive Addiction.* New York: Harper & Row, 1976a.

Articles

DeMarsh, Helen. "Reality Therapy." Unpublished paper on a presentation by Dr. William Glasser also attended by the text author. Toronto: May 13, 1968.

Glasser, William. "Reality Therapy." In *Modern Therapies,* edited by Virginia Binder, Arnold Binder, and Bernard Rimland. Englewood Cliffs, N.J.: Prentice-Hall, 1976b.

Glasser, William. "Glasser's Approach to Discipline." Report. Los Angeles: Dr. William Glasser's Education Training Centre, 1978.

Reilly, Sue. "Dr. Glasser Without Failure." *Human Behavior,* May 1973, 16–23.

Films and Videotapes

Available through the Institute of Reality Therapy. (See address below.)

Training

The Institute of Reality Therapy
11633 San Vicente Boulevard
Los Angeles, California 90040

Institute for Reality Therapy
(Eastern Canada)
Box 402
Midland, Ontario
L4R 4L1

CHAPTER 10

Books

Berne, Eric. *The Mind In Action*. New York: Simon and Schuster, 1947.
Berne, Eric. *A Layman's Guide to Psychiatry and Psychoanalysis*. New York: Simon and Schuster, 1957.
Berne, Eric. *Transactional Analysis in Psychotherapy*. New York: Grove, 1961.
Berne, Eric. *Games People Play*. New York: Grove, 1964.
Berne, Eric. *Principles of Group Treatment*. New York: Oxford University Press, 1966.
Berne, Eric. *What Do You Say After You Say Hello?* New York: Grove, 1972.
James, Muriel, and Dorothy Jongeward. *Born to Win*. Don Mills, Ont.: Addison-Wesley, 1971.
Steiner, Claude, and Carmen Kerr, eds., *Beyond Games and Scripts*. New York: Grove, 1977.
Steiner, Claude. *Scripts People Live*. New York: Grove, 1974.
Woolams, Stan, and Michael Brown. *The Total Handbook of Transactional Analysis*. Englewood Cliffs, N.J.: Prentice-Hall, 1979.

Articles

Barnes, Graham. "Teachings and Practices of the Three Schools of TA." In *Transactional Analysis after Eric Berne,* edited by Graham Barnes. New York: Harper's College Press, 1977.
Berne, Eric. "Ego States in Psychotherapy." *American Journal of Psychotherapy* 11 (1957): 293-309.
Dusay, John M. "The Evolution of Transactional Analysis." In *Transactional Analysis After Eric Berne,* edited by Graham Barnes. New York: Harper's College Press, 1977.
Gardner, Hugh. "Hello Up There Dr. Q." *Human Behavior* 4, (1975): 24-29.
Harris, T.A. "Transactional Analysis: An Introduction." In *Modern Therapies,* edited by Virginia Binder, Arnold Binder, and Bernard Rimland. Englewood Cliffs, N.J.: Prentice-Hall, 1976.

Films

Games People Play: The Theory. 30 min., B & W, 16 mm. Spectrum Motion Picture, National Educational Television. Released by Indiana State University Audio-Visual Centre, 1967. Presents interviews with Eric Berne in which he explains the assumptions upon which his theory of transactional analysis is based.
Learning to Live. Transactional Analysis on film. Series of eight 30-minute colour films on basic TA concepts. Distributed by Marlin Motion Pictures, Toronto. 1973.

Training

International Transactional Analysis Association
1772 Vallejo St.
San Francisco, California 94124
(415) 885-5992

CHAPTER 11

Books

Carkhuff, Robert, and Bernard Berenson. *Beyond Counseling and Therapy.* Toronto: Holt, Rinehart & Winston, 1967.
Ford, Donald H., and Hugh B. Urban. *Systems of Psychotherapy: A Comparative Study.* New York: Wiley, 1964.
Harper, Robert A. *The New Psychotherapies.* Englewood Cliffs, N.J.: Prentice-Hall, 1975.
Hilgard, Ernest R. *Theories of Learning.* New York: Appleton-Century Crofts, 1959.
Hilgard, Ernest R., and Gordon H. Bower. *Theories of Learning.* New York: Appleton-Century Crofts, 1966.
Salter, A. *Conditioned Reflex Therapy.* New York: Capricorn Books/Putnam, 1961.
Wolpe, Joseph. *Psychotherapy by Reciprocal Inhibition.* Stanford, Calif.: Stanford University Press, 1958.
Wolpe, Joseph. *The Practice of Behavior Therapy.* Toronto: Pergamon, 1973.

Articles

Bacharach, Arthur J. "Some Applications of Operant Conditioning to Behavior Therapy." In *The Conditioning Therapies,* edited by Joseph Wolpe, Andrew Salter, and L.J. Reyna. New York: Holt, Rinehart & Winston, 1965.
Eysenck, H.J. "The Effects of Psychotherapy: An Evaluation." *Journal of Consulting Psychology* 16 (1952): 319-24.
Goldfried, Marvin R. "On The Search for Effective Intervention Strategies." *The Counseling Psychologist* 7 (1978): 28-32.
Kisch, Jeremy, and Jerome Kroll. "Meaningfulness Versus Effectiveness: Paradoxical Implications in the Evaluation of Psychotherapy." *Psychotherapy: Theory, Research and Practice* 17 (1980): 401-13.
McNamara, J. Regis. "Behavior Therapy in The Seventies: Some Changes and Current Issues." *Psychotherapy: Theory, Research and Practice* 17 (1980): 2-9.
Shipley, Robert H. "Implosive Therapy: The Technique." *Psychotherapy: Theory, Research and Practice* 16 (1979): 140-47.

Stampfl, Thomas G., and Donald J. Levis. "Essentials of Implosive Therapy: A Learning Theory Based Psychodynamic Behavioral Therapy." *Journal of Abnormal Psychology* 72 (1967): 496–503.

Storms, Lowell H. "Implosive Therapy: An Alternative to Systematic Desensitization." In *Modern Therapies,* edited by Virginia Binder, Arnold Binder, and Bernard Rimland. Englewood Cliffs, N.J.: Prentice-Hall, 1976.

Strupp, Hans H. "A Psychodynamicist Looks At Modern Behavior Therapy." *Psychotherapy: Theory, Research and Practice* 16 (1979): 124–31.

Thoresen, Carl E., and Thomas J. Coates. "What Does It Mean to be a Behavior Therapist?" *The Counseling Psychologist* 7 (1978): 3–21.

Wolpe, Joseph. "The Systematic Desensitization Treatment of Neuroses." *The Journal of Nervous and Mental Disease* 132 (1961): 189–203.

Films

Behavior Therapy in a Case of Over-Dependency. 90 min. B & W, 16 mm. Dr. Joseph Wolpe demonstrates treatment by systematic desensitization. Detailed behavioural analysis and all elements of technique are shown from material taped over thirteen sessions. 1971. Available from Behavior Therapy Presentations, Temple University.

Reinforcement Therapy. 45 min., B & W, 16 mm. Older but classic film demonstration of operant conditioning principles in three experimental behaviour modification programs with severely disturbed children, with retarded children and with chronic schizophrenic adults. 1966. Produced by Smith, Kline & French; available through Film Service Laboratories, 6327 Santa Monica Blvd., Hollywood, California 90038.

See also the *Filmography* of behaviour therapy films and videotapes prepared by Rosemery O. Nelson, Department of Psychology, University of North Carolina, Greensboro, North Carolina 27412.

Index

A

ABC Theory, 255
Abnormality of North American Society, 35
Abreaction, 360
Abstract attitude, 98-100
Acceptance, 46, 122, 176, 250, 284, 314
Accountability, professional, 143
Acting out, 292, 352
Action, by client, 47
Acute mental illness, 58-59
Adapted child, 319, 333
Adaptiveness, 145
Adaptive responses, 352
Addiction, 296
Adler, Alfred, 126
Adult ego state, 318
Advocacy, 35, 40, 63, 129, 132, 138
Affection, 146
Affective disorders, 69
Agape, 115
Aggression, 146
Alienation, 107, 109, 114, 198, 213, 293. See also Estrangement.
  Marx's view of, 109
Allport, Gordon, biography, 119-20
Altruism, 115
Anal stage, 80
Anderson, Walt, 197
Anger, 292
Ansell, Charles, 25
Anticipatory symbols, 100
Anxiety, 81-82, 102, 116, 147, 179, 246, 256, 292, 332, 339, 352, 354, 361, 362. See also Fear.
  defense mechanisms, and, 82
  existential definition of, 113
  Gestalt Therapy, in, 210
  Goldstein's theory of, 99-101
  Tillich's view of, 132
Anxiety hierarchy, 357
Apathy, 338
Arbitrary symbols, 98, 322
  manipulation of, 116
Assertiveness training, 355, 357

Attention span, 149
Autonomy, 315, 331
  achievement of, 321
  definition of, 335
Avoidance, 100, 209, 214, 215, 217, 339, 356, 361, 362
Awareness, 177, 179, 181, 185, 206, 212, 217, 219, 244, 257, 279, 302, 311, 321, 335
Awfulizing, 260

B

Bacharach, Arthur J., 353, 354
Barnes, Graham, 312, 313
Bauhaus, 198
Bebout, Jim, 25
Becoming, 106, 116
Beginning where the client is, xv, 43
Behaviourism, 37, 92, 93, 125, 203, 349, 353. See also Learning.
Behaviour modification, 61, 144, 349, 351
  principles of, 352
Behaviour therapy, 93, 246, 271, 278, 281, 351
  goals of, 352
  introduction to, 348
Being, 19, 27, 185, 206, 223, 250
  existential definition of, 106, 112
Benedict, Ruth, 126
Berenson, Bernard, 22, 23, 26, 31, 35, 348
Berne, Eric, 188, 234, 243, 315-17, 322, 326, 335
Bernstein, Arnold, 83, 85
Beutler, Larry E., 20, 25
Biosocial theroy, 129
Blaming, 262
Body language, 42, 44
  of patients, 65
Bower, Gordon H., 349, 351
Breuer, Joseph, 72, 73
Brill, A.A., 199
Brill, Henry, 66
Brown, Malcolm, 221, 228
Brown, Michael, 330

379

Buber, Martin, 199
Bühler, Charlotte, 190
Burton, Arthur, 20, 21, 247

C

Carew, Rosemary, 144
Caring, 16, 114, 115, 284. *See also* Nurturing.
Carkuff, Robert, 22, 23, 26, 31, 35, 348
Case recording, 142
Casework supervision, 142
Catharsis, 253
 centred, 198, 213, 217
Charcot, Jean, 72
Child ego state, 319, 328
Children, emotionally disturbed, 144, 171
Choice, 15, 28, 99, 102, 106, 112, 113, 116
Choosing, 122, 206, 213, 214, 244, 250, 261, 289, 294, 295, 302, 303, 311, 312, 315, 330, 332, 335
Chronic mental illness, 58-59
Client-centred therapy, 61, 168, 184
Clients, 6
 as consumers, 36-37, 39-40
 rights of, 38-41, 62
Clinical psychology, 173
 graduate training in, 30-31
closure, 94, 198, 205, 206, 208, 209, 212, 216, 343
Cobb, Stanley, 252
Cognitive imagery, 271
Cognitive therapies, 184, 243
Cohen, Mabel Blake, 86
Commitment, 117, 305, 341. *See also* Contract.
Communication, 207, 311, 322
Communion, 102-3. *See* Helping relationship.
Competence, 18
Competition, 147, 150, 283, 288
Compromise, 285, 303
Conditioning, 249, 349, 361
 classical, 350
Confidant, 3, 5, 37. *See also* Helper.
Conflict, 195, 209, 255
Conformity, 14-15, 113, 122, 232, 303, 332
Confrontation, 23, 117, 194, 213, 218, 222, 280, 305, 315
Conscious behaviour, 279
Consciousness, 78, 91, 93
Contract, 244, 313, 315, 341
Coopersmith, Stanley, 9
Counsellor, 3. *See also* Confidant, Helper, Therapist.

Countertransference, 86, 342
Cowichan, 202
Critical parent, 318

D

Days of decision, 338
Death, 112-13
Deductive reasoning, 227
Defense mechanisms, 82-83, 102, 166, 179, 230, 244
Defense system, 230
Deinstitutionalization, 62
Delirium tremens, 68
Denial, 82-83, 179, 198, 209, 231, 290, 333
Dependency, 123, 151, 219, 279, 280, 331
Depersonalization, 178
Depression, 228, 256, 292, 294, 328
 symptoms and treatment of, 60, 70
Destructiveness, 122, 146
Diagnosis, 140, 290, 337
Dickens, Charles, 110
Discounted, 323
Discovery, 207, 214, 215
Disowning, 178, 209, 213
Displacement, 83
Dix, Dorothea, 56, 57
Drive theories, 17
Dusay, John M., 310, 312
Dwyer, Margaret, 138
Dymond, Rosalind F., 184

E

Eclectic, 222, 223, 251, 280, 314
Ego, 76
Egogram, 312
Ego states, 310, 316, 318, 319, 337
Eigenwelt, 115
Electra complex, 80-81
Electro-convulsive therapy (ECT), 53, 57, 71
Ellis, Albert, 5, 34-35, 246-49, 253, 254, 256, 260, 261, 263,, 265, 278
Emergence, 117
Emotion, 252, 254
Emotional disturbance, 255, 256, 262
Empty chair, 217
Encounter, 115, 142, 207, 336, 338, 339
 definition of, 189
 evidence of, 194
Encounter groups, 174, 188, 189-94
England, Mary Jane, 35
Engrams, 321, 361
Enright, John, 217, 218
Environment, 114
Epictetus, 246

Equilibrium, 96. See also Homeostasis.
Erikson, Erik, 316
Eros, 115
Esalen, 202
Essence, 106, 123, 250
Estrangement, 108, 178. See also Alienation.
Ethics
  adult, 335
  definition of, 33
Evaluating behaviour, 302
Existential, 198, 251
Existentialism, 107, 134
  view of reality, and, 107
Existential psychology, 92, 104-34, 199, 203, 281
  definition of, 104-5
Existential therapy, 116-17
  characteristics of, 105
Experiencing, 166, 178, 181, 206, 212, 213, 215, 217, 222, 233
  definition of, 184
Experiential therapy, 184
External behaviour, 203, 204
Extinction, 361
  definition of, 351
Eysenck, J.H., 36, 350

F

Facilitative responses, 23
  discrimination of, 31
Failure, 262
Failure identity, 292, 306
Failure persons, characteristics of, 293
Fantasizing, 272
Fantasy, 151, 210, 355, 358, 361, 363
Farson, Richard, 173
Fatigue, 292
Fear, 99, 102, 234, 314, 363. See also Anxiety.
Federn, Paul, 316
Feedback, 191, 194, 273, 304, 314, 324, 343
Feelings, 181, 183, 191, 193, 221, 222, 229, 230, 246, 302, 312, 333, 356. See also Rackets, Stamps.
  changing, 272
  client, 45
  defintion of, 235
  experiencing, 293
  maintaining, 272
  origin of, 254, 260
  tension, of, 235
Figure-ground relationship, 96
Fischer, Joel, 135, 136

Fixation, anal, 80
  definition of, 79
Flooding, 360
Foley, Henry A., 35-36
Ford, David H., 76
Fragmentation, 223
Frank, Jerome, 34-35, 37
Frankl, Victor, biography and concepts of, 120, 121
Free Association, 86-87
Freedom, 30, 112, 113, 192, 335, 337
  client's, 26, 117
Freudian psychology, 203, 277, 281
Freud, Sigmund, 50, 167, 199, 246
  childhood and adolescence of, 72
  development of theoretical position of, 73
  early followers of, 73
  influence of Joseph Breuer on, 72, 73
  influence on psychiatry of, 60
  major contributions of, 93-94
  medical practice of, 72-73
Friedlander, Sigmund, 198, 199
Friendship, 115
Fromm, Eric, 126
  biography and concepts of, 121-23
Fromm, Marty, 201
Frustration, 122
  tolerance, 149
Fun, 344
Functional disorders, 97
Funding of mental health care, 60

G

Game-playing, 109
Games, 201, 311, 314, 315, 325
  advantages from, 339, 340
  analysis of, 337
  classification of, 340
  definition of, 326
  functions of, 338
Gaylin, Willard, 15-16
Genital stage, 81
Gestalt, 223
Gestalt psychology, 18, 92, 94-95, 198, 199, 203
Gestalts
  formation of, 204, 208, 212
  incomplete, 209, 214
  unfinished, 205
Gestalt Therapy, 165. See also Perls, Fritz.
  concepts and principles in, 203
  development of, 201
  goals of, 196, 212
  introduction to, 196

normal behaviour development, and, 204
personality theory, and, 204-8
Primal Therapy, and, 232
techniques in, 213
theory of and,
  neurosis, 208
Give-up person, 295
Glasser, Ira, 40
Glasser, William, 5, 188, 275, 276, 283, 284, 285, 286, 287, 288, 289, 292, 294, 301, 304, 306
Goal attainment, 305
Goldstein, Kurt, 18, 95, 126, 177, 199, 290
  biography, 123-24
  contributions of, 103-4
  holistic approach to study of behaviour, 95
  theory of anxiety, 99-101
  work with brain-injured soldiers, 60
Goodman, Paul, 201
Greben, Stanley, 20, 21, 22, 31-32
Greenblatt, Milton, 55, 57
Groups
  encounter, 222. *See also* Encounter groups.
  Gestalt Therapy, in, 217
  intensive, 188
  Primal Therapy, in, 241
  Rational-Emotive Therapy, in, 272
  Transactional Analysis, in, 313, 342
Guilt, 78, 261. *See also* Shame.
  ontological, 113-14, 250
Guthrie, E.R., 350, 360

H

Hall, Calvin S., 75, 94, 121, 129
Harlow, Harry, 126
Harper, Robert A., 349
Harris, T.A., 327, 328
Hart, J.T., 182, 183, 184
Health, 228
  psychological, 18
Hebb, D.O., 18
Hefferline, Ralph, 201
Held resentments, 345
Heller, Liane, 38
Helper
  roles, 30, 36, 57. *See also* Confidant, Counsellor, Therapist.
Helping process, 20-25, 47, 140. *See also* Interview techniques.
  aspects of, 6-7
  complexity of, 7
  dynamics, 22
  learning of, 6-7
  synonyms for, 6
Helping relationship, 20, 22, 33, 102-3, 117, 138, 168, 177, 180, 184, 201, 244, 269, 280, 294, 300, 314, 341, 356, 362
Helping techniques, 21, 22
Here and now, 214, 218, 222
  concept of, 206
Heredity, 247, 315
Hierarchy of needs, 126
Hilgard, Ernest R., 349, 351
Hippocrates, 53
Holes, 213, 214
Holistic, 199, 221, 223, 249
  functioning, 204
Homeostasis, 17, 18, 198, 205, 338, 339. *See also* Equilibrium.
Homework, 244, 269, 355, 359, 363
  Rational-Emotive Therapy, in, 271, 272
Homicide, 328
Horney, Karen, 106, 126, 199, 200
Horriblizing, 260
Hostility, 146
Hot seat, 217
Hull, Clark L., 93, 349, 350
Human dignity, 135
Human existence, 116, 121, 123
  Cartesian view of, 105
  guilt as a condition of, 114
  time as dimension of, 116
  transience of, 113
Humanism
  in moral treatment, 57-58
  opposed to the medical model, 51
Humanistic psychology, 104-34, 199. *See also* Existential psychology.
  definition of, 104-5
Hyperventilation, 357
Hypnosis, 72

I

Id, 76
Ideals, 15. *See also* Intrinsic values.
Identification, 13, 209
  with material objects, 110
Identity, 12, 108, 122, 152, 176, 251, 282, 284, 290, 291, 327, 329, 334. *See also* Self-concept.
  effect of Industrial Revolution on, 109
  in industrial society, 109
Identity society, 292
Imagery, 363
Impasse, 343

Implosive Therapy, 271, 351
  effectiveness of, 363
  introduction to, 360
  technique, 362
  theory and concepts in, 360
Impressionism, 110
Individuality, 108, 120, 303
  effect of bureaucracy on, 109
Inductive reasoning, 227
Industrialization, 56, 58
Industrial Revolution, 108, 109, 110
Institutionalization, 29-30
Integration
  loss of, 107, 116. *See also* Alienation.
Internal events, 203
Interpersonal behaviour, 140, 141
Intervention, 117, 218, 343
Interview
  definition of, 139
  initial, 340, 356, 362
Interview techniques
  casework, 138. *See also* Helping process.
Intimacy, 317, 321, 326, 335
Intrapersonal behaviour, 140
Intrinsic values, 15, 19, 26, 116, 121, 228, 261, 284
Introjection, 209, 310
Introspection, 91-92, 93, 125
Involvement, 19, 275, 280, 284, 286, 290, 291, 293, 300, 311
  significance of, 301
Irrational beliefs
  dispelling, 269
  disputing, 272
  ten common, 262
Irrational thinking, 246
Irrational thoughts, 252
Isolation, 108

J

James, Muriel, 330, 331, 335, 336, 340
Janov, Arthur, 188, 221, 222, 223, 230, 231, 236, 237, 240
  biography, 224
Jones, Ernest, 199
Jongeward, Dorothy, 330, 331, 335, 336, 340
Josephson, Eric, 107, 108
Josephson, Mary, 107, 108
Joy, 339
  in fulfilling human potential, 114
  primal, 221

K

Kierkegaard, Søren, xv - xvi, 107
Kisch, Jeremy, 36, 349
Kroll, Jerome, 36, 349

L

Lake, Mrs., 38
Language capacity, 10
Latner, Joel, 196
Learning, 92, 173, 215, 281, 294. *See also* Behaviourism.
  cognitive, 350
  definition of, 347
  Gestalt Therapy, in, 206
  social, 249
  stimulus response, 350
  theory, 93
Levinson, David J., 55, 57
Levis, Donald J., 360, 361
Lewin, Kurt, 190
Lewis, Nolan, 52, 56
Libido, 75
Life
  goals, 253
  plan, 330
  positions, 327
  style, 330
Lindzey, Gardner, 94, 121, 129
Little professor, 319
Lobotomy, 53
Loneliness, 292, 293
Lo, Samuel, 131-32
Losers, 323
  characteristics of, 331
Love, 114, 115, 177, 179, 228, 232, 262, 282, 284, 285, 290, 322
  unconditional, 230, 231

M

MacLeod, Alistair, 133
MacMillan, Harold, 1
Manipulation, 115, 116
  behaviour therapies, in, 353
  existential therapy, in, 115, 116
  Gestalt Therapy, in, 212, 214
  questions with, 215
  Transactional Analysis, in, 311, 325, 332, 340
Marmor, Judd, 21
Marx, Karl, 109
Maslow, Abraham, 91, 288
  biography and concepts of, 124-28
Maturation, 204, 212, 220, 321

Maturity, 207
Maultsby, Maxie, 253
May, Rollo, 104, 105, 106, 107, 113, 114-15, 116-17, 208
  biography, 128
McCary, J.L., 75
McConnell, James V., 128
Medical model, 9, 50
Memory, 214, 223, 229
Mental health care, funding of, 60
Mental hospitals, 55-63
  declining population in, 62
  deinstitutionalization of, 62
Mental illness, 60
  beliefs about causes of, 52, 54
  cognitive therapies, and, 243
  concept of, 50-51
  early treatment methods of, 54
  functional, 69
  organismic psychology, and, 102
  public responsibility for, 63
  Reality Therapy, and, 279, 286, 299
Mental retardation, 352
Millington, Gordon, 32-33
Mitwelt, 114-15
Modelling, 13
Models, for psychological health, 18-19
Mora, George, 53, 55
Moral treatment, 57
Morrison, James, 50
Motivation, 43, 120, 126, 156, 177, 205, 244, 251, 281, 284, 285, 311, 321, 322, 339
  definition of, 16-17
  drive theories of, 17-18
  of patient, 65
Munroe, Ruth L., 76, 87
Murphy, Gardner, biography and concepts of, 128-29

N

Nature
  human relationship with, 108, 132
  human separation from, 109, 110, 114, 122
  Primal Therapy, and, 229
Natural child, 319
Needs
  client, 57
  definition of, 259
  physiological, 322
  psychoanalytic view of, 75
  psychological, 123
  satisfaction of, 177

  social, 16
  states, 18
  substitution of, 231
  symbolic satisfaction of, 231
Need satisfaction, 205, 209, 213, 215. *See also* Gestalts.
  behaviour therapies, in, 352, 357
  feeling and sensation, in, 235
  Primal Therapy, in, 223, 228, 230, 231
  process of, 231
  Rational-Emotive Therapy, in, 251, 267
  Reality Therapy, in, 279, 283, 290
  Transactional Analysis, in, 311, 314, 322, 323
Needs, basic, 244
  Gestalt Therapy, and, 204
  human, 122
  Maslow's, 127
  Primal Therapy, and, 230
  Rational-Emotive Therapy, and, 252
  Reality Therapy, and, 282, 291
  Rogerian, 176, 177
Negatively addicted person, 296
Neo-Freudians, 61, 121
Nervous system
  effect of stimuli on, 96
Neurology, 72
  impact of, on psychiatry, 60
  organismic psychology, and, 95
Neurophysiology, 288
Neurosis, 29, 100, 113, 116, 198
  cure of, 223, 224, 233
  gestalt definition of, 209
  Goldstein's theory of, 102
  influence of early life on, 60
  life positions, and, 334
  maintenance of, 311, 338, 361
  mental illness classified as, 69
  origin of, 78, 165, 243, 246, 251, 283, 360, 361
  Primal Therapy, in, 221, 226, 228, 229
  psychoanalytic theroy of, 81-83
  Rational-Emotive Therapy, in, 252, 254, 255
  sexual origin of, 73
  societal, 210, 213
  societal norm, as, 254
  status quo, and the, 214
  Transactional Analysis, in, 327, 333
  treatment of, 354
Nietzsche, Friedrich Wilhelm, 107
No excuses, 305
Non-directive therapy, 168, 177, 182

Normal behaviour
  characteristics of, 18
Normality, 8-18, 60, 97-98, 120, 132, 166, 174
  cultural-relative, 9-10
  Gestalt Therapy, in, 204
  Primal Therapy, in, 229
  psychological, 10-18
  psychological attributes of, 250
  Rational-Emotive Therapy, in, 249, 265
  Reality Therapy, in, 281, 289
  Rogerian Therapy, in, 176
  statistical, 9
  transcendence as element of, 116
Nordby, Vernon J., 75
Norms, social, 280, 283, 288, 303
Nurturing, 16, 314. See also Caring.
  relationship with client, 22
Nurturing parent, 13, 318

O

Obsessions, 294
Oedipus complex, 80-81
Okness, 314, 328
Openness, 191
Operant conditioning, 271, 349, 361
Opposites, 198
Oral stage, 79
Organic disorders, 96
  brain-injured person, in, 98-99, 101
  mental, 68-69
Organismic behaviour, 18, 25
Organismic experience, valuing of, 178
Organismic psychology, 92, 95-104, 198, 203, 244, 281, 287, 321
  basic concepts of, 123-24
  influence of neurology on, 60
  Primal Therapy, in, 233, 240
Organismic therapy, 101-2
Organisms, 253
  basic needs and operation of, 204
  confusion in, 209
  physiological synthesis, and, 204
Overgeneralizing, 257
Overt behaviour, 223
Owning, 212, 302, 304

P

Pain, 221, 230, 291, 339, 356, 361
  phobic, 215
  primal, 222
  Rational-Emotive Therapy, in, 253
Panic, 357

Paranoid fantasies, 345
Parapsychology, 129
Parental injunctions, 312, 315
Parent ego state, 314, 318
Parenting, 283, 313, 318, 319, 327
Parent messages, 312
Parents, role of, 5, 283
Past, the, 120, 214
  beliefs about, 264
  relevance of, 279
  significance of, 244
Pastimes, 326
Patients, 6. See also Clients.
Paulov, Ivan, 93, 349, 350
Peak experiences, 126
Peebles, Mary Jo, 26
Penfield, Wilder, 234
Perfectionism, 250, 251, 261, 262
Perls, Frederick Solomon (Fritz), 129-31, 188, 208, 210, 212, 213, 215, 216, 217, 219, 278
  biography, 196-203
Perls, Laura, 200
Permission, 343, 344
Permissive environment, 13
Personality
  development, 223, 281
  development in Primal Therapy, 227
  dis-integration, 178, 208
  integration, 196, 212, 230
  re-integration, 212, 213, 217
Personal responsibility, 13, 257, 303
Phallic stage, 80-81
Pharmacotherapy, 61. See also Psychopharmacology.
Phenomology, 92, 114, 175, 177, 249
  view of reality, and, 107
Phobias, 315
Physical examination, 341
Physiological correlates, 321
Pilisuk, Marc, 35
Planning responsible behaviour, 304
Pleasure principle, 75
Polarity, 198, 217, 281
Polier, Justine Wise, 61
Positive addiction, 287
  definition of, 288
Positive regard, 176, 178, 179, 250
  unconditional, 254
Positivists, 106
Potency, 24, 344
Poverty, 255
Preconscious mind, 78

Present, the, 120
Present orientation, 166
Primal group
   dynamics, 241
Primal memory, 234
Primal pain, 232
   implications of, 233
   origin of, 321
Primal Pool, 231
Primal Scene, 230, 231
   major, 232
   minor, 232
Primal scream, 226
Primal Therapy, 165
   development of, 225
   effectiveness of, 222, 224, 241
   goal of, 227, 233, 237
   holistic, 221
   major concepts and principles of, 227-29
   technique, 226, 233, 237-41
Principle of least harm, 41
Problem behaviour,
   maintenance of, 291
   origin and development of, 312
Problem solving, 47
Process recording, 142, 143
   example, 158-64
   guideline, 155
Projection, 83, 213, 217
   Gestalt Therapy, in, 209
Protection, 344
Psychiatrists
   legal authority of, 55
Psychiatry, 5
   classification in, 66-71, 290
   diagnosis in, 64
   interviews in, 63-64
   moral treatment era in development of, 55-58
   "road back" era in development of, 60
   selection of trainees in, 30
   treatment methods in, 71
   treatment modalities in, 50
Psychic determinism, 74-75
Psychoanalysis, 61, 115, 214, 230, 248, ?81
   abstinence in, 84
   defense mechanisms in, 82-83
   effectiveness of, 248
   theory of neurosis, and, 81-83
   origin of, 72-73
   social work, and, 135
   therapeutic technique in, 86-87
   treatment conditions in, 83-84

Psychoanalytic treatment dynamics, 83-86
Psychology, 60
   selection of trainees in, 30
Psychopharmacology, 53, 62. See also
   Pharmacotherapy.
Psychosexual stages of development, 79-81
Psychosis, 294, 352
   mental illness defined as, 69
Psychosomatic symptoms, 292
Psychotherapist, 4, 5. See also Confidant,
   Helper, Therapist.
Psychotherapy
   social institution, as, 29
Punishment, 306, 353

Q

Quantification, 120
Questioning, 44

R

Rackets, 315, 333
Rational-emotive imagery, 272
Rational-Emotive Therapy, 294
   effectiveness of, 251, 274
   goal of, 266
   introduction to, 246
   major concepts and assumptions of, 249
   technique, 267
   theory of neurosis, 252
Rational person
   qualities of, 288
Rational thinking, 253
Reaction formation, 83
Reality, 177, 198, 205, 290
   existentialism, and, 106
   Impressionists' view of, 111
   objective definition of, 107
   subjective definition of, 107
Reality principle, 75
Reality testing, 69, 319, 322, 332
Reality Therapy
   basic assumptions and concepts of, 278
   basic needs, in, 282, 284, 285, 291
   effectiveness of, 277, 307
   goals of, 291, 298
   introduction to, 275
   problem behaviour, and, 289-98
   techniques, 300
   theoretical development of, 280, 281
Rebellion, 15
Receiving, 152
Reciprocal inhibition, 351
Reciprocal inhibition therapy, 354-56

Recognition, 122, 148, 176, 244, 282, 285
Recognition-hunger, 322, 338
Redecision, 312, 314, 315
Reexperiencing, 214, 312, 315
Reflecting feeling, 45, 184
Reflective therapy, 183
Regression, 79, 352
Reich, William, 199
Reilly, Sue, 276
Reinforcement, 350, 354
  definition of, 351
  negative, 353
  positive, 353, 361
Re-integration, 233
Rejection, 291
Relationship
  interpersonal, 116
  therapeutic, 60, 64
Relaxation responses, 355
Relaxation training, 358
Reliability, 227
Renaissance, 108
Re-owning, 214-17
Repetition compulsion, 76
Repression, 78, 82, 166, 198, 209, 221, 223, 229, 230, 231, 234, 235, 246, 333
Rescue, 341
Resistance, 85, 215, 291
Responses, detracting, 31
Responsibility
  awareness, and, 206
  definition of, 153, 282
  learning, 283
  personal, 13, 15, 19
  social, 13
Risk, 27-28
  Gestalt Therapy, and, 213, 214
  in fulfilling human potential, 114
  Rational-Emotive Therapy, and, 273
  Reality Therapy, and, 293, 303
  Rogerian Therapy, and, 191
  Transactional Analysis, and, 336, 339
Rituals, 325
Rogerian Therapy, 165, 166, 281
  basic assumptions in, 180
  conditions for, 177, 180
  developments in, 182, 187
  goals of, 180, 181, 187
  personality dis-integration in, 177
  personality theory in, 175, 188
  Primal Therapy and, 231
  process of, 181
  therapist's roles in, 186-87
  underlying assumptions of, 177
Rogers, Carl R., 9, 23, 131, 167, 168-75, 183, 189, 190, 191, 192, 278
  subjective view of reality of, 107
Role model
  therapist as, 20, 22, 57
Role-playing, 214, 217, 253, 321
Roles, 339
Rothman, David J., 38
Routines, 153, 288, 319
Rush, Benjamin, 55-56

S

Sarason, Barbara R., 52, 53, 67
Sarason, Irwin G., 52, 53, 67
Scene construction, 363
Schizophrenia, 67-68, 173, 184, 314, 328
Schneider, I., 35-36
Schwartz, B.D., 4, 121
Scientific method, 91, 120
  applied to definition of humans, 106
  applied to study of human beings, 107
Screaming, 253
Script matrix, 312
Scripts, 314, 329, 338
  analysis of, 312, 340
  dynamics of, 330
Security, 284
Selective perception, 178
Self-acceptance, 206, 250, 287. *See also* Self-esteem, Self-regard, Self-worth.
  Rational-Emotive Therapy, and, 261
Self-actualization, 12, 15, 18, 24, 25, 101, 102, 166, 244. *See also* Self-fulfillment, Self-realization.
  akin to libido, 75
  Gestalt Therapy, in, 199, 204, 213
  personal qualities in, 126, 127
  Primal Therapy, in, 222
  Rational-Emotive Therapy, in, 249
  Reality Therapy, in, 276, 283, 287, 303
  Rogerian Therapy, in, 175, 180
  Transactional Analysis, in, 321
Self-concept, 152. *See also* Identity.
  Gestalt Therapy, in, 231
  Reality Therapy, in, 284, 294
  Rogerian Therapy, in, 177, 178, 181
  Transactional Analysis, in, 314, 327, 329
Self-control, 13, 14-15, 18, 153, 337
  function of superego, and, 78
Self-depreciation, 257, 263
Self-direction, 178, 212, 250, 303

Self-esteem, 9, 11-14, 18, 21, 72, 127, 176, 250, 261, 327, 333. See also Self-acceptance, Self-regard, Self-worth.
  conditions for, 132
  development of, 12
  in fulfilling human potential, 114
Self-fulfillment, 22, 255, 267, 282, 286, 288, 333. See also Self-actualization, Self-realization.
Self-rating, 250, 261, 263, 282, 288, 327
Self-realization, 196. See also Self-actualization, Self-fulfillment.
Self-regard, 176, 179. See also Self-acceptance, Self-esteem, Self-worth.
Self-regulation, 204, 212, 287, 328
Self-reinforcement, 273
Self-talk, 254
Self-worth, 152, 177, 262. See also Self-acceptance, Self-esteem, Self-regard.
  Rational-Emotive Therapy, in, 261
Sensation, 206, 210, 235, 357, 359
Sensory deprivation, 321
Sensory experience, 231
Sensory imagery, 272
Sexologist, 246
Sexual identification, 81
Sexual response improvement, 355
Shame, 78, 261, 361, See also Guilt.
Shane, Paul, 5
Shaping, 351
  definition and process of, 353
Shaw, George Bernard, 110
Shepard, Martin, 197
Shipley, Robert H., 360, 362
Shoben, E.J., 9, 116
Shuger, Dan, 25
Sickness, 101
Significant others, 178
Signs, 322
Simkin, Jim, 201
Singer, Jerome, 5
Skill
  definition of, 24
Skinner, B.F., 61, 93, 172, 348, 349, 350
Smith, Stuart, 55, 63
Social casework, 136
  behaviour modification, and, 144
Social control, 337
Social Darwinism, 58
Socialization, 287
Social programs
  evaluation of, 40
  funding for, 35

Social reform, 110
Social responsibility, 103, 250, 267. See also Communion.
Social services, negative features of, 38-40
Social work, 60
  training, 30-33
Society, neurotic, 122, 166, 249, 283
Sociology, 60
Spielberg, Gil, 20, 23-24, 31
Splits, 218, 230
Spontaneity, 208, 210, 287, 319, 321, 335
Stampfl, Thomas G., 273, 360, 361
Stamps, 333, 345
Standards, 25. See also Values.
Steiner, Claude, 317, 330, 341, 342, 343, 344
Stereotypes, 58
Stimulation, psychological, 322
Stimulus hunger, 321
Stimulus-response theory, 93
Storms, Lowell H., 360
Strength, 286
  definition of, 287, 295
Strokes, 330, 333, 338
  concept of, 322-23
Structural analysis
  goals of, 337
Strupp, Hans H., 20, 25, 26
Suicide, 294, 328
Superego, 76-77
Supervisor, 3. See also Confidant, Helper, Therapist.
Suppression, 228, 229, 233, 333
Symptomatic relief, 352
Symptom person, 295
Symptom relief, 356
Symptoms, 230, 293, 362
  categories of, 296
  choosing, 294
  definition of, 101
  patterns of, 66
Systematic desensitization, 271

T

Tactile responses, 322
Talbot, John A., 62
Tension, 100, 179, 209, 223, 230, 231, 233, 246, 292, 339
  anxiety vs., 234
  feeling vs. 234
  neurosis, in, 234
Tesher, Ellie, 38
T-group, 190. See also Encounter groups.
Theory, relative to methods, 276

Therapeutic interventions, 21, 22
  impact on client, of, 21
Therapists, 3. *See also* Confidant, Helper.
  as educators, 5
  effectiveness of, 26, 27, 31, 344
  essential values of, 26
  goals of, 10, 117
  interpreting client behaviour, 45
  personality traits of, 20, 22, 30, 166, 167, 301
  responses of, 305
  role of, 43, 46, 63, 181, 182, 187, 201, 213, 215, 216, 218, 244, 269, 275, 280, 289, 300, 304, 306, 313, 314, 315, 341, 344, 356, 357, 362, 363
  skill development of, 23, 24, 117
  supervision of trainees, and, 31
  support of client, and, 22
  training of, 26, 30-33, 173, 190
  values of, 20, 25, 26, 27, 280, 302
Therapy, 5
  categorization of, 8
  comparison and contrast of types of, 275
  effectiveness of, 36, 41, 136, 349, 354, 363
  ethics of, 38
  goal of, 21, 108, 112, 117, 244, 352
  holistic, 54
  interview techinques in, 42-47
  termination of, 359, 363
Thorndike, E.L., 125, 350
Thought-stopping, 357
Tillich, Paul, 131-33, 199
Time, 116
Time structures, 325-26
Titchener, Edward, 91
Tomlinson, T.M., 182, 183, 184
Torrey, E. Fuller, 224
Towbin, Alan, 5, 37
Trainees, supervision of, 31
Trait, definition of, 24
Tranquilizers, 57, 61
Transactional Analysis, 278, 311
  cathexis school of, 314
  classical school of, 313
  communication theory in, 311, 321-27
  concept of transactions in, 321-25
  development of, 310
  effectiveness of, 341
  ego states in, 318-19
  goal of, 311, 312, 314, 315, 324, 330, 334-36
  interventions in, 343
  motivation theory in, 311, 321-27
  neurotic personality development, and, 326-34
  personality structure, and, 311
  personality theory in, 318-27
  redecision school of, 314
  script analysis in, 312
  structural analysis and, 311, 318
  techniques and process of, 340-45
  therapeutic elements in, 336-40
Transactional paradigm, 339
Transactions, 311
  analysis of, 337
  complementary, 323
  crossed, 324
  ulterior, 325
Transcendence, 116, 120
Transfer, 355
Transference, 85, 280, 342
Treatment potential, 65
Trephination, 52
Troemel-Ploetz, Senta, 22
Trust, 191
  client-administrator relationship of, 40

U

Unconditional positive regard, 176, 177, 178, 181, 282
Unconscious behaviour, 279, 312, 326
Unconscious mind, 78
Understanding, 44, 177, 191, 203, 207, 280
  therapist's, 114, 117
Ulrich, Roger, 37-38
Umwelt, 114
Unhappiness, 260
  symptoms and treatment of, 70
Urban, Hugh B., 76
Urbanowski, Martha, 138, 142

V

Validity, consensual, 256
Value judgments, 112, 283, 303, 329
Values, 249
  client, of, 25, 77
  human, 251
  loss of, 108
  relativity of, 314
  social, 244, 255, 280, 288, 303, 335
  social work, 135
  societal, 270-71
  superego development and, 78
Value system, 122

W

Warmth, 24
Watchel, Paul, 42
Watson, John B., 93, 349
Watts, Alan, 202
  biography and concepts of, 133
Weakness, 279
Wertheimer, N[...]
Western cultur[...] t of, 114
  alienation i[...] 285, 290
  neurosis of, 106
  underlying premises about reality in, 106
Weyer, Johann, 54
White, Robert, 9
Whitmer, Gary E., 63
Whole persons, 27, 41, 127, 181, 335
Williams, Donald H., 55, 56, 59
Winners, 331
Wishes, 259

Withdrawal, 325, 333
Wolman, Benjamin B., 74, 91-92
Wolpe, Joseph, 273, 348, 349, 350, 354, 355, 360
Wood, John, 188
Woolams, St[...]
Wundt, Wilhelm, [...]

Y

Yin and Yang, 114, 198
Yontef, G., 206

Z

Zen, 114, 133, 202